The Aerial Atlas of Great Britain & Ireland

BCA

This title has been published exclusively for BCA
CN 136275

The Aerial Atlas of Great Britain & Ireland
© 2005 Wissen Media Verlag GmbH, Gütersloh/Munich
© Cartography: 2005 Wissen Media Verlag GmbH Gütersloh/Munich
All rights reserved

The Aerial Atlas of Great Britain & Ireland was commissioned,
edited, designed and typeset by Book Creation Illustrated Ltd,
Mitre House, 44-46 Fleet Street, London EC4Y 1BN.
www.bookcreation.com

The Aerial Atlas of Great Britain & Ireland

BCA

Contents

Great Britain & Ireland at 1:1,000,000

This series of maps covers Great Britain and Ireland at a scale of 1:1,000,000 and is designed to be viewed alongside the like-for-like satellite images of the same areas that appear between pages 20 and 49. Together they offer a broad overview of the landscape and topography of both countries, along with the main water resources, large conurbations and important towns. The layout of the primary transport routes is also clearly illustrated.

The vivid satellite images provide a unique opportunity to make a direct comparison between the two views of Great Britain and Ireland, with each complementing and enhancing the other.

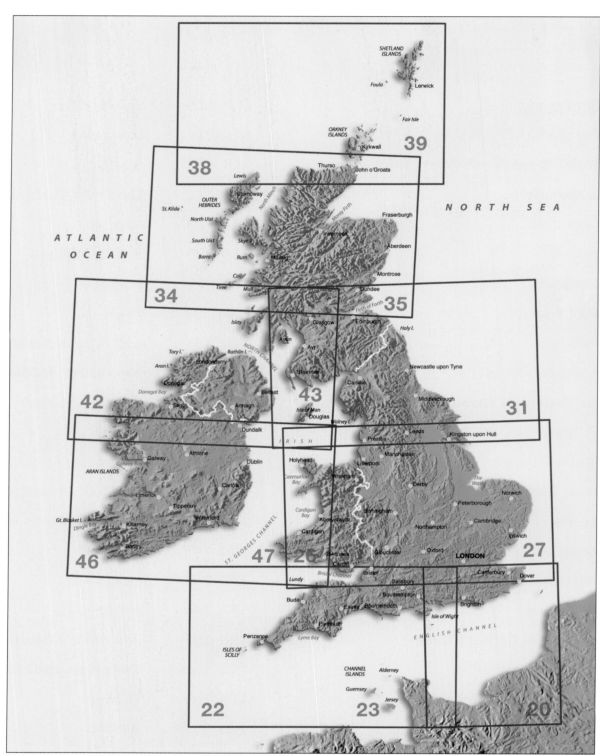

1:1,000,000

| 0 | 10 | 20 | 30 | 40 | 50 miles |
| 0 | 10 | 20 | 30 | 40 | 50 km |

Communications

▬▬▬▬	Motorway and Major Road
▬ ▬ ▬ ▬	Motorway/Major Road (under construction)
═══════	Important Main Road
▬ ▬ ▬ ▬	Important Main Road (under construction)
▬▬▬▬	Main Road

▬ ▬ ▬ ▬	Main Road (under construction)
═══════	Secondary Road
▭ ▭ ▭ ▭	Secondary Road (under construction)
───────	Railway
───────	Freight Railway

Places of Interest

✈	International Airport
✈	Regional Airport
≍	Pass
779	Summit Height (metres)

Other Information

//////////	International Boundary
//////////	County Boundary
▦	Forest
▦	Marshland

Great Britain & Ireland at 1:600,000

These more detailed maps, covering Great Britain and Ireland at a scale of 1:600,000, introduce each regional section between pages 52 and 241. Each of these maps shows the network of roads, both major and minor, that connect with the main transport arteries. They also show the distribution of smaller towns and villages, all of which are listed for reference in the Cartographic index at the end of the book, which provides a detailed index of place names.

Every regional section of the book opens with one of these regional maps, on each of which blue boxes identify the location of the aerial images in the feature pages that follow. Special features of interest are marked on the aerial images with numbers and each is described on the facing page.

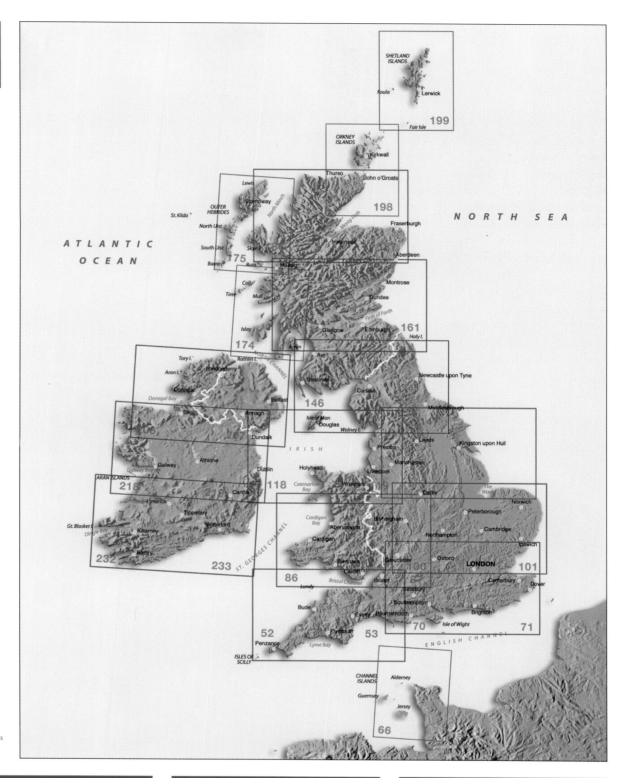

1:600,000

Communications

≣	Motorway	═	Secondary Road
▬ ▬ ▬	Motorway (under construction)	= = = = =	Secondary Road (under construction)
▬▬▬	Dual Carriageway and Major Road	═	Minor Road
▬ ▬ ▬	Dual Carriageway/Major Road (under construction)	= = = = =	Minor Road (under construction)
▬▬▬	Important Main Road	▬▬▬	Car Ferry
▮ ▬ ▬ ▬ ▮	Important Main Road (under construction)	▬▭▬	Railway
▬▬▬	Main Road	▬ ▬ ▬ ▬	Freight Railway
▮ ▬ ▬ ▬	Main Road (under construction)		International Airport
▬▬▬	Trunk Road	✈	Regional Airport
▬ ▬ ▬	Trunk Road (under construction)		

Places of Interest

🏰 *Windsor Castle*	Castle of Interest
⛪ *Muckross Friary*	Church of Interest
✳ *Stonehenge*	Historic Site of Interest
✳ *Cliffs of Moher*	Natural Site of Interest
▨	National Park
⋯⋯⋯	Military Range
⌒	Pass
779	Summit Height (metres)

Other Information

▨▬	International Boundary
▨	County Boundary
▦	Forest
▦	Marshland

1:1,000,000

FRANCE

FRANCE

51°
30'

51°

50°
30'

50°

49°
30'

49°

7°   6°30'   6°   5°30'   5°   4°30'

1:1 000 000

0   10   20   30   40   50 miles

1:1,000,000

NORTH SEA

1°   0°30'   33   0°   0°30'   1°   1°30'   2°

53°
30'

53°

52°
30'

52°

51°
30'

1°   0°30'   0°   21   0°30'   1°   1°30'   2°

1°30'   1°   0°30'   0°   0°30'   1°   1°30'   2°

56°

55°30'

N o r t h   S e a

Farne Islands

55°

Sunderland
Beadnell

Craster
Longhoughton
Lesbury
Alnmouth
Warkworth
Amble
Cocquet Island

Broomhill
Red Row
Widdrington
Cresswell
Ellington

Newbiggin-by-the-Sea
Morpeth
Blyth

Seaton Sluice
Seaton Delaval
Whitley Bay

Tynemouth
Newcastle upon Tyne   South Shields

1 North Tyneside
2 Newcastle upon Tyne
3 Gateshead
4 Sunderland
5 South Tyneside

55°

Gateshead
Washington   **Sunderland**

Ryhope

Houghton
le-Spring
Seaham

Chester
le-Street   Pelton   Seaham
Durham   Hetton
le-Hole

Easington
Peterlee

Bowburn   Blackhall

1 Darlington
2 Hartlepool
3 Stockton on Tees
4 Middlesbrough
5 Redcar & Cleveland

Bishop   Spennymoor   Wingate   Hart
Auckland   Ferryhill   Trimdon   Seaton Carew
Shildon   Sedgefield   **Hartlepool**
Tees Bay

Newton   Billingham   Redcar
Aycliffe   Coatham   Marske-by-the-Sea
Saltburn-by-the-Sea
Brotton

Stockton-on-Tees   **Middlesbrough**   Skelton   Staithes
Ingleby   Loftus   Hinderwell

Darlington   Eaglescliffe   Guisborough   Ugthorpe   Lythe   Sandsend   **Whitby**
Hurworth-on-Tees   Great Ayton   Castleton   Lealholm   Aislaby   Sleights   Hawsker
Croft   Crathorne   Kildale   Westerdale   Egton   Grosmont

54°30'

Scotch   Great   Carlton in   Vale of Moor   454   Robin Hood's Bay
Corner   Smeaton   Cleveland   Swainby   Stoxe Green   Goathland   Ravenscar

East   Great   Kirkby   Ruswarp
Cowton   Langton   Osmotherley   **North Yorkshire**   Rosedale Abbey

Great Langton   Cleveland   Hackness   Scalby
Scruton   Swainby   Cloughton

Northallerton   399   Cleveland Hills

Patrick   South
Brompton   Kirkmoorside   Wrelton   Lockton   **Scarborough**
Bedale   Kennington   Helmsley   Sinnington   Thornton-le-Dale   Ayton
Thirsk   Spaxton   Pickering   Allerston   Brompton
West   Kirby Misperton   Snainton   Salton   Seamer
West Tanfield   Sutton-under-Whitestonecliffe   **Filey**
Easingwold   Yedingham   Filey Bay

Masham   Coxwold   Sherburn   Muston
Brandsby   Hunmanby   Reighton
Ripon   Coxwold   West Lutton

Boroughbridge   Brandsby   Malton   Norton-   Flamborough
Flaxton   on-Derwent   West Lutton   Buckton   Flamborough Head
Minskip   Morton   Stillington   North   Sledmere   West Lutton   Rudston   **Bridlington**
Ripley   Sutton-   Grindale
on-the-Forest   Langtoft   Kilham   Garton-on-the-Wolds   Burton Agnes   Bridlington
Knaresborough   Green   Strensall   Thixendale   Nafferton   Bay

54°

Hammerton   Haxby   York
Harrogate   Stamford Bridge   North Dalton   **Driffield**
Spofforth   Wetherby   Dunnington   Warter   Middleton-   Beeford
Wilberfoss   on-the-Wolds   North   Alnwick
Kirkbymoorside   Pocklington   Frodingham
York   Barmby   Braunton-
Moor   burton   Hornsea
Bramham   Tadcaster   Bishop
Wilton   **East Riding**   Weighton   Long Riston
Leeds   Saxton   **of Yorkshire**   Market
Church   Holme-on-   Weighton   Leven
Fenton   Spalding-Moor   South Skirlaugh
1 City of Kingston upon Hull
2 North East Lincolnshire
3 North Lincolnshire

Leeds   Garforth   Riccall   South Cave   **Beverley**   Burton
Constable
Selby   North Cave   Skidby   Specerary   Tunstall
Barlby   Cottingham   Withernsea
Morley   **Rothwell**   Hemingbrough   Skelton   **Kingston-**   Hedon   Halsham
Batley   **Castleford**   **upon-Hull**   Hollym
Dewsbury   **Knottingley**   Howden   Patrington
Ossett   Featherstone   **Goole**   New Holland
Ryhill   Burton
Wakefield   9   Airmyn   upon Stather   Easington
Skelmanthorpe   S. Ferriby   Barton-upon-Humber   Kilnsea

8   Hemsworth   **Thorne**   Crowle   3   Ulceby   Great   Spurn Head
Ryhill   Coker   Limber
South Kirkby   Bentley   **Scunthorpe**   Kirmington   **Immingham**
Barnsley   10   Hatfield   Brigg   Great   **Grimsby**
Limber   2
Cleethorpes

1°30'   1°   **27**   0°30'   0°   0°30'   1°   1°30'

54°

1:1 000 000

1°30'	1°	0°30'	0°	0°30'	1°	1°30'	2°

56°

55°
30'

55°

54°
30'

54°

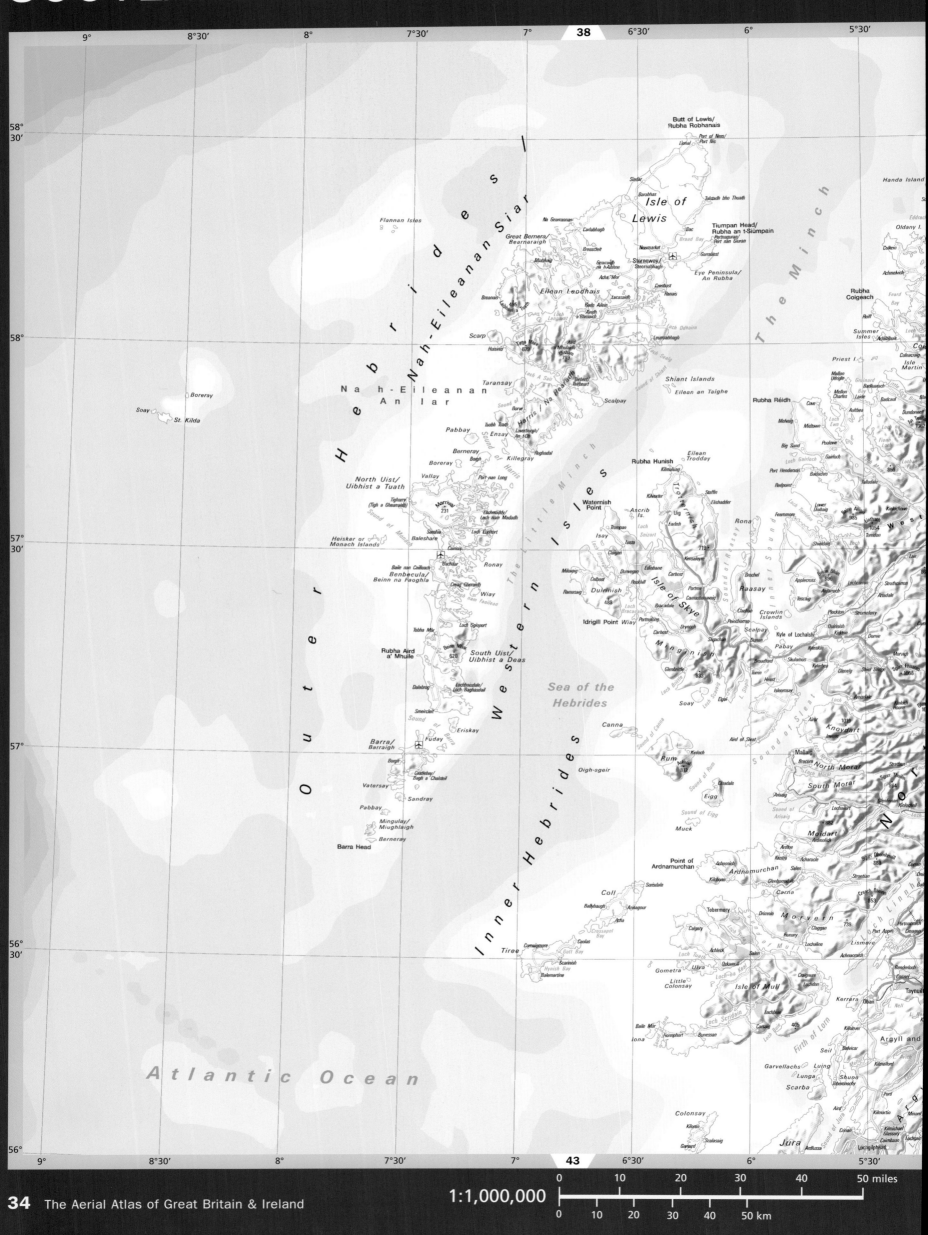

Butt of Lewis/
Rubha Robhanais

Lional
Port of Ness/
Port Nis

Siadar

Barabhas
Isle of
Lewis

Tolstadh bho Thuath

Handa Island

Na Geàrrannan

Carlabhagh

Oldany I.

Culkein

Tiumpan Head/
Rubha an t-Siùmpain
Portnaguran/
Port nan Giuran

Achnahaird

Flannan Isles

Great Bernera/
Bearnaraigh

Breascleit

Newmarket

Eye Peninsula/
An Rubha

Broad Bay

Rubha
Coigeach

Reiff

Geàrraidh
na h-Aibhne

Acha 'Mòr

Stornoway/
Steòrnabhagh

Garrabost

Summer
Isles

Eilean Leòdhais

Lacasaidh

Gleobost
Rànais

Achiltibuie

Priest I.

Isle
Martin

Scarp

Breanais
Baile
Ailein
Àirdh
a'Bhruaich

Loch Odhainn

Leurbost

Scalpay

Shiant Islands
Eilean an Taighe

Mellon
Udrigle

Gruinard
Bay

Badcaul

Hùisinis

Àird
a'Mhulaidh
Bogha Glas

Scotland
Loch A'Siar

Rubha Réidh

Cove

Mellon
Charles

Taransay

Sìobost/
Seilebost

Na h-Eileanan
An Iar

Harris/
Na Hearadh

Big Sand

Dundonnell

Loch
Ewe
Aultbea

Pabbay
Ensay

Lacasdail/
An t-Ob

Roghadal

Rubha Hunish
Kilmaluag

Eilean
Trodday

Port Henderson

Badachro

Poolewe

Midtown

Redpoint

Berneray
Borgh

Sound of Harris
Killegray

Staffin
Digg

Flodigarry

Loch Gairloch

Boreray
Vallay

Port nan Long

Kilmaluag

Uig

Earlish

Rona

Fearnmore
Diabaig

Boreray

North Uist/
Uibhist a Tuath

Waternish
Point

Ascrib
Is.

Tighary
(Tigh a Ghearraidh)

Malaclet/
Loch nam Madadh

Trumpan

Torridon

Soay
St. Kilda

Maraig
231

Isay

Lusta

Edinbane

Snizort

Uig
Portree

Kensaleyre

Shieldaig

Kishorn
Applecross

Lochcarron

Heisker or
Monach Islands

Baleshare

Ùachdar

Rònaigh

Creag Ghoraidh

Milovaig
Colbost

Dunvegan
Roskhill

Skeabost

Raasay

Brochel

Crowlin
Islands

Plockton
Stromeferry

Benbecula/
Beinn na Faoghla

Baile nan Cailleach

Wiay

Ramasaig

Dulrinish

Isle of Skye

Cluanie

Ponchorna

Balmacara

Kyle of Lochalsh

Loch
Bracadale

Bracadale

Inverarish

Kyleakin

Pabay

Kyles ku

Loch Spiggort

Tobha Mòr

Idrigill Point
Wiay

Corbett

Dunvegan

Drynoch

Sligachan
Broadford

Torrin

Inverie

Glenelg

Rubha Aird
a' Mhuile

Beinn Mhòr
620

South Uist/
Uibhist a Deas

Minginish

Glendale

Loch Bracadale

Soay

Loch Scavaig

Elgol

Isleornsay

Knoydart

Daliburgh

Lochboisdale/
Loch Baghasdail

Sea of the
Hebrides

Aird of Sleat

Mallaig

North Morar

Smercleit

Sound of Barra

Canna

Rùm

Kinloch

Sound of Rum

South Morar

Barra/
Barraigh

Fuday

Oigh-sgeir

Glenuig
Arisaig

Loch nan Uamh

Borgh

Eigg
Sound of Eigg

Moidart

Castlebay/
Bàgh a Chaisteil

Vatersay

Sandray

Muck

Ardnish

Acharacle

Pabbay

Point of
Ardnamurchan

Kentra

Loch Shiel

Mingulay/
Miughlaigh

Berneray

Ardnamurchan
Kilchoan
Glenborrodale

Salen
Strontian

Barra Head

Coll

Sorisdale

Carna

Morvern

Morvern

Ballyhough

Arinagour

Tobermory

Drimnin

Calgary

Lochaline

Ardnacross

Tiree

Crossapol
Bay

Caolas

Achnacroish

Scarinish
Hynish Bay

Gometra
Ulva

Kilchoan

Little
Colonsay

Isle of Mull

Kerrera
Oban

Iona

Baile Mòr

Fionnphort
Bunessan

Loch Scridain

Firth of Lorn

Seil

Argyll and

Garvellachs
Luing

Colonsay

Scarba

Kilchattan
Glenan

Kilonain

Gigha

Scalasaig

Jura

Ardfin

Outer Hebrides

Western Isles

The Little Minch

Inner Hebrides

The Minch

Atlantic Ocean

1:1,000,000

| 0 | 10 | 20 | 30 | 40 | 50 miles |

| 0 | 10 | 20 | 30 | 40 | 50 km |

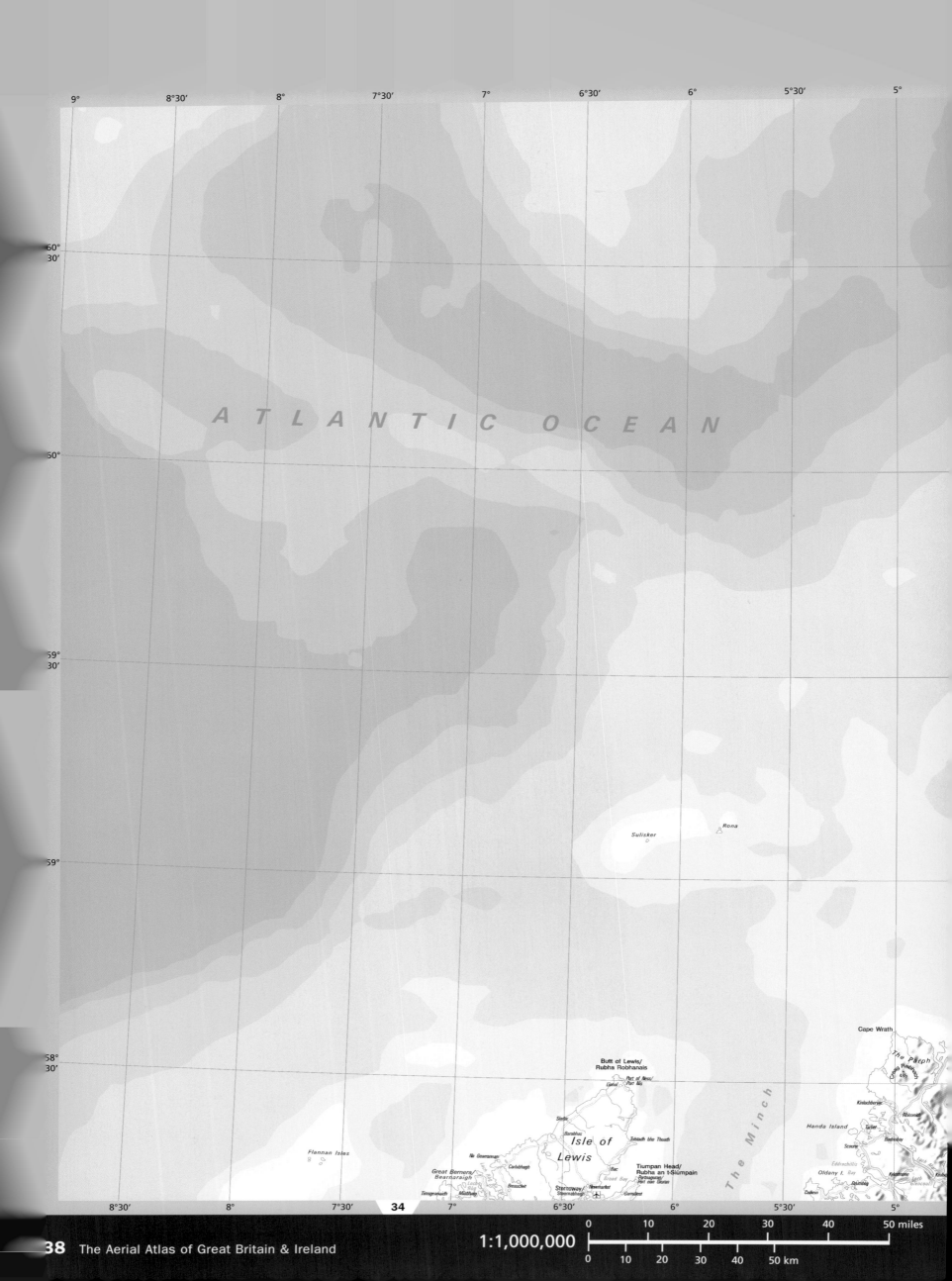

A T L A N T I C   O C E A N

Sulisker

Rona

Cape Wrath

The Parph

Butt of Lewis/
Rubha Robhanais

Port of Ness/
Port Nis

Lional

Kinlochbervie

Handa Island

Flannan Isles

Na Gearrannan

Tolstadh bho Thuath

Oldany I.

Eddrachillis
Bay

Isle of
Lewis

Carlabhagh

Bac

Great Bernera/
Bearnaraigh

Breasclet

Broad Bay

Tiumpan Head/
Rubha an t-Siumpain
Portnaguran/
Port nan Giuran

The Minch

Timsgearraidh

Stornoway
Steornabhagh

Marbhig

Newmarket

Garrabost

1:1,000,000

| 0 | 10 | 20 | 30 | 40 | 50 miles |

| 0 | 10 | 20 | 30 | 40 | 50 km |

1:1,000,000

Northern Scotland

ATLANTIC OCEAN

0   10   20   30   40   50 miles

6 North Lanarkshire
7 Glasgow City
8 East Dunbartonshire
9 West Dunbartonshire
10 Renfrewshire
11 East Renfrewshire
12 Inverclyde

11°   10°30′   10°   9°30′   9°   8°30′   8°

56°

55°
30′

55°

54°
30′

54°

The Aerial Atlas of Great Britain & Ireland

1:1,000,000

0   10   20   30   40   50 miles

0   10   20   30   40   50 km

7°   6°30'   6°   5°30'   5°   4°30'   4°   3°30'

56°

55°
30'

30

55°

54°
30'

54°

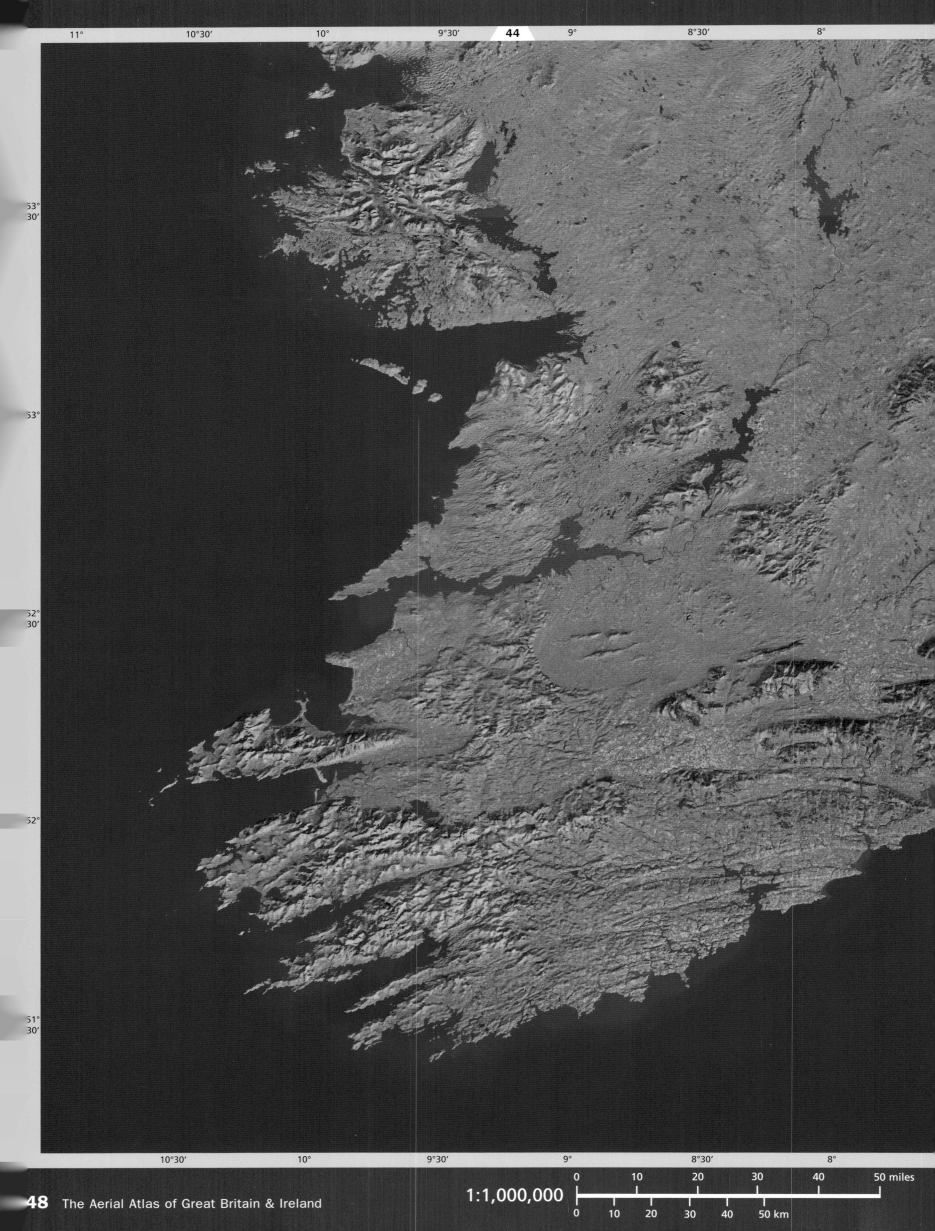

44

11° 10°30′ 10° 9°30′ 9° 8°30′ 8°

53°30′

53°

52°30′

52°

51°30′

10°30′ 10° 9°30′ 9° 8°30′ 8°

1:1,000,000

0 10 20 30 40 50 miles

0 10 20 30 40 50 km

53°
30′

53°

26

52°
30′

52°

51°
30′

Cork-Swansea 8h

C e l t i c

S e a

Lundy
141

Barns
Bid

Hartland Point

Hartland

Woolfardisw

Morwenstow
216
Bradw

Coombe
Kilkham

*Bude
Bay*
Bude
Stratton
Hols
Marhamchurch
Bridu
Poundstock
Whitstone
North
Tamerton
St. Genrys
Wainhouse
Corner
Bo
Warbstow
Boscastle
Eglos
Tintagel Head
Tintagel
Davidstow
307
St. Clether
Launc
Port Isaac
Tintagel
Altarnun
Bay
Delabole
Camelford
Polzeath
St. Teath
Brown Willy
Bolventor
St. Minver
419
Bolventor
390
Nor
Padstow
Rock
Siblyba
St. Merryn
Wadebridge
Camel
L. Res.
Res.
St. Issey
Bodmin
St. Neot
St.
Trenance
St. Column
Major
Lanivet
Fowey
Dobwalls
isk
Tregonetha
Lanhydrock
Newquay
Victoria
Bugle
Lostwithiel
Widege
Cubert
St. Dennis
Lerryn
Sand
Eden
Brighton
St. Blazey
Lanreath
Perranporth
St. Austell
Fowey
Looe
Goonhavern
St. Stephen
Sticker
Polruan
Polperro
St. Agnes
Probus
St. Austell
Bay
Portreath
Grampound
Mevagissey
Chacewater
Trewithen
Tregony
Chapel Point
Truro
Gorran Haven
St. Ives
Camborne
Redruth
Trelissick Garden
Veryan
Bay
Dodman
Point
St. Ives
Bay
253
Penryn
St. Ives
Portscatho
Zennor
Hayle
Crowan
Rame
St. Mawes
Porthmeor
Chysauster
253
Penzance
Crowlas
Leedstown
Falmouth
Pendeen
Cape Cornwall
Marazion
Breage
Glendurgan
Garden
St. Just
St. Michael's
Mount
Helston
Gweek
Mawnan
Falmouth Bay
Newlyn
Porthleven
Sennen
St. Buryan
Mousehole
Garras
Manaccan
St. Keverne
Land's End
Treen
Mount's Bay
Mullion
Coverack
Mullion
Lizard
Ruan Minor
Black Head
Lizard Point

Isles of Scilly

Tresco St. Martin's
Higher Town
Bryher
Crow Sound
St. Mary's
Hugh
Town
Old Town
Isles of Scilly
Gugh
St. Agnes

0   5   10   15   20   25 miles
0   5   10   15   20   25 km

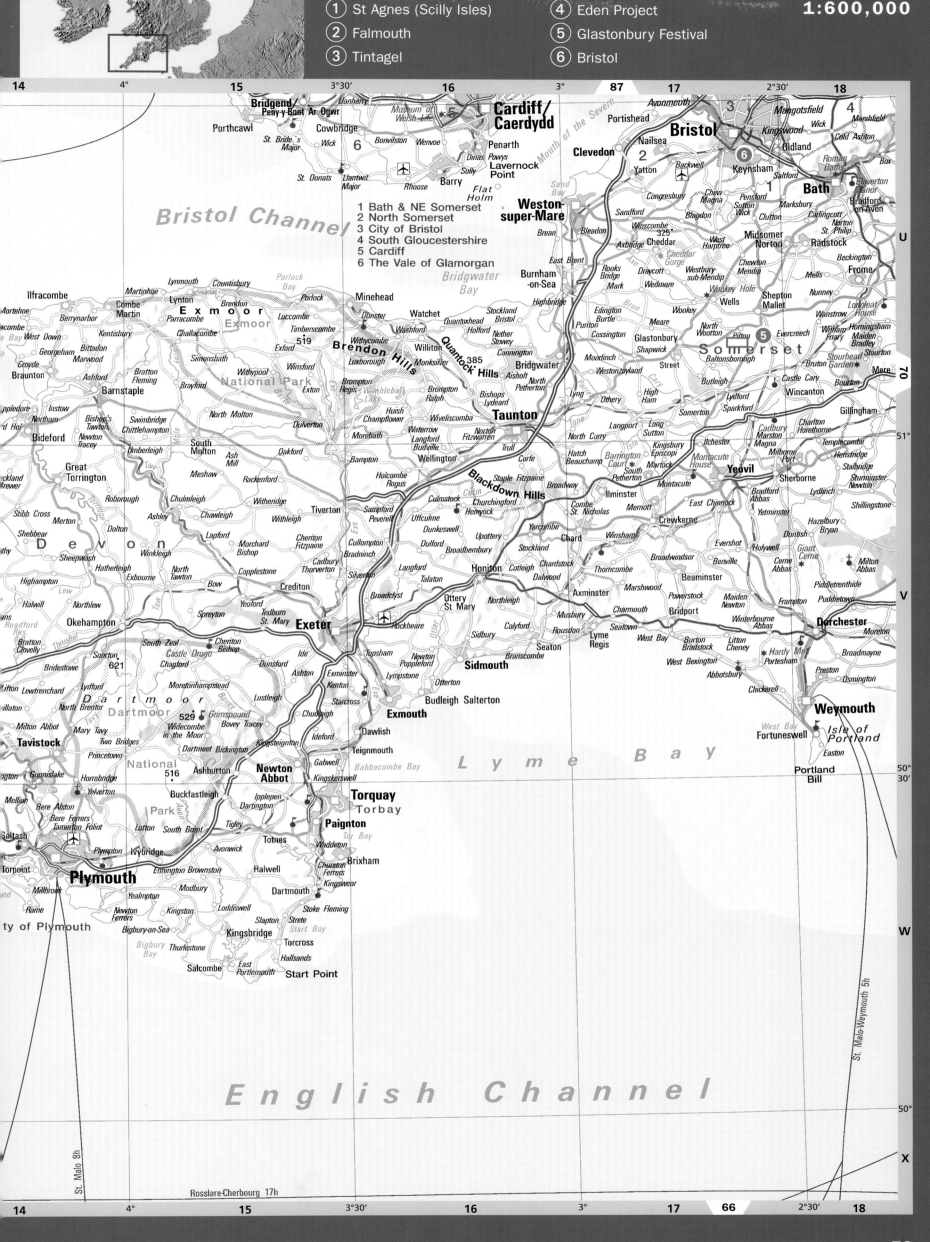

14 4° 15 3°30' 16 3° 87 17 2°30' 18

Bridgend/
Peny-y-Bont Ar Ogwr
Porthcawl St. Bride's Cowbridge Bonvilston Wenvoe Museum of Welsh Life Cardiff/
Major Wick Caerdydd
6 Penarth
St. Donats Llantwit Rhoose Dinas Powys Lavernock
Major Barry Sully Point
Flat
Holm
Bristol Channel

Portishead Avonmouth Mangotsfield Wick Marshfield
3 Kingswood
Bristol Oldland Cold Ashton
Clevedon Nailsea Box
2 Yatton Backwell Keynsham Saltford Roman
Congresbury Chew Pensford Baths
Weston- Sandford Magna Sutton Marksbury Bradford-on-Avon
super-Mare Winscombe Blagdon Wick Clutton Norton
Brean Bleadon 325' Midsomer St. Philip
Axbridge Cheddar West Norton Radstock
East Brent Rooks Draycott Cheddar Harptree Chewton Beckington
Burnham- Bridge Gorge Westbury Mendip Mells Frome
on-Sea Mark Wedmore sub-Mendip Wookey Hole Nunney
Highbridge Meare Wookey Wells Shepton Longleat
Puriton Cossington North Mallet Wanstrow House
Moorlinch Wootton Pilton Evercreech William Horningsham
1 Bath & NE Somerset Shapwick Glastonbury ⑤ Friary Maiden
2 North Somerset Westonzoyland Street Somerset Bradley
3 City of Bristol Baltonsborough Bruton Stourton
4 South Gloucestershire Bridgwater Butleigh Castle Cary Garden Stourhead Mere
5 Cardiff Aisholt North Lydford Wincanton Bourton
6 The Vale of Glamorgan Petherton Cary Sparkford Gillingham
Bridgwater Lyng Somerton Charlton
Bay Othery High Horethorne
Stockland Cannington Ham Cadbury
Bristol Nether North Curry Long Templecombe
Holford Stowey Sutton Itchester Marston Henstridge
Lynmouth Countisbury Quantoxhead Bishops Taunton Langport Montacute Milborne Stalbridge
Minehead Washford Lydeard North House Port
Porlock Watchet 519 Petherton Martock Yeovil Bradford Lydlinch
Combe Porlock Dunster Monksilver 385 Trull Hatch Barrington South Abbas Shillingstone
Martin Luccombe Williton Quantock Beauchamp Court Petherton Sherborne
Martinhoe Timberscombe Hills Corfe Ilminster Crewkerne East Chinnock Yetminster Duntish
Parracombe Withycombe Bishops Staple Fitzpaine Broadway Hazelbury
Exmoor Brendon Withypool Luxborough Lydeard Merriott Bryan
Challacombe Exford Brendon Hills Wiveliscombe Broadway Combe Evershot
Kentisbury Brompton Huish Wellington St. Nicholas Winsham Holywell Giant
Combe Simonsbath Regis Champflower Waterrow Chard Cerne
Ilfracombe National Park Winsford Monksilver Langford Norton Broadwinscombe Benville Milton
Berrynarbor Exton Morebath Budville Fitzwarren Uffculme Thorncombe Abbas
Brayford Bampton Holcombe Staple Churchinford Cerne Milton
Georgeham Bratton North Molton Rogus Fitzpaine Culmstock Stockland Marshwood Abbas Abbas
Marwood Fleming Oakford Hemyock Beaminster
Croyde Ashford Meshaw Dunkeswell Dulford Chardstock Powerstock Piddletrenthide
Braunton South Molton Rackenford Upottery Dalwood Benville Puddletown
Barnstaple Chulmleigh Witheridge Cheriton Broadhembury Honiton Cotleigh Marshwood Maiden Frampton
Swimbridge Chawleigh Fitzpaine Cullompton Bradninch Langford Talaton Northleigh Newton Dorchester
Bishop's Chittlehampton Lapford Bradninch Broadclyst Axminster Bridport Winterbourne Moreton
Tawton Morchard Cadbury Silverton Ottery Musbury Abbas
Instow Bishop Thorverton St. Mary Charmouth Winterbourne Broadmayne
Bideford Copplestone Sidbury Colyford Rousdon Seatown Bridport Abbotsbury
Great Roborough Crediton Tedburn Rockbeare Seaton Lyme West Bay Burton Litton Hardy Mt.
Torrington St. Mary Broadclyst Sidbury Branscombe Regis Bradstock Cheney Portesham
Merton Ashley Yeoford Exeter Topsham Seaton West Bexington Preston Osmington
Shebbear Dolton Spreyton Ide Newton West Bay Osmington
Winkleigh North Ashton Poppleford Chickerell
Highampton Tawton Dunsford Exminster Lympstone Weymouth
Hatherleigh Exbourne Bow Kenton Otterton Fortuneswell Isle of
Halwill Okehampton Lustleigh Starcross Sidmouth West Bay Portland
Northlew Moretonhampstead Chudleigh Exmouth Easton
Bratton South Zeal Castle Drogo Ideford Budleigh Salterton Portland
Clovelly Bridestowe 621 Chagford Dawlish Bill
Lydford Cheriton Bishop Teignmouth
Lewtrenchard Dartmoor Grimspound Bovey Tracey Babbacombe Bay Lyme Bay
Milton Abbot 529 Widecombe Gabwell Portland
Mary Tavy in the Moor Dartmeet Kingsteignton Kingskerswell
Tavistock Two Bridges Bickington Torquay Portland
Horrabridge Princetown National 516 Ashburton Newton Torbay
Gunnislake Yelverton Abbot
Buckfastleigh Ipplepen Paignton
Bere Alston Park Dartington Waddeton Tor Bay
Mellion Bere Ferrers Horrabridge South Brent Tigley Brixham
Tamerton Foliot Latton Avonwick Chuiston Kingswear
Saltash Plympton Ivybridge Totnes Ferrers
Torpoint Ermington Brownston Halwell Dartmouth
Plymouth Yealmpton Modbury Stoke Fleming
Millbrook Kingston Loddiswell Strete
Rame Newton Slapton Start Bay
ty of Plymouth Ferrers Bigbury-on-Sea Kingsbridge Torcross
Bigbury Thurlestone Hallsands
Bay Salcombe East Start Point
Portlemouth

Lyme Bay

English Channel

U 70 51° V 50° 30' W X

St Agnes

The Isles of Scilly consist of more than 200 granite islands and islets 40 kilometres south-west of Land's End, the furthest point west in mainland Britain. St Agnes is one of only five inhabited islands which have a total population of some 2000. Bathed by the warm waters of the Gulf Stream, the Scillies enjoy a mild climate that is almost Mediterranean in the summer. Like the other islands, St Agnes formerly made its living mostly by fishing, but this has given way to tourism and flower-growing. In 1868, William Trevellick, from St Mary's, happened to include a hatbox of cut flowers with his regular consignment of vegetables to Covent Garden in London, so beginning the present industry. Today, many islanders are involved in flower farming.

Part of the Scillies' granite archipelago

❶ St Agnes Lighthouse

Situated near Middle Town, this is the second-oldest lighthouse in Britain – a stone tower approximately 21m (70ft) high – active from 1680 until 1911 when its function was taken over by the Peninnis Head lighthouse. Built for Trinity House – the general lighthouse authority for Britain – the light was much needed, since the Scillies were notorious for shipwrecks, which provided a good living for islanders. Although still owned by Trinity House, the adjacent former lighthouse keeper's dwelling is now leased as a private residence.

❷ Flower fields

Like other islands in the Scillies, St Agnes makes a large part of its living from growing flowers. The warmth of the Gulf Stream ensures that the flowers bloom here before those on the mainland. The cultivation of the plants occupies the months from October to April, when tourism is at its slowest. The plants are grown in small fields boxed in by sheltering hedges of Pittosporum or Hedge Veronica, both from New Zealand, or Escallonia, from South America. Narcissi and daffodils are the staples of the industry.

❸ St Agnes Quay

Boat services to and from neighbouring islands use the small quay, facing onto Porth Conger, the bay separating St Agnes from Gugh on the north side of the sandbar. A good viewpoint is afforded by the Turk's Head which overlooks the quay and is Britain's most south-westerly pub. From April to September these waters feature in gig-racing. Gigs are six-oared boats, designed originally to carry pilots to ships needing navigational assistance in treacherous waters: at one point there were four pilots living on St Agnes. Though gigs are raced elsewhere, the enthusiasm for them here is unequalled, with races held weekly for male and female crews, and every year the World Championships.

❹ Gugh

St Agnes is connected to the islet of Gugh by a sandbar that is only exposed at low tide revealing a fine beach of white sand. The bay to the south of the sandbar is called The Cove; that to the north is called Porth Conger. Among Gugh's mysterious prehistoric remains are the Old Man of Gugh – a Bronze Age standing stone – and Obadiah's Barrow, a burial site. Like St Agnes, Gugh also possesses cairns – monuments of piled stones – and isolated rocks carved into fantastic shapes by the wind.

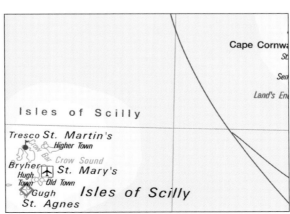

Falmouth

Falmouth is a port town of 20,000 people that historically flourished on fishing but is now largely dependent on tourism. The town developed from a community founded by a local landowner, Sir Peter Killigrew, in the seventeeth century and received its charter from Charles II in 1661. Falmouth grew in importance as the fishing industry expanded. The railway reached the town in 1863, and its eastern extension can be seen here, stopping just short of the docks. The view shows Pendennis Point, a headland extending east from the town into Falmouth Bay. From the top of the headland, Flushing can be seen to the north and St Anthony Head and the village of St Mawes to the east.

View over Falmouth towards the Carrick Roads

❺ National Maritime Museum

The National Maritime Museum Cornwall was opened in 2002 at Discovery Quay and includes exhibitions on boatbuilding, navigation and the fishing life of Cornwall. One gallery tells the story of the packet service for which Falmouth is famous. The town received a great stimulus in 1688, when it became the Westward Station for the Royal Mail's packet ships. These carried mail around the world, and war with France necessitated a new route for ships travelling to Spain, Portugal and the West Indies. The packet service was transferred to Southampton in 1852. The museum also has a lookout tower and a underwater viewing platform with floor-to-ceiling windows looking into the harbour.

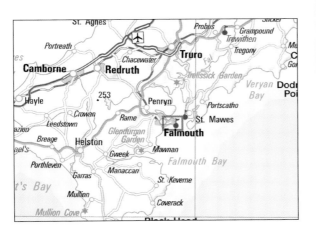

❶ Port Pendennis Marina

Boating for sport and for leisure in general is now an important part of the economy of Falmouth. Many small craft can be seen moored in the basin and alongside the pontoons of the Port Pendennis Marina, adjoining the National Maritime Museum. The marina has been the chosen point of departure and return for many round-the-world yachtsmen and yachtswomen including Ellen MacArthur, who made her record-breaking 71-day solo voyage around the globe between November 2004 and February 2005. The RNLI (Royal National Lifeboat Institution) station is nearby.

❷ Little Dennis Blockhouse

On the rocks below Pendennis Point, at the very tip of the headland, lies Little Dennis Blockhouse, an artillery fort built in the 1540s. Although now roofless, it still retains its D-shaped ground plan and massive walls. The fort's gunports once commanded the estuary and the open sea.

❸ Falmouth Docks

Falmouth possesses the largest natural deepwater harbour in the Northern Hemisphere. An artificial haven is provided for Falmouth Docks by the Eastern Breakwater (jutting into Falmouth Bay at the top right of the picture) and by a complex of wharves to the west, bearing evocative names such as Empire Wharf and King's Wharf. Vessels can be seen here moored alongside the wharves. Four dry docks extend from the southern side of the main dock.

❹ Pendennis Castle ▽

Pendennis Castle has commanded the western side of the anchorage of Carrick Roads since it was built by Henry VIII in the 1540s. The castle was part of Henry's south coast fortification when he foresaw hostility from Catholic Europe after his break with Rome. Its counterpart on the eastern side is St Mawes Castle. Fortunately, Pendennis Castle was never called on to defend the country against the Spanish Armada, whose attack proved abortive. As a Royalist stronghold during the Civil War, the castle briefly housed the Prince of Wales, the future Charles II. It was besieged by the Parliamentarians in 1646. It held out for six months – the last Royalist stronghold to surrender, except for Raglan Castle in Wales. The castle was refortified during the Second World War.

Pendennis Castle dates back to sixteenth century Tudor times

Tintagel

Located on a wild stretch of the Atlantic coast, Tintagel is forever linked with the legend of King Arthur, Lancelot and Merlin. In August 1998, a stone bearing a Latin inscription referring to King Arthur was uncovered at the ancient ruined castle in Tintagel where Arthur was purported to have been born. Originally Tintagel was the name given to the headland but, in the mid-nineteenth century, the village was renamed to promote tourism based on the Arthurian legend.

Tintagel Island, with the earlier castle remains

1 King Arthur's Great Halls

The legend of Arthur has been built on flimsy historical evidence. If such a person did exist, he was possibly a fifth-century warleader engaged in resisting Saxon invaders. The twelfth-century Geoffrey of Monmouth, author of the *History of the Kings of Britain*, described him as a historical figure; subsequently, many people have been fascinated by Arthur, including a retired London businessman, Frederick Glasscock, who built King Arthur's Great Halls which first opened in 1933. Constructed from stone quarried all over Cornwall, the Halls are dedicated to the legend of Arthur and house a version of the famous round table and 72 stained glass windows.

2 Tintagel Island

Twentieth-century excavations, which uncovered a large quantity of Mediterranean pottery, show that Tintagel Island was occupied during the fifth century. At this time it was was still connected to the mainland by a natural causeway. When Geoffrey of Monmouth was writing in the twelfth century, erosion had reduced this to 'a narrow isthmus of rock'. Monmouth described the castle as being 'built high above the sea, which surrounds it on all sides'. The connection to the mainland was so narrow that it was said 'three armed soldiers could hold it...even if you stood there with the whole of the kingdom of Britain at your side'. In the sixteenth century it could only be approached by a bridge made of long elm trees and today the castle can be reached by a steep climb up a hundred rock-cut steps.

Two tunnels run beneath Tintagel Island. The shorter tunnel was produced using metal tools and opens out in the meadow above the cliffs. The larger, known as Merlin's Cave, has been created through tidal erosion. According to local legend, the wizard can still be heard in the cave.

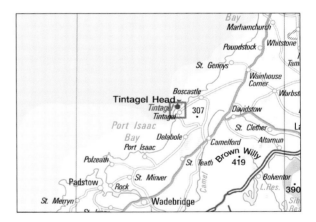

3 Tintagel Castle

The ruins of Tintagel Castle incorporate several phases of development on the island, and include the remains of an entrance on the mainland. Popularly known as King Arthur's Castle, it is in fact a Norman fortress, most of which was constructed in the 1230s by Prince Richard, Earl of Cornwall, the younger brother of Henry III.

Tintagel Castle was built by Richard of Cornwall in the 1230s

Eden Project

An environmental theme park and educational centre near St Austell, the Eden Project opened in March 2001 and was an immediate hit, welcoming nearly two million visitors in its first year. The park contains two vast enclosed conservatories or biomes, made of steel tubing and bubbles of clear plastic, that recreate the natural environments of the tropical rainforest and of warm temperate lands like those in the Mediterranean region. Developed by Anglo-Dutch entrepreneur Tim Smit in disused china clay pits over three years at a cost of £86.5 million, the project recouped this outlay in its first two years.

The James Bond film Die Another Day used the futuristic Eden Project as a set

① China Clay Pits

When Smit and the other members of the Eden development team bought the newly disused Bodelva china clay pits near the village of St Blazey in 1998, the site was a vast hole more than 60m (200ft) deep. Moving 1.8 million tonnes (1.9 million tons) of earth in just six months, they landscaped the area, installed an underground drainage system and added two thousand rock 'anchors' to stabilise the slopes. The development is so large that, for people unable to walk the distance, a train runs from the visitor centre at the entrance down to the lake adjoining the large biomes at the bottom of the site.

② Humid Tropics Biome

The Humid Tropics Biome is the world's largest greenhouse: 50m (160ft) high, 110m (360ft) wide and 240m (790ft) long. More than a thousand plant species thrive inside, in a recreation of the rainforests of tropical South America, the Oceanic Islands, West Africa and Malaysia. Pathways lead among the carefully labelled plants, with educational exhibits, footbridges over waterways and benches for those overcome by the temperature – which is maintained between 18°C and 35°C, increasing with height inside the dome. All the rain falling on the outside of the steel and plastic structure is recycled within; irrigation, waterfalls and artificial misters reproduce the moist conditions prevalent in the rainforests, where typical rainfall is 1,500mm (60ins) every year.

The Malaysian area contains a timber, rattan and bamboo house set within a recreation of a typical Malaysian home garden growing herbs, flowers, vegetables, rice and fruit as well as the horseradish and neem trees. Beyond the garden grows an elegant Bo tree of the kind that the Buddha reputedly settled beneath in northern India when he discovered enlightenment through meditation. The Tropical Islands section contains examples of rare protected plant species including the St Helena Ebony, believed to be extinct for more than a hundred years until two examples were discovered in 1980. The section also includes the remarkable Coco-de-Mer palm from the Seychelles – it has the world's largest seed, which resembles the human bottom. Two of its very rare seeds were donated to Eden by the Seychelles government: one has been planted in the Tropical islands section, the other can be viewed in the project's 'peepshow' attraction. Plants from outside the EU are quarantined at a nursery to comply with regulations for the control of pests and disease.

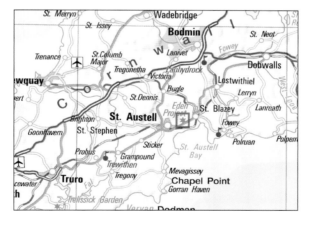

③ Outdoor Landscape

A carefully planted and maintained outdoor landscape – or 'roofless biome' – features the plants that thrive in cooler temperate regions such as Britain, parts of America, Russia and the foothills of India. This includes a section recreating the tall grasses and wild flowers of the American prairies, one celebrating the steppes of Central Asia and Eastern Europe and an outdoor Mediterranean area growing plants such as agave and sisal. Many of the plants for this landscape are grown from seed at the Eden Project Nursery on a five-hectare site at nearby St Blazey.

④ Temperate Biome

A second smaller biome recreates the hot, dry summers and cool, wet winters of temperate areas such as the Mediterranean region, parts of California and South Africa, Chile and South-West Australia. In this biome the soil is dry and dusty, shrubs outnumber trees and many plants have small, hairy leaves, spines or waxy evergreen leaves that develop in the wild as protection against the summer sun. The temperature is kept in the range 15–25°C in summer and no lower than 9°C in winter. The Mediterranean section contains terraced olive groves whilst the South Africa section contains a recreation of the Fynbos, an area of 46,000 sq kms in the Cape that includes 7,000 plant species including 5,000 unique to the region. The California section recreates areas of chaparral grasslands, containing the scrub oak or 'chaparro'.

The geodesic structure of the biomes is light but very hardwearing

Glastonbury Festival

The first Glastonbury Festival – the Pilton Pop Festival – took place in 1970, a three-day event held on a Somerset dairy farm. It was the brainchild of farmer Michael Eavis who, inspired by the Bath Blues Festival, decided to host an event at Worthy Farm near Glastonbury. The first festival attracted 2,000 people who came to listen to T. Rex and drink free milk. Although initially not a financial success, Glastonbury has since become an institution, giving its profits to charity.

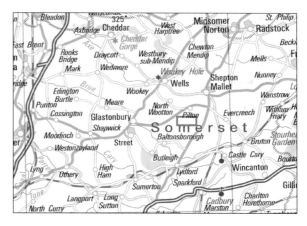

Music lovers at Glastonbury express their enthusiasm

❶ The Pyramid

The first Pyramid stage was built in 1971, on a spot considered to make the most of the natural energies felt at Worthy Farm. The area around Glastonbury is rich in legend and religious connections and Glastonbury Abbey was a place of pilgrimage in the Middle Ages. The performers that year included David Bowie, Fairport Convention and Joan Baez. A permanent Pyramid stage was built in 1979, designed to have a parallel function as a barn the rest of year. This was destroyed by fire in 1994 and the present structure was built in 2000.

❷ Worthy Farm

Worthy Farm is situated close to the small village of Pilton originally a harbour and, according to legend, the place where Joseph of Arimathea landed in Britain. In 1985, an extra hundred acres were acquired.

❸ Michael Eavis

Michael Eavis has been central to Glastonbury throughout the Festival's history. In 1979, he literally put his living on the line when, in order to provide financial backing, he obtained a bank loan on the security of his farm. In 1981, he was able to donate £20,000 to CND; in 2004, more than £1,000,000 was raised for charities including Oxfam, Water Aid and the Sudan Appeal.

A sea of tents looks across to the Pyramid stage with Glastonbury Tor silhouetted in the background

Overleaf: the Bristol Balloon Fiesta

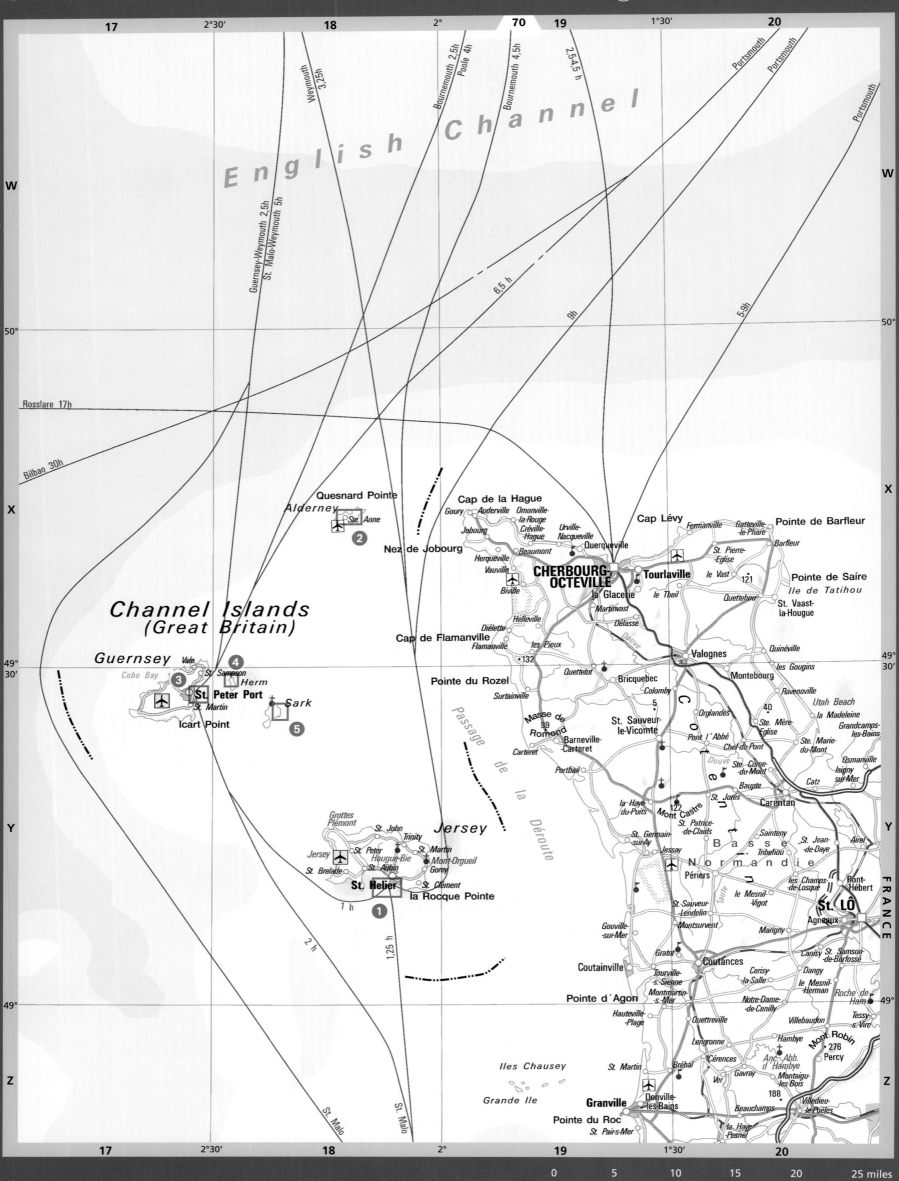

THE CHANNEL ISLANDS

① St Helier   ④ Herm
② St Anne   ⑤ Sark
③ St Peter's Port

English Channel

Guernsey-Weymouth 2.5h
St. Malo-Weymouth 5h
Weymouth 3.25h
Bournemouth 2.5h
Poole 4h
Bournemouth 4.5h
2.54.5 h
Portsmouth
Portsmouth
Portsmouth

6.5 h
9h
5-9h

Rosslare 17h

Bilbao 30h

Quesnard Pointe
Alderney
Ste. Anne ②

Nez de Jobourg

Cap de la Hague
Goury
Auderville
Omonville-la-Rouge
Créville-Hague
Jobourg
Urville-Nacqueville
Querqueville
Beaumont
Herqueville
Vauville
Biville
CHERBOURG-OCTEVILLE
la Glacerie
Martinvast
Délasse
Helleville
Diélette
Flamanville
les Pieux
·132

Cap Lévy
Fermanville
Gatteville-le-Phare
Pointe de Barfleur
Barfleur
St. Pierre-Eglise
le Vast
·121
Tourlaville
le Theil
Quettehou
Pointe de Saire
Ile de Tatihou
St. Vaast-la-Hougue
Quinéville

**Channel Islands
(Great Britain)**

Guernsey
Vale
Cobo Bay
St. Sampson
③ St. Peter Port
Herm ④
St. Martin
Icart Point
Sark ⑤

Cap de Flamanville

Pointe du Rozel

Surtainville

Masse de Romond 99

Carteret

Portbail

Valognes
Quettetot
Bricquebec
Colomby
5
St. Sauveur-le-Vicomte
Pont l'Abbé
Barneville-Carteret
Chef-du-Pont
Ste-Côme-du-Mont
Montebourg
les Gougins
Ste. Mère-Eglise
40
Raveoville
Utah Beach
la Madeleine
Grandcamps-les-Bains
Ste. Marie-du-Mont
Osmanville
Isigny-sur-Mer
Catz

Passage de la Déroute

Jersey
Grottes Plémont
St. John
Trinity
Jersey
St. Peter
Hougue-Bie
St. Aubin
St. Brelade
Mont-Orgueil
St. Martin
Gorey
St. Helier ①
St. Clément
la Rocque Pointe
1 h

la Haye-du-Puits
Mont Castre 122
St. Patrice-de-Claids
St. Jores
St. Germain-sur-Ay
Jessay
Périers
St. Sauveur-Lendelin
Montsurvent
Gouville-sur-Mer
Carentan
Baupte
SaInteny
Tribehou
St. Jean-de-Daye
Airel
Basse Normandie
Pont-Hébert
St. LÔ
Agneaux
le Mesnil-Vigot
les Champs-de-Losque

2 h
1.25 h

Coutainville
Tourville-s-Sienne
Montmartin-s-Mer
Coutances
Cerisy-la-Salle
Canisy
Dangy
le Mesnil-Herman
St. Samson-de-Barfossé
Roche de Ham

Pointe d'Agon

Hauteville-Plage
Quettreville
Notre-Dame-de-Cenilly
Villebaudon
Tessy-s-Vire

Iles Chausey
Grande Ile

St. Martin

Lengronne
Hambye
Abb. d'Hambye
Mont Robin ·276
Percy
188
Villedieu-les-Poêles

Bréhal
Cérences
Gavray
Ver
Montaigu-les-Bois

Granville
Donville-les-Bains
Pointe du Roc
St. Pairs-Mer
Beauchamps
la Haye-Pesnel

FRANCE

St. Malo
St. Malo

1:600,000

0 5 10 15 20 25 miles
0 5 10 15 20 25 km

St Helier, Jersey

St Helier

Jersey's capital is named after the sixth century saint, who was born in Gaul and believed to have lived on Hermitage Rock, near where Elizabeth Castle now stands; he was reputedly beheaded by marauding pirates. Today, the town is a tourist centre and working port with a daily fish market.

1 Island Fortress Occupation Museum

Jersey's proximity to France made it a target for invasion during the Second World War and the Island Fortress Occupation Museum charts the island's experience of occupation and privation. There is also a collection of rare motorbikes, contemporary vehicles and military paraphernalia.

2 Elizabeth Castle

Sir Walter Raleigh named Elizabeth Castle after Elizabeth I, while he was Governor of Jersey. The castle was built on a small islet in St Aubin's Bay as a sixteenth-century replacement for Mont Orgueil, which had become vulnerable to the newly adopted cannon and gunpowder. But since the causeway from Elizabeth Castle was cut off from Jersey by the tide, it was a poor site for defence. After French troops realized this and captured St Helier in 1781, another castle was built above the town. Since 1923, when it was sold to the Jersey government, the castle has been a public monument, although it was used by German forces during the Second World War. It currently houses a local museum and is a conference venue as well as a popular place for weddings and other celebrations.

3 States Chamber

As a British Crown Dependency, Jersey is governed by an appointed governor, and a parliament of elected members called the States Assembly. During the eighteenth and nineteenth centuries the assembly met in the Royal Court House, a twelfth-century building. But in 1887 the States Chamber was opened, and is now the permanent venue for all significant States meetings. The Chamber is decorated in a Jacobean style, lined with oak and plaster carved panels, and is located on the south side of the spacious Royal Square, alongside the Royal Court.

Guernsey, Alderney, Herm and Sark

St Peter Port was a natural anchorage used by the Romans, but it is now Guernsey's main port

Guernsey, Alderney, Herm and Sark

Guernsey is the second-largest of the Channel Islands while Herm, at barely 2.5 km (1.5 mi) long, is the smallest. Alongside Alderney and Sark they are all dependencies that share a history of allegiance to the British crown but independence from the British state. The islands are located closer to France than to Britain.

❶ Castle Cornet, St Peter Port, Guernsey

Castle Cornet is named after the rock on which it has stood since the mid-thirteenth century. Originally an isolated English stronghold protecting Guernsey from the constant threat of attack from France, it was not until the nineteenth century that it was connected to the mainland by a breakwater and bridge. Much of the original castle was destroyed in 1672 as the result of an accidental gunpowder explosion during a thunderstorm, and by the late 1700s its role as a garrison was largely taken over by Fort George, at the other, southern end of St Peter Port. During the Second World War, the German occupying forces modified the building to accommodate modern artillery. King George VI donated the castle to the Islanders of Guernsey in 1947 and it has been a tourist attraction ever since, currently housing a number of museums relating to its history.

St Anne is the main parish of Alderney and it also doubles as the main town

② Guernsey Museum and Art Gallery

Located in the Victorian Candie Gardens, the Museum and Art Gallery has a commanding position looking out over the sea. Opened in 1978, its innovative design incorporates an original cast iron bandstand from the pleasure gardens in its structure. In addition to temporary exhibitions the museum has a number of items that trace the history of Guernsey, as well as information on the island's wildlife and geology. The gardens are a rare example of 19th-century pleasure grounds and include two large statues, of Queen Victoria, and the French novelist Victor Hugo who was exiled to Guernsey between 1855 and 1870.

③ The Breakwater

Alderney's harbour in Braye Bay is exposed to ocean swells, so in 1847 the Royal Navy began constructing a long breakwater to provide a safe anchorage large enough for the entire Channel fleet if necessary. Building was painfully slow and finally abandoned in 1872. Today, only the last 870 m (2,855 ft) are currently maintained; the breakwater providing essential protection to the harbour that underpins Alderney's economy.

④ Alderney Museum

Alderney's Museum is open in the summer months and is run by volunteer members of the Alderney Society. Since 1969 the museum has been based in the former St Anne's School building, built in 1790 in the island's main settlement, St Anne. The collection contains more than 12,000 items; these include coins from a fourth century Roman fort, a rudder excavated from an Elizabethan shipwreck, and memorabilia from the time of the island's occupation in the Second World War.

⑤ Shell Beach, Herm

Herm's reputation as an island paradise comes from its clean sandy beaches, rock pools and the wild flowers along its clifftop paths. The island's chief source of income is tourism and Shell Beach, a stretch of golden sand 1 km (3/4 mile) long near Alderney Point, is one of its major attractions. As its name suggests the beach is made up of millions of small shells washed up by the Gulf Stream.

⑥ Manor House, Herm

The fifteenth century Manor House, with its castellated exterior and well-preserved tenth century chapel, is home to Herm's small school and is situated at the centre of this small community of less than a hundred permanent residents. Until 1737 the Manor was used by the governors of Guernsey while visiting the island for recreational hunting. After that Herm was quarried for its rich granite resources and was then rented by the Crown to Prince Blücher, grandson of the Prussian field marshal who had fought at Waterloo. Blücher, who was credited with introducing a colony of wallabies to the island, made the Manor House his home, as did the next tenant, the novelist Compton Mackenzie. The subsequent tenant, Sir Percival Perry, a chairman of the Ford Motor Company, appropriately enough introduced the first car to the island. Today neither cars or bicycles are allowed on Herm.

⑦ La Seigneurie, Sark

Sark is owned by its hereditary Seigneur, who holds it from the British crown, making it the last remaining feudal state in the world. The family of the present Seigneur, Michael Beaumont, have owned Sark since 1852. The family's residence is the Seigneurie, a late-seventeenth century mansion built on the site of the sixth-century monastery of St Magloire, the island's earliest recorded inhabitant. The house was extended in the nineteenth century, when a watchtower was also added to allow signalling communication with nearby Guernsey.

⑧ Sark Cliffs

Contrasting with the sandy beaches found on other Channel Islands, Sark is a natural rampart surrounded by high cliffs, averaging 90 metres (300 feet) high, all around its 65 km (40 mile) coastline. Above the cliffs, however, the ground is gently rolling, and the island's high point is only some 25 metres (75 feet) above the clifftops. This means that plant and animal species have been unusually isolated since retreating glaciers left some 8,500 years ago. The cliffs are a haven for a wide variety of birds, including Manx shearwaters, common guillemots and peregrine falcons. The absence of motor vehicles on Sark has helped by reducing pollution.

Both cars and bicycles are banned from Herm, the smallest of the Channel Islands

The island of Sark is divided into two areas: Little Sark and Greater Sark

SOUTH-EAST ENGLAND

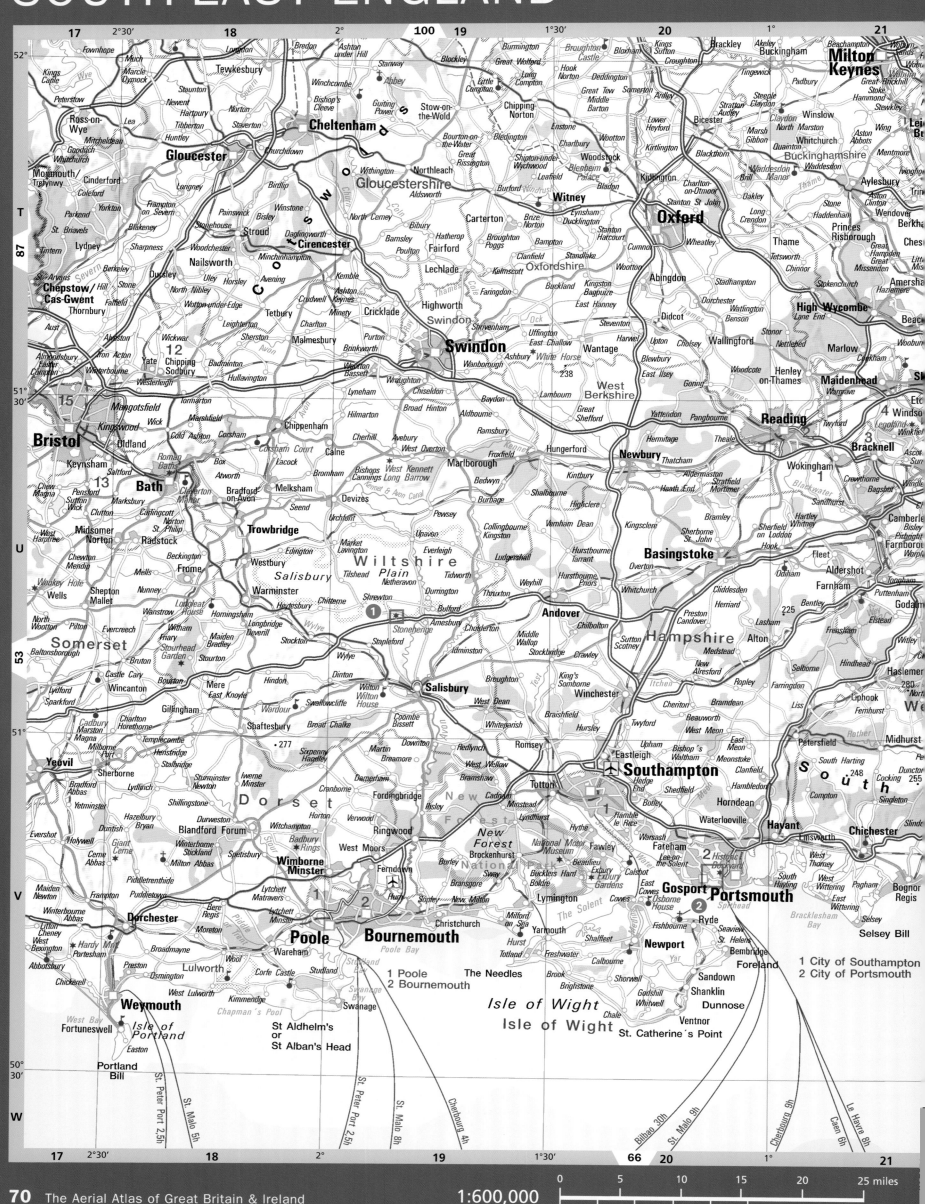

1 Poole
2 Bournemouth

The Needles

1 City of Southampton
2 City of Portsmouth

1:600,000

0	5	10	15	20	25 miles
0	5 10	15	20	25 km	

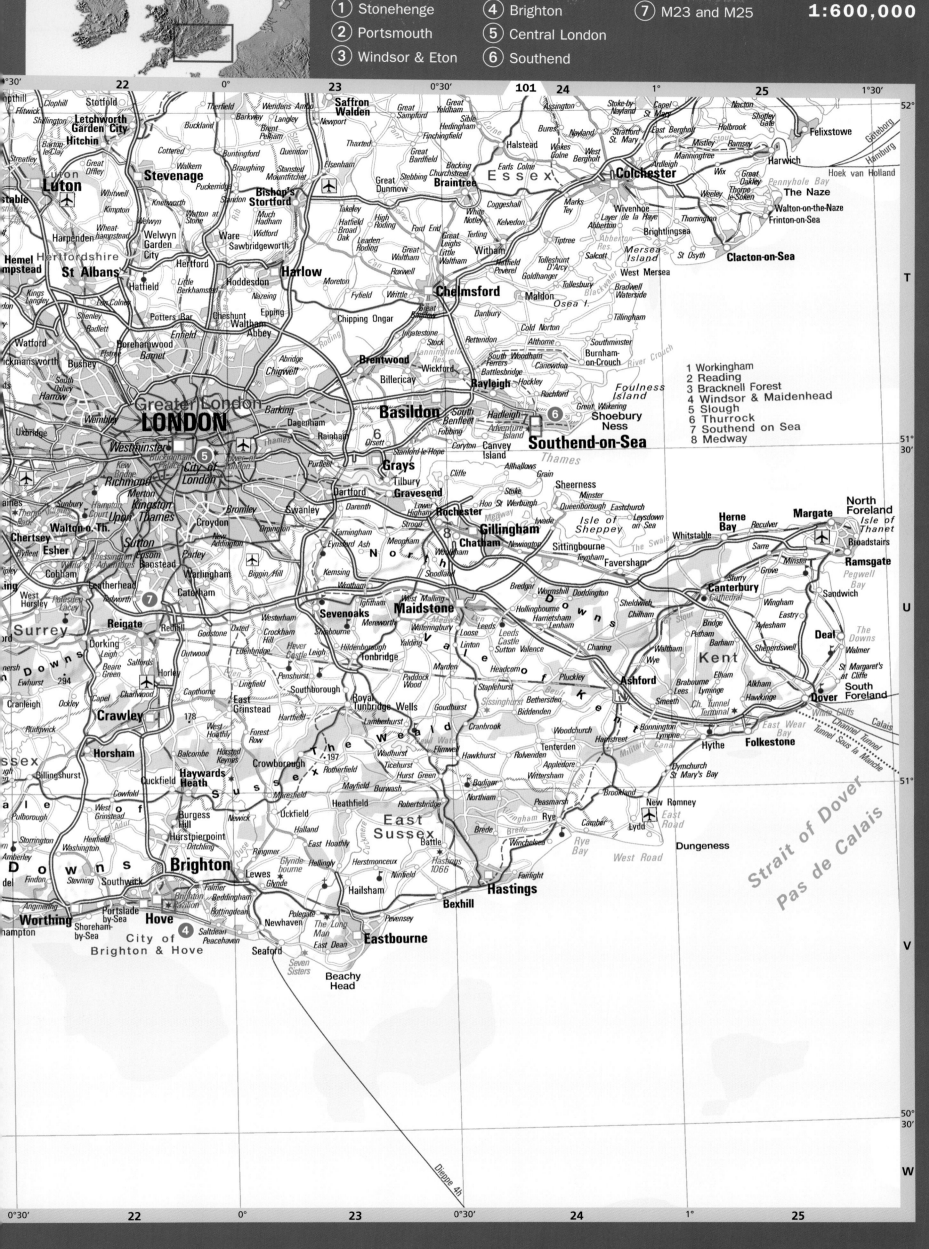

1 Workingham
2 Reading
3 Bracknell Forest
4 Windsor & Maidenhead
5 Slough
6 Thurrock
7 Southend on Sea
8 Medway

Stonehenge

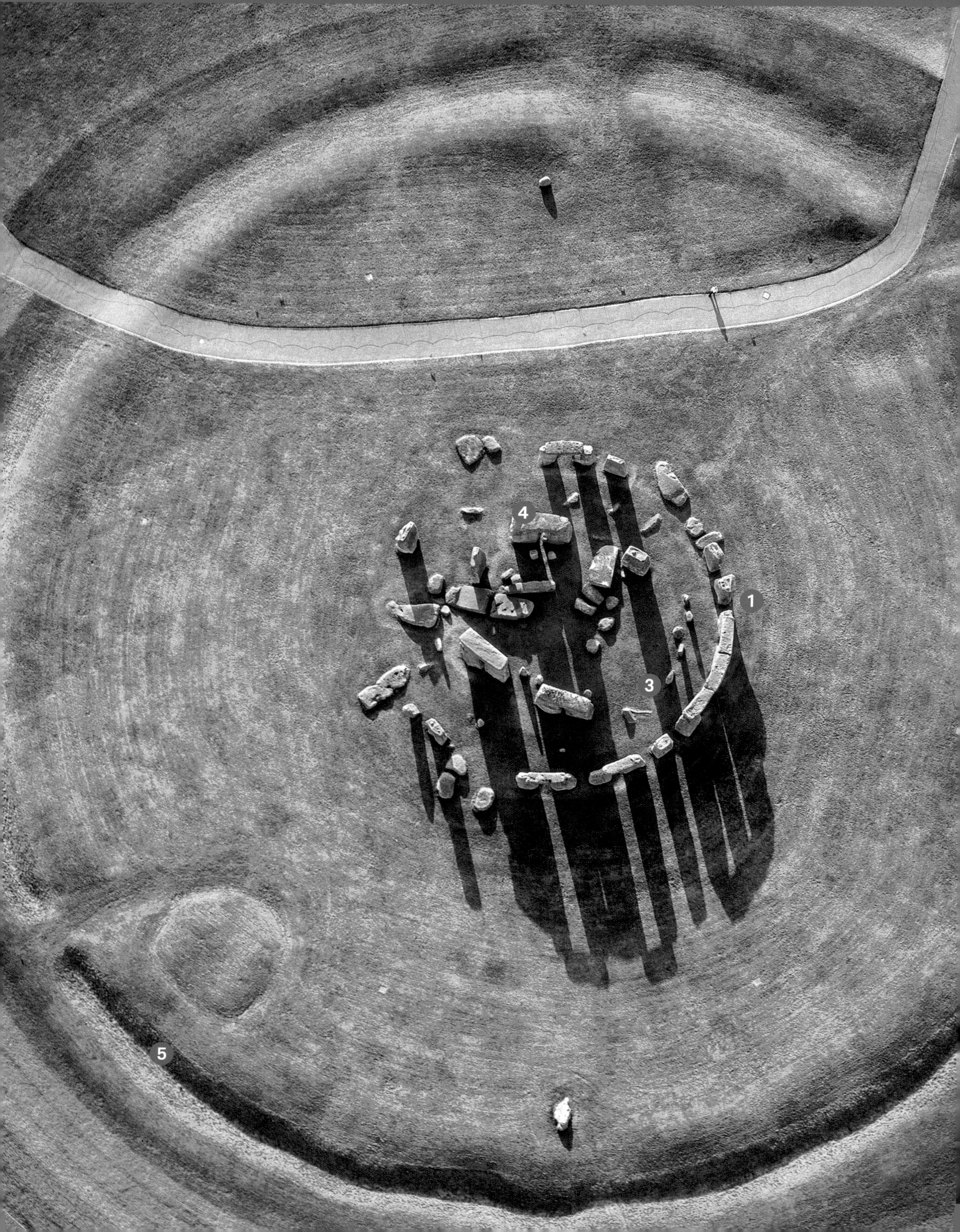

Stonehenge

Standing in a site of great natural beauty high on Salisbury Plain, Stonehenge is an immediately recognizable English icon – a symbol of the mysteries of ancient religion and the past's enduring power to surprise and enthral. The stone circle and earthworks visible today are the ruins of earlier structures, erected in three main stages between 3000 and 1500 BC. How and why Stonehenge was built remains unclear. The site may once have been a temple, an elite burial ground or an astronomical observatory.

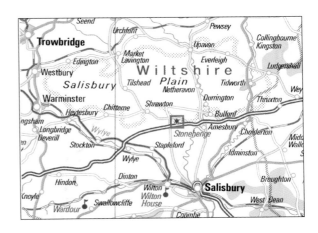

1 Stone circle ▷

Thirty vast sarsen stones brought 20 miles (30km) from the Marlborough Downs to the north were erected in a circle and capped with stone lintels in around 2000 BC. Seventeen of these uprights are still standing, some with their original lintels. The sarsens are as much as 30ft (9m) in length and weigh up to 45,000kg (50 tons). Skilled workers used stone hammers to smooth the rough surface of the rocks and to cut the mortise-and-tenon joints that connect the uprights to the lintels. The lintels themselves were curved to form a continuous circle and were fitted together using tongue-and-groove joints.

Europe's most famous Neolithic site is a triumph of engineering

2 North-east entrance

An entrance in the north-east part of the circle is aligned to the point on the horizon where the sun rises at the midsummer solstice. Two parallel stones were raised to mark the entrance – and one of these survives, now fallen and known as the 'Slaughter Stone'. Arranged around the inner edge of the circle is a series of 56 shallow holes. These were discovered by the seventeenth–century English antiquarian John Aubrey and are called the 'Aubrey holes'. They were not used to hold posts or stones but as burial spots for cremated human remains – perhaps as part of a ceremony to dedicate the site after the completion of the first henge.

Between 2900 and 2400 BC, labourers added wooden structures to Stonehenge. Archaeologists have found holes used to hold wooden posts in the middle of the Stonehenge site and at the north-eastern entrance. They may have supported wooden temples or other buildings, or they may have been freestanding religious totems.

The first stones were raised at Stonehenge around 2600 BC. Eighty pillars of blue stone – specially transported from the Preseli Mountains in south-western Wales, a distance of 385km (240 miles) – were put up in a double crescent within the earthen bank and henge. The bluestones weighed as much as 3600kg (4 tons) each. They were probably transported by sea or river – but may perhaps have been dragged overland by labourers using wooden rollers. The entrance to the bluestone crescent was aligned to the sunrise at the summer solstice. A new approach (the Avenue) was built along this alignment. The bluestones were later taken down and rearranged (see below). Most have since been removed from Stonehenge.

4 Trilithons

Within the stone circle the labourers arranged a horseshoe design of five 'trilithons', each consisting of a pair of sarsen uprights and a stone lintel. Some of the stones in the circle and the trilithon arrangement had designs resembling axes and daggers cut into them. The trilithons were raised in around 2000 BC.

5 Earthwork enclosure

The first construction at Stonehenge was a roughly circular bank and ditch (or henge) about 98m (320ft) in diameter, and is still visible around the outer edge of the site. Native labourers dug the structure using deer antlers as tools. The rubble they dug up was used to build the bank within the circle of the henge.

3 Bluestones

Around 1550 BC about 20 of the Priseli Mountain bluestones were put up within the sarsen circle, in a horseshoe pattern, while the other 60 bluestones were put up in a circle just within the circle of sarsen stones, the arrangement duplicating the pattern. The largest bluestone, now fallen, survives and is known as the 'Altar Stone'.

In the last piece of ancient construction work around 1100 BC, the avenue that leaves the main Stonehenge site to the north-east was extended in an easterly and south-easterly direction and as far as the River Avon around 2,780m (9,120ft) away.

Stonehenge and the circular monument at Avebury about 30km (18.5 miles) to the north were collectively declared a UNESCO World Heritage site in 1986. The monuments lie within a landscape used as a burial ground for more than 1000 years. Near to Stonehenge 10 communal burial chambers or long barrows were built between 4000 BC and 3000 BC. In the Bronze Age (2000–700 BC), 348 round barrows were built in the area to house the remains of community leaders.

Today 800,000 visitors come to Stonehenge and its surrounding area each year to gaze in awe at the vast prehistoric stones and wonder at the remarkable physical strength required to manoeuvre such vast pillars, and consider the skill needed to align the structure so precisely to the ancient midsummer sunrise. Popularly associated with the Druids (ancient Celtic prophet-priests), Stonehenge was in fact completed about 800 years before the first historical records of the Druids around 300 BC. This did not deter groups of revivalists from holding ceremonies at the site and today many people gather each year to celebrate the summer solstice.

Portsmouth

There can be few naval heritage sites anywhere in the world that played such a vital role in any nation's history, and which continue to hold such a grip on a national imagination, as Portsmouth's historic dockyard. Home to *HMS Victory*, Admiral Nelson's flagship at Cape Trafalgar in 1805, in 2005 the dockyard was the focus of the celebrations of the 200th anniversary of that decisive sea battle. However, it holds much more than that, with King Henry VIII's capsized flagship the *Mary Rose*, and *HMS Warrior*, a steam-powered iron-clad warship. The continuity of this heritage can still be observed today in the constant arrivals and departures of the modern 'ships-of-the-line' of Britain's Royal Navy.

❶ HMS Victory

Admiral Nelson's flagship at the Battle off Cape Trafalgar on 21st October 1805 is the world's oldest commissioned warship. Nelson died in the 'orlop' below decks after being fatally wounded at the battle. Launched at Chatham in 1765, it was already an elderly ship by the time of Trafalgar, and was saved for the nation by a campaign led by the wife of Captain (later Admiral) Hardy. He was the ship's captain, best remembered in the dying Nelson's famous remark: "Kiss me (or "Kismet, i.e. fate) Hardy". Weighing 2,162 tons, 227.5 foot (70 metres) long, built mainly of oak and with 100 guns and a crew of over 800 men, she had seen active service off France and Portugal in 1797. Today she provides a unique opportunity to see conditions in a naval ship during the Napoleonic War. She has been in a dry dock since 1922 to ensure her preservation, and was opened to the public in 1928. She is still used by the Royal Navy for ceremonial occasions.

❷ HMS Warrior

Launched in December 1860, *HMS Warrior* was the fastest and most heavily armed warship of her day. She was the first warship with a wrought iron hull, and was powered by both steam and sail. This was because her fuel consumption was so great that she could not carry sufficient coal. She had been built in response to a perceived threat from France's *La Gloire*, though such was her reputation that she never had to fire a shot. So rapid was the development of naval technology in the nineteenth century that she became obsolete within 10 years. After years of serving as a support vessel in Portsmouth, she was sold as a floating oil jetty at Pembroke Dock (Wales) where she served for 50 years, before being rescued as Britain's only surviving iron hull warship. Painstakingly restored, she provides an immaculate example of one of Queen Victoria's great warships.

❸ Mary Rose

The *Mary Rose* was the flagship of King Henry VIII. His development of the navy was an essential riposte to French naval superiority, and the *Mary Rose* was launched in 1511. Originally weighing 500 tons, her weight was increased to 700 tons during two refits. At 38.5 metres (125 feet) at the waterline, she was briefly the largest ship in the English fleet. She was fitted with newly invented gun-ports, and armed with a mix of cannons, demicannons and culverins. She enjoyed a successful career, but sank suddenly and disastrously while sailing from Portsmouth to confront the French fleet in 1545. Substantially preserved on the sea bed, she was finally raised in 1982. Her hull is in the ship hall, constantly sprayed with a wax solution to preserve her, while hundreds of retrieved artefacts (shoes, plates, arms, games, etc.) are displayed in the Mary Rose Exhibition.

❹ Royal Naval Base ◁

Portsmouth naval dockyard was established in 1495 with the building of the world's first dry dock, though the dockyard's traditions go back to at least 1212. Backing onto the Historic Dockyard site is the modern naval base with HMS Nelson at its heart. It is home to a significant part of Britain's Royal Navy, and is the main supply depot. At any time Portsmouth will be home to a number of frigates and destroyers stationed there between commissions for a refit, and the main dockyard will usually contain one the Navy's three small aircraft carriers, designed to operate helicopters and Sea Harriers.

HMS Ark Royal refitting at the dockyard

❺ Spinnaker Tower

Portsmouth's newest attraction is the strikingly elegant Spinnaker Tower, a 170-metre (552.5-foot) high concrete, steel and composite structure that is the focus of a regeneration of the Gunwharf Quays. It has three viewing platforms that give views over the city, Southern Hampshire and towards the Isle of Wight. The 'spinnaker' that gives the tower its name 'billows' out at 35 metres (114 feet) and reconnects with the main shafts at 120 metres (390 feet).

❻ Flagship Portsmouth

This area of the Historic Dockyard is part of the Royal Navy's Portsmouth base. It is handed over every morning to 'Flagship Portsmouth', and then formally handed back to Royal Navy control every evening. Apart from the great historic warships located there, this area also houses the Royal Naval Museum (founded 1911) that tells over 500 years of history of the fleet, and has a fine range of artefacts inc. the great carved figures that once decorated the bows of many ships-of-the-line. Other buildings and docks include the rope hall where the ropes for the rigging of the 'men-of-war' were produced, and landing craft and other small boats from the Second World War.

Windsor and Eton

It is rare to find a castle built on the scale of Windsor, home to British monarchs for over 900 years. It has the double claim of being the largest inhabited castle in the world, and the oldest in continuous occupation. It is in fact only one of numerous royal residences in Britain. Ten monarchs are buried inside the fourteenth century St George's Chapel. Just across the River Thames is Eton College, Britain's most famous public school, a royal foundation from 1440.

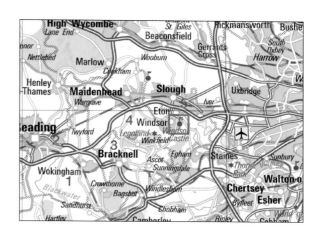

Eton College's chapel played a pivotal role in early English music

① Windsor Castle

Windsor has been the site of a royal residence since Saxon times, and there has been a castle on the site above the River Thames at Windsor since the Norman period, over 900 years ago. The huge Round Tower stands on the site of the original motte and bailey. After centuries of building and re-building, the castle today covers 5 hectares (13 acres), with the Lower Ward to the west of the Round Tower and the Upper Ward to the east. The latter includes the monarch's private apartments as well as the State Apartments and the Grand Reception Room (restored after being badly damaged in the 1992 fire that affected one-fifth of the castle). The castle, which is occupied by the monarch for only part of the year, is also a huge museum, containing priceless paintings by Holbein, Van Dyck, Rembrandt and Rubens, a unique collection of the drawings of Leonardo da Vinci, rare tapestries and furniture. A landscape garden was created to celebrate the Golden Jubilee.

② Eton College and Chapel

Eton College is not the oldest of the great British 'public' schools, but its royal foundation by Henry VI in 1440 gave it a particular status in the social fabric of the nation. He planned that it would have 70 scholars enjoying a free education, and sought their teachers from Winchester College, founded 100 years earlier. It was also well-endowed, thanks to the holy relics given it by the King, and to the right he had granted for it to sell indulgences (pardons) for sins committed. The Chapel became a major European pilgrimage site. It grew in a rather uncontrolled manner, the main school buildings (around the School Yard) proceeding slowly over the centuries. Though the new chapel is a fine example of English Perpendicular Gothic architecture, Henry VI had previously planned a much larger structure. It also contains wall paintings from the late fifteenth century and a fan-vaulted roof that was actually only constructed in 1959. During the Wars of the Roses, however, its association with the Lancastrian cause nearly brought about its closure by King Edward IV. Today the school has around 1,300 boys.

③ St. George's Chapel

This jewel of a chapel was founded by King Edward IV as the home to one of the great chivalric orders, the Order of the Garter, founded by Edward III in 1348. The insignia of the current knights (including banners and swords) are over the choir. All present and past members of the Order live on through their heraldic stallplates, which constitutes one of the world's finest collections of heraldry. With its painted ceiling and stained glass west window, the main structure dates from the late fifteenth century. It also contains more tombs of monarchs than anywhere except Westminster Abbey, the tombs including those the founder Edward IV, Henry VIII and Charles I.

④ The Home Park

The area surrounding Windsor Castle is divided in two. The 200 hectares (500 acres) immediately around the castle are known as The Home Park, and contain Frogmore House and Mausoleum. The 700 hectares (1,800 acres) of Windsor Great Park (the setting for part of Shakespeare's *The Merry Wives of Windsor*) stretch away to the south, and include the Royal Lodge, Cumberland Lodge and Savill Gardens, and many other structures. The Long Walk acts as the western boundary the park where the town of Windsor encroaches, and connects the two areas.

⑤ Frogmore House and Mausoleum

Frogmore House, lying less than a mile from the Castle, has acted as a country retreat for monarchs since the seventeenth Century. Though enjoyed by royal families past and present, the area is most notable for its connection with Queen Victoria. Such were her ties with the place that she chose a nearby site (where her mother the Duchess of Kent was already buried) for the Royal Mausoleum, within days of the death of her husband Prince Albert. The Mausoleum's interior décor, using coloured marbles from all over the world, took 10 years to complete, and out of respect for Albert's artistic preferences, the paintings and sculptures within were in the style of Raphael. Queen Victoria visited it every 14th December, the anniversary of his death, and was buried alongside him after her death in 1901. Frogmore House is no longer a royal residence.

Brighton

Brighton is situated between the South Downs and the Channel on Britain's south coast, and has long been one of Britain's favourite seaside resorts. The centrepiece to the resort is the exotically-domed Royal Pavilion, a nineteenth-century creation of the Prince Regent, later George IV. Fashionable Victorians followed the prince down to the coast, and the resulting development of terraces and elegant squares

enveloped the original fishing village of Brighthelmstone. Of the two piers that were built, the Brighton (formerly Palace) Pier survives today as a well-preserved seaside structure, while the West Pier closed in 1975, and has since fallen into disrepair, mostly collapsing into the sea. Today the city still thrives, and is a lively mixture of commerce, arts, leisure and tourism. The expanding resort was granted city status in 2000, and along with its quieter neighbour, forms the City of Brighton and Hove.

① Royal Pavilion ▷

One of the most exotic and beautiful buildings in Britain, the Royal Pavilion was the seaside residence of the Prince Regent. It was developed from Brighton House, a simple farmhouse that the prince began renting in 1786. The house was transformed and extended regularly, with a mixture of architectural styles, including opulent Chinese and Indian influences that were applied to both the interior and exterior of the building over the years. It also included fashionable Regency features such as bow windows and iron balconies. George IV was rumoured to have cried with joy when he first saw the magnificence of the Pavilion, and it became his favourite creation. At the age of 60 the Prince Regent became king, and spent his last night at the pavilion in March 1827, three years before he died. In the latter half of the twentieth century the Pavilion and gardens have been restored to their former glory, and are a popular tourist attraction.

② The Lanes

The Lanes, a maze of narrow streets, are the oldest part of the Brighton which date back to the time of the old fishing village of Brighthelmstone in the seventeenth century. Bordered by North Street, South Street, East Street and West Street, they were once the location of a monastic farm, poorhouse and fishermen's cottages. Today, the now pedestrianised Lanes are home to fashionable shops, pubs and restaurants, and remain popular with visitors.

③ The Steine

A grassy area of ground next to the old town, the Steine was used by fishermen as a workplace, where they would mend their boats, repair nets and cure fish. As the area became gentrified, the fishermen gradually moved away, and the area was landscaped with flowerbeds and paths where the upper classes could gently promenade and take in the sea views and fresh air. Further into town the main feature of the Steine is St Peter's Church.

The Pavilion is a fine example of the 'orientalist' style in architecture

④ The Dome

Brighton's Dome was part of the Royal Pavilion Estate, and was inspired by the Corn Exchange in Paris. Originally built as riding stables for the Prince Regent in 1805, it was covered by a huge segmented glass dome to top the Regency architecture. It was converted to a concert hall in 1866, with the interior being restored in 1935 with an ornate Grade 1 listed art-deco interior. Today, recently renovated, the Dome continues to be a popular place of live music, and hosts regular concerts from world famous recording artists as well as theatre productions. It is especially busy during the Brighton Festival in May each year.

Central London

The areas along either side of the River Thames in Central London have seen very different development over the centuries. On the northern bank the focus was commerce and government, while the southern shore was more for trade and the pursuit of pleasure. Only as the Industrial Revolution dynamised the expansion of London did the two shores take on a more unified feel. Trafalgar Square, built in the 1820s, became one of the few open spaces where citizens could congregate, and later protest.

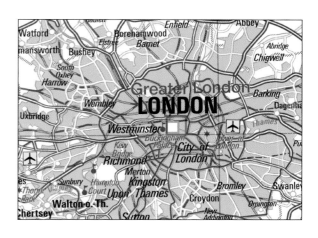

1 The Houses of Parliament and Big Ben

The modern Houses of Parliament (House of Commons and House of Lords) are still referred to as the Palace of Westminster. The Commons was granted a permanent home in 1547 in the palace's St. Stephen's Chapel only after being consigned to various parts of Westminster Abbey for its meetings. The House of Lords has always had accommodation in the palace. The palace's origins go back to Saxon times, but most of the original palace has disappeared, mainly through fire, the last major one being in 1834. It was re-built to designs by Pugin in 'Victorian Gothic' style and re-opened in 1870. The palace occupies approximately 3.24 hectares (8 acres). There are around 1,200 rooms and 2 miles (3 km) of corridor. From the entrance in the central lobby, the House of Commons lies to the north and the House of Lords to the south. The only significant surviving medieval structure is Westminster Hall, built between 1097–1099 by William II. It has the world's largest surviving hammer-beam roof, and has seen many historic occasions. It is here that William 'Braveheart' Wallace was tried; it was the seat of the highest court in the land until 1882; and it has been where many of Britain's great personalities lay in state after their death, most recently Sir Winston Churchill and Queen Elizabeth, the Queen Mother. The 98.50 metre (320 feet) high clock tower on the north-east corner is often referred to inaccurately as Big Ben; this is actually the name of the bell it houses.

Nelson's Column in Trafalgar Square

2 Nelson's Column and Trafalgar Square ◁

The first layout of the square was designed by John Nash in the 1820s but building only started in 1829 and took about 20 years to complete. The focus is the 56-metre (186-foot) high Nelson's Column, dedicated to the victor of the Battle of Trafalgar in 1805. Behind this sits the National Gallery. Former British Dominions feature too – Canada House on the western side and South Africa House to the east. The distinctive classical portico of St. Martin's-in-the-Fields, one of London's best-loved churches, rises above the bottom of Charing Cross Road. On the south side sits the statue of Charles I, from where all distances from London are measured.

3 Waterloo Station

Waterloo Station is one of the largest railway stations in London, and until 2007 is the point where all Eurostar trains arrive from France and Belgium. Opened by the London and South Western Railway in 1848, it is named after the battle in which Britain and its Prussian allies decisively defeated Napoleon in 1815. The original plan was for trains to run through direct to the City business area, but this was never realised. However, trains do run to Charing Cross and London Bridge from Waterloo East. Also, in the nineteenth century Waterloo was next to the terminus (now destroyed) for the funeral trains run by The London Necropolis and National Mausoleum Company, serving Brookwood Cemetery near Woking.

4 Royal Festival Hall and the South Bank

The Royal Festival Hall was designed as a concert, dance and performing arts venue. Built by Sir Hugh Casson for the 1951 Festival of Britain, it was a revolutionary design for the time. Its original appearance has been much compromised by the addition of terraces and walkways that have obscured its lines, but it is a Grade 1 listed building whose continuing survival is ensured by further substantial investment. Additions to the east include the Queen Elizabeth Hall and Purcell Room concert halls, as well as the Hayward Gallery exhibition space.

The wheel takes 30 minutes to go full circle

5 The London Eye ◁

The London Eye, also known as the Millennium Wheel, was the popular success story of the millennium celebrations. Standing 135 metres (443 feet) high, its 32 capsules offer spectacular views of the capital from a site just downstream from the Houses of Parliament. It rotates at 1.6 kph (1 mph) and takes about 30 minutes to complete a revolution, usually never stopping to take on passengers who walk into the slowly moving capsules. It is jointly owned by British Airways, the Tussauds Group and the two architects who designed it. Visitors are advised to book well in advance.

Southend-on-Sea

Southend was originally a village at the 'south end' of Prittlewell Priory. It became a popular seaside resort in the early nineteenth century, booming during the Victorian era, when it spread to embrace surrounding villages. Tourism was helped along by the arrival of the first railway line to Southend from London's Fenchurch Street Station in 1856, and the resort soon became known as Whitechapel-on-Sea, after the town of Whitechapel in London's East End. With London being only 40 miles away, the close proximity to the capital was an important factor towards its appeal. During the 1960s Southend was also developed as a major residential area and centre of commerce, a position which it still retains to this day.

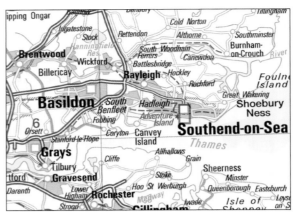

① Southend Carnival

The first carnival at Southend was in the summer of 1906, and was a fundraising exercise for the Victoria Cottage Hospital. Horse-drawn floats travelled from the Bandstand, through the town and finished at The Kursaal Centre. By 1930, the carnival had grown to become a week-long event, raising funds for the new General Hospital. A Carnival Queen attends every year with her court to add a regal air to the festivities. The Southend Carnival continues to be a popular annual event right up to the present day, and will celebrate its centenary year in 2006.

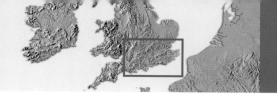

❷ Kursaal Centre

In 1893, a four-acre plot of land at the east end of the town was reserved for the creation of a new amusement park. This was called the Marine Park and was completed in 1894. The popularity of the park soon increased, and in 1901 the Kursaal Centre was opened to the public, complete with a brand new grand entrance topped with a great silver dome. The word 'Kursaal' is German in origin, and means a 'cure hall' or spa. The park was given this name to promote it as a place for healthy amusement. The centre became a major destination for day-trippers and works outings from London, and visitors could also attend such events as the New Year's Eve ball, charity dinners for needy children and the Old People's Dinner. Largely self-supporting, the centre included its own laundry, an ice cream parlour and a seaside rock factory. With the introduction of cheap package holidays to foreign resorts, and the increasing use of the family motorcar, the centre became less popular from the mid 1960s, and closed in the early 1970s. However, the centre was redeveloped and now enjoys a new lease of life as the Kursaal Bowl, a modern computerised ten-pin bowling alley. Other attractions include a circus big top offering amusement machines and cafés.

❸ Pier ▷

The pier at Southend is the longest pleasure pier in the world, first opening to the public in 1889. It has been extended on several occasions, with the final extension being completed in 1929 at a total length of 1.34 miles (2km). The pier was closed during the Second World War, and reopened in 1945. Visitors can access the pier either with a ride on the electric railway, or can enjoy the fresh sea air and impressive views over the Thames estuary with a gentle stroll along the walkway, which extends almost the whole length of the structure.

Attractions held on the pier each year include visits by Tall Ships, a Punch and Judy Festival which attracts over 300,000 visitors as well as sea-fishing which is available to everyone all-year round. There is a half-size replica of Drake's *Golden Hind* next to the pier. Illuminations along the pier were completed in 2000, and can be seen from dusk throughout the year. Over the years, the pier has suffered several fires and even a ship collision, but has been restored to its former glory each time. It remains a popular tourist attraction and a peculiarly-British feat of engineering.

Southend Pier has an electric railway along its 2km length

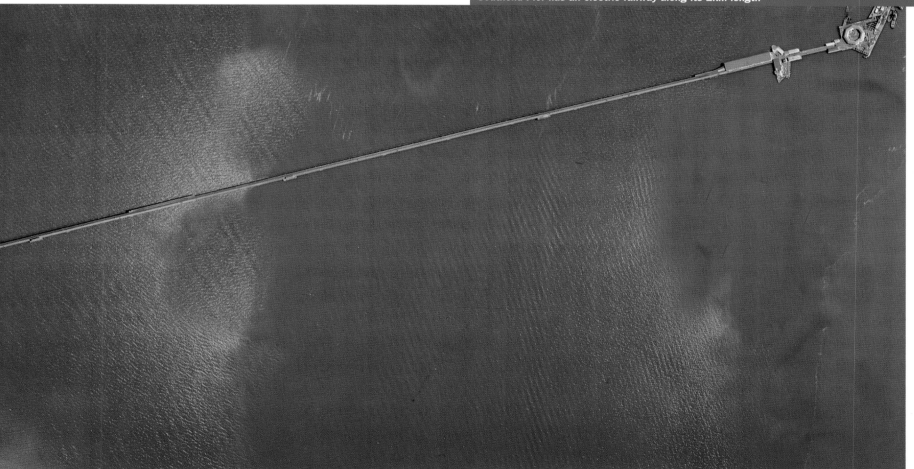

Overleaf: the junction of the M25 and M23 motorways

11 5°30' **12** 5° **118** **13** 4°30' **14** 4°

R

Saint George's Channel

Sarn Meyllteyrn Lleyn Llanbedrog
Aberdaron Rhiw Peninsula Abersoch

Braich y Pwll Port Neigwl or Hell's Mouth Trwyn Cilan

Bardsey Sound

Bardsey Island

Harlech **Gwynedd**
Llanbedr 754 Snowdo

6

Dyffryn Ardudwy

Abbey
Llanelltyd Dolgellau
Llanaber

Barmouth National

Fairbourne Cadair Idris 892 Park

Barmouth Bay Llwyngwril Llanfihangel-y-pennant

Corris
Aberllefn

Abergynolwyn

Llanegryn

Tywyn Talyllyn Railway Pennal Machynlleth

Aberdyfi Dovey

1 City of Wolverhampton
2 Walsall
3 Dudley
4 Sandwell
5 Birmingham
6 Solihull
7 Coventry

Cardigan Bay

Bae Ceredigion

Borth Tal-y-bont 752
Bont-goch or Elerch Plynlimon
Goginan Ponterwyd

Aberystwyth Devil's Bridge **W**

Llanilar 593

Llanrhystud Lledrod Ysbyty Ystwyth
Pontrhydfendig

S Aberaeron *Cilcennin* **Ceredigion** Abbey

New Quay Llanon Llanarth Ystrad Aeron Tregaron 508 Cam
Llwyndafydd Mydroilyn Llangybi Llanddewi Brefi
Llangranog Critbyn Lampeter Llanfair 484
Aberporth Clydogau Llyn Brianne
Ferwig Beulah Llanwenog Ffarmers Rhandirmwyn
Cemaes Head St. Dogmaels **Cardigan/** Ffostrasol Llanybydder Pumsaint Cilycwm Cyng
Moylgrove **Aberteifi** Newcastle Emlyn Rhydcymerau
Pembrokeshire Coast Cilgerran Llandysul
Newport Boncath Llangeler 358 Talley Abbey Talley Llanwrda
Strumble **Dinas** Dinas Cross Eglwyswrw Brechfa Llan
Head **Head** Crymych Llanfyrnach Llanpumsaint
Goodwick National Park Llanfallteg Trelech Carmarthenshire Llangadog
Fishguard/ Foel-cwmcerwyn Cynwyl Elfed Black Mountain
St. Nicholas Abergwaun 536 Cwmfelin **Carmarthen/** 633
St. Davids Head Llanychaer Maenclochog Llanglydwen **Caerfyrddin** Llandeilo Nat
Treleddydfawr Letterston Llanboidy Trapp Dan-yr-Ogof Caves
Llanrhian Puncheston Login Meidrim Llangunnor The National Brynamman Glanaman
St. David's Head Mathry Spittal Clarbeston Llangynin Bot. Garden Llandybie Ystradgynlais
Whitesand Bay 181 St. David's Newton Roch Wiston Whitland St. Clears of Wales Cross Hands Ammanford Ystalyfera
Ramsey Cathedral Solva Treffgarne Llawhaden Narberth Laugharne Llangain Llanddarog Tumble Llannon
Island St. Brides Nolton Taverspite Templeton Llansteffan 283 Pontyates Pontardulais Crynant
Bay Broad Haven Red Roses Kilgetty Pembrey Kidwelly Burry Clydach Pontardawe
Skomer Marloes Pendine Burry Port Skewen
Island Milford Haven Johnston Oakwood Leisure Park Saundersfoot Gorseinon Ne
Skokholm Broad Sound Aberdaugleddau Carew *Carmarthen* **Llanelli** Pontarddulais Briton Ferry
Island Dale Neyland Pembroke Dock/ Tenby *Bay* Whitford **Swansea/** Port
St. Anns Milford Haven Doc Penfro 1 Point **Abertawe** Talbot
Head Angle Pembroke Manorbier Llanmadoc 188 Bishopston Margam
Castlemartin Bosherston Caldey Llanrhidian Port
Pembrokeshire Coast Island Reynoldston Swansea
National Park **Linney** Rhossili The Mumbles Bay
Head **Worms Head** Port-Eynon Oxwich Bay Ken

1 Swansea
2 Neath Port Talbot
3 Bridgend
4 Rhondda Cynon Taff
5 Merthyr Tydfil
6 Caerphilly
7 Blaenau Gwent
8 Torfaen
9 The Vale of Glamorgan
10 Cardiff
11 Newport
12 South Gloucestershire
13 Bath & NE Somerset
14 North Somerset
15 City of Bristol

Brist

Por

Lynmouth Coun

11 5°30' **12** 5° **13** 4°30' **14** **52** 4°

0 5 10 15 20 25 miles

1:600,000

0 5 10 15 20 25 km

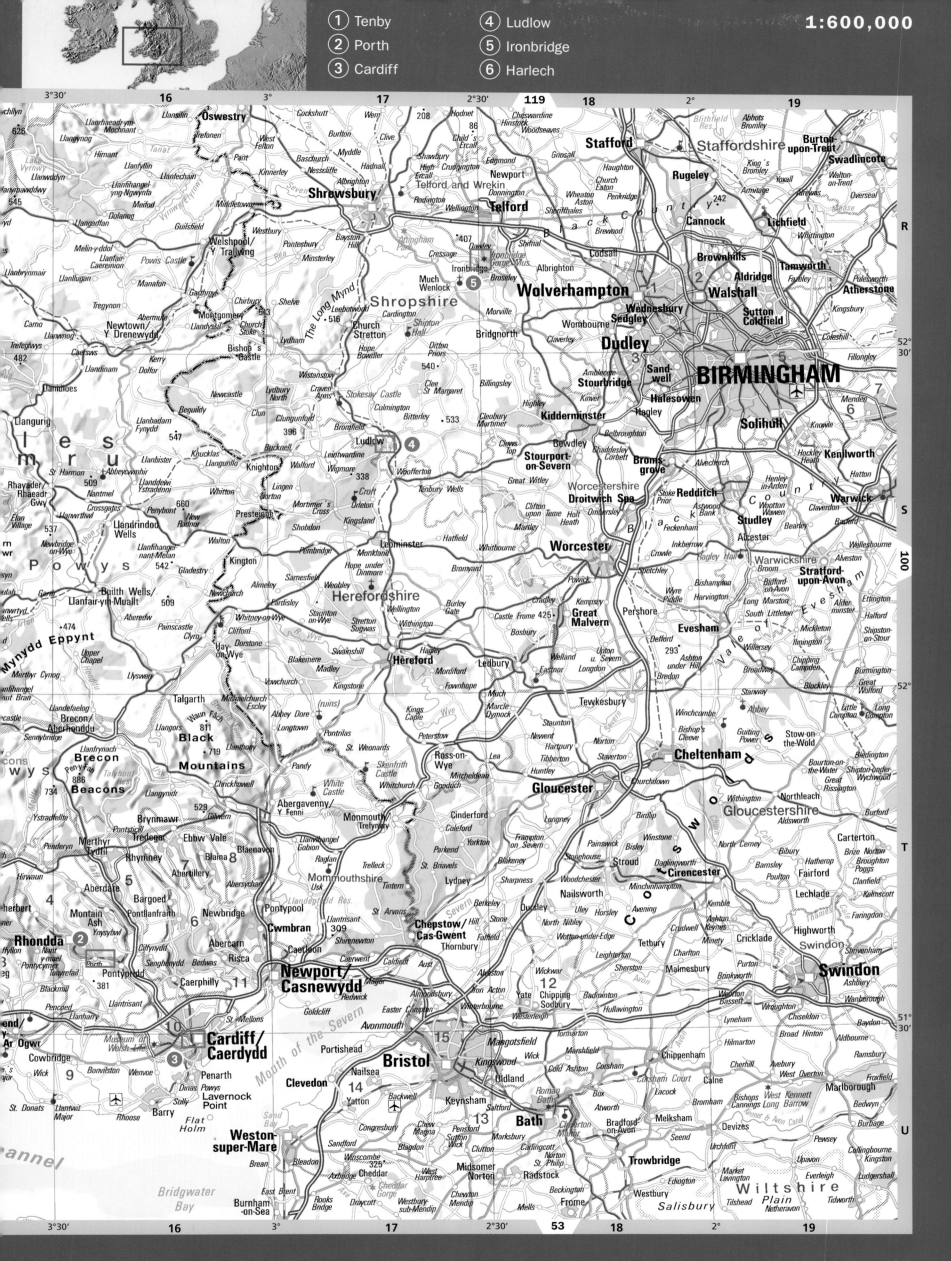

① Tenby   ④ Ludlow
② Porth   ⑤ Ironbridge
③ Cardiff   ⑥ Harlech

1:600,000

2
5

Tenby

On the coast of South Pembrokeshire facing Carmarthen Bay, Tenby combines sheltered sea bathing and a mile-long beach of fine sand against the backdrop of a historic town with the remains of a Norman castle, an ornate medieval church and a thirteenth-century town wall. In the late eleventh century, Tenby became a garrison town and later flourished under the Earls of Pembroke. By contrast, in the nineteenth century the town enjoyed prosperity when Sir William Paxton, a merchant returned from British India, promoted it as a Regency bathing spa.

The medieval heart of Tenby lies behind the nineteenth-century houses

1 Medieval walls

Tenby's position as a Norman stronghold made it a target for violent attacks by the native Welsh. The town's defensive circle of walls, gateways and towers was built following its sacking in 1260 by the Welsh Prince Llewelyn. The walls were strengthened in the early fourteenth century, following Edward III's grant allowing Tenby to impose a levy on all incoming goods, with the addition of extra towers in the wall and the celebrated D-shaped Barbican tower at the West Gate – now known as 'The Five Arches'.

In the mid-fifteenth century the moat (now St Florence Parade) was extended to a width of 9m (30ft), and the existing walls widened. At one time the walls contained 12 towers and three gates. Today only one gate (the West) and seven towers can be seen; the walls are most complete along South Parade and White Lion Street.

2 St Mary's Tower

Those who climb the stairs to the parapet of the tower – 25m (83ft) above ground – are rewarded with splendid views of Tenby's narrow streets, defensive wall and harbour. The church tower, one of the oldest in Pembrokeshire, was built in the thirteenth century. The spire, raised above the tower in the late fifteenth century, rises to 46m (152ft). Its copper weathercock was restored in 1963; according to some authorities, this is the original 1715 weathercock that was torn down and hurled into the harbour by a gale in 1894. In the belfry within the tower are four of the eight bells from a set cast originally in 1789; the tenor bell bears the inscription 'I to the Church the living call and to the grave doth summon all'.

3 Tenby Museum and Art Gallery

Located on Castle Hill, it includes exhibitions on the maritime and social history of Tenby. The paintings collection contains works by Augustus John, who was born in Tenby in 1878, and John Piper.

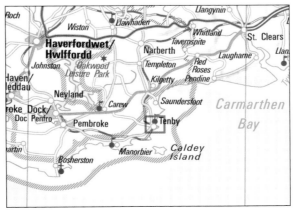

4 The Castle

Tenby Castle occupies a forbidding clifftop position on a headland. A watch-tower and parts of the defensive wall along the north of the headland survive, along with a medieval hall that adjoins the modern castle museum. The oldest surviving stone remains date from the thirteenth century, but an earlier earthwork structure was standing by at least the mid-twelfth century – records tell of its capture by Welsh noblemen Maredudd and Rhys ap Grufydd in 1153, in revenge for an attack on their brother.

5 Tudor Merchant's House

The refurbished fifteenth-century merchant's house is in Bridge Street. The house has period furnishings and a very impressive fireplace.

6 St Catherine's Island

The nineteenth-century fortress on the island – which can be reached by foot at low tide – formed part of the defence for the military docks in Milford Haven.

Porth

Porth lies at the convergence of the two rivers – the Rhondda Fawr ('Great') and Rhondda Fach ('Small') – At its peak, the Rhondda had 53 coal mines in an area 25kms (16m) long – with a population of almost 170,000, including 40,000 miners. The decline of the industry culminated with the closure of the last pit in 1990.

❶ Porth Industrial Centre

In the first half of the twentieth century, Porth and its adjoining settlements of Cymmer and Ynishyr were home to seven working mines. The last survivor of these – until 1983 – was the Lewis Merthyr Colliery that is now the Rhondda Heritage Park. An alternative source of employment was the Porth factory operated by soft drink company Corona. The Corona Pop Company was founded in the 1920s by grocer William Evans, first captain of the Porth fire brigade. The Corona building, with its landmark tower, is now a television studio known as 'the Pop Factory'.

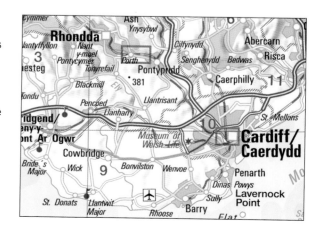

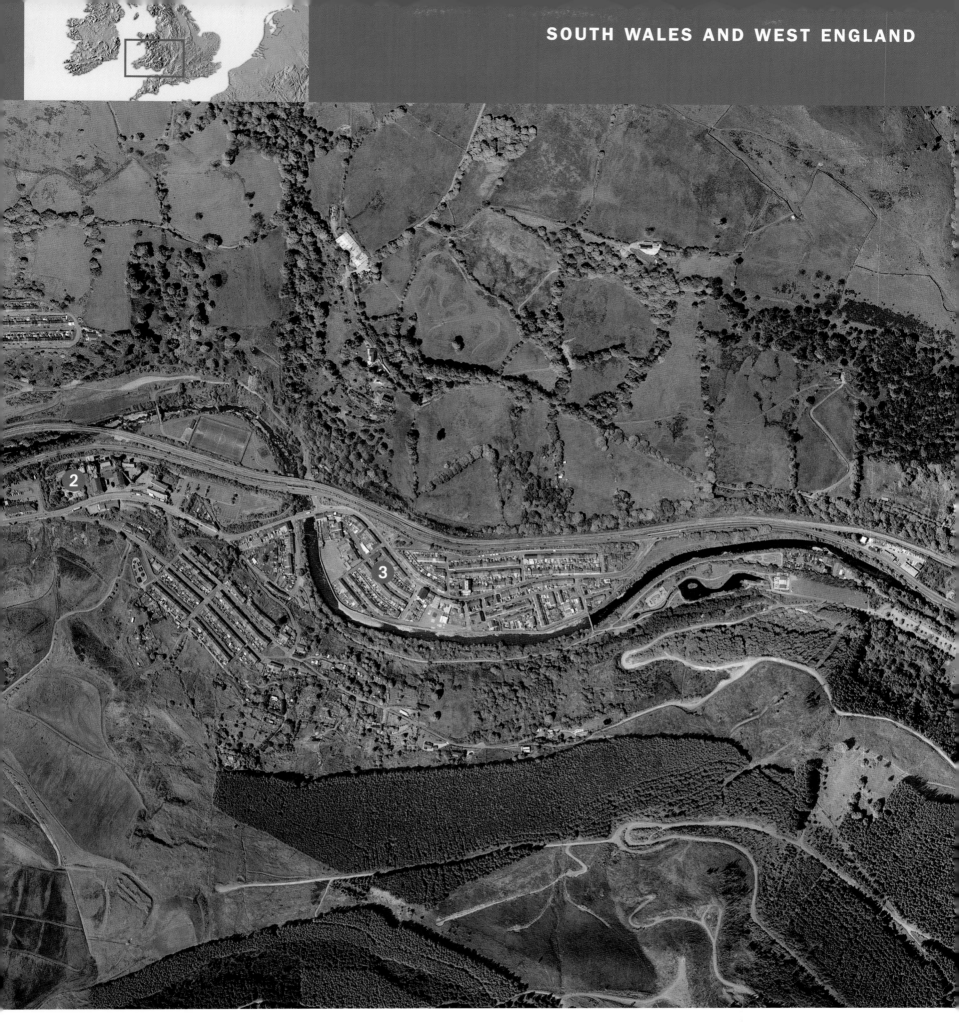

② Heritage Museum for the Coal-mining industry ◁

The Rhondda Heritage Park contains a memorial to the thousands of miners killed or injured in local coalmines. An estimated 30,000 miners were hurt or killed in the mines, or died from work-related diseases. Life could be very hard in these communities: in the depression of the 1930s, local unemployment rose to 47 per cent. Between 1918 and 1939, more than 50,000 people left the Rhondda – many emigrating to the United States and Canada. The museum offers visitors a taste of a working shift in a mine on its underground tour,

including a visit to the coalface. Alternative attractions include a children's adventure playground, 'Trefor and Bertie's Energy Zone' and an audio-visual display – 'Black Gold – the Story of Coal'.

③ Historic village of Trehafod

The village of Trehafod close to the former Lewis Merthyr pit dates from the 1890s and early 1900s. Due to mining activities, the valley floor fell by 4m (14ft) and the village shows the effects of severe subsidence through local buildings and the lie of the land.

The Rhondda Heritage Park from above

Cardiff

Cardiff describes itself as Europe's youngest capital, because it became the capital of Wales as recently as 1955. It had gained the status of a city in 1905. Today it has a population of about a third of a million people – one-tenth of the population of Wales. The heart of Cardiff is seen in the main image, showing most of the buildings that give it the confidence of a great city – ranging from the Norman castle to the new Millennium Stadium. Another vibrant area of the city is the port, to the south. The city once depended on the shipping passing through Tiger Bay, which was the centre of the world's international coal trade. The coal being exported from here was produced in the pits of South Wales. Now Tiger Bay has been re-christened Cardiff Bay, coal is imported, and the imposing Coal Exchange has been turned into a venue for conferences and corporate hospitality.

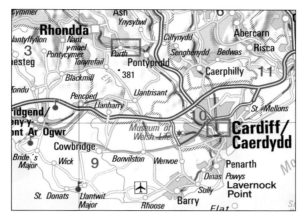

① Millennium Stadium

The largest movable roof in Europe covers the Millennium Stadium, on the site of the former Cardiff Arms Park. The stadium is not only large in area – it is actually the tallest building in Wales because the masts supporting its superstructure at each corner are 93 metres (305 feet) tall. The structure was built in 1999 on the site of the old National Stadium, at a cost of £126 million. During construction, the Welsh rugby team found a temporary home at Wembley Stadium in London, and the Millennium Stadium is now returning the favour by hosting English football events such as the FA Cup final, while Wembley Stadium is rebuilt. (The new Wembley will exceed the Millennium Stadium's capacity of 73,500.) Appropriately, the stadium was the scene of millennial celebrations on New Year's Eve at the end of 1999 that lasted throughout the following day. Fittingly, it has hosted most of the main British sporting events of the twenty-first century as well as rock and music concerts.

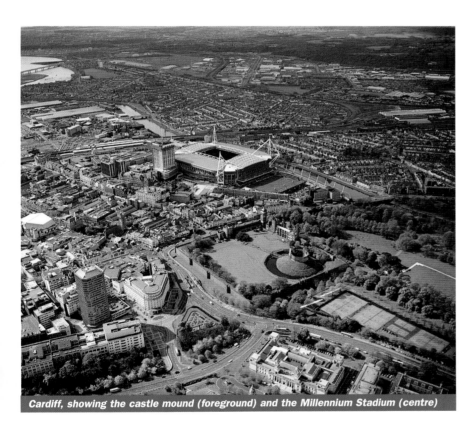

Cardiff, showing the castle mound (foreground) and the Millennium Stadium (centre)

② Cardiff Castle

The magnificent castle that rises over the city is partly authentic Norman and partly flamboyant Victorian makeover. At the base of the walls at the main entrance can be seen the remains of the last of several Roman castles built at this site from about 50 AD onwards. The Norman castle is perched on a motte (artificial mound) that was first built here about 1091 by Robert Fitzhamon, Lord of Gloucester. The first timber castle was reinforced with stonework in the following century. The castle was remodelled in the nineteenth century by the Third Marquess of Bute, John Patrick Crichton-Stuart, and his architect, William Burges. They added such flamboyant anachronisms as a clock tower, fountains, and exuberant interiors with marble fireplaces and Moorish designs.

③ Civic Centre

The heart of Cardiff's municipal life lies in the Civic Centre, an area of distinguished buildings built in white Portland stone, in an architectural style now called 'Edwardian baroque'. The buildings are grouped in Cathays Park, an area north-east of the castle. They include the County Law Courts, the University's main buildings, the Welsh Assembly's main offices and the City Hall. The City Hall was designed by the architectural team of Lanchester, Stewart and Rickards in baroque style and completed in 1906. It has a 59-metre (194-foot) tall clock tower and is topped with a dome carrying an imposing Welsh dragon. Inside, a marble-lined foyer is furnished with images of Welsh heroes.

④ River Taff

The River Taff winds southwards through the centre of Cardiff, one of two rivers to drain into Cardiff Bay (the other is the Ely, entering Cardiff from the west). You can walk alongside the Taff along the Taff Trail, which stretches for 88 kilometres (55 miles) to Brecon. While still in the city you will pass close to the Millennium Stadium and further out of town you will see the Taff Gorge and the adjacent Castell Coch (Red Castle). This fantasy castle was built by the third Marquess of Bute and William Burges in the nineteenth century, the same pair who redesigned Cardiff Castle in accordance with their own tastes. The river is now much cleaner than it was in the industrial days of the nineteenth and early twentieth centuries, and salmon have returned to the waters, alongside other types of fish, to make their home in the Taff.

⑤ Cardiff International Arena

Cardiff's principal entertainment venue, the Cardiff International Arena, can pack in 7,500 people for standing room-only concerts. The arena offers a variety of events as a concert venue and it benefits from its closeness to the Millennium Stadium, which it supports in its capacity as a conference and convention centre.

⑥ Alexandra Gardens

In the heart of the Civic Centre Alexandra Gardens is a small island of tranquility. At the centre is the Welsh National War Memorial, dedicated in 1928. The solemn atmosphere is complemented by the gravity of the surrounding buildings. On the southern side of the gardens is City Hall, flanked by the National Museum and Gallery of Wales.

⑦ National Museum of Wales

The National Museum and Gallery of Wales is built in white Portland stone, matching the nearby buildings of the Civic Centre. The superb art collections include many celebrated pieces, including Renoir's *La Parisienne* (*The Blue Lady*). The collection of Sir Watkin Williams-Wynn, a great eighteenth-century art patron, includes a fine portrait by Sir Joshua Reynolds of Williams-Wynn's second wife, Charlotte, in Turkish costume. The extraordinary Davies Sisters Collection, consisting of the acquisitions of Gwendoline and Margaret Davies from 1908 onwards, contains many French Impressionists and Post-Impressionists, including some of Monet's huge paintings of water-lilies. The museum's other possessions include collections of Bronze Age gold, Celtic artworks, ceramics and fossils.

Ludlow

Ludlow for many is the quintessential English country town, yet between 1536 and 1689 it was effectively capital of Wales for which it is one of the main access points. Set in rolling countryside above the River Teme, a tributary of the River Severn, it boasts a fine Norman castle, medieval churches and a townscape reflecting the prosperity of the Elizabethan and Georgian eras. There is a weekly market and, each summer, an important arts festival. It is also one of the best places outside London to find high-quality restaurants, judging by the number of Michelin rosettes. Everywhere there is a strong sense of a community at ease with itself, confident in and proud of its past. The ashes of A.E. Houseman, author of *A Shropshire Lad*, are buried in the churchyard. The poet John Betjeman reportedly described it as 'the most perfect town in England'.

Ludlow Castle showing the inner and outer baileys or courtyards

① The Town

Ludlow's wealth came from wool, both the raw product and manufactured cloth. It is an example of a planned medieval town, laid out in 'burgage plots' – strips of land, with a building at one end fronting onto the main street, and access at the other end along a back lane. This layout can still be seen around Broad, Mill and Old Streets, where Bell, Brand and Raven Lanes form the residual back lanes. Corve Street may even follow an earlier Roman road down to the ford across the River Teme. Ludlow contains many fine half-timbered houses, including the Feathers Hotel built in 1619 by Rees Jones, a local lawyer. The name comes from the three faded ostrich feathers, symbols of the Prince of Wales, on the building's façade. Rees Jones, like his fellow townsfolk, had Royalist sympathies during the Civil War, and around 1670 his son decided to turn the house into an inn. The inn later became a hotel, and over the years has gradually acquired adjacent buildings, and an international reputation.

During the Georgian period, which also left a strong architectural mark on the town, the wealth of the town was once again assured through trade and the glove industry. A number of the old half-timbered houses were 'georgianised' and their facades remodelled or concealed beneath a new plaster covering. Ludlow's museum tells the story of the town, and explains the complex geology of the region.

② Ludlow Castle △

In contrast with many of the great fortresses that were built to subdue the Welsh in the twelfth and thirteenth centuries, Ludlow's origins go back to the eleventh century with the de Lacy family who came across with William the Conqueror's lieutenant, William fitzOsbern. The castle is ideally situated on high ground, protected in part by two rivers that also supplied its well with water. Unlike many other castles, it was not first built in wood, as the stone for its construction was available on site. Many of the buildings, even though they are now only a shell, stand to their full original height. Some show signs of repeated re-working as the castle expanded. The solar block, where the lord had his private living accommodation, has Gothic as well as sixteenth century windows, most of which would have been glazed for warmth. Other additions at this date include the Judge's Lodgings and the reworking of the keep's main facade. The semi-circular Mortimer's Tower was probably built as a gatehouse controlling a rear exit. The fourteenth century St Peter's Chapel was converted into a court house, and then became the records store for the Council for Wales, the governing body, in the sixteenth century. The castle passed to the Mortimers in the fourteenth century. Roger Mortimer, who was responsible for the brutal death of Edward II, was in turn hung, drawn and quartered by Edward III in 1330.

Richard Plantagenet, Yorkist leader in the Wars of the Roses, son of Anne Mortimer and father of Edward, Earl of March, later Edward IV, lost the Battle of Ludford near Ludlow. The castle and town were then pillaged by the Lancastrians. From the accession of King Edward IV in 1461 until 1811, Ludlow Castle was Crown property, so there are many royal connections. Henry VII's eldest son Arthur, Prince of Wales and first husband of Catherine of Aragon, died here in 1502. Catherine's daughter by Henry VIII, Mary I, spent several winters here. The castle was progressively abandoned in the late seventeenth century. Its present owner is the Earl of Powis, whose ancestor the second Earl bought the site in 1811 and started the repair and consolidation work that continues to this day.

③ Parish Church of St Lawrence

St Lawrence is one of England's finest parish churches, a glorious example of the English Perpendicular Gothic style. Its origins are much earlier, though little remains of the Norman church – except the font – which was completely rebuilt in 1199 in Early English style. The hexagonal south porch, north aisle and south transept were built in the fourteenth century in early Decorated style. The mid-1400s saw a further major re-building in the Perpendicular style, and the addition of the 41.5-metre (135-foot) tower. There are also some fine tombs in the church, amongst them a beautifully carved alabaster monument to Ambrosia Sidney (died 1574), sister of Sir Philip Sidney, the great Elizabethan poet. For visitors, amongst the many glories of the church are the fifteenth century stained glass windows.

Ironbridge

This lush and peaceful valley in Shropshire was, 200 years ago, a hotbed of the young Industrial Revolution. Abraham Darby, a Quaker ironmaster, had his works at the village of Coalbrookdale, just to the north of this area, when he found the secret of smelting iron with coke in 1709. His son improved iron-making still further, and his grandson continued the tradition and built the world's first iron bridge here. This stimulated the growth of the local community; in addition to the iron foundries there were factories making clay pipes, ceramic tiles and china ware. Coal pits worked to fuel this activity, making a quarter of Britain's iron. Even tourism was nurtured here, for a hotel was built specifically to accommodate the visitors drawn by the wonder of the Iron Bridge. This part of the Severn Valley was declared a World Heritage Site by UNESCO in 1986.

❶ Enginuity

Visitors to Ironbridge can learn about science and technology in the Enginuity interactive exhibit. This modern display is located in an old building that once belonged to the Coalbrookdale Corporation, and is on the same site as the Museum of Iron in the Ironbridge Gorge The themes often begin with engineering artefacts old and new, from steam engines to mobile phones. But visitors are invited to play with them, design them anew, and generally push, pull and handle exhibits. They also get the experience of operating X-ray machines or 'floating on air', thanks to magnetic levitation.

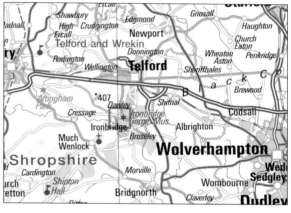

❷ The Iron Bridge ◁

Construction of the world's first bridge made wholly of iron began in late 1777, and it was formally opened on New Year's Day 1781. It was the creation of the architect Thomas Pritchard and the iron-maker Abraham Darby III. Pritchard died a month after work on the bridge began, but Darby was to receive a gold medal from the Royal Society of Arts for his achievement. Though repainted and smartened up in recent years, the bridge can no longer take vehicles. But pedestrians can cross it, admire the beauty of the gorge, and visit the tollhouse on the south bank, where a tariff of tolls dating from Victorian times can still be seen posted on the outside of the building.

The Iron Bridge is the focus of the town and the surrounding area

❸ The Greenwood Trust

The Greenwood Trust is devoted to keeping alive old country crafts and finding new solutions for modern living. The community room here is of a unique construction, made of local timber and positioned to make the best use of sunlight for warmth. Non-toxic plant materials were used in place of conventional paints and stains, and recyclable materials were used for insulation. Waste water is filtered through reed beds and flows into a 'wildlife-friendly' pond. The Trust uses experts in forestry and country crafts, together with artists and teachers, to keep alive ancient skills.

❹ River Severn

The Ironbridge Gorge is home to a short stretch of the longest river in Britain. The Severn rises in the Cambrian Mountains in Mid-Wales and flows 354 kilometres (220 miles) to the Atlantic Ocean, its estuary forming the Bristol Channel. There are six bridges over the river in the Ironbridge area. The Iron Bridge was built following the loss of a previous bridge during floods. The riverside dwellers used coracles, small bowl-shaped craft still made at Ironbridge until the death of their last constructor, Eustace Rogers, in 2002.

❺ The Museum of the Gorge ▽

A short walk along the river from the Iron Bridge is the Museum of the Gorge. It is housed in a building erected in 1834 in a striking Gothic style – yet this is the Old Severn Warehouse, once used for storing goods by the Coalbrookdale Company. The exhibition inside includes a scale model of the gorge as it was in 1796.

The unique gothic building at the Museum of the Gorge

Overleaf: the castle and village of Harlech

1:600,000

| 0 | 5 | 10 | 15 | 20 | 25 miles |

| 0 | 5 | 10 | 15 | 20 | 25 km |

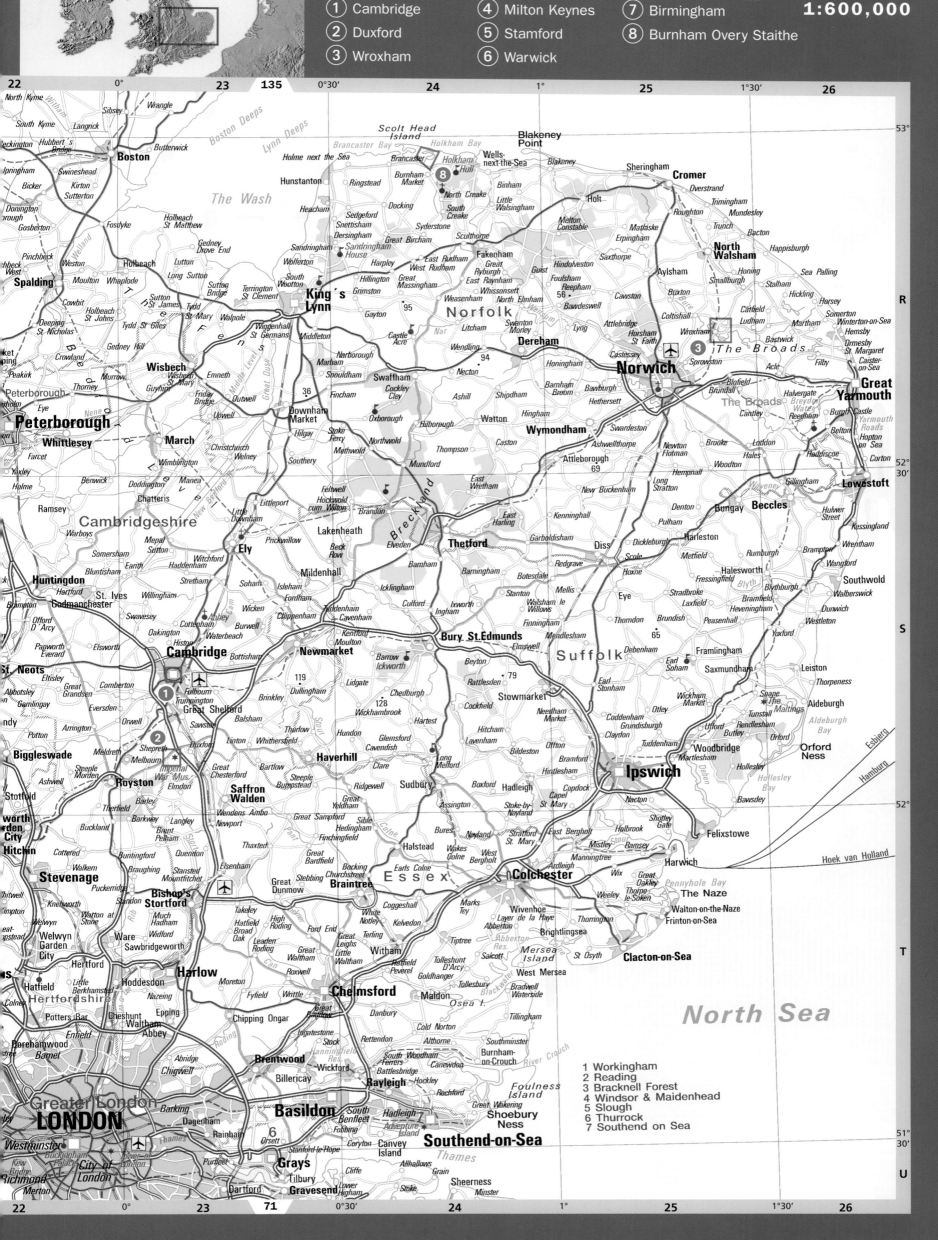

Cambridge

Cambridge University is one of Europe's oldest universities and, after Oxford, the second oldest university in the English-speaking world. It produces more Nobel prize-winners than any other university in the world and is also an architectural jewel, richly endowed by generations of patrons and containing some of the finest examples of craftsmanship anywhere in Britain. The university's main expansion took place in the later middle ages when the academic focus switched from church law to classical studies and mathematics. The first all-women colleges were added in 1869 (Girton) and 1872 (Newnham). Robinson College, built in 1979, brought the total of colleges to 31.

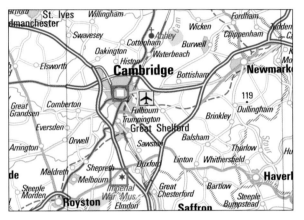

1 Pembroke College

Pembroke was the third college to be founded in Cambridge, in 1347. Its founder was Mary de Pol, wife of the Earl of Pembroke, and the college was originally called Marie Valence Hall. First Court is the original college, containing all the accommodation and catering facilities originally required, as well as the chapel, the first college chapel in Cambridge. During the Reformation period Mary I had several college fellows martyred, including the Master, Nicholas Ridley. The chapel was re-designed by Sir Christopher Wren in classical style in 1665. The college has a strong tradition of oriental studies, especially Arabic, and has produced a number of distinguished alumni, both literary and political, including Edmund Spenser and Ted Hughes.

2 King's College

In a university where colleges jostle for special recognition, King's still manages to stand out, thanks to its glorious Chapel and internationally renowned choir. King's was founded by Henry VI in 1441 as a college for pupils from Eton, and the choir too owes its existence to him. The choir includes 16 boy choristers, and the annual nine lessons and carols service before Christmas from King's College chapel has a worldwide audience. The Chapel took a century to built and has twelve huge windows on on each side and the world's largest fan-vaulted ceiling. King's also boasts one of the best college libraries, with 130,000 items, including many rare manuscripts and books, and estate records going back to its foundation year. The universities of Oxford and Cambridge, and their colleges, are amongst the biggest landlords in Britain.

3 Queen's College

The college was founded in 1448 by Margaret of Anjou, and re-founded in 1465 by Elizabeth Woodville, Edward IV's wife. Its official name is The Queen's College of St Margaret and St Bernard. It is only one of two colleges that has buildings on either side of the River Cam; indeed, the President's Lodge is the oldest building on the river. The two sides of the college are connected by the Mathematical Bridge, supposedly designed and built by Sir Isaac Newton, but actually by one James Essex the Younger.

4 Trinity College

Trinity is the largest and richest of the Cambridge colleges, with around 900 undergraduate and postgraduate students. It was founded by Henry VIII in 1546, and most of the college's buildings were built over the next 100 years. A key influence in its development was Thomas Nevile, who became Master in 1593, and re-built many of the existing buildings. One of the quadrangles (Nevile's Court) bears his name.

The grass-covered banks of the Cam are known as 'the Backs'

5 Gonville and Caius College

The original college foundation was by Edward Gonville, Rector of Terrington, in 1348 as Gonville Hall, a place for prayer and study. However, the college went into a prolonged decline and was re-founded in 1557 by a former student, Dr John Keys, a name he subsequently changed to Caius. He is best remembered for the elegant Caius Court and the college's three gates - 'Honour', 'Humility' and 'Virtue'. The college's fortunes rose and fell over the years, declining between the seventeenth and nineteenth centuries.

6 St John's College

St John's is the university's second largest college. It was founded in 1511 on the site of the Hospital of St John by Lady Margaret Beaufort, who died soon after. Nothing now remains of the original hospital, part of which had formed the First Court until it was demolished in the nineteenth century. The court had been used to house prisoners in the English Civil War. The college chapel is by George Gilbert Scott. The Second Court was built between 1589 and 1599, and is claimed to be England's finest Tudor court. Other important features include the Old Library (1624) and New Bridge over the River Cam. This leads to the nineteenth century Gothic New Court on the west bank. St John's also boasts one of Britain's finest college choirs.

7 Peterhouse

The oldest and smallest of the Cambridge colleges, Peterhouse was founded by Hugo de Balsham, Bishop of Ely, in 1284. The early founders expected students to pray for their souls. It has been traditionally strong in the sciences, and counts Charles Babbage (inventor of the first computer), Henry Cavendish (after whom the great Cambridge research laboratory was named), and Christopher Cockrell (inventor of the hovercraft) amongst its alumni.

Duxford

Located a few miles south of Cambridge, Duxford is only one of several museums operated by the South London-based Imperial War Museum (IWM). It is one of the world's most important air museums, on an airfield that played a vital role in the defence of Britain in two world wars. Today the First World War hangers and new state-of-the-art displays contain a rich selection of aircraft and military vehicles, helping to interpret twentieth century history for a new generation.

❷ The Land Warfare Hall

Duxford's focus for many years was aviation heritage, but in recent years a major initiative has been the development of the Land Warfare Hall. Tanks, trucks and artillery from various countries, allies and former enemies, are displayed singly, or in special dioramas that recreate some of the atmosphere of a battle scene. A series of rotating exhibitions allows visitors to study some of the activities of the British Army in both world wars, and more recent conflicts.

A Soviet-made tank outside the Land Warfare Hall

❹ The American Air Museum

Opened by George Bush in 2002, the museum is the most dramatic display of historic aircraft to date at Duxford. By suspending several aircraft from the ceiling of the display hall, some 20 aircraft, from a First World War SPAD to the vast B-52 Stratofortress bomber (still in service with the U.S. Air Force) are accommodated. There are numerous immaculately preserved examples of many of the legendary aircraft produced in the U.S. and flown by American and allied airmen in the Second World War. These include the three classic heavy bombers, the B-17 *Flying Fortress*, the B-24 *Liberator* and B-29 *Superfortress*, the type that dropped the first atomic bombs on Japan. For many the highlight is the futuristic SR-71 *Blackbird*, the extraordinary, once top secret high speed spy plane produced by Lockheed. Speculation abounds as to whether its successor is already out there, somewhere.

❶ The Fighter Collection

Duxford's pre-eminence as the European centre for the restoration and display of historic warbirds is the result of the IWM's enlightened collaboration with the founder of The Fighter Collection, Stephen Grey, Britain's largest 'warbird' operator. This has provided a base, and a core of restoration and operational expertise, that has helped a range of other 'warbird' specialists. Their aim is to bring back as many classic aircraft to flying condition as possible, using rigorous historical research to ensure that the restorations are accurate. Some of the smaller specialists rebuild classic aircraft for sale to collectors worldwide, while others focus on the preservation of aircraft as varied as Boeing's B-17G bomber and the Bristol Blenheim light bomber.

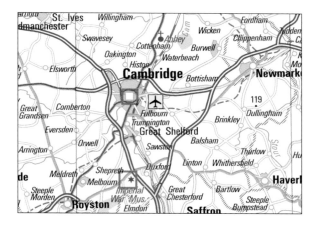

❸ AirSpace

The Superhanger will be replaced by the state-of-the-art AirSpace display by the end of 2006. Over the years the Superhanger's collection has been re-shuffled, but has always had a strong British flavour. Pride of place went to the Anglo-French Concorde supersonic airliner, withdrawn from service at the end of 2003, and the TSR.2, a strike aircraft that was cancelled in the 1960s after only four prototypes were produced. Naval aircraft are currently exhibited along with a myriad of other types that help display the rich variety (and eccentricity) of British aircraft development over the last century.

Concorde is always a major attraction at Duxford

Wroxham and the Norfolk Broads

The Norfolk Broads comprise a multitude of wide, shallow lakes in north-east Norfolk. Often called the capital of the Broads, Wroxham and the adjoining village of Hoveton are surrounded by large stretches of water, once thought to be natural phenomena but only relatively recently revealed to be a series of artificially created waterways, the product of medieval peat digging since flooded. From the late nineteenth century the Norfolk Broads have been a major tourist attraction.

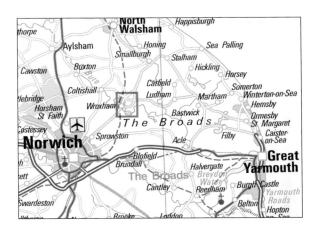

❶ Wroxham and Hoveton

Situated about seven miles from Norwich, the villages of Wroxham and Hoveton are linked by a small hump-back bridge spanning the River Bure. Together, these villages form the boating heart of the Norfolk Broads. In the summer months, the local population of 3,200 is swelled massively by tourists taking cruises around the local area, hiring leisure craft and using Wroxham as a base for exploring the 303 square kilometres (117 square miles) of the surrounding broadland. One of the major attractions of the actual village is Roys of Wroxham, a large shop spread across multiple sites.

The kidney-shaped Wroxham Broad with the village of Wroxham in the background

❷ The River Bure ▽

The River Bure is one of the major rivers flowing through the Norfolk Broads. It is especially busy where it reaches Wroxham due to the great demand for leisure use at peak tourist times in the summer. Intense arable farming in the immediate catchment area has caused agricultural phosphates to drain into the river causing a reduction in oxygen supply and a growth of algae, a process known as eutrophication. However, this is slowly being reversed.

❸ The History of the Broads

The true origins of the Norfolk Broads were not uncovered until the late 1950s when research into the vertical banks of the lakes revealed that the vast areas of water were actually man made, the result of peat collection as a source of fuel. This occurred on a massive scale until the fourteenth century when flooding caused these diggings to be abandoned. The resulting waterways became a haven for wildlife and an essential aid to commerce.

❹ Wroxham Broad

Wroxham Broad is one of the largest Norfolk Broads covering nearly 50 hectares (120 acres) at an average depth of 1.3 metres (4.3 feet). The lake itself lies to the south-east of the village of Wroxham in the middle reaches of the Bure; a narrow bank of trees separates it from the main river channel. Small areas of wet woodland also surround the Broad. Wroxham Broad is host to a great diversity of wildlife, including species such as Bitterns, Marsh Harriers, Swallowtail butterflies and the Norfolk Hawker dragonfly, all of which are rare or absent from the rest of the country.

The recent suffocation of the broad, caused by the discharge of treated sewage effluent, has been tackled through a rigorous programme of phosphorus removal.

The River Bure divides Wroxham in the south from Hoveton in the north

Milton Keynes

The new town of Milton Keynes lies 50 miles (80 km) to the north-west of London, and is unique in Britain as a plan for a new community that would be rationally designed to balance industry, leisure and transport; in it shopping, the arts and housing are carefully zoned. The sprawling town, with its population of over 200,000, embraces ten mediaeval villages, 15 lakes and 11 miles (18 km) of canals. Twenty-two percent of Milton Keynes' area is parkland. The view (left) shows Willen Park.

The Peace Pagoda is one of two Japanese sites in Willen Park

① Peace Pagoda ▷

The pagoda in North Willen Park was built by a Japanese Buddhist group, the Order of Nipponzan Myohoji. It was inaugurated on 21st September 1980 by the Order's founder, the Most Venerable Nichidatsu Fujii. The order had begun building such pagodas around the world after the Second World War, the first being in Hiroshima. The first in the Western Hemisphere was this one at Milton Keynes. Around the outside of the pagoda is a sequence of carvings representing eight stages in the life of the Buddha, from his birth to his death. Inside the pagoda there are relics of the Buddha.

② Cathedral of Trees ▽

The Cathedral of Trees, designed by the landscape architect Neil Higson and planted in 1986, reproduces the ground plan of Norwich Cathedral. Evergreens define the central tower, the spires and the walls. The nave is lined with hornbeam and limes. The choir is planted with golden ash and the chancel with holm oak. Variations in tree species define points of interest throughout the cathedral: for example, flowering cherries and apple trees mark the chapels. A large, slightly sunken square on the south side represents the cathedral cloisters. A mound to the south-east is the chapter house and also provides a viewing point. At different seasons patches of colourful bulb plants within the cathedral represent the effect of sunlight shining onto the floor through stained-glass windows.

③ Japanese temple and gardens

Near the Peace Pagoda the monks and nuns of Nipponzan Myohoji live in a Buddhist temple of traditional Japanese design and cultivate the gardens around the temple. There are prayers every morning and evening, and special ceremonies on New Year's Day. The temple is a centre of instruction for Buddhism, one of the most flourishing religions in the area.

④ Willen Maze

Willen Maze is an elaborate pattern cut into the turf near the North Lake. It is not a puzzle maze but rather a labyrinth, consisting of a single winding path that leads you by a circuitous route from the outside to the centre. It is a larger version of the labyrinth cut into the turf at Saffron Walden in Essex. Willen Maze is 230 ft (70 m) across, making it one of the largest in the world. The full path is 1.9 miles (3 km) long.

⑤ Circle of Hearts Medicine Wheel

The Circle of Hearts Medicine Wheel was designed by Roy Littlesun, who drew on the traditions of the Hopi people of North America. The Wheel consists of two concentric circles of 108 limestones. They include larger stones marking north, south, east and west. Extra marker stones align with the rising sun at midsummer. The area between the circles represents the elements of air, earth, fire and water.

⑥ Road network

This intersection hints at the nature of Milton Keynes' road network. When the town was first being designed, it was proposed that transport would be provided by a public transport system based on monorail. As it became clear that the private car was to be the preferred mode of transport, the town adapted and is now based on a sprawling grid of roads. Roads have numbers as well as names: those running roughly north–south have numbers beginning with V (for 'vertical'); those running roughly east–west have numbers beginning with H (for 'horizontal'). The large road running vertically here is Brickhill Street, V10. The large road running horizontally is Portway, H5. Traffic flow is congestion-free, through intersections that are roundabouts rather than junctions. Around 200 km of cycle routes complement the system.

The trees reproduce Norwich Cathedral's ground plan

Stamford and Burghley House

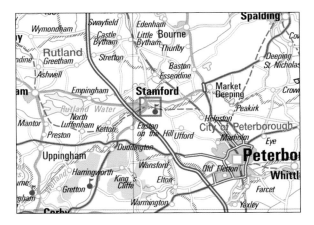

For many centuries the 'Great North Road' ran through Stamford, though the town now sits a mile or so away from the modern A1 road. It was the nearby ford crossed by Ermine Street that gave the town the name of Stane ('Stone') Ford. Under Viking rule, Stamford was capital of one of the five boroughs of the 'Danelaw'. Henry III confirmed its status when he granted the town's charter in 1254. Until the town lost out to other medieval towns further south in East Anglia, its fortune was made on the backs of sheep (the local wool being turned into 'Stamford cloth'), as well as local pottery. The fifteenth century Wars of the Roses saw the town's fortunes decline briefly, but development continued, with a further burst of building activity in the Georgian period. The combination has created an attractive townscape with many elegant streets. Small wonder then that it is so popular as an outdoors set for television historical dramas.

Burghley House is the backdrop for the annual Burghley Horse Trials

❶ Burghley House and Grounds △

Burghley House is one of the finest Elizabethan Houses in England. Built between 1555 and 1587, it was not only commissioned but designed by William Cecil, Queen Elizabeth I's Lord High Treasurer, and one of the most powerful men in the kingdom. Though the Elizabethan house, with its 35 large rooms and more than 80 smaller ones, was sumptuous enough, later Cecils were keen to change it. John Cecil, the 5th Earl, and his wife Anne transformed the house in the seventeenth century. Lord Exeter too, and his wealthy wife, Anne Cavendish, daughter of the Duke of Devonshire, collected innumerable paintings, sculptures and *objets d'art* on their 'Grand Tour' in Italy to add to the wealth on display. A substantial number of state rooms are open to visitors, and it is as much the rooms as the contents themselves that are of interest. The park was laid out by the great landscape gardener Capability Brown in the eighteenth century. His carefully manufactured views from the house, such as the lake seen from the Blue Silk Bedroom, are breathtaking. To the north, the spires of Stamford's many fine churches can be seen through the trees.

❷ St Martin's Church

St Martin's was founded in 1146, though it may be older. A ruin by the late fifteenth century, it was comprehensively rebuilt in English Perpendicular Gothic style by 1482. Today, it is the only medieval church to have survived outside the old town walls. St Martin's houses the mortal remains of William Cecil, Lord Burghley, who died in 1598. He was the builder of Burghley House and trusted advisor and confident to Queen Elizabeth I. His tomb shows him in armour, with his badges of office.

❸ Stamford Town Centre

The prosperity of medieval Stamford, from the 'haberget' or 'Stamford cloth' it made, is still very evident in the town, even though the Norman castle mound was bulldozed to make a car park, and only a postern gate and a tower remain from the original town walls. Brasenose College's gateway still stands in Bath Street as witness to the brief period when academics and students from Brasenose and Merton Colleges in Oxford tried to set up a breakaway university in 1333. A medieval legacy is also apparent in the fine churches throughout the town. St Mary's, with its thirteenth century 50-metre (163-foot) tower, stands surrounded by Georgian houses. The original church of All Saints in Red Lion Square was recorded in the Domesday Book of 1086. Stamford has suffered little industrialisation and still enjoys the reputation of being the 'finest stone town in England'.

Warwick

Warwick, the county town of Warwickshire, lies on the Avon River at a place that was historically important as a crossing-place. The line of the river curves from the bottom centre of the picture, through the centre, to the top right-hand corner. The town received its first charter, granting certain rights and privileges to its merchants and other citizens, in 1545. Its castle is the most famous feature of the town, but the town centre is rich in ancient buildings – both those medieval structures that survived the town's great fire in the seventeenth century and those from the eighteenth century. The history of the city was dominated for centuries by the Earls of Warwick who owned the castle until 1978.

❷ Collegiate Church of St Mary

One of the Earls of Warwick, Robert de Newburgh, founded St Mary's in Church Street in 1123. Some of the original Norman features of this splendid building can still be seen in the crypt, which also houses a genuine ducking stool, a device for publicly dipping miscreants into water. The nave and tower were rebuilt following the fire of 1694, as were so many other of Warwick's buildings. Visitors can climb the tower for magnificent views of the castle and of the town. The interior of this, one of the largest churches in England, includes the Beauchamp Chantry, regarded by some as the finest medieval chapel in England.

❸ Lord Leycester Hospital

Towards the end of the fourteenth century, Thomas Beauchamp, 12th Earl of Warwick, built the Chantry Chapel of St James at Warwick's West Gate, and later granted it to one of the town's powerful guilds, the Guild of St George, who were later joined by the Guild of the Blessed Virgin. These guilds, later called the United Guilds of Warwick, built several buildings at the site, including fine halls and living quarters. The guilds were dispersed by Henry VIII in 1546, and the property here was acquired in 1571 by Robert Dudley, Earl of Leicester (also spelled 'Leycester' at the time). He founded a 'hospital', or charitable home, for aged or disabled soldiers and their families. The hospital survived Warwick's great fire of 1694. It is occupied today by eight ex-servicemen and their wives. On the same site is the regimental museum of the Queen's Own Hussars, an armoured regiment.

❶ Castle Park and River Avon

The town's population of just over 25,000 people can take its leisure in the extensive park, across the river from the town and taking its name from the castle. It is officially classified as a Grade I landscape. Its boundaries are marked on three sides by the River Avon. Below the castle, the Avon is regulated by weirs. (The name 'Warwick' means 'dwellings by the weir'.) The river is linked with the Grand Union Canal, which passes north of the town, north-westward to Birmingham and southward to London. From the great Hatton flight of 21 locks 5 kilometres (3 miles) to the northwest of Warwick there is a fine view of St Mary's and the castle.

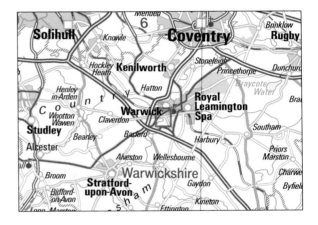

❹ Warwick Racecourse

Warwick Racecourse has its home on Warwick Common, and lays claim to be the oldest racecourse in the country. Races have been held here since 1728, with a major interruption during the Second World War, when much of the common was given over to a prisoner-of-war camp. The course holds both flat and National Hunt (steeplechasing) events, which means that there is racing around the year, with 26 fixtures in all. Flat racing takes place from April until October, and steeplechasing from November until May.

The biggest event held at the racecourse is the Warwick National, held in January. The main Flat event is the two-day Warwick Festival, held in June. The first grandstand here was built in 1808. The present grandstand was refurbished in 2000, and now holds over 1,200 spectators.

❺ Warwick Castle ◁

One of England's best-preserved castles, Warwick Castle lies on the north side of the Avon River. Queen Ethelfleda, daughter of Alfred the Great and sister of Edward the Elder, ordered an earth rampart to be built here in the tenth century to defend the area against the Danes. William the Conqueror ordered that the existing fort be enlarged. The wood of the castle was replaced with stone in the 13th century, and the castle was continually strengthened, remodelled and extended in the centuries that followed. Most of what can be seen today dates from the 14th and 15th centuries. In 1750 'Capability' Brown landscaped the gardens. The castle is now owned by the company that operates Madame Tussaud's Waxworks in London, and the castle's visitors can see wax figures of historical personages occupying some of the rooms, and a waxwork recreation of a royal weekend party held in 1898.

The mound of the early motte and bailey fort abuts Warwick Castle

Birmingham

Home to a million people, the bustling metropolis of Birmingham covers an area of 80 square miles – making it one of the largest cities in Europe. In the nineteenth century it was a thriving centre of industry, producing almost 50 per cent of the globe's manufactured goods, making it known as 'the workshop of the world'. Birmingham has retained its name as a centre of enterprise, supplemented in the late twentieth and early twenty-first century by a growing reputation as a cultural centre. Since 1991 the city has been home to one of the world's finest concert venues in the Birmingham Symphony Hall.

❶ St Chad's Cathedral

Birmingham's Roman Catholic Cathedral is a magnificent neo-Gothic building designed by Augustus Pugin, celebrated architect of the Houses of Parliament in London. Opened in 1841, St Chad's was the first Roman Catholic church constructed in England since the Reformation in the sixteenth century. The Cathedral, built of brick with stone facing, contains a medieval statue of the Virgin Mary, a fifteenth-century Flemish pulpit and stalls and stained-glass windows designed by Pugin and made by John Hardman of Birmingham. Pugin also designed the six vast candlesticks that stand on the impressive Bath-limestone altar. The United Kingdom's largest new manual organ was installed in 1993.

The centre of Birmingham features the new Bullring.

❷ Bullring ◁

Birmingham's state-of-the-art Bullring shopping complex began life in the twelfth century as a marketplace. In the early 1960s an enclosed shopping centre – one of the world's biggest outside North America – was built on the site. The Bullring opened in 1964, but fell into decline in the 1980s and 1990s and was demolished between June 2000 and March 2001 to make way for a new £500 million complex containing more than 140 shops and kiosks. The new Bullring – featuring the eye-catching 'bubble-wrap' surface of Selfridge's futuristic department store – opened on 4 September 2003. More than 10 million shoppers visited the new centre in its first twelve weeks of trading.

❸ The Rotunda

Overlooking the Bullring centre is the 81m (265ft)-tall Rotunda in New Street, one of the enduring icons of Birmingham. Designed by James Roberts and opened in 1965, the 23-floor Rotunda building houses offices. In August 2000 English Heritage granted this much-loved Birmingham landmark the status of a Grade II listed building.

❹ St Martin's in the Bullring Church

A church has stood on this site since the Norman period: the original was rebuilt in the 13th century, but most of today's building was constructed in the 19th century. Sometimes called the 'Cathedral of the Bull Ring', St Martin's – like Birmingham's Anglican Cathedral, St Philip's – contains fine stained-glass windows designed by artist Edward Burne-Jones. The church has recently been renovated.

❺ Birmingham Town Hall

This splendid Grade 1 listed pillared building was designed by Joseph Hansom, creator of the hansom cab, in 1831. Construction work began the following year and although the town hall was formally opened on 19 September 1834, building continued until 1849. Made of local Selly Oak brick with Anglesey marble facing, the town hall has the appearance of a Greek temple and when first built dominated the Birmingham skyline from its elevated position at the top of Hill Street. Initially a venue for Birmingham's Triennial music festivals, the building became a celebrated concert hall, hosting premieres by Edward Elgar and Felix Mendelssohn and, in later years, rock concerts by Bob Dylan and The Beatles. It was the home of the City of Birmingham Symphony Orchestra until the orchestra moved to the Symphony Hall in 1991. It was closed to the public in 1996 and following rennovation was reopened in 2005.

❻ Symphony Hall

Opened in 1991 as part of Birmingham's International Convention centre, Symphony Hall is the performance home of the City of Birmingham Symphony Orchestra. Its 10th anniversary year was celebrated with the installation of a 6,000-pipe symphony organ. Each year around 350,000 people attend events in the Hall, which hosts music concerts, conferences and other promotions.

❼ Council House

The Council House was built to designs by architect Yeoville Thomason between 1874–79. Its clock – known as 'Big Brum' – was once lit by gas. Thomason also designed the adjacent Birmingham Museum and Art Gallery, built in 1885, which contains a celebrated collection of Pre-Raphaelite paintings. Above its entrance, the carved inscription declares 'By the gains of Industry we promote Art'. In Victoria Square in front of the Council House stand contrasting pieces of public art: a nineteenth–century statue of Queen Victoria, a 6.6m (21ft)-tall figure entitled *Iron:Man* (1993) fashioned by sculptor Antony Gormley and a fountain with a reclining River Goddess designed by Indian-born artist Dhruva Mistry, also in 1993.

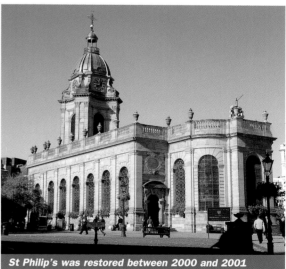

St Philip's was restored between 2000 and 2001

❽ Birmingham Cathedral △

Consecrated in 1715, St Philip's Church in Colmore Row was designed as a parish church by the leading English baroque architect Thomas Archer. It was then named the Cathedral for the newly created diocese of Birmingham in 1905. Birmingham-born Pre-Raphaelite painter Edward Burne-Jones designed four stained-glass windows – depicting the Nativity, the Crucifixion, the Ascension and the Last Judgement – between 1885 and 1891. The windows were made by William Morris & Co at no cost. St Philip's Churchyard was restored in 2000–2001 and contains a double line of plane trees.

Overleaf: the salt marshes at Burnham Overy Staithe, Norfolk

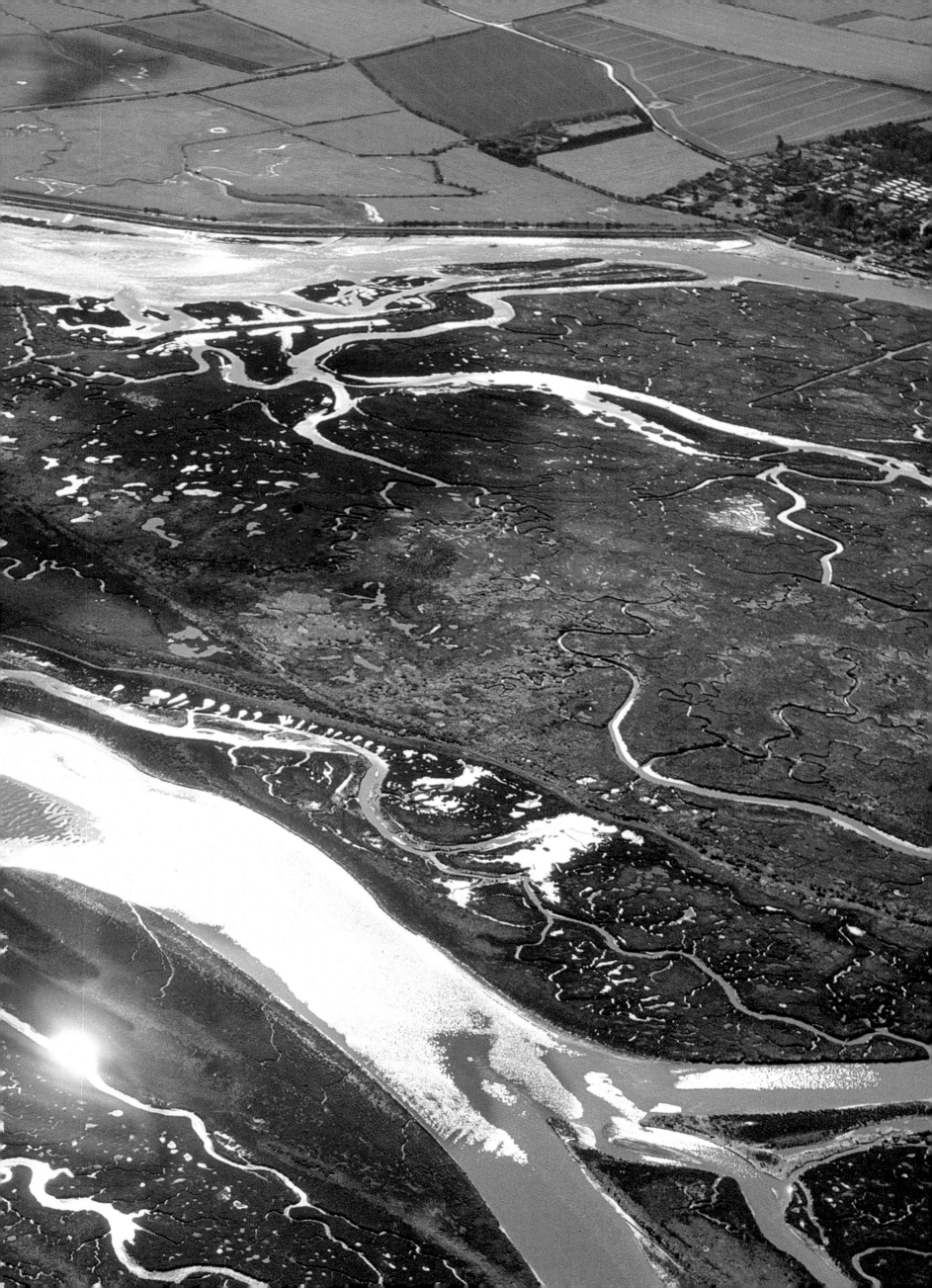

6°30'   10   207   6°   11   5°30'   12   5°   13   4°30'

Tandragee
Banbridge
Clare
Markethill
Poyntz Pass
Mountnorris
Scarva
Loughbrickland
Katesbridge
Moneyslane
Ballyroney
Rathfriland
Jerrettspass
Down
Dromara
Drumaroad
Inch Abbey
Downpatrick
Saul
Clough
Ballyward
Castlewellan
Hilltown
Mayobridge
Bryansford
Newcastle
535
Kilclief
Killough
Ardglass
Strangford
Ballyquintin
Point
Lecale
Pen.
Dundrum
Tyrella
St. John's Point
Dundrum Bay

Bessbrook
Camlough
Newry
Forkill
557
Warrenpoint
Rostrevor
Lisnacree
Annalong
Mourne Mtns. 852
Slieve Donard

Omeath
Carlingford
Boharboy
Kilkeel
Greencastle
Cranfield Point

Dundalk/
Dun Dealgan
54°
Blackrock
Dundalk
Bay
Castlebellingham
Annagassan

Louth
Togher
Dunleer
Grangebellew
Clogher Head
Clogherhead
Termonfeckin
Collon
Abbey
Ballymakenny
Newgrange
Drogheda/
Droichead Átha
Bettystown
Julianstown
Duleek
Gormanston
Balrath
Rathfeigh
Ardcath
Naul
179
Balbriggan
Skerries
Garristown
Ballyboghil
Lusk
Loughshinny
Ratoath
Rush
Ashbourne
Killsallaghan
Swords
Donabate
Lambay
Island
53°30'
Dunboyne
Clonee
Lucan
Malahide
Portmarnock
St Mary's
Abbey
Howth
DUBLIN/
Baile Átha Cliath
Dublin Bay
Dublin
Clondalkin
Rathcoole
Saggart
Tallaght
Dún Laoghaire
Dalkey
Killiney
Brittas
Kilbride
Killiernan
Kippure
754
Enniskerry
Bray/
Bré
Bray Head
Powerscourt Gardens
Mullaghcleevaun
850
Roundwood
Newtown
Greystones
Delgany
Newcastle
Wicklow
Mountains
Wicklow
N.P.
Ashford
Mount Usher Gardens
Laragh
Glendalough
Rathnew
Wicklow
Gleneally
Wicklow Head
53°
Rathdrum
Aghavannagh
Ballinclash
Kilbride
Avoca
Mizen Head
Aughrim
Woodenbridge
607
Arklow/
An tInbhear Mór
Inch
457
Kilmichael Point

REPUBLIC OF IRELAND
219

Larne, Belfast
Isle of Man
Andreas
Sandygate
Regaba
The Cronk
Sulby
Kirk Michael
Sulby
Res.
621
Snaefell
Laxey Wh
Glenmaye
Foxdale
Crosby
Onchan
Douglas
Peel
St. John's
Close
Clark
Braaid
Port Erin
Ballasalla
Port St.Mary
Castletown
Calf of Man

Anglesey
(Môn)
Carmel
Head
Cemaes
Holyhead
Bay
Llyn Alaw
Llanfaethlu
Llanenchy
Llanfachraeth
Bodedern
Y Fali
Holyhead
Caergybi
Trearddur
Holy Island
Rhoscolyn
Cymyran Bay
Rhosneigr
Anglesey
Aberffraw
Gwalchmai
Llanfaelog
Niwbwrch
Caernarfon
Bay
Llandw
Clynnog-
fawr
Llithfaen
Nefyn
Edern
Tudweiliog
Boduan
Dinas
Sarn Meyllteyrn
Llanbedrog
Pwllheli
Braich y Pwll
Aberdaron
Rhiw
Port Neigwl or
Hell's Mouth
Abersoch
Bardsey Sound
Trwyn
Cilan
Bardsey Island
Lleyn Peninsula

Irish

St. George's Channel

Caernarfon Bay

1:600,000

0   5   10   15   20   25 miles
0   5   10   15   20   25 km

1 Blackburn with Darwen
2 Bolton
3 Bury
4 Rochdale

1 Wirral
2 Liverpool
3 Knowsley
4 Halton
5 St Helens
6 Warrington
7 Trafford
8 Manchester
9 Stockport
10 Tameside

3

Snowdonia

The Snowdonia National Park is named after Mount Snowdon which at 1,085m is the highest peak in England and Wales. The park itself was established in 1951 and covers 2,132 square kilometres. Formed mainly from glacial activity during the last ice age, the great U-shaped valleys form a stunning area of outstanding natural beauty.

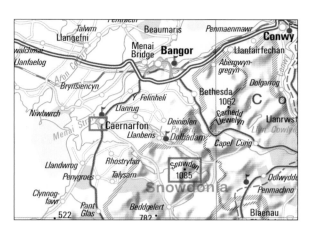

Westerly winds often bring spectacular cloud formations to Snowdonia

1 Paths

The Snowdonia Upland Paths Partnership was launched to rebuild and repair eroded mountain footpaths throughout the Snowdonia National Park. The paths leading up to the summit are well-trodden but there are less well-known routes around the similarly spectacular and often quieter nearby peaks such as Crib y Ddysgl (1,065 metres). Local guides are available to show visitors such byways, but a reasonable level of fitness is required to explore them in a day.

2 Summit ▽

Over 350,000 visitors reach the summit of Snowdon every year, either on foot or by taking the mountain railway. The summit building was designed by the renowned architect Clough Williams Ellis in 1935 and has recently been refurbished. From the top of Snowdon visitors can see Anglesey, Pembrokeshire, the Isle of Man and even as far as Ireland. The Welsh name for the mountain – Yr Wyddfa – means 'the Tomb'. Legend tells that it is reputedly the burial place of the giant ogre Rhita vanquished by King Arthur in the ancient kingdom of Gwynedd. The peak often appears higher than it really is because unlike some mountain ranges the ground rises from sea level to the summit in quite a short distance.

The railway carries thousands to the summit each year

3 Snowdonia Mountain Railway △

Opened in 1896, the Snowdonia Mountain Railway runs four miles from the base station at Llanberis to within 66 feet of the summit. Most of the carriages are still in working order and run on a rack and pin system that provides the necessary traction for the steep climb, but also acts as an effective brake on the descent. This is the only such system on any British railway due to the incline of the Snowdonia mountainscape. Each carriage can carry 54 passengers plus a guard. When the service first began, the carriages were open to the elements, but were modified to include roofs in the 1950s. The average speed of the railway is 5mph.

The trigonometrical point at the summit of Snowdon

Snowdonia, Gwynedd **121**

Caernarfon

Caernarfon

Celts were already in the area of Caernarfon when the Romans first settled this site on the Menai Strait, overlooking and controlling the sea route to Anglesey. When the Romans withdrew from Britain in the late fourth century, their fort was occupied by local chieftains, and there are remains of a fifth century Celtic church. Although the Normans did make brief forays, during which they built a small motte (fortified mound) on the present castle site, the area was controlled by Welsh princes, who built a

manor there. The site was transformed by Edward I who built not only a castle that was to be an occasional royal residence and military strongpoint, but also laid out a carefully planned, walled town alongside it. The borough received its royal charter in 1284, and became capital of North Wales. The port area along the walls of the castle was probably used from Roman times, but its main development was in the nineteenth century when it was used for shipping slate from local quarries.

❶ Caernarfon Castle and Old Town

The inspiration for the design and aesthetics of the walls of Caernarfon Castle came supposedly from the fortifications (fifth century onwards) of the great Byzantine city of Constantinople, which Edward would have known from his crusading years. He was fortunate too in having James of St. George as his master builder, but as a result of his ambitions the castle's costs (over the 46 years that it took to build) exceeded those for any of his other Welsh fortresses. His castle-building programme had already started in 1283 at Conwy on the north coast and, after Caernarfon, Harlech was to be his next. The still substantial ruins of Segontium provided cut stone for parts of the castle, while extra stone was brought in by sea. A moat was created, and to the north the 740 metres (800 yards) of town walls added further protection.

It was in the greatest of the towers, Eagle Tower, that Edward's son, the future King Edward II, was born in 1284 and declared Prince of Wales. Formal investitures of the sovereign's eldest son as Prince of Wales have only actually taken place in the castle since 1911. During the Civil War it was besieged three times by the Parliamentarians, falling to them in 1646. Gunpowder had finally prevailed over stone. However, unlike many other great fortresses, it was not destroyed and, despite some 250 years of neglect until the late nineteenth century when serious restoration started, it is still substantially intact, as a potent reminder of power projection over a subject people. The size of the King's Gate and the elegance and grandiose proportions of the Eagle Tower help set it apart from almost any other castle in Britain except Windsor. Indeed, few others in Europe would stand comparison. Caernarfon Castle is today notable as Wales' most prominent UNESCO World Heritage site.

❷ Roman Segontium

Segontium Roman fort plays a significant role in both local history and legend, as it is connected to the legend of Magnus Maximus, who tried to usurp the title of Roman emperor. He appears as Macsen Wledig in the 'Dream of Macsen', part of the Mabinogion, the great collection of 11 Welsh legends, where he supposedly dreams of a land of mountains across from an island, and a great city, full of multi-coloured towers. It is this story that, supposedly, helped to inspire Edward I's plans for Caernarfon Castle. The fort was built as an auxiliary fort in 77 AD by the Roman Governor of Britain Agricola on a low hill south-east of the modern town centre, and had the longest continuous occupancy of any Roman fort in Wales. The fort would have held around 1,000 auxiliary troops (i.e. not Roman citizen soldiers), who would have each signed on for 25 years' service. The unit was stationed here until Rome withdrew its forces from Wales around 394 AD. The fort was the largest in the area, and also functioned as the administrative centre for North-West Wales. It was responsible for tax collection and mining activities. The sea approaches to Anglesey were covered from the observation point on Twt Hill to the north. The camp was originally protected by a wooden palisade and an external ditch, corresponding to Roman practice throughout the Empire. From 140 AD this was rebuilt in stone. Excavations have revealed extensive rebuilding on the site, and the foundations of a number of barracks (each containing 80 infantrymen) have been left exposed to give visitors a clearer idea of the layout. The two bathhouses are located to the south, across the modern road, in an area reserved for Roman officers and higher officials. East of the walls are the remains of a third century temple dedicated to the Roman god Mithras. The small museum at the site contains a number of finds.

❸ Museum of the Royal Welch Fusiliers

The museum of the Royal Welch Fusiliers Regiment is an unexpected bonus for the visitor to the castle. Like so many of Britain's infantry regiments, its history is a reflection of the tumultuous times during which the reach of the British Empire was worldwide, in countries and territories that they colonised and in those where they merely attacked and withdrew. Wars with the French loom large in the exhibitions, including the 1808 defence of and subsequent retreat from Corunna, after the death of General Sir John Moore (the museum holds the keys of one of the town gates), and the invasion of the French island of Martinique in 1809. The latter, more successful, expedition is one of the battle honours on the Regiment's colours. The First World War also provides mementoes that are on display.

The investiture of the Prince of Wales has taken place here since 1911

Aintree Racecourse

Aintree Racecourse near Liverpool is home to one of the world's most celebrated horse races, the Grand National steeplechase, watched on television each April by more than 10 million people in the UK alone – and upwards of 600 million people globally. The race has a proud history, dating back to its first running on 26th February 1839, when the 5-1 favourite 'Lottery' was the winner over a course including a ploughed field and a stone wall. Today's course contains thirty often hazardous jumps and demands extraordinary stamina of the competing horses. Often, few are left in the race by the time the winner crosses the line.

❶ Racecourse

The racecourse takes its name from the nearby Saxon village of Aintree. The word 'Aintree' is believed to mean 'a tree standing alone' – according to some authorities, the ancient oak tree that stood in Bull Bridge Lane, Aintree, until 2004, when its diseased state made it necessary to cut it down. Aintree racecourse was developed by Liverpool hotelier William Lynn, who leased ground from local landowner Lord Sefton on which he erected a grandstand and laid out a course prior to holding the first official horse race at Aintree on 7th July 1829. This was a flat race rather than a steeplechase. Following the running of the first steeplechase on the course in 1839, the Aintree steeplechase took the name 'Grand National' in 1847.

The modern race consists of two laps of a roughly triangular course, totalling 7.2km (4 miles 855 yards). There are 16 fences, each jumped twice during the race apart from 'The Chair' and 'The Water Jump', which are jumped only once. The maximum number of runners allowed is forty.

2 The Chair

The Chair is the course's deepest fence. Riders must time their jump perfectly to clear a ditch 1.83m (6ft) across before soaring over the fence itself, which stands 1.42m (4ft 8in) tall.

3 Mildmay Course and Motor racing track

In the mid-twentieth century Lord Sefton sold the land on which the course stood to a local family named the Tophams. Mrs Mirabel Topham laid out a new course named after amateur jockey Lord Mildmay. The Mildmay course ran within the circuit of the Grand National course; around the perimeter of the Mildmay, Mrs Topham also established a motor racing circuit. Both the Mildmay and the motor circuit opened in 1953.

The British motor racing Grand Prix was held at the Aintree circuit on five occasions in 1955–62. Amid wild excitement at Aintree on 16 July 1955, British driver Stirling Moss won his first Grand Prix, driving a Mercedes-Benz. He beat his fellow Mercedes driver Juan Manuel Fangio by one-tenth of a second in front of a crowd estimated at 150,000.

4 Stands and winners'enclosure

The Queen Mother Stand, which commands a view of the winning line, stands in front of the Winners' Enclosure. The Princess Royal Stand nearby was completed in 1998. Two new stands are planned alongside the Queen Mother Stand, as well as a new parade ring with space for 4,000 spectators and a new winners' enclosure.

5 Becher's Brook

The most celebrated fence is 'Becher's Brook', the sixth and the 22nd jump on the course. Riders who succeed in clearing a fence 1.47m (4ft 10in) high must negotiate a drop of 2.07m (6ft 9in) to lower ground while also clearing a brook 61cm (2ft) across. The combination is named after Captain Martin Becher, who in the very first steeplechase in 1839 fell from his mount 'Conrad' into the brook while leading the race.

6 Golf course

A nine-hole golf course is laid out on the land within the Grand National course, in full view of celebrated course features such as Canal Turn and Becher's Brook. It is the UK's longest nine-hole course, measuring a total of 6,056m (6,624 yards). Golfers must cope with a lake and stream, as well as a brook and a line of fir trees across the fairway of the third hole.

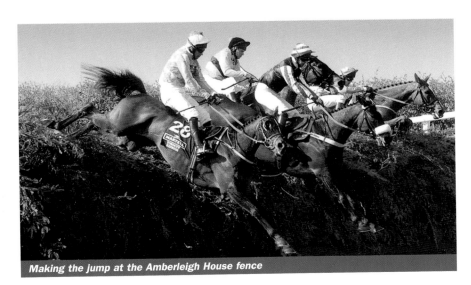

Making the jump at the Amberleigh House fence

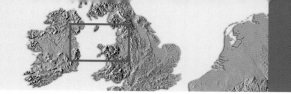

Blackpool

Blackpool is Europe's largest seaside resort. It lies on Britain's northwest coast, where the coast runs almost due north–south, and faces onto the waters of the Irish Sea. It is surrounded by the county of Lancashire, but is itself governed by its own unitary authority. Its permanent population of about 142,000 plays host to over 6 million visitors every year. The buildings along the promenade and even the trams that ply the length of the shore are illuminated during September and October with fantastic designs picked out in neon, fibre optics and light-bulbs. All the traditional pleasures of the English seaside resort are to be found at Blackpool in abundance. The resort is most famous for its tower, but it also has three piers providing public entertainment. The North Pier and Central Pier are visible in this view (left and below).

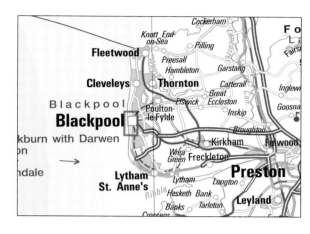

Blackpool's homely family entertainment image may change with the advent of big casinos

❶ Blackpool Tower

Blackpool Tower casts a long shadow across the front in the main picture. This famous structure is 158 metres (519 feet) high, including the 18.3-metre (60-foot) flagpole. It is constructed from 3,534 tonnes of steel and 358 tonnes of cast iron. It is protected by 9 tonnes of paint and adorned with 10,000 light bulbs. The tower is half the height of its inspiration, the Eiffel Tower in Paris. Work on building the Blackpool Tower began in 1891. At the foot of the tower there is a complex of buildings including the Tower Circus, which has been there since 1904, and the Tower Ballroom, boasting the largest sprung dance-floor in the world. To the north-east of the tower are the Winter Gardens, which function now as a conference centre. Inside this magnificent structure there are foibles and follies of many places and eras, including Tudor England, Seville, and Strauss's Vienna. The Opera House here is Britain's largest theatre.

❷ Golden Mile ▽

Blackpool boasts 11.6 km (7.2 miles) miles of some of the best beaches in Britain. The central region of the front is called the Golden Mile. This is the home of the kiss-me-quick hat, the comic postcard and the fish-and-chip shop. It is also where the RNLI (Royal National Lifeboat Institution) has its station, just north of Central Pier. The first lifeboats were based at Blackpool in 1864; the latest addition to the service comprised several inshore rescue craft. Among the latest leisure attractions on the Golden Mile are the six-million-pound Sea Life Centre, which includes an underwater tunnel from which visitors can get a close-up view of sharks. Nearby is Louis Tussaud's waxworks, founded by a great-grandson of London's Madame Tussaud.

❸ Central Pier

The Central Pier was the second of the three piers to be built, and was opened in May 1868. Its entertainments of music and dancing were more boisterous than those of the more decorous North Pier and its 'quality' entertainments. Today the pier is dominated by a Ferris wheel 32.7 metres (108 feet) high – its shadow can be made out in the main picture, on the beach above the shadow of the pier. The present length of the pier is 340 metres (1,118 feet). The Central Pier is still very popular with visitors who come to see the end of the pier shows. South of the Central Pier lies the South Pier and the South Shore, which includes the Pleasure Beach, with its permanent funfair and extravagant rollercoaster rides.

❹ North Pier

The first pier to be built at Blackpool was the North Pier, which was designed by master pier-builder Eugenius Birch. It began construction in 1862 and was opened on 21 May 1863. It continued the line of Talbot Road, where Blackpool's first railway station had been constructed. The pier was later extended with a jetty that brought its length up to 503 metres (1,650 feet). The pierhead was enlarged with two 'wings' to accommodate an Indian-style pavilion, bandstand, restaurant and shops. The pavilion and a successor were both destroyed by fire, to be replaced by a 1,500-seat theatre. Today there is also a helipad, from which flights can be taken around the Tower and along the shore. Even today, the North Pier provides a quieter and more staid leisure environment than Blackpool's other two piers.

The Golden Mile offers amusements, tram transport and access to the beach

Port Erin

The small town of Port Erin is at the south-western tip of the Isle of Man, which lies in the Irish Sea, roughly equidistant from England, Scotland, Wales and Ireland. The island has an area of 572 square kilometres (221 square miles). The Isle of Man is politically not part of the United Kingdom, but a Crown Dependency, having its own government. It was this political independence that enabled the island in 1905 to begin the tradition of closing major parts of the road system to permit first car racing and then the internationally famous TT (Tourist Trophy) motorcycle races. Port Erin lies on an inlet of the Irish Sea. It is connected by road and steam railway to Douglas, the capital of Man. Neighbouring settlements include the village of Cregneash to the south, where there is a notable outdoor Folk Museum, and Port St Mary to the south-east, a yachting centre.

The dockyard and town at Port Erin

② Bradda Headland

To the north of Port Erin lies Bradda headland, a favourite route for walkers. Rugged beaches fringe the headland, whose tip is called Bradda Head. The most notable landmark here is Milner's Tower, standing at Bradda Head itself. This monument was erected in 1871 by the townspeople of Port Erin, in honour of William Milner, who was a benefactor to the fishing families and poor people of the town. Milner had made his fortune as a safemaker in Liverpool, and so the tower was built in a form suggesting a huge key.

③ Steam Railway

There was once an extensive railway network on the Isle of Man. The trains were mostly hauled by steam locomotives, though there were also electric trains and horse-drawn trams, and some of these survive today. Today a narrow-gauge line with steam-hauled trains runs between Port Erin and Douglas. This is the last surviving line of the 74 kilometres (46 miles) of the former Isle of Man Railway Company. Its locomotives date back to 1874, and it is the longest stretch of narrow-gauge steam railway in Britain.

④ Railway Museum

Next to the railway station in Port Erin, which has been restored to its original Victorian décor, lies the Railway Museum, occupying a former engine shed. Visitors can see full-size trains, additional carriages and numerous memorabilia of the age of steam from the island. The museum also houses the workshops and smithy that keep the working railway in operation, and visitors can view maintenance work being carried out on rolling stock before it goes out on service again.

① Port Erin

Port Erin has long been a popular tourist resort, and hotels line the bay. The scenic sands and rocky inlets attract photographers and walkers, as well as scuba divers and pony-trekkers. There are interesting walks to Bradda Head to the north, as well as along the coast to the south. Visitors can take boat trips to the Calf of Man, an islet off the tip of Man, to the south-west. The town is home to the Erin Arts Centre, which organizes many arts events, including the three major Mananan International Festivals every year. The festival is named after the ancient Irish god who was the mythical first ruler of Man. The bay on which the town stands is almost circular.

⑤ Port Erin Bay

The Bay's sheltered waters are fringed by fine sandy beaches but also some rocky ones. Occasionally fierce storms cause the seas to run high: the remains can still be seen of a breakwater of concrete blocks erected in 1854 which lasted for just 10 years before it was wrecked by a storm. At the southern side of the bay the University of Liverpool maintains its Port Erin Marine Laboratory.

Peel

Peel

Peel is the most significant settlement and only city on the west coast of the Isle of Man. Enclosing the harbour is St. Patrick's Isle, dominated by the extensive ruins of Peel Castle and by St German's Cathedral. The town's origins date from the thirteenth century, but Bronze Age remains have been found. St Patrick's Island was the site of a Celtic monastery from 550 AD, and after the Viking invasions around 800 AD it became the capital of a Norwegian dependency that included the Hebrides.

1 Peel Castle

Magnus Barefoot, the Viking Chieftain who landed in 1098, built a wooden fort on St. Patrick's Isle, remains of which were found in the 1980s. Peel Castle probably owes its name to the 'peel tower' form of the castle keep, a type widely used in the Scottish borders, though a wooden defensive fence or 'paling' has also been suggested. The substantial but ruined red sandstone fortifications seen today are fifteenth-century curtain walls with fourteenth-century towers, though some structures pre-date this. Peel Castle was capital of the northern part of the island until the mid-1600s. Building re-started in the early and then mid-nineteenth century, in response to perceived or real threats from the French, and several earlier buildings, including the residence of the Lords of Mann, were torn down to provide extra defences.

The thirteenth century cathedral at Peel

② St German's Cathedral

St German's dates from the thirteenth and fourteenth centuries, though the nave and transept may have been earlier. It is named after a follower of St Patrick who is supposed to have settled here 550 AD, and was an integral part of the capital city for the Kingdom of Mann and the Isles. In the late fourteenth century it was crenellated for extra protection. The cathedral crypt was used as a prison by the bishop for sabbath-breakers, a sin that could involve fishing, farming or playing music on Sundays. The last Bishop was appointed in 1785, by which time the cathedral's fabric had already deteriorated, and in 1824 the roof collapsed in a heavy storm. This ruin is little changed today. Nearby is a 16-metre (50-foot) round tower, also crenellated, that pre-dates the cathedral, and which would have been a belfry and lookout post, and the ruined tenth century St Patrick's Church. This appears to have collapsed and been re-built in the twelfth century, but continued in use as the parish church until 1884. Its present state is due to a fire in 1958.

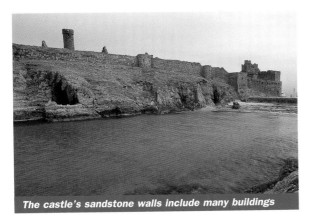

The castle's sandstone walls include many buildings

③ House of Manannan

Built in 1997, this award-winning museum is located on the harbour, overlooking St. Patrick's Isle, in the old Peel railway station that has been substantially modernised. It is named after the island's mythological sea god, and covers much of the early Celtic and Viking history of the area. It charts the interaction of the pagan invaders and the early Christian missionaries, and the gradual conversion of the island to Christianity. Maritime traditions, from smuggling to fishing, are also reflected in the exhibits, including a full-size replica Viking longship.

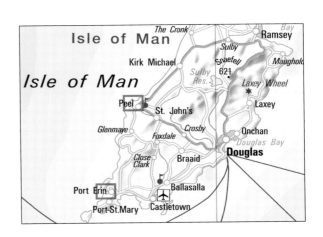

Overleaf: the seafront at Liverpool including the Royal Liver Building

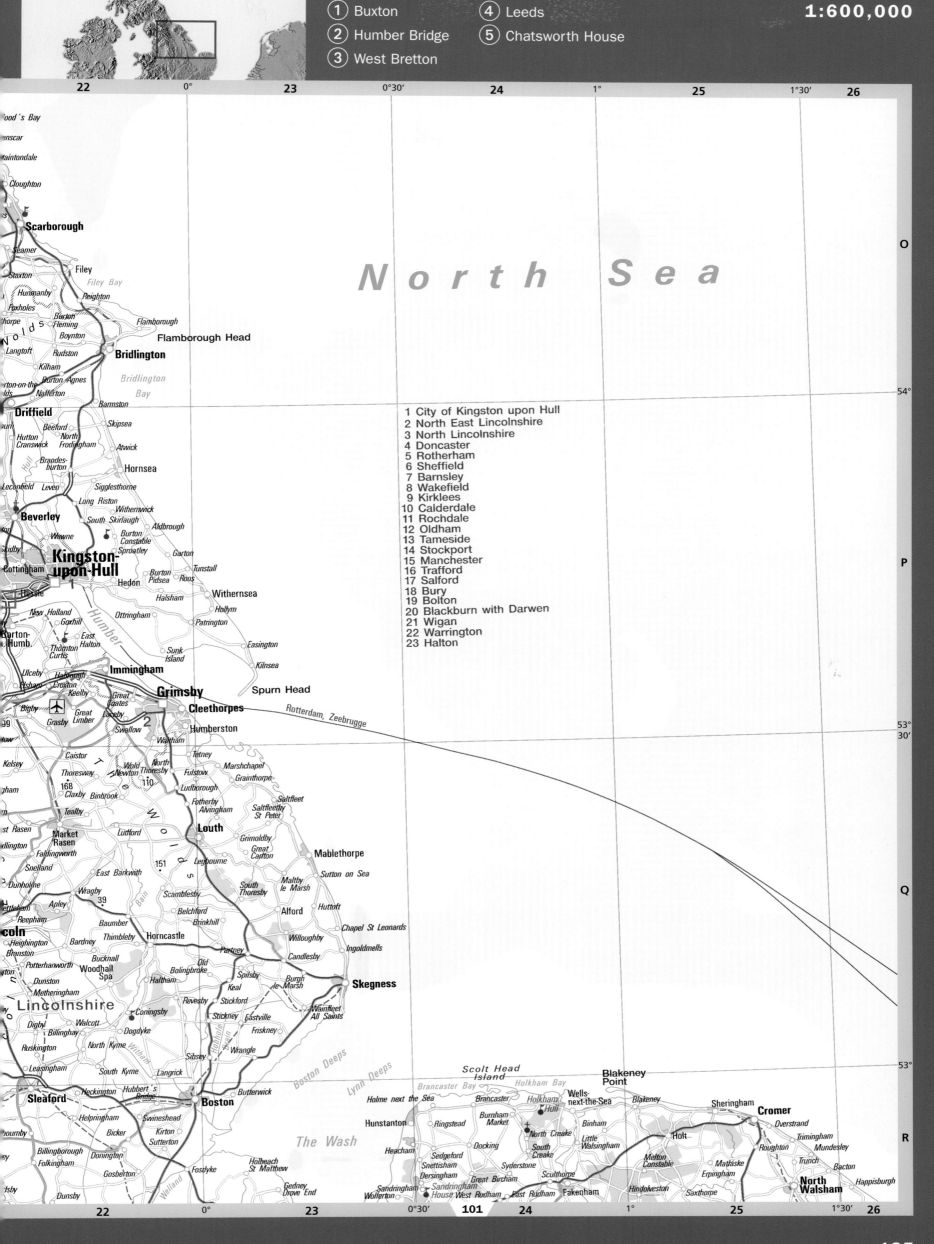

North Sea

1 City of Kingston upon Hull
2 North East Lincolnshire
3 North Lincolnshire
4 Doncaster
5 Rotherham
6 Sheffield
7 Barnsley
8 Wakefield
9 Kirklees
10 Calderdale
11 Rochdale
12 Oldham
13 Tameside
14 Stockport
15 Manchester
16 Trafford
17 Salford
18 Bury
19 Bolton
20 Blackburn with Darwen
21 Wigan
22 Warrington
23 Halton

Scarborough
Seamer
Staxton
Filey
Filey Bay
Hunmanby
Reighton
Foxholes
thorpe
Langtoft
Flamborough
Burton
Fleming
Boynton
Rudston
Kilham
Burton Agnes
Flamborough Head
rton-on-the
lds
Nafferton
Bridlington
Driffield
Bridlington
Bay
Barmston
urn
Hutton
Cranswick
Beeford
North
Frodingham
Skipsea
Atwick
Brandes-
burton
Hornsea
Leconfield
Leven
Sigglesthorne
Long Riston
Withernwick
Beverley
South Skirlaugh
Wawne
Skidby
Cottingham
Burton
Constable
Sproatley
Aldbrough
Garton
Tunstall
Kingston-
upon-Hull
Hedon
Burton
Pidsea
Roos
Hessle
Withernsea
New Holland
Goxhill
Halsham
Hollym
Barton-
Humb.
East
Halton
Ottringham
Patrington
Ulceby
Thornton
Curtis
Sunk
Island
Easington
Habrough
Croxton
Keelby
Kilnsea
Bigby
Great
Coates
Immingham
Spurn Head
gg
Grasby
Great
Limber
Laceby
Grimsby
Cleethorpes
Rotterdam, Zeebrugge
Kelsey
Caistor
Swallow
Humberston
Thoresway
Wold
Newton
North
Thoresby
Waltham
ham
168
Claxby
Binbrook
110
Fulstow
Marshchapel
Grainthorpe
Tealby
Ludborough
Fotherby
Alvingham
Saltfleet
Saltfleetby
St Peter
Market
Rasen
Ludford
Louth
Grimoldby
st Rasen
dlington
Faldingworth
Snelland
151.
Legbourne
Great
Carlton
Mablethorpe
Sutton on Sea
Dunholme
East Barkwith
Malthy
le Marsh
Wragby
Apley
39
Scamblesby
South
Thoresby
ettleham
Reepham
Belchford
Alford
Huttoft
coln
Heighington
Bardney
Thimbleby
Baumber
Brinkhill
Chapel St Leonards
Branston
Bucknall
Horncastle
Willoughby
Ingoldmells
Potterhanworth
Woodhall
Spa
Partney
Candlesby
Dunston
Old
Bolingbroke
Spilsby
Burgh
le Marsh
Metheringham
Haltham
Keal
Stickford
Skegness
Revesby
Stickney
Lincolnshire
Digby
Coningsby
Eastville
Friskney
Billinghay
Walcott
Dogdyke
Wrangle
Wainfleet
All Saints
Ruskington
North Kyme
Sibsey
Leasingham
South Kyme
Langrick
Boston Deeps
sby
Sleaford
Neckington
Hubbert's
Bridge
Butterwick
Lynn Deeps
Scolt Head
Island
Holkham Bay
Blakeney
Point
Helpringham
Swineshead
Boston
Brancaster Bay
Wells-
next-the-Sea
Blakeney
Sheringham
Cromer
Bicker
Kirton
Sutterton
The Wash
Holme next the Sea
Brancaster
Holkham
Hull
Binham
Overstrand
Billingborough
Donington
Hunstanton
Ringstead
Burnham
Market
North Creake
Little
Walsingham
Holt
Trimingham
Mundesley
Folkingham
Gosberton
Fosdyke
Heacham
Sedgeford
Docking
South
Creake
Sculthorpe
Melton
Constable
Matlaske
Roughton
Bacton
Happisburgh
sby
Dunsby
Holbeach
St Matthew
Gedney
Drove End
Snettisham
Dersingham
Sandringham
Great Bircham
Syderstone
Hindolveston
Erpingham
Trunch
Sandringham
Wolferton
Sandringham
House West Rudham
East Rudham
Fakenham
Saxthorpe
North
Walsham

Buxton

Buxton in the Derbyshire Peak District, at more than 300 metres (984 feet), is the highest market town in England. Thanks to thermal springs providing a constant water temperature, it has been a spa town since Roman times. It benefited from the Georgian and Victorian obsession with 'taking the waters'. It has fine Georgian buildings, as well as the Victorian Pavilion Gardens and covered winter gardens. Buxton's importance as a tourist destination was enhanced by the opening of the Midland Line railway in 1863. The beautifully restored Edwardian opera house is the focus of an opera festival every July. Tourists also come to Buxton for the annual 'well dressings' – a reminder of the pre-Christian past.

Buxton's crescent can be clearly seen from the air

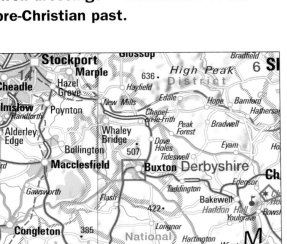

❶ The Crescent

The Dukes of Devonshire saw Buxton as a northern equivalent of Bath, catering for the newly rich industrial and commercial middle classes of Lancashire, and set out to create a city centre worthy of comparison. John Carr left the most enduring mark by designing the fine Crescent (modelled on Bath's) in 1784. Built in local sandstone, with nearly 400 windows, it was badly in need of restoration for many years, but work was finally put in hand in the late 1990s to secure the fabric for the future.

❷ The Devonshire Hospital

In 1790, John Carr was also commissioned by the fifth Duke of Devonshire to build the Great Stables and Riding School, with accommodation for more than a hundred horses. In 1858, two-thirds of the stables were converted into The Devonshire Hospital (later the Devonshire Royal Hospital). It was completed, in 1881, with a clock tower and a soaring slate dome 48m (156ft) across the central courtyard. At the time it was the largest unsupported dome in the world. The building is now being transformed into a campus for the University of Derby College, Buxton.

❸ Poole's Cavern

Just outside Buxton, to the south, is one of the finest and most accessible underground limestone cavern systems in England. Probably created by the eroding action of flood waters, Poole's Cavern is some 650m (700yds) long, divided into a series of chambers such as the Roman Chamber and the Great Dome, some 12m (40ft) high. Stalactites and stalagmites hang from the ceilings or rise up from the cavern's floor. Several areas are dyed red, the result of the effects of iron oxide, while elsewhere the calcite formations owe their colouring to manganese.

❹ Opera House

When in 1901 the Gardens Commission decided to build a new theatre in Buxton, they turned to Frank Matcham, the architect for prestigious theatres such as London's Palladium and Coliseum. The site did not allow for anything so large, but the resultant building, now beautifully restored, is an exquisite, finely proportioned, gold and filigree jewel. It was opened in 1903, and attracted some of the finest talent in theatre and music, including Gertrude Lawrence, Anna Pavlova and Gracie Fields. The advent of 'talkies' saw a gradual decline in live performance, and from 1945 to the late 1970s it functioned mainly as a cinema. After substantial repairs, it was re-opened in 1979, in time for the first Opera Festival. Thanks to more local and national funding, it now been restored to its former glory.

Humber Bridge (north bank)

Designed to cross the last major unbridged estuary in Britain, the Humber Bridge was opened by H.M. The Queen in 1981 having been 8 years in construction. Both Roman records and the Domesday Book record the use of a ferry to cross the Humber, the journey in more recent times lasting a minimum of twenty minutes, with boats subject to the twin hazards of weather and tide. The bridge opened up both sides of the estuary to further economic and social development, where communities previously miles part were now joined by road. More than six million vehicles cross the structure every year.

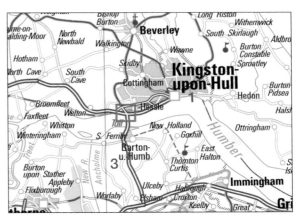

❶ The Estuary

The brown appearance of the Humber Estuary is often thought to be a sign of pollution; however the colour derives from the river's natural turbidity as a large tidal estuary. The waters are heavily laden with sediment and support a wide range of wildlife. The enormous width of the river prevented economic development for many years. The ever-shifting bed of the river meant a tunnel could not be constructed easily and so the bridge was finally erected between Hessle in the north and Barton-upon-Humber in the south.

❷ Humber Bridge Country Park

The Country Park and local nature reserve is located near to the northern approach of the bridge in a disused chalk quarry known in the local area as Little Switzerland. Aside from the wildlife on offer, the park features the Phoenix Sculpture Trail and a black painted windmill, now minus sails, that was used to crush the chalk in the old quarry.

❸ Yorkshire Wolds Way

Beginning in the shadow of the bridge at Hessle, the Yorkshire Wolds Way is a National walking trail that extends for nearly 80 miles north to Filey in Cleveland. The first 5km (3 miles) of the way is alongside the estuary where walkers can see chalk pebbles on the foreshore left behind by the quarrying activities that produced the area now known as Little Switzerland.

The Humber Bridge's two main cables each contain 14,948 wires

❹ The Bridge △

At the time of its completion and for 17 years thereafter the Humber Bridge was the largest single-span bridge in the world. The suspension structure was chosen because the cost of tunnelling was prohibitive and a single span bridge would not obstruct the flow of river traffic along the navigable estuary. The main central span of the bridge is 1,410 metres in length, clearing the water by an average of 30 metres. About 480,000 tonnes of concrete were used in building the bridge alongside 11,000 tonnes of steel wire in the main cables which is long enough to stretch one and a half times around the world. The Humber Bridge was designed perfectly for its environment; it has the ability to bend inward at the top by more than 3 metres in high winds. The main support towers at the top are 36mm further apart than at the base, to allow for the curvature of the earth.

West Bretton

Near Wakefield, West Yorkshire, the village of West Bretton is the site of the nationally renowned Yorkshire Sculpture Park, displaying works by Auguste Rodin, Barbara Hepworth, Elisabeth Frink and many others in the outdoor setting of its eighteenth-century landscaped grounds. Adjacent to the park is the stately home, Bretton Hall, now part of the University of Leeds, and the Bretton Country Park, housing an outdoor display of works by Henry Moore, one of the twentieth century's most celebrated sculptors.

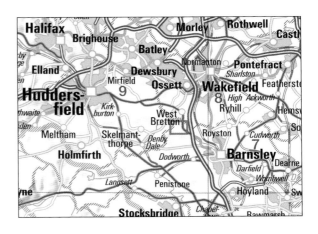

1 Yorkshire Sculpture Park ◁

After opening in 1977, the park won a wide reputation for its pioneering work in exhibiting work within the natural forms of its 105 hectare (260 acre) landscape. Sculptures on display from the park's collection are changed periodically. They include works by Jonathan Borofsky, Sol LeWitt, Edward Allington, David Nash and Richard Serra as well as Barbara Hepworth and Elisabeth Frink. Hepworth is renowned for her flowing, largely abstract sculptures in bronze, marble or wood, often showing the influence of natural shapes. Born locally in 1903, she reported that her youth in the West Yorkshire landscape 'discipled me to the life of form and sculpture'. Frink produced mainly figurative sculptures in bronze: her works on display include the celebrated *Running Man*.

In addition the park puts on temporary exhibitions which have included works by such leading figures as Eduardo Paolozzi, Christo and Jeanne Claude, Anthony Caro and Richard Long.

With more than 300,000 visitors annually, the park has expanded with the acquisition of more land and a new visitor centre. This incorporates a glass concourse through woodland with views of the formal gardens; the upper level contains a balcony overlooking the display of Henry Moore works in Bretton Country Park alongside.

Modernist sculpture in the parkland at West Bretton

2 Display of Henry Moore works in Bretton Country Park

The monumental bronze sculptures of Henry Moore are at home in the setting of the 40-hectare (100-acre) Bretton Country Park. Moore was born in 1898 in the West Yorkshire town of Castleford and, like Barbara Hepworth, told of the influence of the local landscape on his artistic vision. He is best known for bronze and marble abstract forms and partly abstracted renderings of mother-and-child pairs or reclining figures. His reclining figures were influenced by the recumbent sacred sculptures of the Toltecs and Maya of ancient Mexico and Guatemala; these figures, thought to be images of the rain god and known as chacmools, were used for the display of the extracted heart of a human sacrificial victim. The display of Moore's bronze sculptures at Bretton – on loan from the Henry Moore Foundation, the Tate Gallery and other sources – is periodically changed.

3 Bretton Hall

The hall was built in about 1720 following the designs of amateur architect Colonel James Moyser. It sits in a landscaped park with pleasure grounds and formal gardens. The lakes and planting were laid out in the 1770s by the surveyor, Richard Woods, whose work is also to be seen at Lulworth Castle, Dorset, and Hatfield Priory, Essex. The fine camellia house was constructed in about 1817 by Jeffry Wyattville. The estate has a long and well documented history. Listed in the Domesday Book (1086) as Bretone, the land was held from at least the thirteenth century by the Dronsfield family. The Dronsfields intermarried with the Beaumonts of Whitley Hall and Beaumonts occupied the estate from 1792 until 1948, when the house was sold to West Riding County Council. After some years as a teacher training college, the hall became part of Leeds University in 2000.

Other sculptures in the park can take on surprising forms

Leeds

The centre of Leeds contains a splendid Victorian Town Hall and Grand Theatre that stand as monuments to its great nineteenth century prosperity, when it was celebrated as the industrial capital of Yorkshire. In the late twentieth century Leeds – while valuing and restoring its rich heritage of historic buildings – also established itself as a thoroughly modern multicultural centre for commerce, finance and the arts, home to people of more than 75 nationalities.

The domed roof of the Corn Exchange

➊ Leeds City Art Gallery

Established in 1888, the gallery's collection was designated by the government in 1997 as being of national importance – the best gathering of twentieth-century British art outside London. It includes watercolours by JMW Turner and John Sell Cotman, drawings by Yorkshire sculptor Henry Moore and work by Paula Rego. It also has a fine display of Pre-Raphaelite art and one of the country's leading collections of modern sculpture.

➋ The Grand Theatre

The Grand Theatre was built in 1878. It is widely regarded as a landmark of Victorian theatre construction, designed by architects George Corson and James Robertson Watson with seating for 2,600 people. Because two earlier Leeds theatres had been destroyed by fire, the design for the gas-lit establishment included an elaborate water-sprinkler system using the gas pipes. Electric lighting and a new stage were added in 1898. Great theatre names including Lily Langtry, Sarah Bernhardt, Henry Irving and Ellen Terry all appeared at the Grand in the late 19th and early 20th centuries. With a current capacity of 1,550 it attracts more than 240,000 theatregoers and opera-lovers each year. However, its age has made restoration necessary, and a £31 million renovation programme was launched in 2005.

➌ Leeds Town Hall

Leeds' most celebrated and recognisable building was opened by Queen Victoria in 1858. The town hall was designed by a young architect, Cuthbert Broderick, whose plans for the building won a competition and the first prize of £200 in 1853.

Built of honey-coloured millstone grit and local sandstone, with a splendid colonnaded front, the hall was intended to be an expression of Leeds' civic pride. The main building was begun in 1853, with the tower and dome added in 1857. Initially the town hall – hailed by contemporaries as a municipal palace – contained the council chamber, the Lord Mayor's offices, the law courts as well as the police headquarters. Today, however, the Victoria Hall at the centre of the building is a premier venue for music concerts in Leeds.

➍ Corn Exchange △

The oval hall of the Corn Exchange was designed by Cuthbert Broderick, architect of Leeds' landmark town hall, and opened in 1864. A tribute to the corn exchange in the French capital Paris, the Leeds exchange was laid out beneath a glass dome roof that allowed plenty of light to fall on the trading floor, where merchants needed to be able to examine corn samples in good lighting conditions. Broderick also designed the Leeds Mechanics Institute.

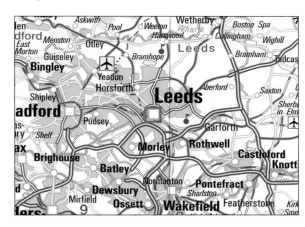

➎ St John's Church

The Church of St John the Evangelist stands behind Allders department store on the Headrow, in a bustling part of Leeds city centre. Built in 1632–34 by local wool merchant John Harrison in the Gothic Survival style, it contains original plasterwork, pews and pulpit – but its glory is probably the magnificent carved wooden screen, featuring vines and flowers together with human and animal heads. John Harrison was also a benefactor to Leeds grammar school, providing land and some new buildings, and his name was given to one of the 'houses' within the school. He is buried in St John's, to the right of the altar.

St John's Church is no longer in use for worship but is maintained by the Churches Conservation Trust and local volunteers. In the 19th century the parish wanted to demolish the church to replace it with a modern building; Late - Victorian architect Richard Norman Shaw campaigned for its survival and was subsequently entrusted with the church's restoration.

➏ City Station

Leeds City Station was established in 1938 by the merger of two previous rail terminals – the Leeds Wellington Station and the Leeds New Station, owned by different companies. Leeds City Station was rebuilt in 1967. Its origin as two separate stations lives on its present design with two concourses – the North and South.

➐ St Paul's House, Park Square

St Paul's House is a Grade-II listed office building, built in 1878 by architect Thomas Ambler as a warehouse for the clothes' manufacturer John Barron. The building's generally plain lower floors are complemented by extravagant detail on the upper floors suggesting the influence of Moorish and Venetian architecture – in particular the Alhambra palace in Granada, Spain, and the Doge's Palace in Venice, Italy.

Overleaf: Chatsworth House, home to the Dukes of Devonshire

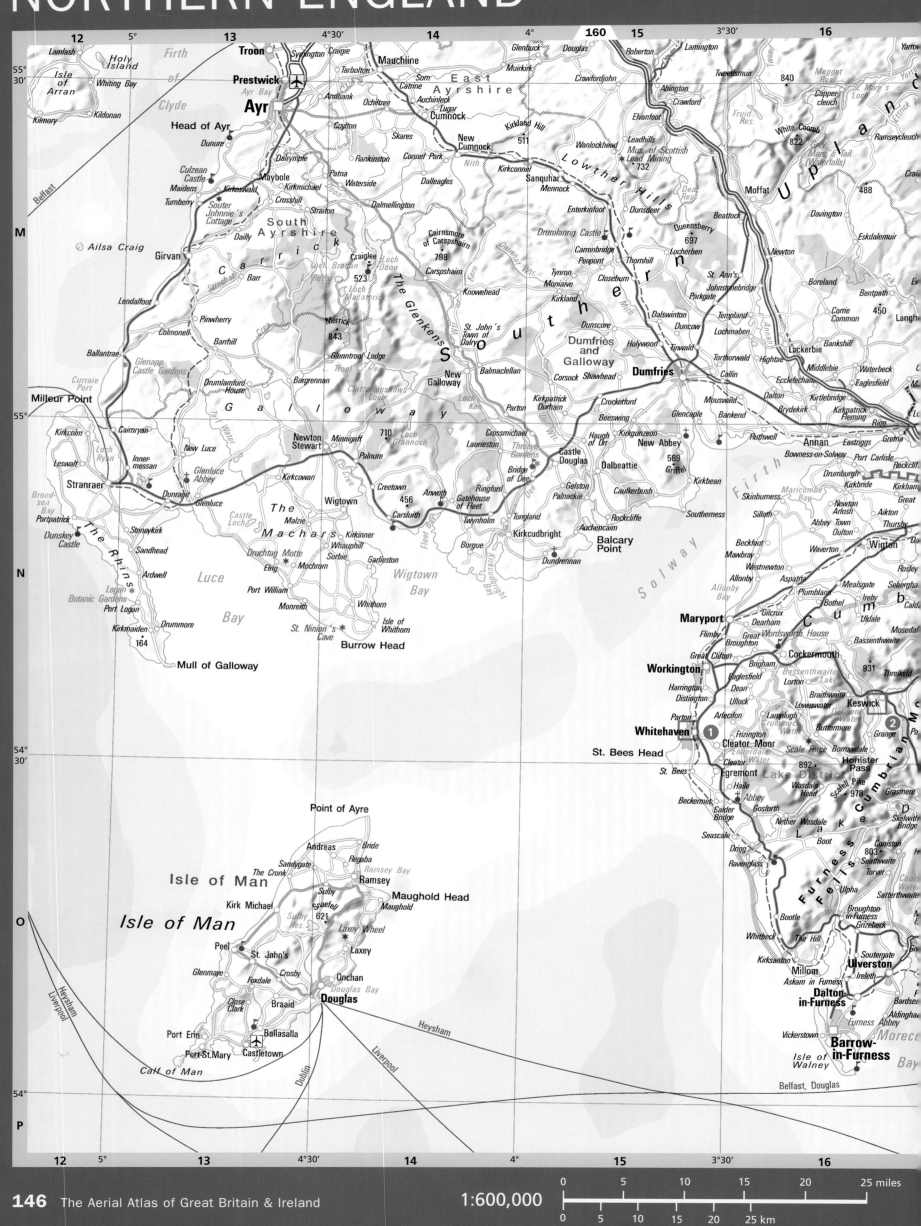

1:600,000

0   5   10   15   20   25 miles

0 5 10 15 20 25 km

① Whitehaven
② Keswick and Derwent Water
③ Chesters Fort
④ Newcastle and Gateshead
⑤ Tynemouth
⑥ Warkworth

1:600,000

1 North Tyneside
2 Newcastle upon Tyne
3 Gateshead
4 Sunderland
5 South Tyneside

1 Darlington
2 Hartlepool
3 Stockton on Tees
4 Middlesbrough
5 Redcar & Cleveland

Whitehaven

Laid out in the seventeenth century, the elegant seaport of Whitehaven was the first planned town built since the Middle Ages – and its grid design was reputedly the inspiration for the streetplan of New York City. In Whitehaven's heyday, in the mid-eighteenth century, the port grew rich exporting local Cumbrian coal, building ships and importing tobacco and rum from North America and the Caribbean. The town supports a small fishing fleet and its harbour and architecture make it a popular holiday spot.

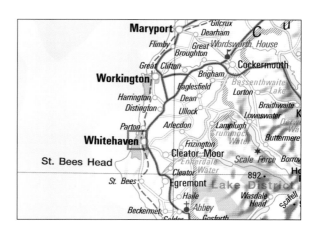

❶ Whitehaven Harbour ◁

Sir Christopher Lowther, Sheriff of Cumberland, bought the fishing village of Whitehaven in 1630 in order to develop a port from which to export salt from the saltpans he owned. He built a stone pier in 1633. On his death in 1644 the estate passed to his son, Sir John, then a baby. Sir John subsequently developed Whitehaven as a coal port. He extended the pier twice, in 1665 and 1687. The harbour expanded over the next 60 years and by the mid-1700s, Whitehaven was Britain's third largest port, after London and Bristol. The town prospered particularly on trade in coal across the Irish Sea, notably to Dublin. In the nineteenth century, however, Whitehaven's trade dwindled because the new larger ships could not navigate the shallow waters of the Solway Firth off Whitehaven and merchants turned to deep-water ports such as Liverpool and Glasgow. The Whitehaven Beacon, on the West Strand, is today a visitor centre housing a weather station and an exhibition celebrating the town's mining and merchant shipping past.

In the harbour area, a statue at the end of the Old Quay commemorates the daring night raid carried out on Whitehaven in April 1778 by American naval hero John Paul Jones. Originally born in Scotland and known as John Paul, Jones had changed his name when he settled in Virginia, after making a fortune and then running into trouble in the West Indies. At the time of the American Revolution he become a notable figure in the American colonists' 'Continental Navy' and in April 1778 was in command of the privateer *Ranger* during a raid from a base in France through the Irish Sea. He knew Whitehaven, having undergone his seaman's apprenticeship there, and came ashore with a landing party to spike the port's defensive guns and set fire to the ships in the harbour. Jones and his raiders succeeded in putting the guns out of action, but were discovered when they had set fire to just three ships and fled back to the safety of the *Ranger*. This raid remains the most recent invasion of the English mainland. The statue near Old Quay represents Jones in the moment of spiking one of the cannon – that is, rendering the gun useless.

A replica eighteenth-century ship in Whitehaven harbour

❷ Whitehaven Castle

The original building on the site of Whitehaven Castle was a mansion called the Flatt, purchased by Sir John Lowther on 1st October 1675. Almost a hundred years later, Sir James Lowther had to rebuild the house after the Flatt was destroyed in a fire in 1769. He renamed it Whitehaven Castle, and the Lowther family occupied the building until 1920, when it was auctioned off. In 1926 the Castle opened as Whitehaven and West Cumberland Infirmary and continued until the opening of a new hospital at Hensingham in 1964. The building is now privately owned.

❸ St James's Church

Celebrated for its Georgian interior, St James's Church was built in 1752. Its architect was a Whitehaven engineer, Carlisle Spedding, designer of an early type of safety lamp for use in local coal mines. Italian craftsmen named Arture and Baggiotti created the ceiling plasterwork, while the altarpiece was once in the Escorial monastery and palace outside Madrid before being brought to England. St James's has been the parish church of Whitehaven since the 1970s, when St Nicholas's Church burned down.

❹ Market place and streets

The lord of the manor was granted the right to hold a market in Whitehaven in 1654 and most of the buildings surrounding the market place have been standing since the mid-1600s. Chapel Street, King Street and Roper Street were built in the 1640s near the site of the market place. Church Street was laid out in the 1660s and College Street, Duke Street, James Street, Lowther Street, New Street, Queen Street and Strand Street were all built in the 1680s. In this period, Whitehaven's population was growing quickly, up from around 1,000 in 1685 to about 3,000 in 1700. In the market place the market hall, opened in 1881, stands on the site of an earlier hall, built in 1814–19 and designed by Sir Robert Smirke.

❺ St Nicholas's Church tower and graveyard

St Nicholas's Church was built in 1883, replacing an earlier church that was constructed in 1693. In August 1971, a major fire left only the tower standing and the building lost its status as the parish church of the area.

Records show that Mildred Gale, grandmother of the first American President, George Washington, was buried in St Nicholas's graveyard – but the exact location of her grave still remains unknown.

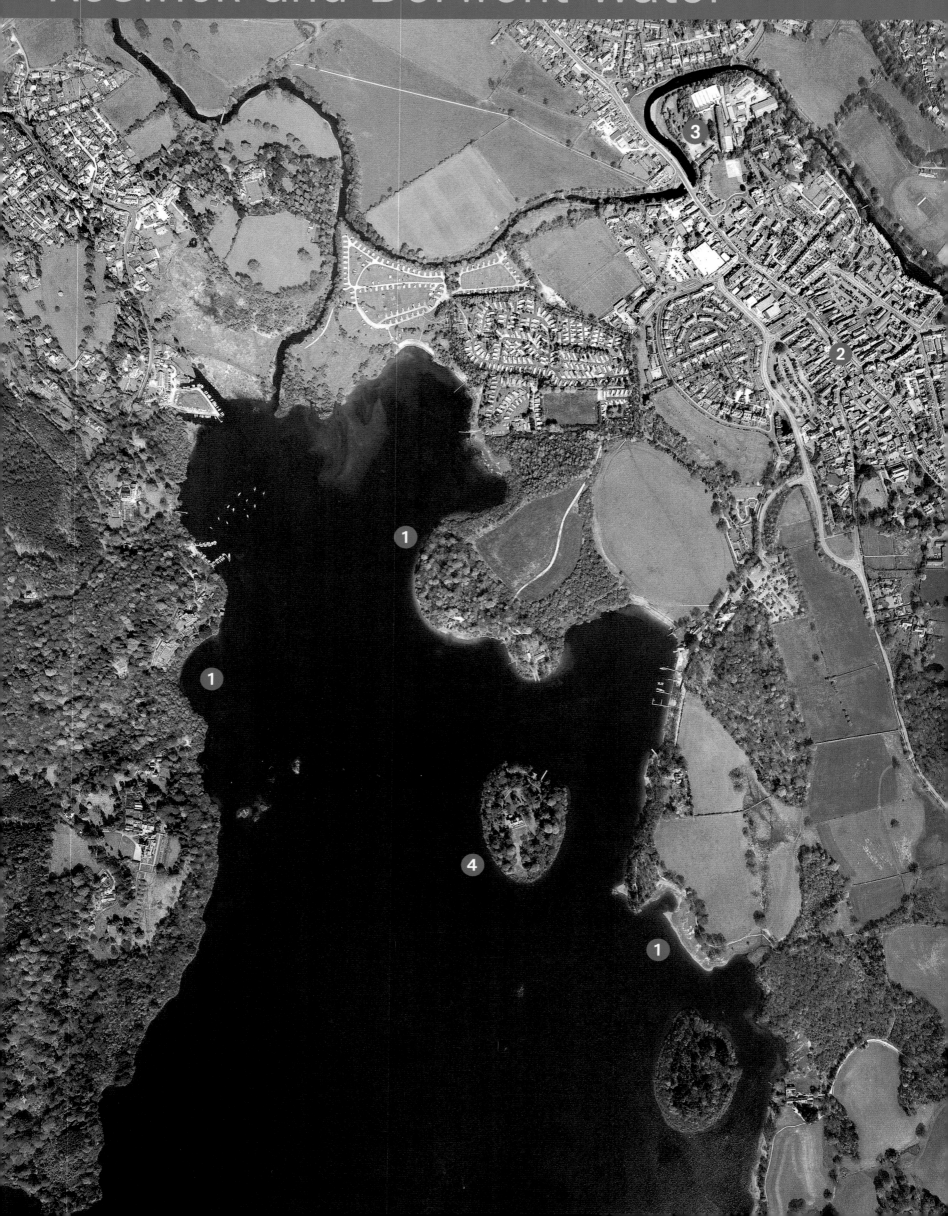

Keswick town and Derwent Water

In Old English 'Keswick' (like London's Chiswick) means 'outlying cheese-producing farm', and its gently sloping pastureland is ideal for dairy farming. Granted a charter to hold markets in 1276, Keswick still has a market every Saturday in the town centre. For 300 years it was the centre of world pencil manufacturing, but began a new chapter as a tourist destination when the railway arrived in 1865. It is now the main centre from which walkers and boaters set out to explore the northern Lake District.

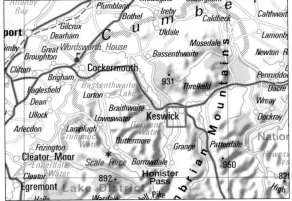

❷ Keswick town centre

Keswick is still today a small market town, with a population of about 5,000 – not much more than it was a century ago. Keswick's centre is its medieval marketplace, where stalls sell local produce every Saturday and the town's tourist information centre is located. North of the town runs the River Greta before it joins the River Derwent. On its northern bank lies Keswick's Fitz Park, home of the Keswick Museum and Art Gallery. As the regional base for most outdoor activities, many of the town's shops are devoted to walking, camping and sailing gear.

Derwent Water is 5 kilometres long and a major tourist attraction

❶ Derwent Water lakeside △

Keswick grew up by a lake, but was not a lakeside town until tourism began in the nineteenth century. West of the town, on the low-lying ground around the River Derwent, are the fields that now serve as Keswick's main camping and caravanning grounds. West of the river is the marina of the Derwent Water Boat Club, south of which are the private houses of Fawepark and Lingholm, where Beatrix Potter spent many summers and in whose grounds she set her stories of Squirrel Nutkin and company. To the south of Keswick, the town is separated from Derwent Water by the crest of Hope Park and Crow Park, owned by the National Trust and with wonderful views across the lake to Newlands Valley and the fells. The parks' protected status has ensured Keswick lakeside's preservation from private development and its continued accessibility to the public. South of Crow Park are the landing stages from which the Keswick Launch embarks on a six-stop, hour-long tour of the lake in summer. Next to the landing stages is Cockshott Wood, home to Theatre by the Lake – a new purpose-built theatre and year-round repertory company – opened in 1999.

❸ Cumberland Pencil Works and Museum

The history of the pencil began in 1555 in Borrowdale, the valley south of Derwent Water, when shepherds discovered lumps of a black rock that they found useful for marking sheep. Encased in a narrow cylinder of wood, the pencil was born. Until a process for making artificial pencil leads was developed in France in 1795, Borrowdale was the source of all the world's pencil graphite, and many of the actual pencils were made, by hand, in Keswick. In 1832 the first industrial-scale pencil factory opened in the town. The Cumberland Pencil Company was founded in 1916 and is now home to the Cumberland Pencil Works (still producing Derwent fine art pencils) and Museum, where visitors can see displays about the history of graphite mining and pencil making, as well as the world's longest pencil, a behemoth measuring 7.91 metres (26 feet) long and weighing 446 kg (985 lb).

❹ Derwent Isle

Derwent Isle, the only one of Derwent Water's four islands still to be inhabited, was originally owned by the monastery of Fountains Abbey in North Yorkshire. In 1778, the eccentric Joseph Pocklington built the core of the present-day house in the centre of the island. He also built several follies and outbuildings of which only a chapel remains. The island was bequeathed to the National Trust in 1951.

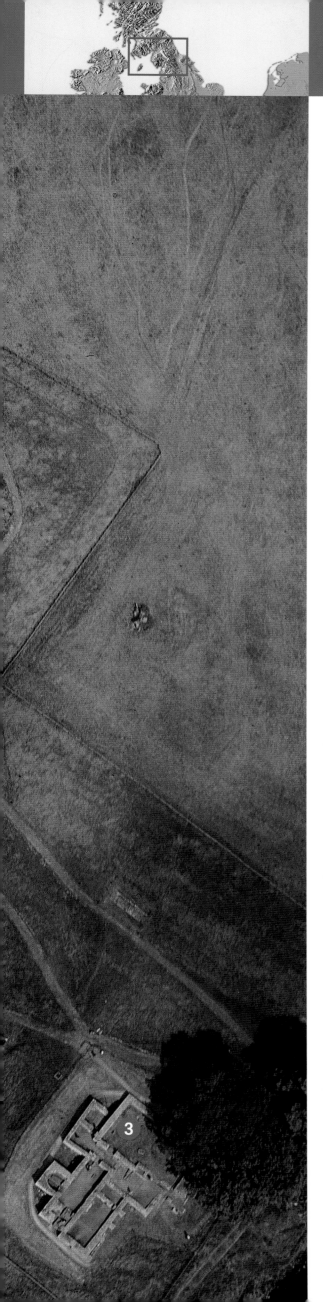

Chesters Fort

Hadrian's Wall is ancient Rome's most substantial legacy to Britain, stretching 117 kilometres (73 miles) from Wallsend on Tyneside to Bowness on the Solway Firth. Lying on the west bank of the River Tyne on Hadrian's Wall, between milecastles 27 and 28, Chesters Fort (Roman Cilurnum) is the best preserved Roman cavalry fort in Britain. It was built around 123 AD, and the unit stationed there was probably a reserve strike force to be deployed in case of trouble with the northern 'barbarian' Picts. The site was designed for a unit of 500 mounted troops and their horses (though later it held legionaries), and contained a substantial *praetorium* with an open courtyard, barrack blocks and a bath complex between the fort and the river. The wall is carried over the nearby river by a Roman bridge, of which very little remains today.

❶ The Praetorium

This was the headquarters building of the fort, and a visitor would have walked in off the street into a courtyard colonnaded on three sides. Some of the paving (one carved with a phallus for good luck) and guttering is still visible. Beyond was a hall with a tribunal from which the commander could address his troops. On the south side are five rooms used for administration, storage of the standards and the strong room, whose vaulted roof (second room from the right) still sits proud of the ground level. What are seen today are the Hadrianic remains.

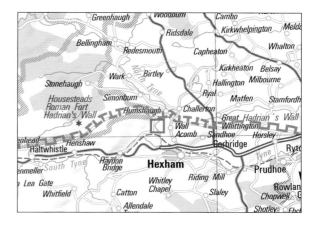

❷ Barracks and Stables

Close to the North gate are the remains of some of the main barrack blocks. The narrow rectangular rooms, probably with wooden partitions, were for the troopers, while the officers had more spacious accommodation at the end of the blocks. Remains of columns indicate the presence of broad, supported eaves, probably with rainwater gutters. Backing on to the south of the two rows of barracks is a third building that probably housed the horses.

❸ The Bath House Complex

Proximity to the river and fear of fire dictated the location of the bath complex outside the fort. It contains some of the most substantial remains on the site, with walls standing up to 3 metres (10 feet) high and 0.9 metres (3 feet) thick. It was developed in different stages – the first with changing rooms, and the main hot and cold rooms, while the second added a porch, larger changing rooms, and more heated rooms. There is significant buttressing along the latrine wall, though few of the 'fixtures' remain apart from part of the sewer. The roof was probably made of tiles and tufa (a volcanic stone).

The remains of the Roman bath block at Chesters Fort

❹ East Gate

There were six gates into the fort, four main ones in the centre of the walls and two smaller ones midway between the East and West gates and the southern wall of the fort. The walls of the fort were originally some 1.5 metres (5 feet) thick and 4.6 metres (15 feet) high. The East Gate would, like the other main ones, have had two substantial square towers, and a double entrance. The extensive remains show the towers reduced back to their original Hadrianic foundations. The north wall projects significantly beyond Hadrian's Wall, and in gates such as the North Gate, the original post holes for the gates can still be seen. With the angled corner towers, interval towers and battlements, the fort would have been a potent symbol of power on the northern edge of the Roman Empire.

Newcastle and Gateshead

Lying 13 kilometres (8 miles) inland from the North Sea on the banks of the River Tyne, Newcastle and Gateshead were renowned industrial centres in the nineteenth and early twentieth centuries, known for coalmining, iron and steel production and shipbuilding. Newcastle's fine Victorian civic

architecture is testament to the wealth generated by these industries. Today visitors and residents are attracted to Newcastle and Gateshead for their renowned cultural centres, shops and nightlife.

❶ Millennium Bridge ▷

This remarkable pedestrian and bicycle bridge runs for 126 metres (413 feet) across the River Tyne, linking Gateshead and the Quayside area of Newcastle. When ships need to pass, the bridge's roadway is tilted upwards on pivot mechanisms sited on both sides of the river, with a motion like that of a giant eyelid opening. The bridge was opened for public use on 17 September 2001 and has since won several awards for design and ingenuity. The Millennium Bridge was designed by Wilkinson Eyre Architects with Gifford and Partners Engineers.

The eyelid-mechanism Millennium Bridge

❷ Baltic Centre for Contemporary Art

Standing near the Millennium Bridge, on the river's south bank, the former Baltic Flour Mills in Gateshead was transformed into an international centre for visual arts in a £46 million project during the late 1990s. The Baltic Centre for Contemporary Art – which contains five art galleries, a cinema, artists' studios, a library-archive, media laboratories and restaurants – was opened on 13 July 2002. The design for the art centre was produced by Ellis Williams Architects. The Baltic, which has no permanent art collection, commissions new contemporary artworks and appoints artists in residence. The original Baltic flour mills complex operated from 1950–82 as a flour mill and animal-feed factory. The building converted into the Baltic centre was the original mill silo.

❸ Sage Centre ▽

The Sage Centre for music in Gateshead includes two concert halls, a rehearsal space, a 25-room music education centre, dining and bar spaces and a large concourse. Above the entire complex rises a curved steel roof containing 250 glass panels amid 3,000 stainless-steel sheets. From the concourse visitors can enjoy

The Sage Centre was opened in 2004

magnificent views of the quayside and river area. Designed by Foster and Partners it is home to the Northern Sinfonia chamber orchestra. It opened on 17 December 2004 after eight years of construction.

❹ Bridges

When it was opened in 1928, the Tyne Bridge was the world's largest single-span bridge. However, it lost this record within five years to the Sydney Harbour Bridge. Immediately to the west is the Swing Bridge, constructed in 1876 on the spot where the Romans built the first bridge across the Tyne in the second century AD. Next, is the High-Level Bridge designed by Robert Stephenson and opened in 1849 by Queen Victoria.

❺ Castle Keep and Black Gate

Newcastle takes its name from the 'new castle' built in 1080 by Robert Curthose, William the Conqueror's son, when returning from a military raid into Scotland. Robert's original wooden castle was rebuilt in stone in 1172, during the reign of King Henry II. The keep of this castle survives and can be visited today. The Black Gate was added in around 1250. The castle keep stands on the site of the original Roman fort, Pons Aelius, built in approximately 120 AD.

Tynemouth

The town of Tynemouth, part of the district of North Tyneside, lies on a promontory on the north side (top in the main picture) of the River Tyne, where it flows into the North Sea. To the south of the river mouth lies South Shields, in the district of South Tyneside. A large area of water around the harbour is sheltered by long twin piers. The place-name 'Shields' derives from the old word 'shiel' or 'shieling', meaning 'hut', and refers to the fishermen's huts that once stood here – fish have been landed at the mouth of the Tyne for many centuries. The military importance of the site is shown by fortifications that have existed since Roman times. Three kings are buried in the area – in the priory that overlooks the harbour. They are represented by three crowns in the priory's coat of arms.

The castle suffered badly in the Civil War

① Priory and Castle △

The ruins of the ancient priory and castle stand on Penbal Crag, overlooking the sheltered Prior's Haven. The priory is supposed to have been founded by Edwin, king of Northumbria, in the early 7th century, and rebuilt by King Oswald in 634. St Oswin, king of Deira (part of what was to become Northumbria), was buried there in 651, which is why the priory is dedicated to St Mary and St Oswin. The priory was later fortified. A Benedictine priory was built there in 1090. Henry VIII included the Spanish Battery, a gun emplacement manned by Spanish mercenaries, in the fortifications. Only the name survives, but a restored Second World War gun battery can be seen today. The castle was a Royalist stronghold in the Civil War, but fell to the Parliamentarians.

② Clifford's Fort

The ruins of Clifford's Fort, built in 1672 on the outbreak of the Third Dutch War to protect the mouth of the Tyne, can still be seen. Its main firepower was directed seawards. There was a lighthouse and a three-storey keep within the fort. In 1804, as a result of a drunken bet, companies of regular soldiers attacked the fort across the water from South Shields, but were repulsed by a Volunteer force. The fort continued as a battery until 1888, when it became a depot for Tyne Division, Royal Engineers (Volunteers) Submarine Miners. It again saw service as a coastal battery in the Second World War.

③ Roman Fort and Museum

One of the finest Roman forts has been excavated and partly reconstructed here in South Shields. The fort of Arbeia was first constructed in 160 AD on the site of an Iron Age roundhouse. Its original cobbled parade ground can now be viewed by visitors. The fort soon became a supply base, equipped with granaries, to provision the 17 forts along Hadrian's Wall, which lies to the west. When the camp was burned down in 300, it was rebuilt with the addition of a fine house for the commanding officer. The house had two dining rooms, baths, kitchens, stables and central heating. Among the treasures recovered from the site are pieces of jewellery carved from jet.

④ Black Middens

These treacherous rocks, hidden at high tide, were once the cause of many shipwrecks in heavy seas. Ships were likely to run into them as they tried to avoid Herd Sand, a shallow sandbank on the south side of the harbour. The schooner *Friendship* and the steamer *Stanley* were wrecked on the Black Middens on 24 November 1864, with the loss of 36 lives. This tragedy inspired the formation of the first Volunteer Life Brigade to assist in future rescue efforts from the landward side. The building of the piers was begun in 1854 and was only completed in 1895, when the North Pier was finished. Only two years later the North Pier was breached by a storm, and it was 14 years before its reconstruction was completed. The result was a tranquil harbour, which made the rocks less deadly.

⑤ Fish Quay

The Fish Quay was already the site of a small fishing community as early as the thirteenth century. It developed to become the heart of an important fishing port. In the nineteenth century, the North Shields dockside were frequented by the famous fishwives of Cullercoats, a village a short way along the coast to the north. Less white fish is landed here nowadays, owing to the depletion of North Sea fish stocks. However, Tynemouth is still the country's major port for prawn and it is busiest in the prawn season, between September and March.

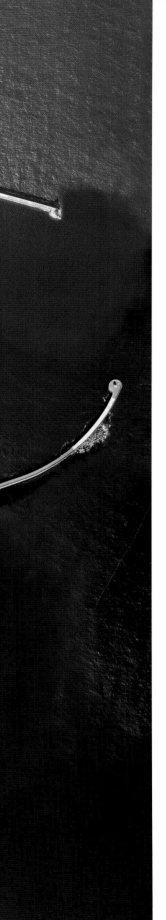

The reconstructed Fort gateway of Arbeia

Overleaf: the village and fourteenth century castle at Warkworth

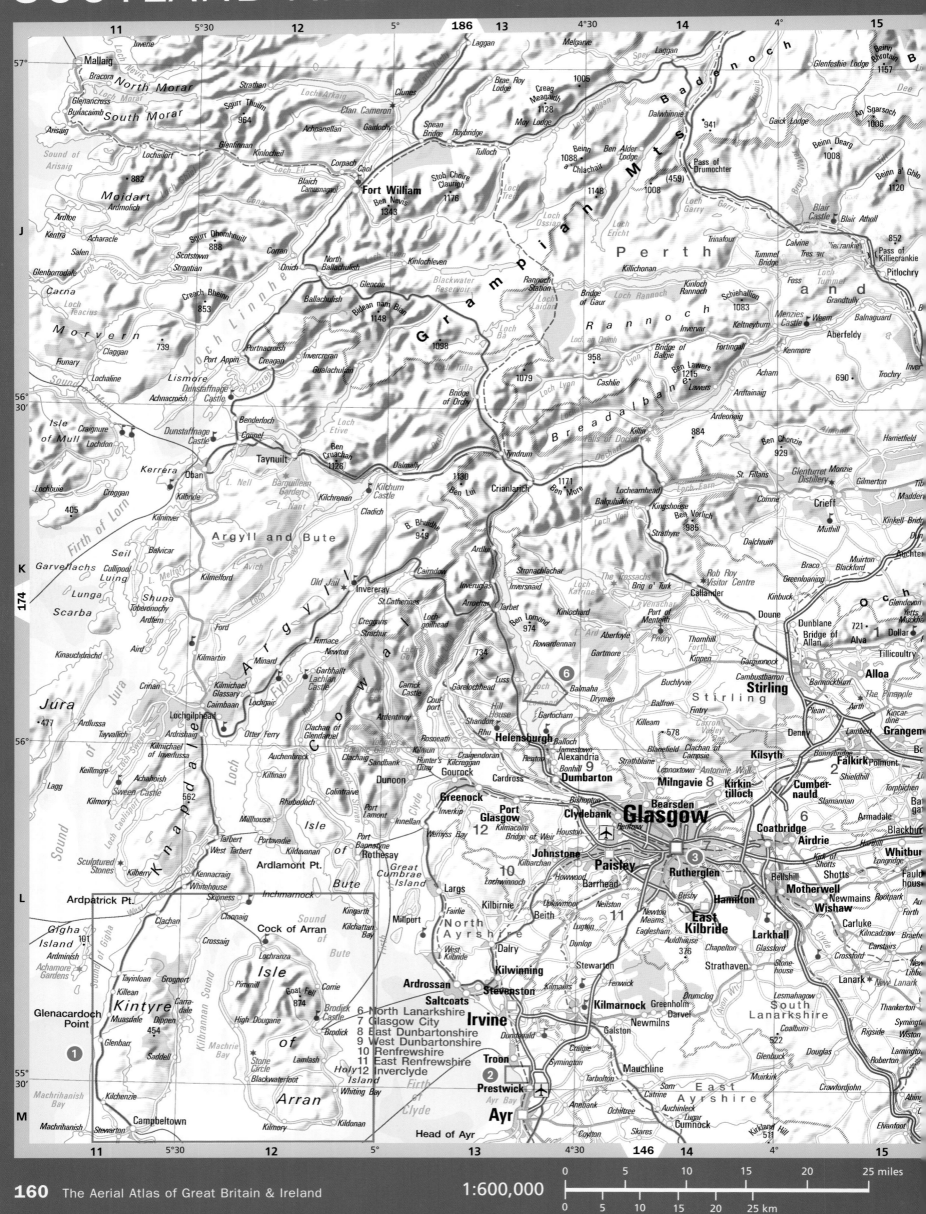

1:600,000

6 North Lanarkshire
7 Glasgow City
8 East Dunbartonshire
9 West Dunbartonshire
10 Renfrewshire
11 East Renfrewshire
12 Inverclyde

0   5   10   15   20   25 miles

0   5   10   15   20   25 km

1:600,000

① Isle of Arran   ④ Edinburgh
② Royal Troon   ⑤ Holy Island of Lindisfarne
③ Glasgow   ⑥ Loch Lomond

N o r t h   S e a

1 Clackmannanshire
2 Falkirk
3 West Lothian
4 City of Edinburgh
5 Midlothian

1 Dundee City

The Isles of Arran and Bute

Arran is a mountainous island in the Firth of Clyde with an area of 426 sq kms (165 sq miles) and a population of some 4,500. Its landscape of hills, streams, glens and lochs has been described as 'Scotland in miniature'. The most dramatic scenery is in the north: the top of Goat Fell looks over one of the best panoramic views in Scotland. Earlier settlers left their mark on the island with stone circles and the remains of their huts and burial places. Eight kilometres (five miles) across the water from Arran is the island of Bute which, despite a rocky coastline, has a fertile soil suitable for crop-growing and dairying.

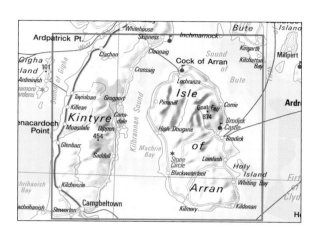

Isle of Bute viewed from the south

2 Isle of Bute △

Bute covers an area of 120 sq kms (46 sq miles) and granite, red sandstone and slate are found on the island. The resort of Rothesay has sandy beaches, Winter Gardens and the ruins of a thirteenth-century castle that was destroyed by Oliver Cromwell. Mount Stuart, built in the late nineteenth century, lies six kilometres (four miles) south of Rothesay and is one of the seats of the Marquis of Bute. Tourism and agriculture are the backbone of the economy and there are ferry services connecting the island with the mainland and with Arran. Bute is separated from the Cowal peninsula by a stretch of water called the Kyles of Bute. Cattle used to make the crossing by being forced to swim across.

3 Standing Stones

Arran is well known for its fine collection of prehistoric standing stones. The most famous are the stone circles at Machrie, on the western side of the island, which include stone circles, single stones and hut circles dating from the Bronze Age around 2000 BC. Near Blackwaterfoot, also on the western side, are bronze-age cairns. Just opposite the school in Brodick is a single standing stone by the side of the road. There is another stone in the forested area just south of the bridge over Glenrosa Water. Drumadoon Point is the site of an Iron Age fort.

1 Brodick, Isle of Aran ▽

Brodick on the east coast is the main town, resort and port on Arran. The name derives from the Norse invaders who captured the site in the ninth century - Brodick means 'broad bay'. The Bay is commanded by the red sandstone bulk of Brodick Castle, the earliest part of which dates from the thirteenth century. Its defences were strengthened many times in the sixteenth and seventeenth centuries, but the biggest change came in the mid-nineteenth century when it was transformed from a fortress to an opulent Victorian stately home. The castle was in the possession of the Dukes of Hamilton from 1503, when James IV granted it to his cousin, Lord Hamilton later Earl of Arran, until 1957, when the Duchess of Montrose, the daughter of the 12th Duke died and it was bequeathed to the National Trust for Scotland.

The island benefits from the Gulf Stream that gives it a mild climate – mild enough to grow palm trees in the Castle's Edwardian-style garden. There is also an internationally famous collection of rhododendrons in the woodland garden, begun in 1923. Behind Brodick Castle rises Goat Fell, at 874m (2,866ft) the highest peak on Arran. Brodick village provides the island's main centre for shops and services and, behind the sandy beaches of the bay, protected by the dunes, is a fine 18-hole golf course in the classic Scottish links style. Just north of the village on the main road is the Arran Heritage Museum, where visitors can enjoy a picnic by the river before seeing demonstrations of horse-shoeing and other work.

The peaceful landscape around Brodick

4 Lamlash Bay

Lamlash Bay on the east side on the island is a centre for yachting. It is protected by Holy Island, the site of a hermit's cell – St Molais's cave – dating from the sixth century.

5 Lochranza

Arran has a connection with Robert the Bruce who, after the uprising which ended in the execution of William Wallace, headed another rebellion against the English king, Edward I. He landed at Lochranza on what was called 'the loch of safe anchorage' from Ireland in 1306 and was crowned at Scone the same year. He sheltered in caverns near Blackwaterfoot, known as the King's Caves.

1

3

2

4

The clubhouse at Royal Troon

Royal Troon Golf Club

Golfers rate the windswept, undulating Old Course at the Royal Troon Golf Club as one of the world's best. The celebrated British Open Championship has been held on the course eight times including 2004, when American Todd Hamilton was triumphant. The Club, which has two other courses, lies to the south of the Ayrshire coastal resort of Troon. The town was at one time a coal port and shipyard, and more recently a marina and a base for ferry operations to Ireland.

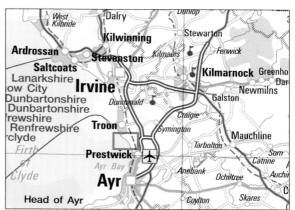

1 Clubhouse

A group of 24 golf enthusiasts founded the Troon Golf Club on 16 March 1878. The first course, laid out by 1880, had six holes but an 18-hole course 1,950m (2,125yds) long had been completed by 1888. The first clubhouse was no more than a converted railway carriage, but this was replaced in the late 1870s with a small wooden building. The present clubhouse was begun in 1886, and the Smoke Room and the Dining Room were added in the early twentieth century. The club was honoured as Royal Troon in 1978, its centenary year.

The 8th hole is known as the Postage Stamp

2 Old Course

The Old Course measures 6,470m (7,079 yds) of uneven country overlooking the waters of Ayr Bay; the prevailing north-westerly wind is a particular threat on the second half of the 18-hole course. The most celebrated hole is the par-3 eighth, known as the Postage Stamp because, when viewed from the tee, the green – only 7.5m (25ft) across at its widest point – looks no larger than a stamp. The Postage Stamp is also the shortest hole on any Open Championship course, measuring just 115m (126yds) in length.

The British Open Championship was held on the Old Course at Troon for the first time in 1923. Arnold Palmer won the Championship in 1962. The Ladies British Open Amateur Championship was first held at Troon in 1904.

3 Par-3 Course

This course, consisting of nine holes, provides a series of challenges. It is mainly used by older and junior players. It is 1,080m (1,191yds) long.

4 Portland Course

The Portland, initially known as the Relief Course, was opened in June 1895 when Willie Fernie was the club's professional. In 1924, its name was changed to the Portland Course. The Portland is more sheltered than the Old Course and shorter, measuring about 5,700m (6,274yds). Running across moorland terrain with broom and gorse, it has five Par-3 holes and four more demanding Par-5s. In 1979, the qualifying rounds for the European Open Championship were held here.

Glasgow

Glasgow has come a long way from its beginnings as a small fishing village on the River Clyde to its present-day position as a centre of culture, and winner of the 1990 European City of Culture award. Though little of the medieval city remains, the cityscape is coloured by its past as a centre for shipbuilding, textiles and the coal and steel industries. The nineteenth century brought poverty and overcrowding, but also grand public architecture, and art collections amassed by the wealthy. The city today has a reputation as a centre for entertainment and the arts.

① Charles Rennie Mackintosh buildings ▽

A Glaswegian by birth, architect and artist Charles Rennie Mackintosh's early-twentieth century Art Nouveau buildings, furniture and interiors impart a minimalist elegance. He was involved in designing a chain of tea rooms – part of an unsuccessful campaign to fight drunkenness in the city – an outstanding example being the Willow Tea Rooms on Sauchiehall Street, with an opulent Salle de Luxe decorated in silver and white on the first floor. The Glasgow School of Art on Renfrew Street is perhaps his best-known larger building, and has an imposing exterior as well as many examples of his furniture inside its grand Library. An overview of Mackintosh's unique and innovative style can be seen in the Mackintosh House at the Hunterian Art Gallery, part of the University of Glasgow.

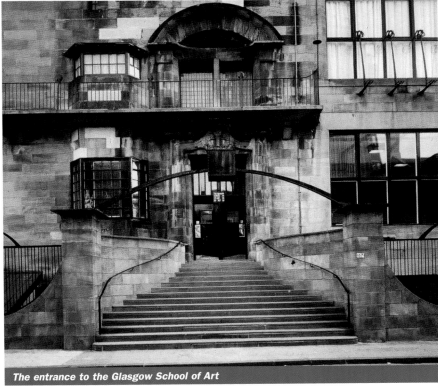

The entrance to the Glasgow School of Art

② St Mungo's Cathedral ▷

Glasgow Cathedral is built on the site believed to have been that of a sixth-century church established by the city's founder and patron saint, St Kentigern – who was baptised as 'Mungo' or 'dear one'. The present cathedral was consecrated in 1197, and building was completed in the early sixteenth century. A previous stone cathedral, consecrated in 1136, was destroyed by fire. In 1560, Archbishop James Beaton fled to France to escape the Reformation, saving many relics and artefacts. Though the Cathedral did not escape Reformation damage completely it was repaired by voluntary subscription in 1574, and has been restored over the centuries. Originally Episcopalian, it became Presbyterian in 1689. Remarkable interior features include the Laigh Kirk (lower church), whose fine Gothic crypt holds St Mungo's tomb, and the fifteenth-century nave, divided by a stone choir screen. In 1993, the St Mungo Museum of Religious Art was opened in a large purpose-built building.

The Cathedral was rebuilt after a fire in the sixteenth century

③ Sauchiehall Street

With a name derived from the Gaelic words for willow and meadow – saugh and haugh – Sauchiehall Street has a long history as Glasgow's most popular and famous thoroughfare. Running from Buchanan Street to Charing Cross, it was originally a winding lane. In the nineteenth century it was widened and straightened to become the location for the finest city shops and, in later years, home to the Regal, La Scala and Gaumont cinemas, and the Locarno Ballroom. The few older businesses that remain include the Willow Tea Rooms, and Watt Brothers.

④ Provand's Lordship

Provand's Lordship was built in 1471 as part of St Nicholas's Hospital, although its name comes from the nineteenth century when it was the home of the Lord of Provand. It is the oldest surviving house in Glasgow and a rare example of pre-Reformation domestic building. Unlike its contemporary near neighbour, St Mungo's Cathedral, it has a simple 'random rubble' exterior with no artistic pretensions. Mary, Queen of Scots is believed to have stayed there when visiting Glasgow in 1566, and over the years it has been a bishop's manse, an alehouse and a sweetshop. It is now a museum maintained by the City Council, who renovated the building in 1983 and subsequently restored the original St Nicholas physic garden behind the house. The three-storey museum has a fine collection of Scottish furniture and medieval artefacts.

Edinburgh

Edinburgh evolved in the Dark Ages around the nucleus of the naturally fortified Castle Rock to become the capital of the nation that unified Lowland Anglo-Saxons and Britons with the Celts of the Highlands and Islands. Its magnificent architectural heritage and distinguished intellectual history gave it the title 'Athens of the North' and, along with its museums and world-renowned summer festival, they continue to be a magnet for visitors today.

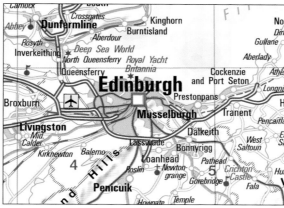

❶ Royal Mile

The Royal Mile is the straight road – made up of the High Street and its continuation, Canongate – that slopes down from the Castle at one end to the Royal Palace of Holyroodhouse at the other. The route as a whole forms the northern boundary of Edinburgh's Old Town. Part way along the High Street is St Giles' Cathedral, founded in the twelfth century. The combination of royal power, military might and the city's cathedral made the Royal Mile the ceremonial and processional artery of Edinburgh during its centuries as the capital of an independent Scotland.

❷ Edinburgh Galleries ▽

The narrow valley between Castle Rock and the New Town houses two neo-classical galleries, both designed by William Playfair. The Royal Scottish Academy was completed in 1826 and the National Gallery of Scotland opened in 1859. In 2004, the two buildings were connected by an underground link housing a lecture theatre, cinema, and restaurant. The National Gallery building now houses the permanent collection, while the Academy hosts international exhibitions. The Scottish National Portrait Gallery can be found in Queen Street.

The Castle as seen from the Old Town

❸ Edinburgh Castle △

The great plug of volcanic rock that dominates the city of Edinburgh has been fortified since prehistoric times. The oldest surviving building on it is probably the twelfth-century St Margaret's Chapel. James VI (later James I of England) was born in the castle in 1566, and it served as a prison for American prisoners of war in the 1770s as well as a royal arsenal and barracks.

❹ Old Town

To the east and south of the castle lies Edinburgh's Old Town. This is the medieval city that, alongside the markets and the famous multi-storeyed tenements, also included the Palace of Holyroodhouse, Parliament House (home of parliament in the seventeenth century), Edinburgh University and St Giles' Cathedral.

❺ New Town

As the Old Town became more crowded, suggestions were made to build a spacious new urban centre on the north side of the castle. James Craig laid out the masterplan in 1766 and the individual buildings were constructed over the next 30 years by architects such as Robert Adam and William Chambers.

The National Gallery of Scotland

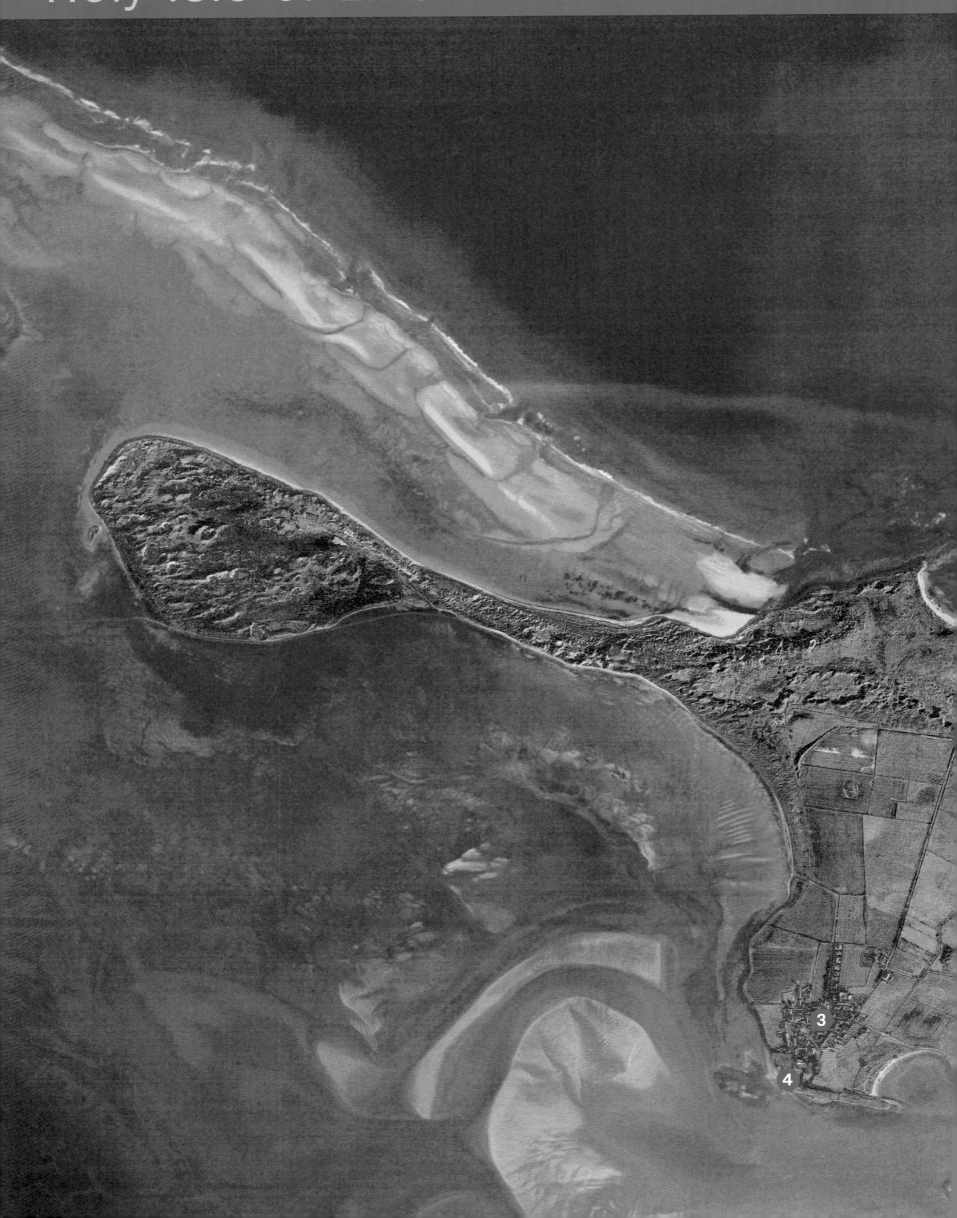

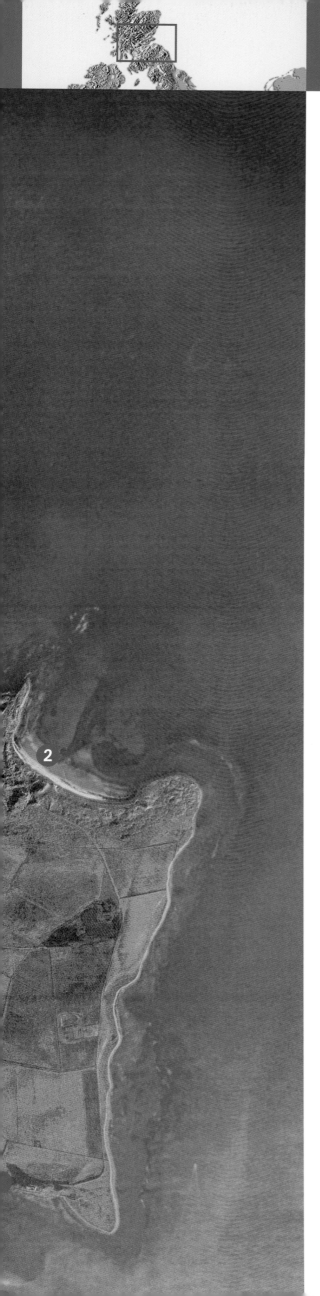

2

Holy Isle of Lindisfarne

Lindisfarne, the largest of the Farne Islands off the coast of Northumberland in north-east England, is only an island part of the time: at low tide a causeway built on a sandy spit connects it to the mainland. Isolated—but not too isolated—it was an ideal place to build a monastery that was not only a place of retreat, but one of the spiritual powerhouses of Dark Ages Britain, from which missionaries spread out to convert the Anglo-Saxons to Christianity.

① Castle ▽

A timber and earth defensive structure was built on the island's most prominent outcrop of rock in 1548–49, then rebuilt in stone in 1565–71. It was held by Parliament during the Civil War, but the small garrison was finally removed in 1819, after which the castle was abandoned and became derelict. In 1901 it was bought by Edward Hudson, the owner of Country Life magazine, and he commissioned the architect Edwin Lutyens to renovate and redesign it as an intimate, domestically scaled retreat. The rooms are mostly small, with low, sometimes vaulted ceilings. The stonework is plain and massive, and the heavy, dark wooden furniture is largely seventeenth century, or in a similar style. A garden, laid out by the famous garden designer Gertrude Jekyll, is intended to be at its peak in high summer. In 1944 the castle was given to the National Trust, and today is open to the public.

The castle was rebuilt by Edwin Lutyens

② Wildlife

The tidal sand flats around the island make it an important staging post for birds migrating north and south, particularly waders. Arctic and common terns are also seen, and among resident birds the eider duck, an emblem of St Cuthbert, is here near the southern limit of its range. The dunes and marshes—which are concentrated on the northern shore, away from the main area of settlement—also support some rare plant life, including orchids (the Northern Marsh Orchid), cord grass, eel grass, and marram grass. This area is now protected by English Nature as one of its National Nature Reserves.

③ Island History

The meaning of the island's original name, Lindisfarne, is uncertain, but most probably combines the Celtic words for stream or pool (perhaps referring to the nearby River Low or to the island's own small lake) and for land (farran). The island first clearly appears in history in 635 when King Oswald of Northumbria granted Lindisfarne to St Aidan, the Irish monk who had come from Iona at Oswald's request to evangelise his people. The monastery Aidan founded became famous as the spiritual home of northern England's most beloved saint, Cuthbert, from 664–76. In the eighth century Cuthbert's cult made it a rich and sophisticated monastery and this drew the attention of Vikings, who made the first recorded attack on the British Isles there in 793. Shortly afterward the monastery was abandoned, and not re-established until the early twelfth century; there is no record of the island being inhabited between those times. In the 1540s, Lindisfarne's position near the Scottish border, and the sheltered harbour on its southern side, made it an important English defence.

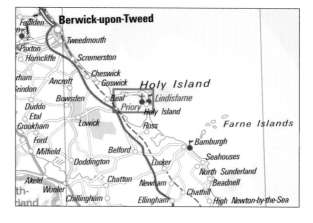

④ Priory

The ruins that can be seen today are of the medieval priory that began around 1130 and were completed around 1200, by which time it was home to a community of around a dozen monks. It was also at this time that the island was first called Insula Sacra, Holy Island. The priory—built on the same site as the remains of the smaller eighth century monastery—was an outpost of Durham Cathedral, and its church may have been designed as a miniature replica. In the mid-fourteenth century political tensions led to the fortification of the priory. War, bad harvests, and the Black Death cut its income severely and, by 1400, the much smaller community had abandoned some of the buildings, taking up residence in the prior's lodging. In 1537 the dissolution of the monasteries saw the priory closed, its buildings used as storehouses. By the early seventeenth century the lead had been stripped from the roof.

Overleaf: a ribbon of islands stretches across Loch Lomond

THE HEBRIDES

1. Iona and Mull
2. Eriskay
3. Skye and the Cuillins
4. Stornoway
5. Staffa

1:600,000

0 5 10 15 20 25 miles

0 5 10 15 20 25 km

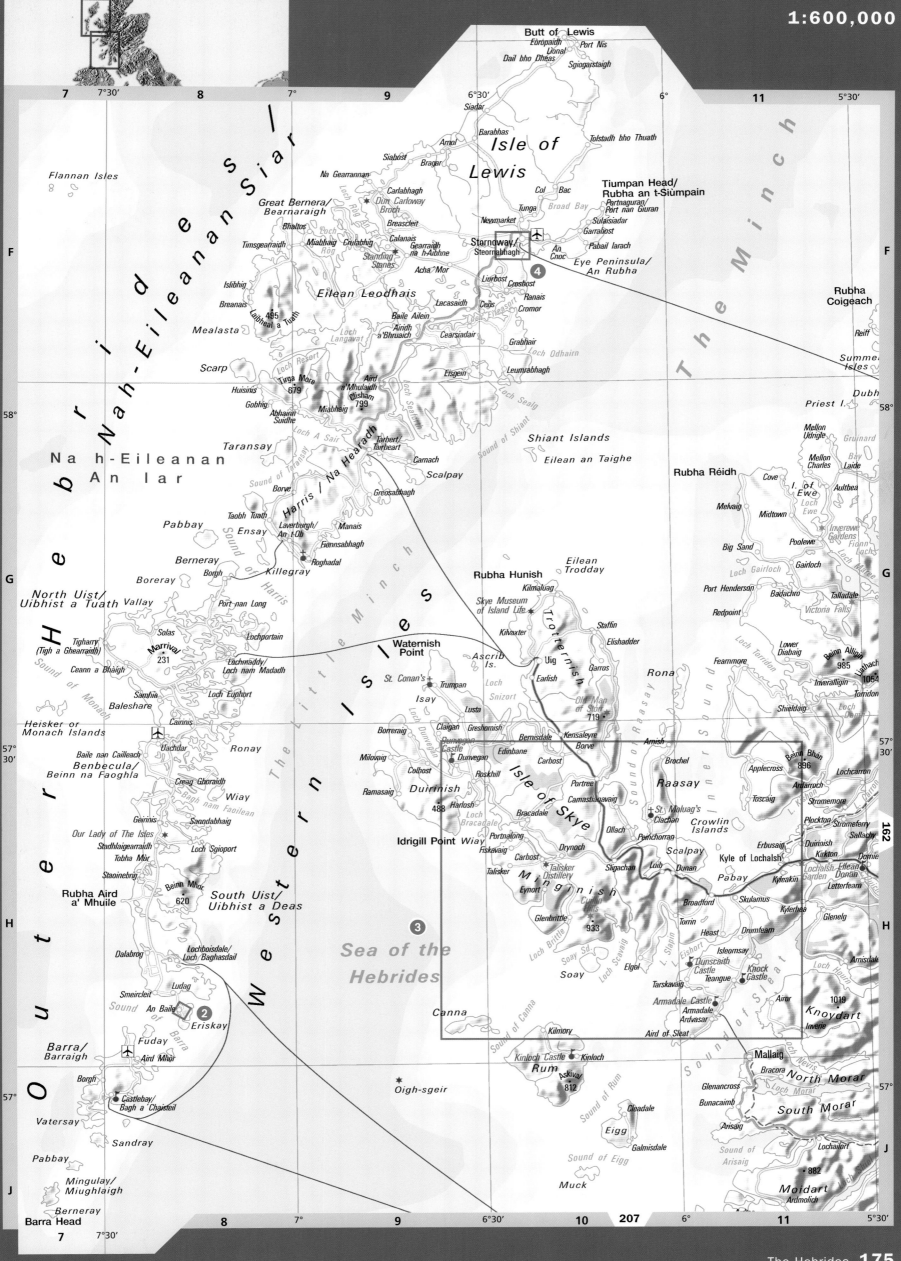

Butt of Lewis
Eòropaidh
Lional
Port Nis
Dail bho Dheas
Sgiogarstaigh

Siadar

Arnol
Barabhas
Isle of
Lewis

Siabost
Bragar
Na Gearrannan

Tolstadh bho Thuath

Col
Bac

Tiumpan Head/
Rubha an t-Siùmpain

Carlabhagh
Dùn Carloway
Broch

Great Bernera/
Bearnaraigh

Bhaltos

Breascleit

Tunga

Portnaguran/
Port nan Giùran
Sulaisiadar
Garrabost

Newmarket

An
Cnoc

Timsgearraidh
Miabhaig
Crulabhig
Calanais
Gearraidh
na h-Aibhne
Acha'Mor

Stornoway/
Steornabhagh

Pabail Iarach

Eye Peninsula/
An Rubha

Islibhig

Eilean Leodhais

Baile Ailein

Liurbost
Crosbost

Ranais
Cromor

Breanais
Lallbheal a Tuath
485

Mealasta

Airidh
a'Bhruaich
Cearsiadair

Grabhair

Rubha
Coigeach

Reiff

Loch Langavat

Eisgein

Leumrabhagh

Summer
Isles

Scarp

Tirga More
679

Aird
a'Mhulaidh
Clisham
799

Loch Sealg

Priest I.
Dubh

Huisinis
Gobhig
Abhainn
Suidhe
Miabhaig

Shiant Islands

Rubha Réidh

Mellon
Udrigle
Gruinard
Bay

Taransay

Tarbert/
Tairbeart

Carnach

Eilean an Taighe

Mellon
Charles
Cove
I. of
Ewe

Na h-Eileanan
An Iar

Borve

Scalpay

Laide
Aultbea

Pabbay

Taobh Tuath
Ensay

Greosabhagh

Melvaig
Midtown

Loch
Ewe

Big Sand

Inverewe
Gardens

Manais

Laverburgh/
An t-Ob
Fionnsabhagh

Poolewe

Berneray
Borgh
Roghadal

Rubha Hunish

Eilean
Trodday

Port Henderson
Badachro

Gairloch

Killegray

Boreray

Kilmaluag

Redpoint

Skye Museum
of Island Life

Loch Gairloch

North Uist/
Uibhist a Tuath

Valley

Port nan Long

Kilvaxter

Staffin

Elishadder

Fearnmore

Lower
Diabaig

Beinn Alligin
985

Liathach
1054

Tigharry
(Tigh a Ghearraidh)

Solas

Marrival
231

Lochportain

Waternish
Point

Ascrib
Is.

Uig
Garros

Trotternish

Rona

Inveralligin
Torridon

Ceann a Bhàigh

Lochmaddy/
Loch nam Madadh

St. Conan's
Trumpan
Earlish

Old Man
of Storr
719

Shieldaig

Sound of Monach

Samhla
Baleshare

Loch Euphort

Isay
Lusta

Claigan
Greshornish

Bernisdale
Kensaleyre
Borve

Arnish

Beinn Bhàn
896

Heisker or
Monach Islands

Cainnis

Ronay

Borreraig
Dunvegan
Castle
Dunvegan
Edinbane
Carbost

Brochel

Applecross

Lochcarron

Uachdar

Milovaig
Colbost
Roskhill

Portree

Raasay

Toscaig

Ardarroch
Stromemore

Benbecula/
Beinn na Faoghla

Creag Ghoraidh

Ramasaig

Duirinish
488

Camastianavaig

St. Moluag's
Clachan

Plockton
Stromeferry
Sallachy

Wiay

Harlosh
Bracadale

Crowlin
Islands

Erbusaig

Duirinish
Kirkton

Geirinis
Sanndabhaig

Loch
Bracadale

Portnalong

Ollach

Scalpay

Kyle of Lochalsh

Domie

Our Lady of The Isles

Idrigill Point
Wiay

Fiskavaig

Pemchorran

Pabay

Kyleakin

Eilean
Donan

Stadhlaigearraidh
Tobha Mòr

Carbost

Drynoch

Sligachan
Luib
Dunan

Kyle of Lochalsh

Letterfearn

Staoinebrig

Talisker

Talisker
Distillery

Eynort

Cuillin
Hills
933

Broadford
Skulamus

Kylerhea

Glenelg

Rubha Aird
a' Mhuile

Beinn Mhor
620

South Uist/
Uibhist a Deas

Minginish

Glenbrittle

Loch Brittle

Torrin
Heast

Drumfearn

Isleornsay

Amisdale

Loch Scavaig

L. Slapin
L. Eishort

Dunscaith
Castle

Knock
Castle

Dalabrog

Sea of the
Hebrides

Soay Sd.
Soay

Elgol

Tarskavaig

Teangue

Airor

Lochboisdale/
Loch Baghasdail

Armadale Castle
Armadale
Ardvasar

1019
Inverie

Smeircleit
Ludag

An Baile
Eriskay

Canna

Aird of Sleat

Knoydart

Barra/
Barraigh

Fuday

Aird Mhòr

Sound of Canna

Kilmory

Mallaig

Bracora
North Morar

Borgh

Kinloch Castle
Kinloch

Oigh-sgeir

Rum

Glenancross
Bunacaimb

South Morar

Castlebay/
Bagh a 'Chaisteil

Askival
812

Arisaig

Vatersay

Cleadale

Lochailort

Sound
of Arisaig

Pabbay

Eigg

Galmisdale

882

Mingulay/
Miughlaigh

Sound of Eigg

Moidart
Ardmolich

Berneray

Muck

Barra Head

Mull and Iona

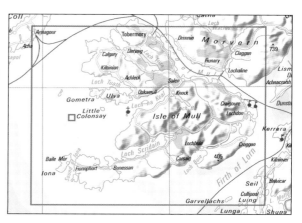

The tiny island of Iona covering a mere 850 hectares (2,100 acres) in the Inner Hebrides was the site of a monastery founded by St Columba in 563 AD, part of his mission to convert pagan Scotland to Christianity. It became an important Christian centre, a place of learning and pilgrimage, and was also the burial place of 60 Scottish, Irish and Norwegian kings. By contrast, Iona's neighbour, the Isle of Mull, covers an area of 950 square kilometres (367 square miles) – a beautiful landscape that includes mountains, waterfalls, forests, sea lochs and beaches. Mull has one of the best ferry services in the Scottish islands.

① Tobermory

Tobermory is the capital and fishing port of Mull, its harbour lined with brightly painted houses. A centre for yachting and diving, Tobermory played a small part in the rout of the Spanish Armada. A galleon, the *Florida*, took refuge in the bay in 1588 and was blown up by the local inhabitants. During the summer months, boat trips for viewing wildlife or sea fishing take place daily from the town. There are local walks and a museum, as well as a multimedia exhibition at the Hebridean Whale and Dolphin Trust.

Iona's beaches offer spectacular views

② Isle of Iona △

Iona can be reached by ferry from Fionnphort on Mull. Its place is secured in history by the presence of St Columba who, paradoxically, went there as an act of self-imposed penance for causing a battle in his home in Ireland. Iona was the first place that he landed from which he was unable to see his homeland. He founded a community there which became famous for its scholarship and craftmanship: the early ninth-century manuscript of the *Book of Kells* – now in Trinity College, Dublin – bears witness to this. The community suffered attacks from Viking raiders, but survived as a Benedictine abbey until the Reformation. Restoration began again in 1899. Former British Labour party leader John Smith is buried on the island.

③ Ulva

The island of Ulva off the west coast of Mull can be reached from there by ferry. Ulva has had a procession of distinguished visitors over the past two centuries, including Samuel Johnson and his biographer and friend, James Boswell, who came there to inspect Ulva's caves and basalt cliffs in 1773. They were followed by the missionary explorer, David Livingstone.

④ Carsaig Arches

The Carsaig Arches on the southern coast of Mull, form a fitting climax to one of the most spectacular coastal walks in Britain. Created as a result of long-distant volcanic activity, the cliffs are a form of living geology with the two arches demonstrating the eroding power of the sea. One is a huge tunnel, the floor of which is covered in boulders that are ground ever smoother as the ocean rolls over them. The other is a tower some 35 metres (114 feet) high which is pierced by a keyhole-shaped arch. The walking on this coast is not easy but worthwhile: colonies of kittiwakes and fulmars nest here in the spring and the cliffs are home to eagles and goats.

⑤ Fionnphort

Situated on the southwest peninsula of Mull, known as the Ross of Mull, the village of Fionnphort is a busy ferry port serving Iona and the island of Staffa. Tourism plays an important part in the local economy together with fishing and agriculture. The distinctive pink and red granite quarried there has been exported worldwide.

Eriskay

The island of Eriskay is located at the southern tip of South Uist, named after the Norse 'Eirisgeidh' meaning Eric's Isle. In Gaelic it is also referred to as Eilean na h-Oige, or Isle of Youth. It is hoped that the addition of a causeway linking the island directly with the nearest mainland will prevent a further decline in population on the island which, by the time of the census in 2001, had fallen to fewer than 180.

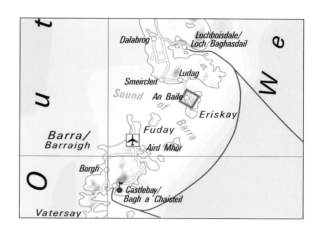

1 Prince Charlie's Bay

On 23 July 1745, Charles Edward Stuart, better known as Bonnie Prince Charlie, landed on Eriskay in a small boat from the French ship *Du Teillay*. Now named Coilleag a Phrionnsa, which translates roughly as 'the prince's cockleshell strand', the white sand beach on which he landed features a white-striped pink sea bindweed not found anywhere else in the Hebridean islands. It is believed that that the seeds for this plant fell from the Prince's handkerchief (gathered during his exile in France). From Eriskay he moved to the mainland and then south to England. His campaign ended with the bloody Battle of Culloden in 1746.

The new causeway has improved island life

2 Am Politician ▷

Eriskay's only public house, the Am Politician, is named after the SS Politician that struck rocks off the north east of the island in February 1941. En route to New York, the cargo contained 264,000 bottles of Scotch whisky. After the crew was saved, it is believed that over 2,000 cases were salvaged from the wreck before the authorities arrived. Compton Mackenzie's best-selling novel *Whisky Galore* was based on this story, as was the subsequent film in 1949. Local rumours suggest that bottles can still be found, washed up on the shore or discovered in long-forgotten hiding places.

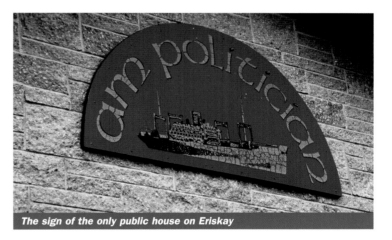

The sign of the only public house on Eriskay

Ann Baile, a tiny settlement near Haunn

3 The Causeway

At the time of its construction, between 2000 and 2001, the causeway linking Eriskay to South Uist was the largest civil engineering project in the United Kingdom. The geology of the local area helped to provide materials for the foundation and protective layering of the roadway – gneiss from the quarries of South Uist and Eriskay itself. The new road ended the isolation of the island community, and is the latest in a series of causeways built between the other Western islands linking all the way to Northern Uist 135 miles away.

Skye and the Cuillins

Skye is the largest island in the Inner Hebrides with an area of 1,740 square kilometres (672 square miles). The coastline is deeply indented by many sea lochs and the central part of the island contains the Cuillin Hills which provide some of the best and most dangerous climbing in the United Kingdom. The economy of the island is based on crofting, tourism, livestock and craft industries. The island briefly gave refuge to Bonnie Prince Charlie after the Battle of Culloden in 1746.

❶ The Skye Bridge

Until 1995, Skye was dependent on ferry services for contact with the mainland. The construction of a privately funded toll linked Kyleakin on Skye – formerly the main ferry port – with the Kyle of Lochalsh.

❷ Portree

Portree is the capital of Skye, a harbour and an ideal centre for touring the island. The town hosts the annual Skye Agricultural Show and the Highland Games. The town's name derives from the Gaelic Port-an-Righ or 'King's Port' following a visit by James V of Scotland in 1540.

The beautiful Cuillin Hills dominate southern Skye

❸ The Cuillin Hills △

These are considered to be the most dramatic mountains in Britain, comprising the eastern Red Cuillin formed of red granite, and the main ridge, the Black Cuillin, formed of a dark, coarse rock known as gabbro. Sgurr Alasdair is the highest peak at 993 metres (3,257 feet).

Stornoway

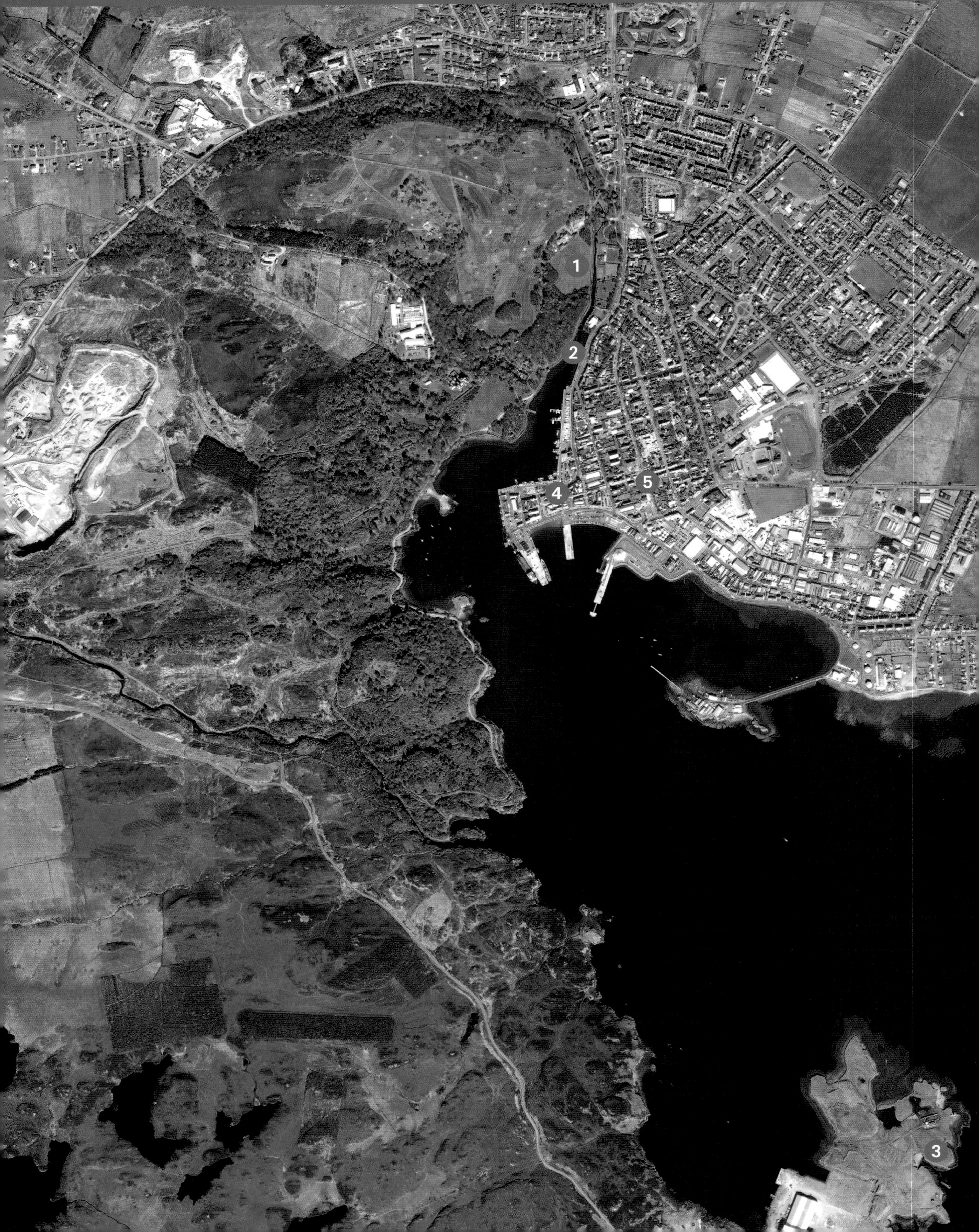

Stornoway, Outer Hebrides

With a population of some 7,000, Stornoway is the largest town on Lewis, and the unofficial capital of the Outer Hebrides. Renowned as a bastion of Gaelic culture and Free Kirk tradition, it is also a fishing port, the centre of world-famous Harris tweed production and the commercial and services hub for the region, as well as the base from which visitors can explore the distinctive peat moorland landscape of Lewis and Harris.

Lews Castle overlooks the harbour

① Lews Castle

In 1844, Sir James Matheson, laird of Lewis, began constructing a mock-medieval castle as his residence, incorporating Seaforth Lodge, the home of previous lairds, on a site west of the town. The grounds were extensively landscaped, with conservatories growing tropical plants. The castle was sold along with the island to Lord Leverhulme in 1918, and castle and grounds were deeded to the people of Stornoway. It became the home of Lews Castle College until the 1990s. Possible future plans include a museum and hotel.

③ Arnish Point Lighthouse

Arnish Point marks the western side of the entrance to Stornoway Harbour, and its rocks, projecting into the harbour entrance, have been a danger to shipping for centuries. This was rectified in 1852 when an innovative hollow iron lighthouse, built by Alan Stevenson, began service on the point. The tower was automated in 1963.

② Lewis Loom Centre

The Lewis Loom Centre, located near the centre of town on Bayhead, displays the techniques of weaving that have made Harris tweed famous around the world. There are hands-on examples of raw materials and yarns, and the looms are demonstrated by the expert proprietor. The building itself has a long history and was built as a weaver's workshop in 1799.

④ Stornoway Town Hall

Stornoway Town Hall stands in Cromwell Street on the town's waterfront, its clock tower a familiar sight to incoming ferry passengers. The first town hall was completed in 1905 and incorporated a library endowed by Andrew Carnegie, but was destroyed by fire in 1918. Its replacement opened in 1929. This building, in a turreted, baronial style, also housed a library, until 1979.

⑤ Museum nan Eilean

The Museum nan Eilean was founded in 1983, the first museum in the Western Isles. In 1995, it moved from the Town Hall to a former secondary school in Francis Street, that was specially redesigned. It holds documents, and objects relating to the history of Lewis and the Western Isles.

Overleaf: the towering columnar basalt cliffs of Staffa

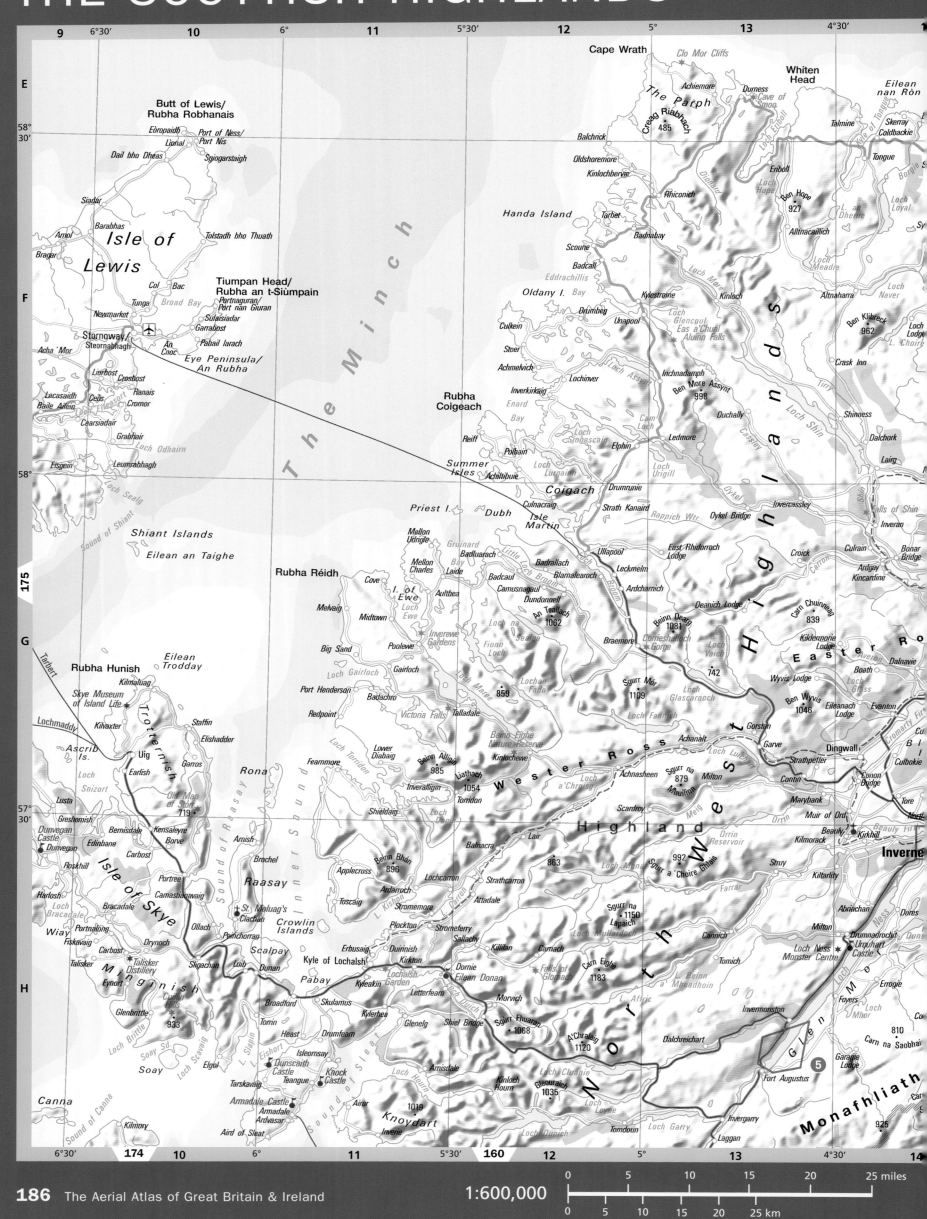

1:600,000

① Aberdeen
② The Cairngorms
③ Inverness
④ Findhorn
⑤ Loch Ness

1:600,000

North Sea

Moray Firth

Strath of Kildonan

Strathspey

Cairngorms

Grampian Mountains

National Park

Braemar

Moray

Aberdeenshire

Buchan

Aberdeen
1 Aberdeen City

Aberdeen

Aberdeen is the capital of the Grampian Highlands, and is often known as the Granite City because of its many striking stone buildings. With enduring close connections to the sea, it was once the point of departure for clipper ships trading in Chinese tea. Now, as a result of the discovery of North Sea oil in the twentieth century, it is a prosperous and growing city, the third largest in Scotland. The city has won the 'Britain in Bloom' award on many occasions.

1 Aberdeen Maritime Museum

This award-winning museum is situated on the Shiprow, near the Aberdeen City docks. It is housed in a purpose-built structure, completed in 1997, which incorporates the sixteenth century Provost Ross's House. The house was the museum's original home.

Considered by many to be one of the finest visitor attractions in Scotland, the museum offers a wonderful view of busy Aberdeen harbour, and provides a detailed history of sailing and shipbuilding in the city, as well as a unique exhibit on the offshore North Sea Oil industry. With many multimedia and interactive exhibits, the museum's high point – literally – is the model of the Murchison oil production platform, which stands 8.5m (28ft) high. The collections also feature exhibits on land transport as well as the maritime attractions.

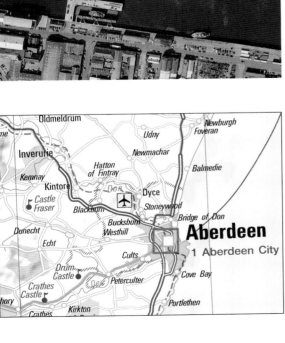

The seventeenth century tolbooth was built as a prison

② The Tolbooth △

The Tolbooth was built in the 1620s as a jail for criminals awaiting punishment or trial. Stone-built, with a clock tower and steeple, its small cells are connected by narrow winding staircases. Apparently, seventeenth century jailers were somewhat lax in their duties: there are several stories of prisoners simply walking out of the Tolbooth. Today it is a museum of civic history, but also includes exhibits of medieval instruments of torture.

④ Provost Skene's House

Originally built in 1545, the house was bought in 1669 by George Skene, a wealthy landowner who was provost from 1676 to 1685 and who virtually rebuilt it in contemporary style. One of the few remaining example of seventeenth century domestic architecture, it stood on Guestrow, a street dating from the 1450s, now no longer in existence. Over the years the area became a less desirable part of the city, and Provost Skene's House fell into decay. Fortunately it was saved from demolition and is now open as a museum of local history. Most notable in the house are the remarkable ceiling paintings, and a series of ten tempera panels of the Life of Christ, which were discovered in 1951 when the council began restoration of the building.

⑤ Marischal College and Museum

Marischal College was founded in 1593 by the fourth Earl Marischal of Scotland on the site of a Franciscan priory disestablished during the Reformation in 1560. The existing college building, an ornate mid-nineteenth century 'Tudor Gothic' edifice with a central tower, is the second largest granite building in the world. Once the city-centre site of the University of Aberdeen, most of the building was empty for some time but now houses offices, though it is still used for the university's ceremonial events. The Marischal Museum was founded in 1786, largely through donations of materials by former graduates and benefactors. It has significant collections of both Egyptian and Classical antiquities, non-Western artefacts and major exhibits on Scottish prehistory. The art collection is mostly of Scottish paintings from the seventeenth century onwards.

③ Cathedral Church of St Andrew

Situated in the centre of the city, St Andrew's has been a cathedral since 1814 and, as the Episcopal Church in the Diocese of Aberdeen and Orkney, serves the whole of north-east Scotland. The eighteenth-century Gothic sandstone building was designed by Archibald Simpson, and an extension was built in the 1930s, though not completed until after the Second World War. It was later described by John Betjeman as 'Aberdeen's best modern building'. In 1784, Dr Samuel Seabury, of Connecticut, was consecrated Bishop for America by Bishop Kilgour of Aberdeen, extending the church's reach to the New World for the first time.

Aberdeen harbour's main activity is supporting the offshore oil industry

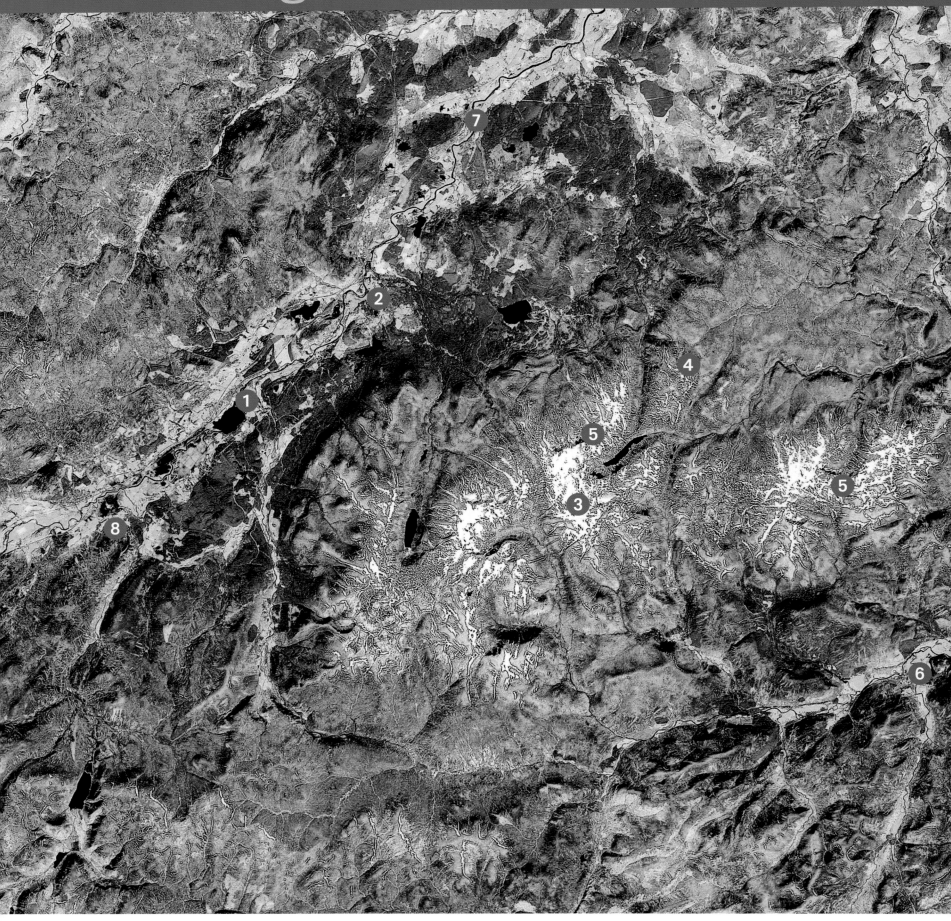

The Cairngorms

The Cairngorms are among the most rugged environments in the British Isles. Feared and rarely penetrated for centuries, their mixture of sublime mountain beauty and inhospitable remoteness have in recent decades made them a major attraction for climbers, walkers, and naturalists. In 2003 their unique value was recognized when the range was made one of Scotland's first two national parks. With a high winter snowfall and four of the five highest peaks in Britain, the area is a magnet for climbers and skiers. The landscape of the mountains is amongst the most spectacular in Europe and is home to a range of wildlife including golden eagles, ptarmigans and wildcats.

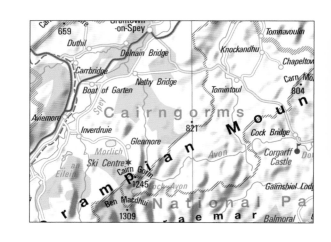

Skiing has been popular on Cairn Gorm since the 1960s

① Transport and Tourist Infrastructure △

The River Spey runs along the Cairngorms' northern flank, and in its valley are the road and rail links that form the major transport access routes to the mountains. Aviemore, some 16 km (10 miles) northwest of the summit of Cairn Gorm, is the main base from which walkers and climbers, and in the winter skiers and snowboarders, set out to enjoy the mountains. Since the early 1960s skiing has been developed on Cairn Gorm. The resort as a whole includes 17 lifts, which service 30 ski runs of widely varying difficulty. In 2001 a new funicular railway, with picture windows, was built to take passengers year-round to the Ptarmigan Restaurant, which has a northward-facing viewpoint at a height of 1,125m (3,700ft), about 120m (400ft) below Cairn Gorm's summit. Many protested at the impact of the railway's construction but supporters hope that, by preventing railway and restaurant users from climbing on the mountain itself, the overall human impact on fragile plant and animal species will be reduced.

② Aviemore

Aviemore, together with Carrbridge and Grantown-on-Spey, is one of the main ski resorts, lying in the foothills of the Cairngorms. Its transformation from a village into a winter sports centre took place in the 1960s with the construction of a large holiday complex. As well as catering for skiers, Aviemore also provides a good base for walkers.

③ Ben MacDhui

Ben MacDhui, at 1,309m (4,296ft), is second in height in Britain only to Ben Nevis. Legends abound of eerie presences sensed by climbers who make the ascent to the summit, including one account, in 1925, of a professor from London University who ran down the mountain to escape the footsteps that he felt were pursuing him.

⑤ Mountain range

The Cairngorm range forms the northern arm of the chevron-shaped massif of the Grampian Mountains, separated from the southern arm by the River Dee. The Cairngorms encompass the highest summits in the Grampians, including four of the five highest mountains in the Britain (only the highest, Ben Nevis, is not here). The range is named after one of its mountains, Cairn Gorm (1,245 metres (4,084 feet), which means 'blue mountain', though the highest summit of the group is Ben MacDhui (1,309 metres (4,296 feet).

The millions of years during which the Cairngorms were covered with glacial ice sheets have worn down its mountains to a high plateau punctuated by a series of domed summits. This plateau, because of its height and latitude, forms the only arctic ecosystem in Britain, with patches of year-round snow and unusual, distinctive plant species that are more commonly found in Siberia.

⑥ Braemar

Braemar Castle was built by the second Earl of Mar in 1628. After the Jacobite Rising of 1715, it was garrisoned by English troops in order to control the Highlanders and rebuilt some 30 years later. In the nineteenth century, Queen Victoria brought a different atmosphere to the area by popularising Braemar as a holiday resort; the Royal Highland Games - which include sports such as tossing the caber and putting the shot, as well as dancing and bagpipe playing - are held in the town every year.

⑦ Grantown-on-Spey

Situated on the River Spey, Grantown is the creation of an eighteenth-century landowner, Sir James Grant, who planned and built the town as a centre for the linen industry.

④ Geology and wildlife

The rock of the highest part of the Cairngorms, including most of the high plateau over 900 metres (3,000 ft), is mostly granite, polished smooth by the friction and pressure of ice. The granite includes a type of reddish-brown quartz native to the area, known as Cairngorm quartz. At lower elevations, metamorphic rocks such as schists are found. These are more easily eroded, so tend to form more craggy features and steeper-sided valleys, giving rise to the deep north-south clefts that cut the Cairngorm range on both flanks. Typical plant species of the high tundra landscape include moss campion, starry saxifrage, and least willow. Birds to be found here include golden eagles, osprey, and the Scottish crossbill, while the rivers contain rare freshwater mussels and lampreys as well as the trout and salmon for which the Dee and Spey are famous.

⑧ Ruthven Barracks

The stark walls of the ruins of Ruthven Barracks on the road south of Kingussie bear grim testimony to the unrest in the Highlands during the eighteenth century. The uprising in 1715 by the Jacobites - an attempt to restore the Stuarts to the throne - brought a strong military response from the English. Ruthven was built between 1716 and 1718 to accommodate English troops stationed there to subdue the Scots, and enlarged in 1734 by General Wade, the architect of the military roads that crisscross Scotland. After defeat at the battle of Culloden in 1746, which effectively brought the challenge of the Jacobites to an end, the Highlanders assembled at Ruthven to wait for their leader, Prince Charles. When he failed to arrive, but sent a message of farewell instead, his supporters blew up the barracks to stop them falling into English hands.

Inverness

Known as the Capital of the Highlands, the ancient town of Inverness (which means 'mouth of the Ness') was granted city status by the Queen in 2000 as part of the millennium celebrations. Its position near the sea at one end of the Great Glen has long made it a focal point for road, canal, and rail networks, as well as the administrative centre for the Highlands, while its fine buildings and attractive riverside continue to draw visitors from far and wide.

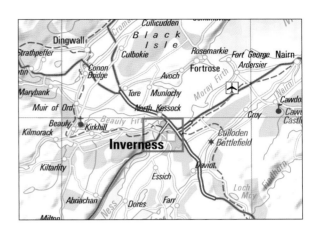

The Victorian churches on the riverbank

1 Inverness Castle

The site of the current castle, on a commanding site beside the east bank of the River Ness, has been fortified for centuries. A succession of medieval wooden forts were sacked in the 14th and 15th centuries before the castle was rebuilt in stone in 1548. After withstanding a siege in the Civil War and being enlarged and strengthened in the 1720s, this castle was finally blown up by retreating Jacobite forces in 1746.

The red sandstone castle seen today dates from 1835 and was designed by William Burn. Despite its fortified appearance, it was built for administration, serving as Inverness-shire's county hall and court house, a function it still serves today for the Highland unitary authority. Next to it is the North Block, completed in 1848 in a similar style, which was originally the town prison but now houses court rooms.

2 Caledonian Canal ▽

Inverness is where the Caledonian Canal emerges into the sea at the Beauly Firth. Plans for a canal along the Great Glen between Inverness and Fort William had first been drawn up by James Watt in the 1770s, but it was finally constructed by the great engineer Thomas Telford between 1803 and 1822, then further deepened in the 1840s to its current depth of 5.5 m (18 ft). The best place to see it in Inverness is at the Muirtown basin, where boats can moor or turn around before entering or leaving the canal. Just south of it, the Muirtown locks is a series of four locks that raise the canal water some 10 m (33 ft) to the level of Loch Ness. The canal passes through western Inverness (walkers can follow along the towpath, part of the 118 km / 73 mi Great Glen Way footpath), and just south of the city it merges with the River Ness, 2.5 km (1.5 mi) from where the river meets Loch Ness.

3 The Town House

Like the Cathedral and Castle, the Town House is a Victorian creation, completed in 1882. It was designed by Inverness architect William Laurie in a style that, like other Scottish town halls of the period, mixed red-brick municipal construction with gothic detailing, stained glass windows, and baronial turrets along the roofline. Inside, it is notable for its grand dividing staircase leading up to the formal Council Chamber, with its horseshoe-shaped table, and Committee Room. The Council Chamber is notable as the site of the only British government cabinet meeting ever held outside Westminster, Lloyd George held an emergency session there in 1921.

4 St Andrew's Cathedral

On the west bank of the river, opposite the castle, stands St Andrew's Cathedral. Like the castle, it is medieval in appearance but was built during the 19th century renaissance of the city. The Episcopalian (Anglican) cathedral—the first new cathedral to be built in Britain since the Reformation—was the brainchild of Robert Eden, who became Bishop of Moray and Ross in 1851. He first proposed a new cathedral for Inverness in 1853, construction began in 1866, and was completed in 1869. After a bout of fund-raising finally paid off the building costs, the cathedral was finally consecrated in 1874. It was designed by a member of the congregation, Alexander Ross, who had envisaged a rather larger building.

5 Kessock Bridge

East of Inverness, the Kessock Bridge carries the A9 from Perth over the strait separating the Beauly and Moray firths. Replacing an earlier ferry, the cable-stayed bridge, with a main span of 240 m (787 ft), was begun in 1976 and completed in 1982, and is credited with helping revitalize the northern Highlands, to which it is a gateway. Its design, by the German engineer Hellmut Homberg, is based on that of a bridge across the Rhine at Düsseldorf.

The castle at Inverness controls access to the sea

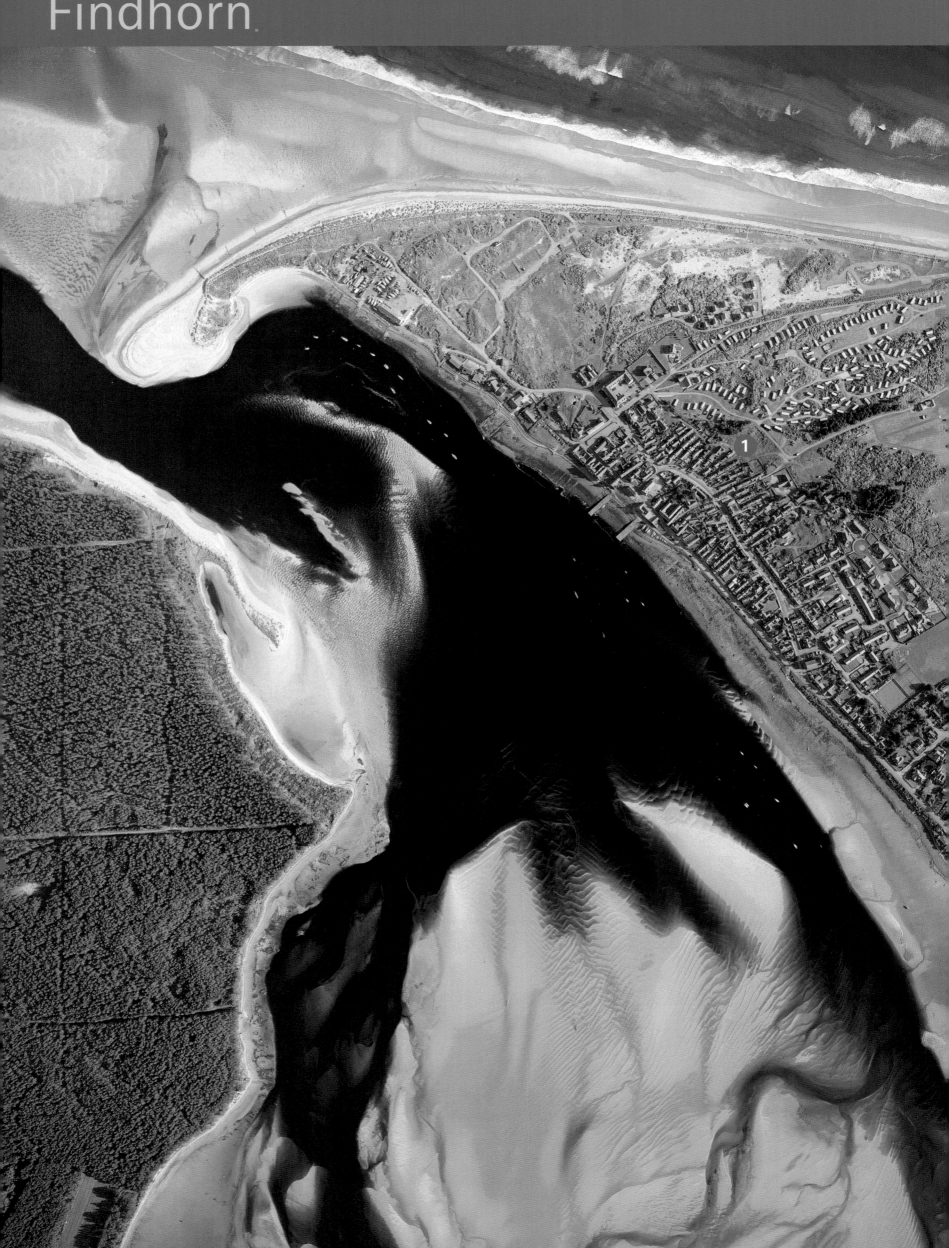

Findhorn

The village of Findhorn lies between the north-facing seacoast and the sheltered inlet of Findhorn Bay, where mudflats and dunes provide a haven for wildfowl and wading birds. Once a fishing port and shipbuilding base, Findhorn is today a renowned centre for sailing and watersports and since the 1960s has been home to a spiritual community that runs globally renowned courses in music, the visual arts and spiritual living. At the south end of Findhorn Bay, just outside the village of Kinloss, an RAF air base has been operational since 1938.

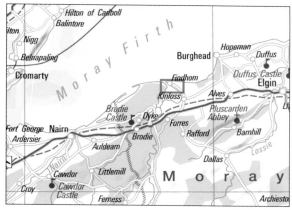

1 Findhorn Heritage Centre

At the northern edge of Findhorn village, the Heritage Centre occupies two huts formerly used by salmon fishers. The first building recreates the conditions of a salmon fishery, while the second contains an exhibition of local history. There has been a settlement at Findhorn since at least 1189. Today's village is the third to have been built here: one was buried in sand dunes by seventeenth-century storms, while a second was destroyed by floods in 1701. The thriving port once had trading links with Scandinavian and Baltic settlements.

2 Findhorn Foundation and Ecovillage ▽

The Findhorn Foundation charity, established in 1972, grew from the seeds of the Findhorn spiritual community that began in the village in 1962. In addition to offering many courses, the Foundation is today the hub of some 30 ecologically sustainable local businesses. The community, which lies just to the south of Findhorn village, offers guided tours in the summer months. Community founders Eileen and Peter Caddy and Dorothy Maclean came to the area in 1957 to manage the Cluny Hill Hotel in the ancient royal town of Forres, 6.5km (4 miles) inland from Findhorn. In business they tried to follow divine guidance that Eileen received in the form of an inner voice. The hotel was a success but the trio lost their jobs in 1962 and moved to a caravan site in Findhorn. Here in the dry, sandy coastal land they established a remarkable garden, in their planting and growing again seeking to follow divine guidance. Their astonishing results – including cabbages weighing 18kg (40lb) – attracted likeminded individuals and a spiritual community was born. Permanent buildings were constructed and the community began educational work. The Findhorn community expanded. In 1975 it bought the Cluny Hill Hotel as an educational centre and in 1982 purchased the Findhorn Bay Caravan Park. Findhorn won an international reputation, in part through the publication of Eileen Caddy's guidance in the books *God Spoke to Me* and *Opening Doors Within*. In the late 1980s the community built an 'ecovillage' designed to be an ecologically, economically and spiritually sustainable living place. The Findhorn Foundation is recognized as a United Nations non-governmental organization, and its representatives have taken part in United Nations summits.

Houses at the ecovillage

3 Seashore habitats

The Findhorn Bay area is a nature reserve. At low tide large parts of the bay, which extends to just over 3km (2 miles) in width at its widest point, are exposed mudflats. Ornithologists flock here to observe wildfowl and wading birds, and in winter to view visiting geese and duck. Botanists also visit to examine a wide range of lichens and fungi. To the north of the village, the North Shore extends for 11km (7 miles) of sand and dunes alongside Burghead Bay to the village of Burghead on a short headland. Grey and common seals live in the area and can be seen basking on the North Shore. In the Moray Firth, bottlenose dolphins. Orca, sperm and pilot whales and porpoises can be seen.

Overleaf: Loch Ness featuring Fort Augustus' Benedictine Abbey

Atlantic

Ocean

Mull Head

Noup Head
Noltland Castle
Pierowall
Westray
Midbea

Papa Westray
Hollandstoun
North Ronaldsay

The North Sound

North Ronaldsay Firth

Scar
Northwall

Rapness
Broughtown ②
Overbister
Start Point

Carrick Ho.
Kettletoft
Sanday

Fara
Eday
Backaland
Quoyness Cairn
Braeswick

Rousay
Washbister
Sanday Sound

Brough
Head
The Barony
Brinian
Skaill
St. Magnus
Egilsay
Cubbie Roo's ①
Wyre
Whitehall
Aith
Stronsay

Redland
Gairsay
Rothies-holm

Twatt
Tingwall
Gorseness
Edmonstone
Firth
Lamb
Head

Aith
Doomby
Loch of Harray
Balfour
Shapinsay

Skara Brae
Newlot
Orkney Islands

Yesnaby
Wide Firth
Auskerry
Orkney Islands

Ring of Brogar
Maes
Howe
Finstown
Shapinsay
Sd.

Stromness
268
Kirkwall
Mull Head

Graemsay
Swanbister
Skaill
Gritley

Ward Hill
481·
Quoyness
Houton
St. Mary's
Italian Chapel
Copinsay

Old Man of Hoy
Rackwick
Cava
Scapa Flow

Rora Head
Fara
Flotta
Hunda
Burray

Hoy
Hoxa
St. Margaret's Hope

Lyness
Little Ayre
Bow
Herston

Longhope
South
Ronaldsay

Hurliness
South Walls

Swona
Burwick

Pentland Firth

Island
of Stroma

Dunnet
Head
Mey Castle
Duncansby Head

Scarskerry
Gills

Brough
Mey
Huna
John o'Groats

Totegan
Dunnet Bay
Dunnet
Freswick

Strathy Point
Scrabster
St. Mary's
(ruin)
Nybster
Keiss

Armadale
Dounreay
Forss
Thurso
Castletown
Sortat

Strathy
Portskerra
Westfield
Roadside
Kirk
Sinclair's
Bay
Noss Head

Skerray
Melvich
Reay
Shebster
Halkirk
Reiss
Sinclair Castle

Kirtomy
Bettyhill
Calder Mains
Watten
Ackergill
Staxigoe

Skelpick
Dalhavaig
Olgrinmore
Mybster
Wick

Syre
Westerdale
212
Thrumster

Forsinard
Altnabreac
Station
Sarclet

Loch
Rimsdale
Dalnawillan
Lodge
Achavanich
Ulbster

L. nan
Clar
L. an
Roathair
Houstry
Lybster

Kinbrace
Glutt Lodge
Latheron

Loch Choire
Lodge
Braemore
Dunbeath

Creag Mhòr
713
Morven
705

Kildonan Lodge
Berriedale

Balnacoil
Strath of Kildonan
Helmsdale

Muie
Dalreavoch
Lothmore

Rogart
Loch
Brora
Brora

Spinning-dale
Pittentrail
Golspie
Dunrobin Castle

Embo
Littleferry
Loch
Fleet

Proncy
Dornoch

Edderton
Glenmorangie Dist
Tarbat Ness
Wilkhaven

Tain
Inver
Portmahomack

Dornoch Firth

North Sea

Aberdeen

Lerwick

Mainland

Hoy

Westray Firth
Eynhallow Sd.
Stronsay Firth
Deer Sound
Wick W.
Helmsdale R.
Thurso R.
Berriedale W.
Dunbeath W.

186

D   D
E   E
F   F
G   G

59°
58°30′
58°

1:600,000

0   5   10   15   20   25 miles
0   5   10   15   25 km

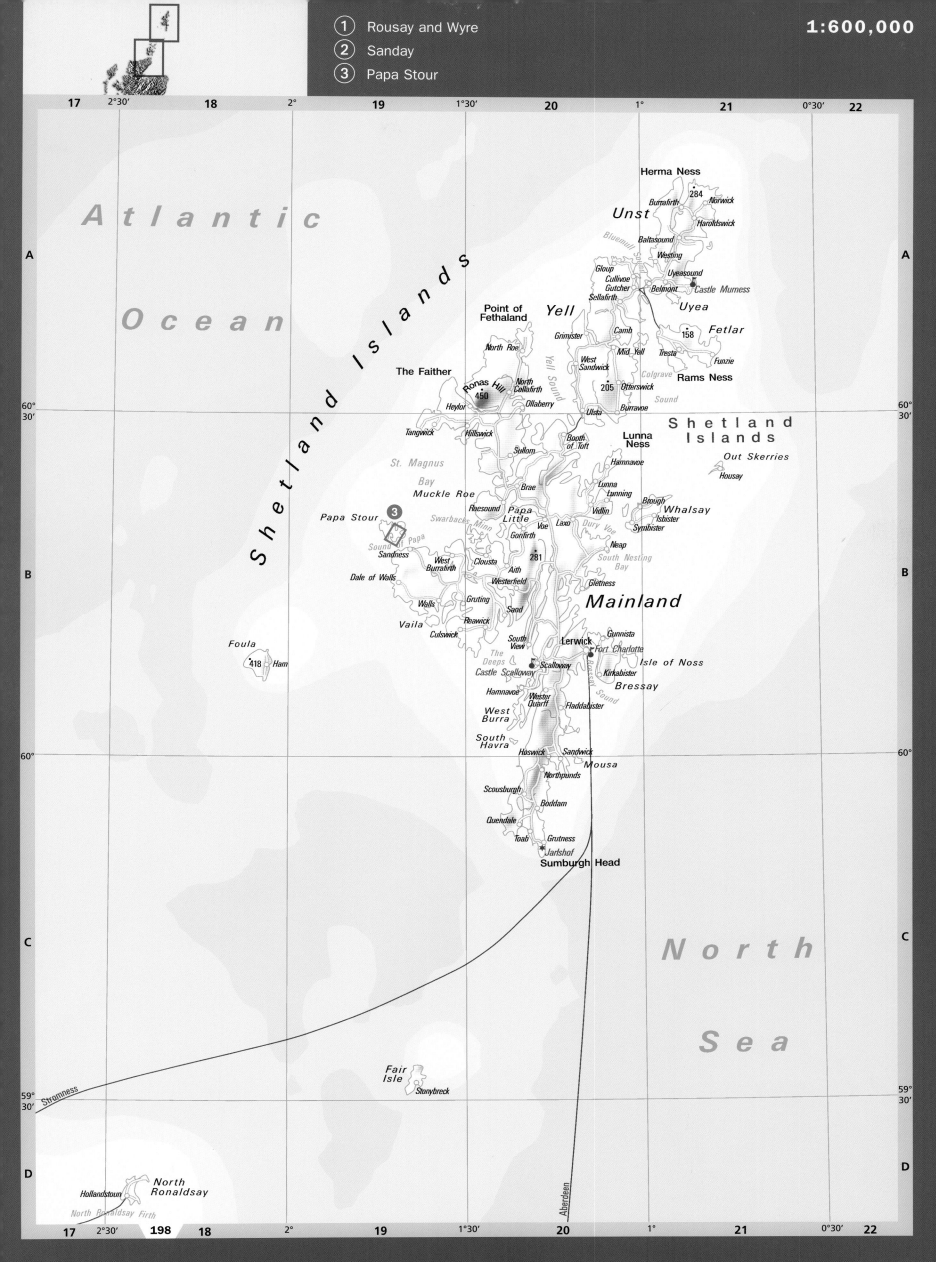

Atlantic

Ocean

Shetland Islands

North

Sea

Herma Ness
284
Burrafirth   Norwick
Unst   Haroldswick
Bluemull   Baltasound
Westing
Gloup   Uyeasound
Cullivoe   Belmont   Castle Murness
Gutcher   Uyea
Sellafirth   Fetlar
Point of   Yell   Camb   158
Fethaland   Grimister   Mid Yell   Tresta
North Roe   West   Otterswick   Funzie
Sandwick   Rams Ness
The Faither   North   205   Burravoe
Ronas Hill   Collafirth   Ulsta   Shetland
450   Ollaberry   Islands
Heylor   Booth   Lunna   Out Skerries
Tangwick   Hillswick   of Toft   Ness   Housay
Sullom   Hamnavoe
St. Magnus   Brae   Lunna
Bay   Lunning
Muckle Roe   Brough   Whalsay
Raesound   Papa   Vidlin   Isbister
Papa Stour   ③   Little   Voe   Symbister
Swarbacks   Gonfirth   Laxo
Minn   281   Neap
Sound   Papa   Aith   South Nesting
Sandness   West   Clousta   Bay
Dale of Walls   Burrafirth   Westerfield   Gletness
Walls   Gruting   Sand   Mainland
Vaila   Reawick   Gunnista
Culswick   South   Lerwick   Fort Charlotte
View   Castle Scalloway   Isle of Noss
The   Scalloway   Kirkabister
Foula   Deeps   Bressay
418   Ham   Hamnavoe   Wester
West   Quarff   Fladdabister
Burra   Hoswick   Sandwick
South   Mousa
Havra   Northpunds
Scousburgh   Boddam
Quendale
Toab   Grutness
Jarlshof
Sumburgh Head

Stromness

Fair
Isle
Stonybreck

Aberdeen

Hollandstoun   North
Ronaldsay
North Ronaldsay Firth

Rousay and Wyre

The islands of Rousay and Wyre, with Egilsay reveal the unique heritage of the Orkney Islands. Together they showcase the best preserved archaeological sites in the Orkney Islands, which has led to the area being dubbed the 'Egypt of the North'. Situated a short distance from the north-east coast of the Orkney Mainland, Rousay is both the largest, at five miles in diameter, and most hilly of the islands. Rousay has been designated a Site of Special Scientific Interest for its flora, birdlife and natural features and archaeology. Connected by ferry, the islands have experienced a rapid depopulation from about 1,000 people in 1831 to fewer than 300 in 2001.

③ The Bu

The island of Wyre (from the Old Norse 'Vigr' meaning spearhead), only 3.5km (2 miles) in length, features in the Viking sagas as the domain of Kolbein Hruga, a notable landowner and Viking chieftain from Norway. It is thought that the farm of The Bu stands on the site of Hruga's original farmhouse. The Bu also has more recent fame as a childhood home of the Scottish poet Edwin Muir (1887-1959). Muir is remembered by the island through an exhibition at the nearby heritage centre.

① Trumland, Rousay

Trumland is the main settlement on Rousay with the nearby Trumland House forming most of the island's recent history. General Sir Frederick William Traill-Burroughs or 'The Little General' became known as Orkney's worst landlord after he increased rents and evicted more than 200 people from Rousay. His actions contributed to the passing of the 1886 Crofters Act in parliament that subsequently protected smallholders from eviction and arbitrary rent increases. Later, in the 1930s, Trumland became home to Walter Grant, whose fortune helped bring archaeologists to the island and excavate all the sites that are currently in the care of Historic Scotland. The Trumland visitors centre, near the pier, has a restaurant and provides tourist information.

② MV Eynhallow

The ferry that connects Rousay and Wyre to the rest of the Orkney Islands and the mainland is named after the uninhabited island that lies to the north of Rousay. Built in Bristol in 1987, it carries up to 95 passengers and nine cars. The MV Eynhallow begins and ends its day at Wyre. Catching the ferry early in the morning allows the visitor to see Rousay, Wyre and Egilsay in a single day.

④ Wyre Heritage Centre

Originally built as a school and then converted into a community hall, the heritage centre at Wyre contains several collections, notably a history of island life and of the poet Edwin Muir. There is also detailed information on the excavation of nearby Cubbie Roo's Castle and its Norse links.

The remains of Cubbie Roo's Castle

⑤ Cubbie Roo's Castle ◁

Cubbie Roo, a corruption of the name Kolbein Hruga, variously described as a Viking Chieftain, tax collector and giant played an influential role in the early development of Wyre. His castle, the oldest dated square keep in Scotland, was built around 1145 and is mentioned in the Orkneyinga Saga of Norse legend as 'a fine stone fort...a really solid stronghold'. Excavated in the 1930s, it is a well-preserved site, the tower of which has survived to a height of 15m (49ft) in places with walls approximately 1.7m (5.5ft) deep. A considerable height in its day, the archaeological site remains an impressive feature of the island. The castle is thought to have withstood at least one siege in 1231 when the assassins of Earl Haraldson took refuge there to avoid the wrath of their victim's allies. A successful castle, it has been described as a 'very unhandy place to attack'.

⑥ St Mary's Chapel

The well-preserved St Mary's Chapel, close to the castle, was founded either by Cubbie Roo himself or his son Bjarni Kolbeinsson, the Bishop of Orkney and a noted poet of the period. The chapel is accessible via the road and signposted from the castle.

⑦ Chambered Cairn

A common sight around the Orkney Islands, a Chambered Cairn is a Neolithic burial tomb.

Such sites have provided fascinating insights into Stone Age life through the remains of people and possessions found there. Other cairns discovered on Rousay and Wyre have multiple burial areas where whole groups of people would have been buried.

The MV Eynhallow at Rousay

5

4

1

Sanday

Lying 24km (15 miles) north-east of Kirkwall on the Mainland and offering the best farmland of all the Orkney Islands, Sanday is the largest of the North Isles Group. Literally meaning 'sand island', Sanday is thought to have been underwater at one stage, emerging to create the long coastline found today. Its white sandy beaches are a favourite with shell collectors and otter spotters alike. In 2001 the population of Sanday was 478, having shrunk from a reported 2,000 people in 1883.

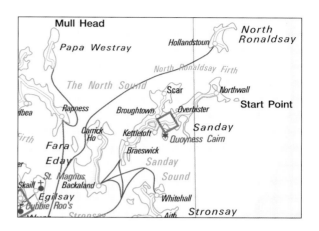

1 Lady

Sitting approximately in the centre of the island, the village of Lady is one of the main settlement areas on Sanday, aside from Kettletoft. With its central location, the parish of Lady is bounded on all sides by sea. In the east its coast is deeply indented by the nearby Otterswick and Stywick bays. The National Gazetteer of Great Britain and Ireland in 1868 described the area of Lady as 'one-fourth...pasture or under cultivation, and the rest is either heath or waste.' The parish of Lady comprises the north-eastern part of the island.

2 Wildlife

Sanday is famed for its wildlife. Common and grey seals, known as selkies are frequent visitors and can often be seen in Otterswick Bay during June. Otters, by contrast, are much more elusive. Birds such as the Arctic tern, Oystercatchers, Redshanks and Short-eared owls have all been spotted on the island.

A view of Sanday looking south across the low-lying island

3 Ladykirk ▽

Located off the main road to Kettletoft (outside the main image), Ladykirk is a ruined church of the village. A well-known feature of the building is the Devil's Clawmarks, a strange, unexplained set of grooves in a balustrade at the top of the church steps.

The Devil's Clawmarks

4 Agriculture and Industry

The good soils of Sanday, derived from flagstone of Old Red sandstone age, have served the island well agriculturally. Improvements in farmland occurred at the beginning of the nineteenth century as the kelp industry declined and landowners saw the need to provide an injection of capital into farming. A regular link with the Mainland in 1836 allowed further development with a 75 per cent increase in arable acreage between 1842 and 1860. Links with outside markets also allowed the number of cattle kept to increase to 22,830 head in 1871 with 13,586 sheep. Innovation on the island was generally the result of individual enterprise, mainly from small producers who were both crofters and poultrymen – the sale of eggs being a valuable asset to the Orkney economy.

Today, the main activities of Sanday include knitwear, the farming of beef cattle, lobster and crab fishing, and electronics (there is a factory on the island).

5 Myrtle Lane

In the nineteenth century, the crofters of Sanday suffered from the increasing value of their fertile land and the ever-present threat of eviction. Successive rises in rent made those who had improved their farms increasingly resentful of the lairds who made them pay more in rent and taxation. A case in point would be John Grieve who was given leave to settle on 18 acres of hill land at Myrtle Lane in 1847. He originally paid ten shillings a year for the uncultivated site, and saw this rise in three stages to seven pounds by 1889. During that time he had lost some of his hard-won land and, in its place, was given instead infertile fields. However, the people of Sanday were, in general, more fortunate than those in the Orkney island of Rousay who, twice in a lifetime, had to start from scratch, farming on a bare hillside.

Ladykirk is one of two ruined churches on the island

Papa Stour

On the western coast of Shetland at the southern tip of St Magnus Bay lies Papa Stour. The name derives from the Norse *papi* (priest) and *stòrr* which means large. The island was inhabited between the sixth and seventh centuries by a Celtic missionary community although there is evidence of prehistoric settlement. It was owned by Norway until the late fifteenth century when it was pledged to Scotland. In 1975 it was designated a Site of Special Scientific Interest for its wildlife and geology. Today the 32 islanders are mainly crofters supplementing their income through fishing and tourism.

① Brei Holm
One of the first of many impressive sights of Papa Stour is gained approaching the island by ferry. At Brei Holm a large tunnel has been eroded by the sea against the rocks. Here, the sea caves are accessible but only by small boat when conditions permit.

② Da Biggins
Archaeological excavations at the Da Biggins have unearthed the impressive foundations of a thirteenth-century Norse House. The remains of wooden floors suggest that this may have once been a significant building on the island and probably one of the oldest settlements in the area. Shetland's oldest document, a witness statement alleging slander, was signed here 1299 at King Haakan's Royal Farm. The farm may well have been a 'stofa' or log-timbered house imported from Norway. Archaeologists from St Andrews University have explored the area for clues.

③ Housa Voe
Ferry services to the island arrive at Housa Voe pier after a 45 minute journey from West Burrafirth on the west mainland most days of the week. The passenger-only ferry very rarely carries cars because there is only one short road on Papa Stour and walking is the best way to see the landscape.

Gardie House is near to the pier and was once used by the Earl of Balcarres in the nineteenth century to confine his son, the Hon. Edwin Lindsay. The young man, an officer in the Indian army, was punished for his refusal to fight in a duel and was subsequently imprisoned in the house for 26 years.

④ Maiden Stack
Maiden (or Frau) Stack is the tallest of the dramatic sea stacks on the approach to the island. Here, tradition says that a Norse lord imprisoned his only daughter in 1300 for refusing an arranged marriage. However, she was rescued from her confinement by a humble fisherman to whom she had given her heart and together they eloped to safety.

⑤ Ting
Above the beach at Housa Voe is a circle of 46 stones thought to be where the Vikings held a local assembly. Here, Lord Thorvald Thoresson, accused of corruption in the oldest document found on the island (1299), fought and won a duel. In this period the island was the property of King Haakon of Norway.

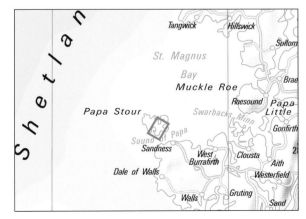

Papa Stour viewed from Sandness

⑧ Miniature Shetland ponies
Miniature Shetlands are mainly bred in a stud on the south-east of the island. They are exceptionally hardy, being able to weather the strong winds that sweep in from the Atlantic Ocean. Shetland ponies tend to graze on the East side of the island on grass and the kelp washed ashore at the nearby beaches. Such ponies have been used on the island for hundreds of years and are bred with a calm temperament.

A Robins Brae Mareel Shetland pony

⑥ The Church
The original church on the island is a listed building dating from the mid-nineteenth century. A new window added in 1918 features Jesus calming the storm and was paid for by public subscription in memory of the six men of Papa Stour who died in the First World War. Services are still held every Sunday in a nearby chapel but the old church is no longer used after being declared unsafe.

⑦ Wildlife
The wealth of marine life around Papa Stour has led to the waters being designated a Special Area of Conservation (SAC). The island is internationally recognized as an important area for terns that nest there in the summer breeding season. Puffins may also be found along the coast. Seals may be spotted in June and July and occasionally killer whales and porpoises can be seen swimming near the island.

⑨ SS Highcliffe
In February 1940 the 3,847 ton steamship *SS Highcliffe* sank off Forewick Holm to the south-east of Papa Stour. All 35 members of the crew were rescued safely by the local lifeboat. The wreck is one of the best-known scuba-diving attractions amongst the many sunken vessels in the area.

1:600,000

| 0 | 5 | 10 | 15 | 20 | 25 miles |

| 0 | 5 | 10 | 15 | 20 | 25 km |

8 7° 9 6°30' 10 6° **174** 11 5°30' 12

Malin Head

orman
Malin
Portaleen
Culdaff Bay
Culdaff
Ballyliffin
Gleneely
Carndonagh
Inishowen Head
Slieve Snaght
615 •327
Moville
Greencastle
Magilligan Point
Downhill
Portstewart

I n i s h o w e n

uncrana
Quigley's
Point
Burnfoot
Muff
Foyle
Lough

E End
wn
Londonderry ④
New
Buildings
ohnstown
gham
Eglinton
Ballykelly
Limavady
Glebe
•384
Macosquin

Coleraine

Portrush
Dunluce Castle
Bushmills
Portstewart

Benbane Head ⑤
Giant's Causeway
Rathlin Island
Church
Quarker
Rathlin Sound
Ballintoy
Ballycastle Bay
Ballycastle
Ballyvoy
Fair Head
Murlough Bay
Torr Head

Mull of
Kintyre
Beinn na Lice
•428
Feochaig
Machaioch
Southend
Carskiey
Sanda Island

M

North Channel

Derrykeighan
Dervock
Stranocum
The Drones
Armoy
Knocklayd
517
Antrim
Carnanmore
382
Cushendun

Claudy
Dungiven
Feeny
Park
464
•
Garvagh
Kilrea
Ballymoney
Agivey
Finvoy
Dunloy
Rasharkin
Clogh
Mills
Newtown-
Crommelin
Trostan
554
Antrim Mountains
Glens of Antrim
Glenariff
Cushendall
Red Bay

Dunnamanagh
Artigarvan
Ballynamallaght
Glenshane
Pass
683
•
Sperrin Mts
Swatragh
Upperlands
Maghera
Cullybackey
Portglenone
Ahoghill
Whitesides
Corner
Ballymena
Moorfields
Broughshane
Carnlough
Carnlough Bay
Glenarm
The Sheddings
Ballygalley
Carncastle
Kilwaughter
Glynn
Larne
Larne Lough
Mullaghboy
Island Magee
The Gobbins

vnstewart
Plumbridge
Glenelly
Gortin
542
Greencastle
Mountfield
Cranagh
Rousky
Draperstown
Desertmartin
Slieve Gallion
529
Magherafelt
Gulladuff
Bellaghy
Lough Beg
Toome
Randals-
town
Kells
Tildarg
Ballyclare
Doagh
Ballynure
Ballycarry
Whitehead
Copeland Island

N o r t h e r n
I r e l a n d
Omagh
Mountjoy
Creggan
Carrickmore
The Loup
Ballyronan
Moneymore
Coagh
Cookstown
Ballinderry
Newport
Trench
Lough
Neagh
Round Tower
Antrim
Temple-
patrick
Killead
Greenisland
Carrickfergus
Belfast Lough
Newtownabbey
Holywood
Bangor
Donaghadee
Millisle

Ulster
American
Folk Park
Omagh
Carrickmore
Pomeroy
T y r o n e
Sixmilecross
Stewartstown
Coalisland
Crumlin
Dundrod
Glenavy
BELFAST ①
Dundonald
Newtownards
Mt. Stewart Gard.
Greyabbey
Abbey
Carrowdore
Ballywalter

hogan
Beragh
Seskinore
Castlecaulfield
Dungannon
Lower
Aghalee
Upper
Ballinderry
Dunmurry
Lisburn ②
Carryduff
Comber
Ballygowan
Strangford Lough
Kircubbins
Greyabbey
Ballyhalbert

more
Fintona
Garvaghy
Ballygawley
Greystone
Moy
Lurgan
Moira
Lurgan
Craigavon
Hillsborough
The Temple
Saintfield
Gardens of
Rowallane
Killyleagh
Audley Castle
Cloghy
Portaferry

Clabby
Augher
Clogher
Aughnacloy
Carnteel
Benburb
Ardress
Blackwatertown
Portadown
Armagh
Richhill
Tandragee
Gilford
Banbridge
Ballynabragget
Dromore
Ballynahinch
Crossgar
Inch Abbey
Strangford
D o w n
Dromara
535
Drumaroad

Fivemiletown
383
•
Brookeborough
Tedavnet
Glaslough
Emyvale
Caledon
Navan Fort
Clare
Markethill
Scarva
Loughbrickland
Katesbridge
Moneyslane
Clough
Saul
Lecale
Pen.
Downpatrick
Kilclief
Ballyquintin
Point

uiresbridge
Eshnadarragh
Rosslea
Middletown
Cladymilltown
Keady
Mountnorris
A r m a g h
Ballyroney
Ballyward
Killough
Ardglass

Maghaveely
Newtownbutler
Smithborough
Clontibret
Monaghan/
Muineachán
Carnagh
Newtown-
hamilton
Camlough
Bessbrook
Hilltown
Mayobridge
Rathfriland
Castlewellan
Bryansford
Slieve Donard
Newcastle
Dundrum
Tyrella
St. John's Point
Dundrum Bay

naskea
Rossiea
Monaghan
Newbliss
Clones
Rockcorry
Ballybay
Carrickmacross
Newry ③
557
•
Forkill
*Mourne Mtns.*852
Annalong

C a v a n
Cavan
Stradone
New Inn
Bellanagh
Cross Keys
Ballyhaise
Cootehill
Castleblayney
Broomfield
Shantonagh
Crossmaglen
Cullaville
Omeath
Warrenpoint
Rostrevor
Lisnacree
Carlingford Lough
Kilkeel
Greencastle
Cranfield Point

Bailieborough
Shercock
Chanonrock
Carlingford
Boharboy
Irish Sea

Ballyjamesduff
254
•
Virginia
Lough Sheelin
Kingscourt
L. Sillan
Iniskeen
Dundalk/
Dun Dealgan
Blackrock
Dundalk Bay
Castlebellingham
Annagassan

Finnea
Ballymachugh
Lisduff
Oldcastle
Mullagh
Moynalty
Nobber
Drumcondra
Ardee
Dunleer
Togher
Grangebellew
Clogher Head
Clogherhead
Ballymakenny
Collon

8 7° **219** 9 6°30' 10 6° 11 5°30' 12

55°
N
54°30'
O
54°
P

Stranraer, Troon
Cairnryan, Fleetwood
Heysham
Liverpool

Belfast

Belfast has been the capital of Northern Ireland since the partitioning of the island in 1922. It is the province's largest city, with a population of about 300,000.

The Lagan is Belfast's most important river. It flows into Belfast Lough, where the docks, seen here, are located. Although Belfast was founded in 1603 by Scots and English settlers, it developed significantly only in the nineteenth century, when it grew because of industrialisation. There were iron foundries, engineering works and whiskey distilleries and, although the cotton industry declined, the linen industry expanded. As a result, most of Belfast's grander buildings date from no earlier than the mid-nineteenth and early twentieth centuries. The city is the home of Queen's University, and the University of Ulster also has a campus here. The city is served by two airports.

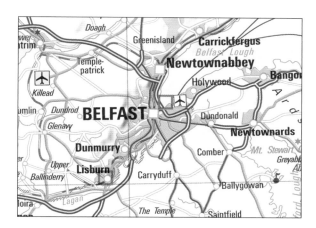

① Queen's Island

Queen's Island was formed when a channel was dug to bypass a bend in the Lagan River in the mid-1840s. It was first called Dargan Island, but was renamed in honour of Queen Victoria in 1849. The major occupant of the island has been the shipyard of Harland and Wolff which began in 1853 when Robert Hickson set up the first yard in Ireland to build iron ships. In 1854, Edward James Harland bought the yard, and in 1861 he took on Gustav Wilhelm Wolff as his partner.

One of the Titanic's propellers weighing 38 tons

② Harland & Wolff

The company built many great ships, including more than 70 for the White Star Line. Among these were the ill-fated *Titanic*, and her sister ships the *Britannic*, sunk in 1916 during the First World War, and *Olympic*, which continued in service from 1911 to 1935. The last cruise liner built by the company was *Canberra* in 1960. The company was nationalised for a period but is now back in private hands, though with a much-reduced workforce of 3,000. Today the yard's order books are filled mostly with ferries, oil tankers and floating drilling rigs. The company has also diversified into other areas such as offshore construction and bridge-building.

③ Bombardier-Shorts

Belfast is home to the aircraft plant of Bombardier-Shorts, a subsidiary of the Canadian company Bombardier. Shorts (also known as Short Brothers), said to be the oldest aircraft company in the world, had been wholly located in Belfast since 1948 and was acquired by Bombardier in 1989.

④ Samson and Goliath

Two enormous gantry cranes, 'Samson' and 'Goliath', tower over Harland and Wolff's yard and are visible from most parts of Belfast. Their span is 140 metres (459 feet) and they can lift 840 tonnes each – 1,600 tonnes in combination.

⑤ The docks △

The first record of a ship being built in Belfast dates from 1636. The vessel was constructed by a group of Presbyterian clergymen. Shipbuilding began in earnest, however, when William Ritchie, a Scot, founded a shipyard in July 1791. His first ship was the 300-tonne *Hibernia*. Soon, his brother Hugh had launched a second shipyard in partnership with Alexander McLaine. Their yard was the first in Ireland to build a steamboat – the *Belfast*. In December 1838 the third yard, Thompson and Kirwan, opened and, in 1851, they moved to the newly created Queen's Island.

The Odyssey Arena is a huge entertainment venue

⑥ Odyssey Arena ◁

Next to the Abercorn Basin is the Odyssey Arena, the largest indoor sports and entertainment venue in Ireland, which opened in December 2000. It can seat as many as 1,000 spectators and accommodate a huge variety of sporting events – boxing, running, basketball, tennis and motorcycling. It can be converted into an ice-rink. On the same site is W5, an interactive science and technology centre, with an IMAX giant-screen cinema, shops and restaurants.

⑦ Belfast City Airport

Belfast City Airport is in the heart of Belfast and right next to the docks. Flights go to destinations in Britain and the Isle of Man, and to Cork in the Republic of Ireland. Its runway is 1.83 kilometres (1.14 miles) long. Despite being subject to strict pollution controls, the airport handles two million passengers annually.

Lisburn

Lisburn has enjoyed the status of a city since 2002, when it was created such as part of the Golden Jubilee celebrations for the accession to the throne of Queen Elizabeth II. With a population of about 110,000, it lies south-west of Belfast on the River Lagan in County Antrim. Many important agencies of government are sited here, including the headquarters of the Belfast Region of the PSNI (Police Service of Northern Ireland), and the headquarters of the British Army in Northern Ireland at

Thiepval Barracks. After Louis Crommelin, a Huguenot (French Protestant), was appointed Overseer of the Royal Linen Manufacture in Ireland in 1698, the city became a centre of the Irish linen industry, and attracted a French community. Though flax had already been grown and spun in Ireland, the Huguenots possessed many secrets of the manufacture of linen which were unknown to the local people. This soon made Irish linen into a byword for quality with a worldwide reputation.

① Railway station

The first rail service from Lisburn was opened on 12th August 1839, when an 11-kilometre (7-mile) stretch of track between Lisburn and Belfast was inaugurated with 3,000 people travelling on that day alone. This was the first rail service in Northern Ireland (it had been preceded in the south by a service from Dublin to Kingstown in December 1834). The railway station that can be seen today in Lisburn dates from 1890. The railway network in today's Northern Ireland is much reduced from its heyday in the mid-twentieth century.

Lisburn's historic centre was damaged by fire in 1707

② Castle Gardens

The Castle Gardens form part of the city's Historic Quarter. The castle from which they take their name is Lisburn Castle, a manor house built by Sir Fulke Conway in 1622. It burned down in the great fire of 1707, and only the entrance gateway survives. Currently the gardens are being developed, and archaeological investigation is proceeding as they are cleared. The improvements in the park include the restoration of the war memorial, the seventeenth-century garden terraces and the Wallace Monument. This last is dedicated to Sir Richard Wallace, a benefactor of the town.

③ Historic Quarter △

The oldest part of Lisburn has been designated as the Historic Quarter. It contains many ancient buildings that survived the city's great fire of 1707, and others that were built shortly afterwards. It is now the subject of municipal regeneration and development plans. Among the features to be found in the Historic Quarter are the railway station and Market Square as well as the County Antrim Infirmary, founded in 1767 by Act of Parliament and supported by private subscription. There is also a building that was the city's French Church in the eighteenth century, used by the Huguenot families engaged in the linen trade. It later became the courthouse, and then, with the adjoining building, became the town hall, continuing to be used for civic purposes until 2001. The Lisburn Museum and the Irish Linen Centre share a building dating from the eighteenth and nineteenth centuries.

④ Lagan Valley Island

This island was formed when the Lagan Navigation (waterway) was constructed in the middle of the eighteenth century. A section of canal was built to cut off the bend in the river here. The island became known as Vitriol Island because it was used as a chemical works producing bleach for the linen industry. Later, a linen spinning-mill was built there and linen thread was produced on the island until 1983. The canal was subsequently filled in and has only been restored in recent times, so that Lagan Valley Island has once again become an island. The island is now home to a major complex of buildings that house the City Council offices, conference facilities and an arts centre. It is built on the site of a derelict linen mill and is surrounded by gardens. The arts centre has an extensive programme of classes and workshops. There is also a sculpture trail on the island.

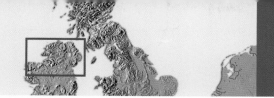

Newry

In March 2002, Newry was granted the status of a city in celebration of the Golden Jubilee of Queen Elizabeth II's reign. Lying partly in County Armagh and partly in County Down, this historic market town once stood at the head of the now disused Newry Canal. Newry retains its long-established reputation as a centre for trade and shopping and attracts visitors to nearby areas of outstanding natural beauty – the Mountains of Mourne and the Ring of Gullion.

Newry's classical town hall sits in both Armagh and Down counties

1 Historic town

Newry's original Irish name, An iu(bh)ir C(h)inn Tra(ha) ('The Yew at the Head of the Strand') derives from a story that St Patrick planted a yew tree here, at the head of the strand of Carlingford Lough, in the fifth century. The saint is also reputed to have established a monastery, which is said to have burned down – together with the yew tree – in 1162. Slightly earlier, in 1157, Maurice McLoughlin, the King of Ireland, founded a Cistercian monastery at Newry. After the dissolution of the monasteries in the sixteenth century King Edward VI granted the monastery to Sir Nicholas Bagenal (Marshall of the King's Army in Ireland), who established a garrison there. The building later became McCann Bakery on Abbey Way, which closed in 1996; in 2004, architects won funding to restore the building to its former glory.

Sir Nicholas Bagenal developed a significant part of the town and also built the Parish Church of St Patrick, Ireland's first Protestant church, in 1578. A sixteenth-century map shows 'Bagenal's Castle' – thought to be the former Abbot's House – on the east side of the new area of town that he laid out within ditches and earth banks. Several two-storey houses are depicted, together with a tree stump, perhaps a representation of the founding yew tree. In 1575 Bagenal played host to an important visitor in Lord Sydney, who approved of the 'well planted' town.

In 1689 Newry was burned almost to the ground by the forces of James II, during the campaign in Ireland to regain his throne from William and Mary. Only the rebuilt castle and six houses survived the flames. But the town's fortunes soon revived. By the mid-1700s Newry was Ulster's most prosperous port, its trade greatly stimulated by the construction of the Newry Canal. The coming of the railways in 1849 brought further development by which time the population of the town had increased to nearly 16,000.

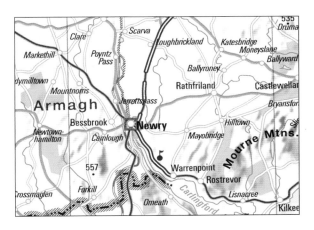

2 Newry Town Hall △

Designed by William Batt in the Classical style, Newry Town Hall was built in 1893. It stands on a three-arched bridge across the River Clanrye, which divides County Armagh and County Down – a location chosen following disputes between the people of the two counties over which should lay claim to the town hall building. The crest of the Newry Town Commissioners, with the date 1891, adorns the front of the building.

3 Newry and Mourne Museum

The museum, opened in 1986, contains very diverse collections and includes exhibitions relating to Newry's prehistoric past, the coming of the Cistercians and the building of the monastery, the development of the town, the building and use of the Newry canal and local working life and folk traditions. Early eighteenth-century architectural features from Newry's Upper North Street were rescued during redevelopment work in that part of town in the 1960s and placed on display in the museum. An exhibition about 'Bagenal's Castle', the building used as a garrison by Sir Nicholas Bagenal, attracts many visitors. There is also an oral history project which captures the experiences of local people.

4 Cathedral of St Patrick and St Colman

The Cathedral was designed by Newry-born architect Thomas J Duff. Construction started in 1823 and lasted for six years using local granite. It was the first Catholic Cathedral built in Ireland after the Reformation in the sixteenth century. The Cathedral was dedicated on 6th May 1829, shortly after the passing of the Emancipation Act that allowed Catholics to sit as members in the Westminster Parliament. Two transepts were added in 1888 and a bell-tower was built in 1891; the nave was lengthened by 12 metres (40 feet) and a new sanctuary area created between 1904 and 1909. Craftsmen from Italy worked for five years to install the marble and mosaics in the cathedral's interior.

5 Newry Canal

The canal was built using 15 locks across 28 kilometres (18 miles) of difficult country that rose to a height of 23 metres (78 feet) above sea level. Work began in 1731 under the supervision of Sir Edward Lovett, and was completed by first Richard Cassels and then Thomas Steers. Opened in March 1742, it connected Newry to Whitecoat Point, two kilometres (about a mile) south of Portadown on the River Bann. The Newry canal was the first 'summit-level' canal in the British Isles, predating those in Manchester and St Helens by more than 20 years. Barges on the canal carried cargoes including coal, grain, flax seed and linen cloth. But as the railways spread, fewer goods were carried by water and the last working journey on the canal was in 1936. Today, the route of the canal can be followed on the south bank, starting by the Town Hall. Close to the Steenson's Bridge section lies Goragh Wood, which was Newry's main railway station and, as the last stopping place before the Irish Republic, a customs point.

Londonderry

Sitting astride the River Foyle, Londonderry – or Derry – is Northern Ireland's second largest city, after Belfast. The original seventeenth-century settlement, on the west bank, is the only fortified city in Ireland whose defensive walls survive intact. The city survived a siege by the forces of James II in 1689. Between the 1960s and 1990s the city, in particular the Bogside area, was a flashpoint for the sectarian violence popularly known as 'the Troubles'.

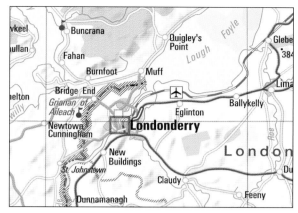

An evening view across the River Foyle

① City walls

Visitors can walk the ramparts of the city's seventeenth-century walls, which are 5.4 metres (18 feet) thick and 2 kilometres (1.2 miles) in circumference and still have the air of impregnability. The original black cannon remain in place. In 1987, sculptor Antony Gormley, creator of the celebrated *Angel of the North* in Gateshead, designed and installed three pairs of figures standing back-to-back with outstretched arms on the walls.

The walled city was built in the early seventeenth century as part of King James I's policy for the 'Plantation of Ulster', in which the region was colonised by Protestant English and Scottish migrants. The new settlement, designed and constructed under a charter of 1613 granted to the City of London, was named 'Londonderry'. Its elegant layout, with four main streets leading out from a central point to the four gates – Butcher's Gate, Shipquay Gate, Ferryquay Gate and Bishop's Gate – has survived to this day.

After the city's foundation, it grew slowly, and by the 1680s had around 2,000 inhabitants. During the English Civil War, Londonderry supported the Parliamentarians: in 1649 it survived a siege by a troop of Scottish royalists. Then on 18th April 1689 James II arrived at Londonderry and demanded the city's surrender. But the people of Londonderry refused to accede to his demand and the celebrated slogan 'No Surrender' was born. The Siege of Derry lasted 105 days and cost thousands of lives, both within the city and among the besiegers. Finally, in late July, a relief ship (the *Mountjoy*) brought the siege to an end.

② River Foyle

Craigavon Bridge connects the old walled city of Londonderry on the west bank to the modern development on the east bank of the River Foyle. The bridge was built in 1933, replacing an earlier steel bridge (Carlisle Bridge), which had been erected in 1863. Carlisle Bridge was itself a replacement for Londonderry's first bridge, made of wood, and built in 1790 around 90 metres (300 feet) north of the present bridge in the Bridge Street area.

③ Bogside

The traditionally Roman Catholic Bogside area has been at the centre of the Irish 'Troubles'. In 1968 riots erupted there while in August 1969, the Siege of Bogside, involving fighting between the Catholic residents and the police, followed another flare-up after a march. These events have been identified by some as the start of 'the Troubles'. In January 1972 British soldiers shot dead 13 men there during a civil rights demonstration – another later died, one of 13 wounded in the incident known as 'Bloody Sunday'.

④ St Colomb's Cathedral

The Gothic Cathedral of St Columb was built in 1633 as part of the city's seventeenth-century development by the master builders of the City of London. In its porch visitors can read the inscription: 'If stones could speake then London's prayse should sounde Who built this church and cittie from the grounde'. Memorials and relics relating to the Siege of 1689 were later installed in the Cathedral. The keys to the city gates that were locked against James's army are displayed in the chapter house, while in the Cathedral there is a memorial to Colonel Baker, the city governor who died on the siege's 74th day, and to Captain Browning, who was killed as the *Mountjoy* broke through the boom across the River Foyle to lift the siege. The Cathedral's stained-glass windows celebrate scenes from the siege.

St Columb's was the first Protestant cathedral built in Ireland following the Reformation. The Honourable Irish Company, formed in London under King James I's 1613 charter to build Londonderry, sent a silver-plate chalice and paten, still used in the Cathedral on special occasions.

Overleaf: the polygonal columns of the Giant's Causeway, County Antrim

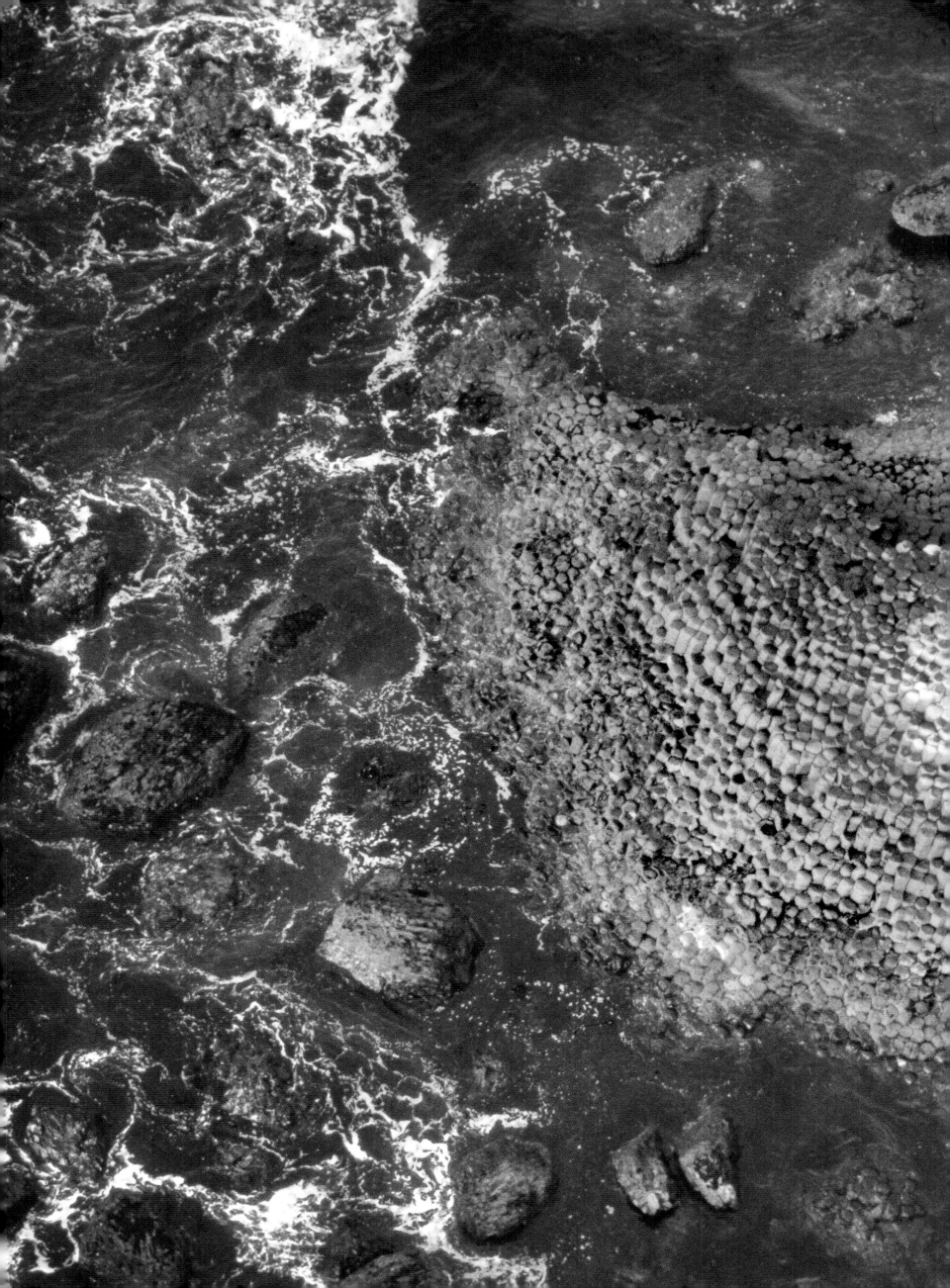

CENTRAL IRELAND

1:600,000

0		5		10		15		20		25 miles
0	5	10	15	20	25 km					

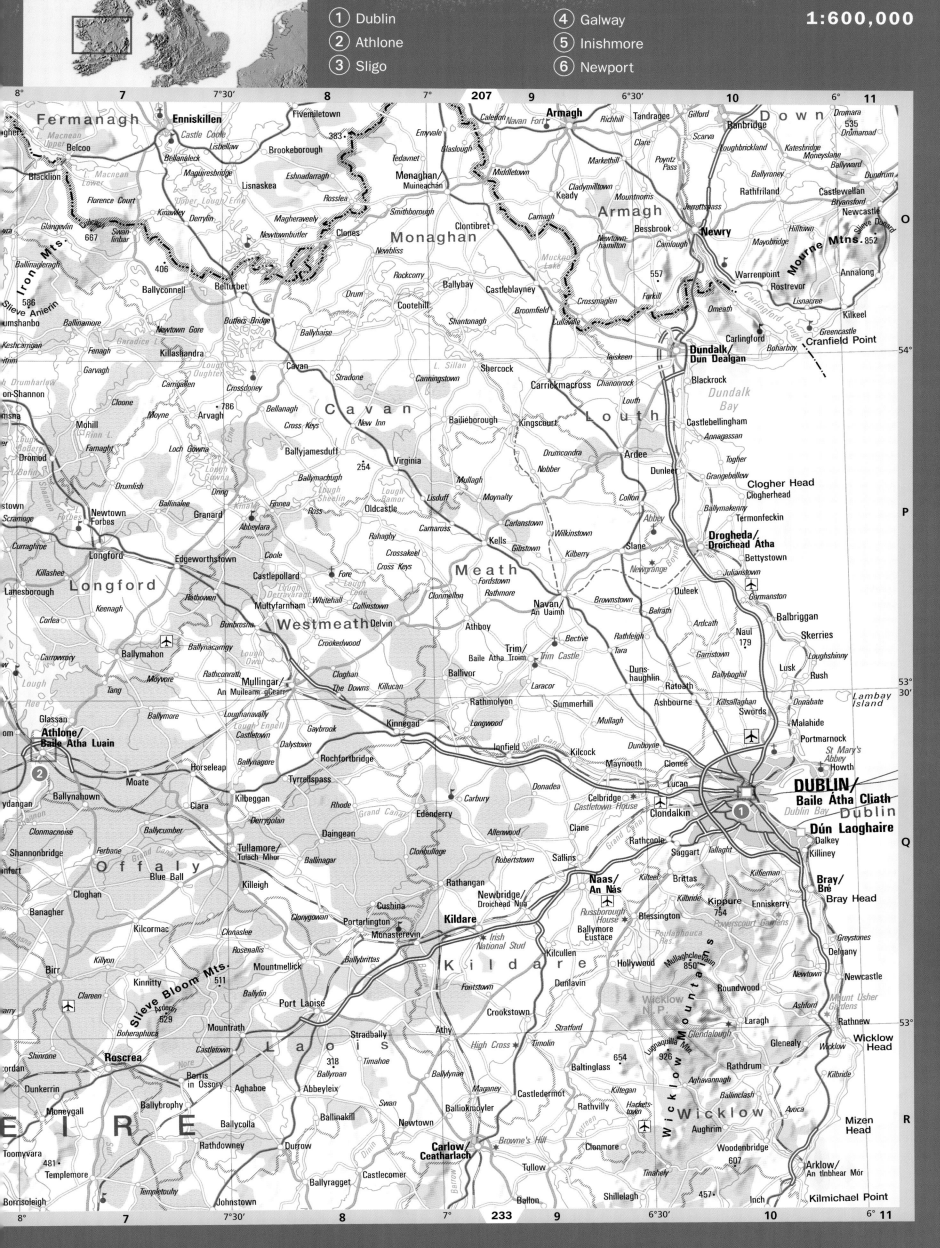

Dublin

Ireland's capital city takes its name from the ninth-century black pool, or 'dubh linn', that formed at the meeting of the Poddle and the River Liffey. Founded by Vikings in 841, the fortified settlement became a trading centre. Its chequered past is one of unrest and change. The Great Famine of the 1840s brought destitution, while the twentieth century saw the ill-starred 1916 Easter Rising. But throughout its history Dublin has remained a vibrant cultural centre, and has produced some of the world's most influential writers, most famously James Joyce, whose *Ulysses* immortalises much of the city. Today Dublin is a sophisticated European metropolis undergoing a new renaissance, partly through an influx of high-technology industries.

❶ Dublin Castle

Situated on high ground, Dublin Castle occupies a commanding position of defence. The Plantagenet king, Henry II, came to Dublin in 1171 to receive the submission of the Irish chieftains after his troops had taken the city, and the old Viking fortifications were strengthened. Henry's son, John, was responsible for the construction of the stone castle which began in 1204 and was completed by 1230. As the seat of English colonial administration, the castle acted at various times as the parliament building, official residence for royal representatives and as a prison. Now it is largely used to entertain heads of state and as the location for European Union summit meetings. In 1684, most of the medieval building was destroyed by fire; only the Record Tower remains. Most of today's building, with its imposing Great Gate and palatial state apartments, dates from the Georgian period.

❷ Guinness Brewery and Guinness Storehouse

Ireland's most famous export started life in 1759 at the St James's Gate Brewery, when Arthur Guinness started producing a beer made from roasted barley. By 1838, the brewery was the largest in Ireland. The Guinness Storehouse, in a renovated fermentation building, provides an extensive audio-visual history of the brewery as well as a top-floor bar. Guinness is now part of Diageo PLC.

❸ Trinity College

Founded by a royal charter of Elizabeth I in 1592 on the site of the former All Hallows monastery, Trinity College is the oldest university in Ireland; it first admitted women as students in 1904; It remains a thriving seat of learning whose graduates include Jonathan Swift, Oliver Goldsmith, Bram Stoker, Oscar Wilde and Samuel Beckett. Trinity College Library's Long Room, over 65m (213ft) long and dating from 1712, houses an outstanding collection of Irish manuscripts, including the *Book of Kells*. Other interesting campus buildings are the 30m (100ft)-high campanile and the eighteeth-century printing house, with its impressive Doric temple front.

The River Liffey dominates the centre of the city

❹ River Liffey △

Also referred to as 'Anna Livia', from its Irish name An Life, the River Liffey divides the city into north and south. The mouth of the river provided a landing-place for the ships of the ninth-century Viking invaders. It is spanned by many bridges from the pedestrian 'Ha'penny Bridge' – originally a toll bridge, and the unofficial symbol of Dublin – to the starkly minimalist James Joyce bridge.

❺ Christ Church Cathedral

Originally founded in the eleventh century by the first Bishop of Dublin, the present structure dates from 1172 when the first Anglo-Norman archbishop, John Comyn, started a new building. The Romanesque cathdral was completed in 1240, and in the fifteenth century an extended choir was added. The south nave wall collapsed in 1562, the temporary repair lasting until the 1870s. The overhaul of the entire building by the architect George Street was at the expense of a Dublin whisky distiller. The massive Romanesque crypt was restored in the 1990s.

One of Dublin's elegant eighteenth-century squares

❻ Georgian Cityscape ◁

Georgian buildings like the Bank of Ireland, City Hall, Four Courts, and Leinster House remain as evidence of Dublin's eighteenth-century architectural glory. At a more domestic level, the Georgian legacy endures in the many gracious terraces, spacious streets and squares that characterise much of the central area. Particularly interesting are the variety of Georgian doors, windows and fanlights, which managed to escape the strict building regulations of the period.

❼ The Dublin Spire (the Needle Monument)

At 120m (393ft) high, the Dublin Spire is the tallest structure in the city centre. It was completed in 2003, and was built to replace Nelson's Pillar, a nineteenth-century monument blown up by the IRA in 1966. The swaying stainless steel 'needle' is three metres (nine feet) wide at its base and 15 centimetres (five inches) wide at its top, where it is illuminated by 1,200 small lights.

Athlone

Athlone's position as a crossing point on the River Shannon has characterised its history in terms of economic development and strategic significance. The first recorded bridge – a wooden structure – built by the King of Connaught in 1120 was quickly supplemented by a protective castle in 1129. Frequently a place of battle for control of the crossing, the town of Athlone is perhaps best known for the siege of 1691 after the Irish armies had retreated following their defeat by William III's army at the Battle of the Boyne in 1690.

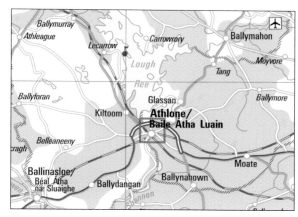

Athlone guards the mouth of Lough Ree

1 Athlone Castle

On the West bank of the Shannon the castle has always been the town's line of defence. The current structure was rebuilt and remodelled several times since the first construction in 1210 by the Normans on the site of an earlier wooden fort. The drum-shaped towers date from the thirteenth century. It was badly damaged in the siege of 1691, in no little part due to the 12,000 cannon balls that were fired by the advancing English forces.

2 Connaught Street

A well-known street of Old Athlone, Connaught Street once contained many of the town's major businesses. Even today some of the most interesting and curious shop fronts still survive, the most interesting of which is the doorway of the Noggin Inn. Connaught Street has been immortalised by the poet Desmond Egan and the author John Broderick, who both lived on the street.

3 The Batteries

At the end of the eighteenth century, eight batteries were built on the western edge of Athlone as defences against the French. Only part of one remains but the name 'The Batteries' refers to the whole area – the first location of the Athlone Golf Club.

4 St Peter and St Paul's Church

In the Square, St Peter and St Paul's Church is often mistaken for a cathedral. A priory of the same name had existed on the site since before the thirteenth century, but the first St Peter's Church was not built until the end of the eighteenth century. Enlarged in 1809, St Peter's served as the parish church until the Church of St Peter and St Paul, designed by Ralph Byrne, was completed in 1837.

Athlone, County Westmeath **223**

Sligo

Located on Sligo Bay at the mouth of the River Garavogue and close to the picturesque inlet of Lough Gill, Sligo thrives as a port, a salmon-fishing base and a holiday destination. The town and bay derive their name, which means 'the Place of Shells', from the large numbers of shellfish found along the coast and in the river. These plentiful natural resources made the area an attractive place to settle in ancient times, and at nearby Carrowmore there is a group of megalithic monuments, parts of which may date to the fourth millennium BC.

① Sligo Abbey

Sligo Abbey was founded as a Dominican friary in 1252–53 by Anglo-Norman Maurice Fitzgerald. The building's name is the Convent of the Holy Cross, although it is commonly referred to as Sligo Abbey. The abbey has had a troubled history including destruction by fire and attacks in the 1595 Tyrone War and the 1641 Ulster Rising. The Dominicans remained until 1760, when they moved to the Holy Cross Priory. There are six thirteenth-century lancet windows in the choir, as well as a carved fifteenth-century stone altar. There is also a 1624 monument in the choir to Sir Donagh O'Connor, Lord of Sligo.

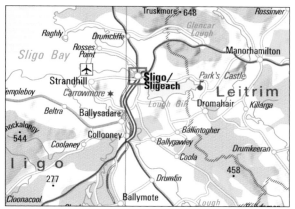

② Cathedral of St Mary the Virgin and St John the Baptist

A much-modified Georgian building, Sligo's Protestant Cathedral in John Street was designed by German architect Richard Cassels in 1730, and constructed on the site of a thirteenth-century almshouse and a seventeeth-century mortuary built by Sir Roger Jones of Banada, Governor of Sligo. The grave slab from Sir Roger's tomb can be seen in the church's west wall. The glass and fittings date from the Victorian period. Near the pulpit a brass plaque commemorates Susan Mary Yeats who was from a wealthy Sligo family and mother of the poet William Butler Yeats and the painter Jack Yeats. Her father, William Pollexfen, lies buried close to the church's main gate. Also in the graveyard is the family plot of the Thornleys, whose daughter Catherine was the mother of Bram Stoker, the author of *Dracula*.

Sligo is the largest town in Ireland's north-west

③ The Cathedral of the Immaculate Conception

Designed by English architect George Goldie in the Romanesque style, Sligo's Catholic Cathedral was built by Laurence Gillooly, Bishop of Elphin, and dedicated in 1874 by the Archbishop of Dublin, Cardinal Cullen. The Cathedral's main entrance faces away from Sligo – a requirement of the Protestant landowner who sold the land on condition that, if used for a Catholic Church, the church's doors must face away from the town. The peel of nine bells is struck rather than rung because of fears that their loud ringing might cause the spire to crumble.

④ Sligo Town Hall

Built in the Italian Renaissance style to designs by Dublin architect William Hague, the town hall was built in 1865–72 using limestone dressed with contrasting County Donegal rock. It stands on the site of a seventeenth-century stone fort. The statue in front of the Town Hall celebrates a former Lord Mayor of Sligo.

⑤ Niland Centre

Situated in a former schoolhouse dating to 1862, the Niland Centre has a permanent display of paintings by Jack Butler Yeats, brother of the poet William Butler Yeats. Both brothers had strong Sligo connections – Jack was educated there and William spent many childhood holidays in the town. William is buried in the graveyard of the Protestant church at Drumcliffe, as he had asked in a poem in his final collection. His grave is marked with the epitaph he wrote: 'Cast a cold eye on life, on death. Horseman, pass by!'

Galway

From its roots as a small fishing village named after the mythical princess Galvia, reputed to have drowned there, Galway evolved into a bustling medieval port, made wealthy through importing wine and exporting wool. It prospered after gaining a Royal Charter in 1396. In the fourteenth and fifteenth centuries it was dominated by 14 powerful merchant families, giving the city its enduring nickname of 'city of the tribes'. In recent years Galway has benefitted from the development of the computing industry, and is now one of the fastest-growing cities in Europe. Present-day Galway is noted for its young population, its internationally-renowned arts festival and for the Galway Races, which draw huge crowds from all over Ireland and beyond.

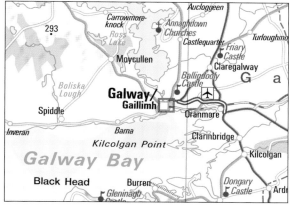

① Salmon Weir Bridge

Completed in 1819, Salmon Weir Bridge is so called because dozens of spawning salmon pass under it in June and July as they make their way up the River Corrib. The weir is upstream from the bridge; it is the largest in the country and, with a flow of four million gallons per second at full strength, is a tourist attraction in itself. Downstream, salmon traps are set in what is known as Queen's Gap. The bridge is built as a series of elegant stone arches.

② Lynch's Castle and Window

Built in the early seventeenth century for the Lynch family, one of the powerful merchant 'tribes' of Galway, this impressive building has an ornate façade. The Lynch Memorial Window, in the wall adjacent to St Nicholas's Church, commemorates the alleged hanging – the first lynching – by James Lynch FitzStephen of his own son for killing a Spaniard.

③ Galway Cathedral

The largest building in the city, Galway Cathedral has a copper dome, 44m (145ft) high, visible for miles around. Officially known as the Cathedral of Our Lady Assumed into Heaven and St Nicholas, the cathedral was built between 1958 and 1965, on the site of the former city jail. The cathedral is built from local limestone, in a style blending Renaissance architecture with medieval influences, with opulent green Connemara marble floors, stained glass windows and mosaics.

④ Galway's Medieval Walls

Thirteenth-century Galway was fortified by the Normans, who built walls around the thriving port to protect its increasing wealth from the native Irish, many of whom were forced to live outside the walls, where they settled on the west bank of the River Corrib to form a Gaelic-speaking fishing community, which was still in evidence in the 1950s. Today, only a few remnants of the original medieval town walls remain, since most either decayed or were destroyed by Cromwellian forces in the 1650s. These remnants include one near the Eyre Square Shopping Centre, and the Spanish Arch, which was a later addition, built in 1584 to protect the estuary of the River Corrib. First known as the 'Ceann an Bhalla' or 'head of the wall', the Spanish Arch acquired its later name in the eighteenth century in reference to the Spanish traders who unloaded their ships there.

⑤ St Nicholas's Church

Dating from 1320, the Anglo-Norman St Nicholas's Church is the oldest surviving building in Galway, and one of the best-preserved medieval churches in Ireland. St Nicholas – the original Santa Claus – is the patron saint of both children and sailors, and legend has it that in 1477 Christopher Columbus visited the church. The building was enlarged in 1486, and again in the 1500s. There is a private chapel for the Lynch family and, although some monuments were defaced by Parliamentarian forces when Cromwell captured the city in 1652, there are still many interesting carvings of mermaids, animals, angels and some fearsome gargoyles.

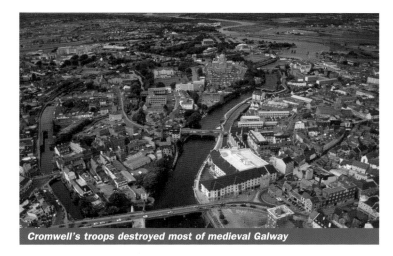
Cromwell's troops destroyed most of medieval Galway

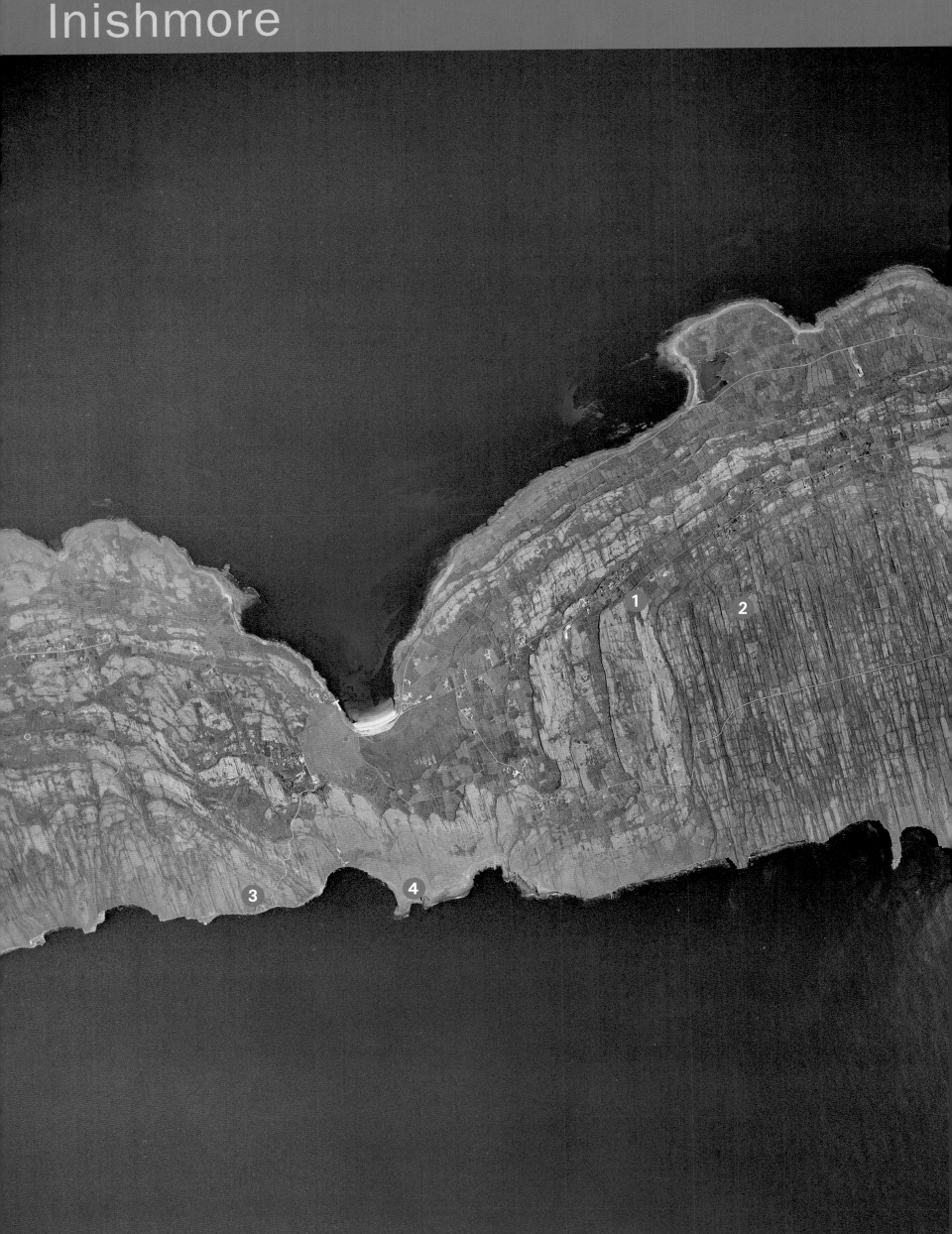

Inishmore

On the east coast of Ireland, in Galway Bay, on the very edge of Western Europe, the Aran Islands lie stark against the full force of the Atlantic Ocean. Inishmore, the largest, elongated island, has a population of 900 and is well-known for its spectacular jagged limestone cliff scenery and prehistoric sites. The economy of the island relies heavily on tourism and the community there is still predominantly Gaelic-speaking.

❶ Dún Eochla

One of the great stone forts of the island, Dún Eochla, stands near the highest point on the island. Its massive circular walls, terraces and stairways are well-preserved and heaps of stones inside the fort mark the remains of huts. Nearby, the name 'EIRE', outlined in stone, was one of a series of coastal markers placed around the country during the Second World War.

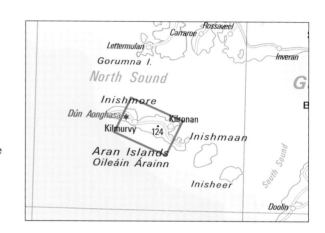

❷ Teampall an Cheathrair Álainn

The fifteenth-century church at Teampall an Cheathrair Álainn is dedicated to the 'four beautiful saints' – Fursey, Conal, Brendan and Berchan – supposedly buried on Inishmore. A holy well nearby inspired J.M. Synge's play The Well of the Saints.

❹ Serpent Hole

Located close to the village of Gort na gCapall, the Serpent Hole is a perfectly rectangular shaped pool of unidentifiable origin. It is connected to the ocean by an underwater channel.

❸ Dún Aonghasa ▽

The triple-walled cliff top fort at Dún Aonghasa is known as one of the finest prehistoric monuments in Western Europe. Standing almost 82m (270ft) above sea level, it has a defensive structure known as 'chevaux de frise', literally bands of stone standing on edge, placed to deter attackers. Dún Aonghasa is perched on the edge of a sheer cliff that falls immediately away into the sea. Theories have abounded as to whether it was purposely constructed this way or simply the full ring of the fort eroded over time. It is believed that it was built by the prehistoric tribe Fir Bolg whose chief, Aonghus, is part of medieval literary legend.

Dún Aonghasa is a spectacular triple-walled fort

Overleaf: the Irish coast at Newport stretching westwards to Achill Island

Map of Southern Ireland

Irish Sea

Kilkenny

Home to many Irish parliaments between 1293 and 1408, Kilkenny is today renowned for its well-preserved medieval buildings. It is known as 'the Marble City' because of its distinctive locally-quarried limestone which resembles marble. Kilkenny has been a brewing centre since the early eighteenth century, and is the site of Ireland's oldest brewery (Sullivan's) as well as the birthplace of the well-known Kilkenny and Smithwick's ales. With a population of 24,000, Kilkenny is the Republic of Ireland's smallest city.

❶ St Canice's Cathedral

Kilkenny takes its name – in Irish, Cill Chainnigh meaning 'Church of Canice' – from the saint who founded a monastic settlement here in the sixth century and who is celebrated in the splendid St Canice's Cathedral. This was begun in the 1190s, under Bishop Felix O'Deleaney, on the site of the monastery. Built of limestone in the early Gothic style, it was largely complete by 1280.

The Cathedral still has its original thirteenth-century baptismal font, together with one of the finest collections of carved stone memorials found in Ireland.

The building was badly damaged in 1650 by Oliver Cromwell's Parliamentarian forces who used it as a stable; restoration work was carried out in the nineteenth century. To the south of the Cathedral stands a ninth-century round tower, 30 metres (100 feet) high, probably used as a refuge and watchtower.

Visitors enjoy the sunshine under the battlemented walls of Kilkenny Castle

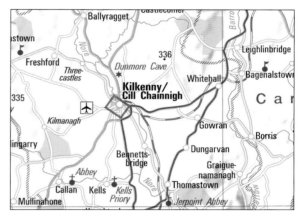

❻ The Tholsel

The Tholsel was built in 1761, on the site of Kilkenny's medieval courthouse and guildhall. It takes its name from the Old English words toll (tax) and sael (hall). Today it is used for art exhibitions and street theatre performances in the arcade that was once a covered marketplace.

❷ Kilkenny Castle △

This imposing building occupies a 30m (100ft) hill at the south-eastern end of the city, looking down on the River Nore. The present building has three of the four original towers erected when the first stone castle was built on the site by William Marshall, Earl of Pembroke, in 1192. This stone building replaced an earlier wooden fortress built in 1172 by the Norman knight, Richard de Clare, known as 'Strongbow'. James Butler, 3rd Earl of Ormonde, bought the castle in 1391 when he was Lord Lieutenant of Ireland. The building was restored in the nineteenth century, and in May 1922 it was occupied by Irish Republican forces, who were defeated after a two-day siege. The castle remained the home of the Butler family until 1935 and, in 1967, Arthur Butler, 23rd Earl of Ormonde, handed over control of the castle to a restoration committee. The building opened to the public in 1976.

❸ The Black Abbey/Holy Trinity Church

The 'Convent of the One and Undivided Trinity' was founded by the Earl of Pembroke in 1225 for the Dominican friars. Located outside the walls of the city, it became known as the Black Abbey because of the dark habits worn by the friars. In 1349, during the Black Death, eight friars died in a single day. The abbey was repressed in the early 1540s, and used as a courthouse until the end of the seventeenth century. In the late eighteenth century it was partially restored and in the mid-nineteenth century became Holy Trinity Church. Visitors can view the original thirteenth-century nave, a fourteenth-century transept and the fifteenth-century stained glass windows. Close by, on Abbey Street, is Black Freren gate, the only surviving part of the entrance gates in the medieval city walls.

❹ St Francis's Abbey

Kilkenny's Franciscan abbey was founded in the 1230s by Richard Marshall, Earl of Pembroke, and quickly expanded and grew in importance. It was repressed in 1540 during the dissolution of the monasteries, but the friars remained in residence until 1550, when they were made to leave by John Bale, Bishop of Ossory. They briefly returned under the Catholic Queen Mary I (1553-58) but were expelled once more following the accession of her half-sister, the Protestant Queen Elizabeth I. The monastery was rededicated following the accession of James I in 1603, but the buildings were little more than ruins. The Franciscan community survived but dwindled, and the abbey's last Franciscan friar, Father Philip Forristal, died in 1829. In the early eighteenth century, Richard Cole and John Smithwick started a brewery in the abbey grounds.

❺ The Maltings

This building was probably constructed around 1810, as an expansion site for Sullivan Brewery, established on James's Street and High Street in 1702 and the oldest brewery in Ireland. For much of the twentieth century the brewery was operated by Smithwick's, who bought it in 1910. The Kilkenny Corporation is overseeing the redevelopment of The Maltings.

❼ Shee Alms House

The alms house was built by Sir Richard Shee, a powerful Kilkenny lawyer, in 1582 'to accommodate twelve poor persons'. The Shees lost their possessions in the era of Oliver Cromwell in the mid-seventeenth century but finally regained control of the Alms House in 1756. The last known inmates were resident in 1830. Since 1978, it has belonged to Kilkenny Corporation and has been carefully restored.

❽ Rothe House

In 1594, wealthy Kilkenny merchant John Rothe built a fine house on Parliament Street (at that time called the Coal Market) for his wife, Rose Archer. Its three buildings stand around cobbled courtyards, which contain a well dating from 1604. The restored building contains a kitchen, bakery, brew house and reception room, with a collection of period costumes. It is now the headquarters of the Kilkenny Archaeological Society and the Heritage Council of Ireland.

Blarney

North-west of the City of Cork lies the village of Blarney, its name derived from the Irish An blarna which means 'the plain'. Best-known for the castle and, within the battlements, the Blarney Stone, the village has also entered the English lexicon through a comment made by Elizabeth I. The monarch's response to the elaborate excuses made by the owner of the castle (asked to give up his property as a sign of loyalty to the crown) was that it was all 'Blarney', later defined as 'pleasant talk, intending to deceive without offending'.

1 Blarney House

The picturesque Blarney House was built in Scottish baronial style to the south of the castle and completed in 1874 by the Colthurst family, whose descendants reside in the property to this day. Recently restored, it is open to visitors in the summer months. The house has a collection of early furniture, tapestries and works of arts and there are also extensive gardens, forests and parklands.

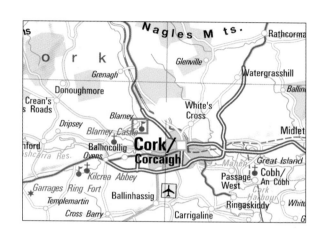

2 The Rock Close

The previous owners of the castle, the Jeffreyes family, planned a garden area consisting of a collection of boulders and rocks arranged around a possible prehistoric Druid site. The Rock Close, as it is known, remains an eerie place to visit after nightfall as within the area survives a Dolmen or ancient burial place shaped in the form of a tomb with a large flat stone laid on uprights.

3 The Blarney Stone

Tradition dictates that kissing the Blarney Stone bequeaths eloquence upon a person. The stone is believed to be half of the Stone of Scone, originally used in the coronation of Scottish kings and presented to Cormac McCarthy by Robert the Bruce in gratitude for his support at the Battle of Bannockburn in 1314. Situated high in the battlements of the castle, the stone can only be reached by bending backwards with the support of others until, hanging upside down, the stone can be kissed.

The castle (foreground) and house at Blarney

4 The Woollen Mills

Opened in 1824, the success of the mills shielded the village of Blarney from the worst effects of the Irish famine. Destroyed by fire in 1869, the factory was operational again by 1871 and employed as many as 700 people by 1950. The mill closed in 1975 but is now a hotel and restaurant.

5 Blarney Castle △

The existing keep structure of Blarney Castle was built by Dermot McCarthy, King of Munster, in 1446. However, this is the third castle to stand on this site. The first structure was a wooden castle of the tenth century which was replaced by a stronger stone building in 1210. At 26 metres (86 feet) high, the surviving keep is the sole remnant of a much larger fortress that was able to withstand long sieges. The tower walls were broken by the cannon force of Cromwell's general Lord Broghill. The building remained under the control of the McCarthy family until it was forfeited by Donagh McCarthy, because of his support for James II at the Battle of the Boyne in 1690. It was subsequently sold to the Governor of Cork, Sir James St John Jeffreyes soon after. The castle stands in 139 hectares (344 acres) of land currently managed by the Trustees of the Blarney Castle Estate.

Limerick

Limerick

Situated at the head of the River Shannon estuary, Limerick has been a major seaport since the Vikings sacked the early native settlement and founded a town in 812. After Irish hero Brian Boru drove out the Vikings in 967, Limerick first became a medieval stronghold and later, in 1769, an elegant Georgian new town. As part of the Irish economic revival of the 1990s, Limerick established itself as a centre for hi-tech industry, while sustaining a reputation as a holiday centre.

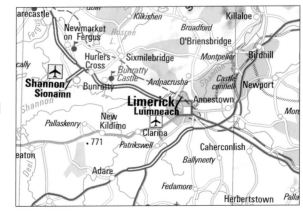

❶ John's Square and Georgian architecture

This was the first of the Georgian developments in Limerick, begun in the 1750s in advance of the planning and laying out of the Georgian part of the city, Newton Pery. The elegant houses of John's Square are built in local limestone.

The symmetrically designed terrace at numbers 1–6, Pery Square, is claimed by some authorities as the finest Georgian architecture in the whole of Ireland. A great deal of the original marbling, woodwork and plasterwork can still be seen. Gable entrances adorn numbers 1 and 6. Number 2 has been restored by the Limerick Civic Trust and is now open to the public.

③ Bishop's Palace

The Bishop's Palace was built in the late seventeenth century. With a five-bay classical façade, this building exhibits a form of the English Palladian architectural style adapted for Irish climatological conditions. It was once the palace of the Protestant Bishop of Limerick, but is now the headquarters of the Limerick Civic Trust. It stands across the road from King John's Castle.

④ Limerick Civic Offices

This modern development stands on the site of the city jail and Courthouse. It was built for the Limerick Corporation and the City Council and was the first building in Limerick to follow a new policy of orientating new constructions towards the river. Visitors can tour the gallery within the building.

⑤ King John's Castle

The Viking settlement, chief town of their kingdom of Limerick, was established on an island beside a ford across the Shannon; after Brian Boru and his brother King Mahon of Thomond had defeated the invaders, the island settlement became the capital of the kings of Thomond. Then in the twelfth century an Anglo-Norman army took the town and named the spot King's Island. King John, 'Lord of Ireland', ordered the construction of fortifications and King John's Castle was built around 1200. The castle's curtain walls and D-shaped towers on its north face were unique for the period.

The castle was besieged and overpowered by Oliver Cromwell when he captured Limerick in 1651, then besieged twice more by the 'Williamite armies' fighting in support of William and Mary in 1690-91. The Treaty of Limerick, ending the second of the sieges and bringing to an end that phase of the struggle between 'Williamites' and 'Jacobites' (supporters of the exiled James II), was signed on 3rd October 1691 on a stone now mounted as 'the Treaty Stone' on the opposite bank of the river beside Thomond Bridge. The Treaty Stone can be seen from the battlements of King John's Castle.

Visitors can walk the battlements, enjoying views of the Shannon and the city, and examine excavations of Viking and other houses that occupied the site before the castle was built.

The River Shannon runs through Limerick

② Custom House and Hunt Museum

Limerick's Palladian-style Custom House was built in 1765-69 to designs by the Italian architect Daviso de Arcort (also known as Davis Ducart), designer of a number of Irish country houses. The Custom House was the administrative headquarters of the Revenue, and the site of a post office when the new Penny Post was introduced in the 1840s. Today it is the home of the Hunt Collection, a miscellany of around 2,000 objects brought together by John and Gertrude Hunt who collected the pieces – from all eras – on the basis of their craftsmanship, artistic merit and standard of design. The collection contains medieval statues, crucifixes and jewellery, ancient Egyptian pieces, ancient Greek and Roman items, the personal seal of King Charles I and a bronze horse by Italian artist Leonardo da Vinci. Pieces of Irish interest include some Neolithic flints dating from c.4000–2000 BC, Bronze Age gold (c.2000–700 BC) and an 8th-century AD Antrim cross.

⑥ St Mary's Cathedral

Founded in 1168 and completed nearly 30 years later, the Cathedral of St Mary the Blessed Virgin combines Gothic and Romanesque architectural styles. It was built on the site of a palace given by Donal Mor O'Brien, King of Munster, and is believed to incorporate parts of the palace structure. Experts suggest that the Cathedral's Romanesque West Door was once the palace entrance; around the door marks in the wall are said to have been made by soldiers who sharpened their swords and crossbows there during the sieges of the city. The site of King Donal Mor's palace was previously the Viking meeting house.

The West Door is now only in ceremonial use – a new bishop knocks and is admitted by this entrance during his installation ceremony. Within the Cathedral, visitors can see beautifully sculptured fifteenth-century oak misericords (carvings on the underside of seats). After Oliver Cromwell's troops captured the city in 1651, they used the Cathedral as a stable. The choir today wears scarlet cassocks as a mark of its royal origins.

Overleaf: Great Blasket Island off the Dingle Peninsula

Index to place names

A

Abberton Essex GB **71** T 24
Abbey Galway IRL **218** Q 5
Abbey Galway IRL **218/219** Q 6
Abbey Essex GB **71** T 23
Abbey Dore Herefordshire GB **87** T 17
Abbey St. Bathans Scottish Borders GB **161** L 18
Abbey Town Cumbria GB **146** N 16
Abbeycwmhir Powys GB **87** S 16
Abbeydorney Kerry IRL **232** S 3
Abbeyfeale Limerick IRL **232** S 4
Abbeylara Longford IRL **219** P 8
Abbeyleix Laois IRL **233** R 8
Abbots Bromley Staffordshire GB **100** R 19
Abbotsbury Dorset GB **53** V 17
Abbotsley Cambridgeshire GB **100/101** S 22
Aberaeron Ceredigion GB **86** S 14
Abercarn Caerphilly GB **87** T 16
Aberchirder Aberdeenshire GB **187** G 17
Abercraf Powys GB **86/87** T 15
Aberdare Rhondda Cynon Taff GB **87** T 16
Aberdaron Gwynedd GB **118** R 13
Aberdaugleddau Milford Haven Pembrokeshire GB **86** T 12
Aberdeen Aberdeen City GB **187** H 18
Aberdour Fife GB **161** K 16
Aberdyfi Gwynedd GB **86** R 14
Aberedw Powys GB **87** S 16
Aberfeldy Perth and Kinross GB **160/161** J 15
Aberffraw Anglesey GB **118/119** Q 14
Aberford Leeds GB **134** P 20
Aberfoyle Stirling GB **160** K 14
Abergavenny Y Fenni Monmouthshire GB **87** T 17
Abergele Conwy GB **119** Q 15
Abergwaun Fishguard Pembrokeshire GB **86** T 13
Abergwesyn Powys GB **86/87** S 15
Abergwyngregyn Gwynedd GB **119** Q 15
Abergynolwyn Gwynedd GB **86/87** R 15
Aberhonddu Brecon Powys GB **87** T 16
Aberlady East Lothian GB **161** K 17
Aberlemno Angus GB **161** J 18
Aberllefenni Gwynedd GB **86/87** R 15
Abermule Powys GB **87** R 16

Abernethy Perth and Kinross GB **161** K 16
Aberporth Ceredigion GB **86** S 13
Abersoch Gwynedd GB **118** R 13
Abersychan Torfaen GB **87** T 16
Abertawe Swansea Swansea GB **86/87** T 15
Aberteifi Cardigan Ceredigion GB **86** S 13
Aberteifi Pembrokeshire GB **86** S 13
Abertillery Blaenau Gwent GB **87** T 16
Aberystwyth Ceredigion GB **86** S 14
Abhainn Suidhe Na h-Eileanan an Iar GB **175** G 9
Abingdon Oxfordshire GB **70** T 20
Abington South Lanarkshire GB **146** M 15
Aboyne Aberdeenshire GB **187** H 17
Abriachan Highland GB **186** H 14
Abridge Essex GB **71** T 23
Accrington Lancashire GB **134** P 18
Acha Argyll and Bute GB **174** J 9
Acha´Mor Na h-Eileanan an Iar GB **175** F 9
Achahoish Argyll and Bute GB **174** L 11
Acham Angus GB **161** J 16
Achanalt Highland GB **186** G 13
Acharacle Highland GB **174** J 11
Acharn Perth and Kinross GB **160** J 14
Achavanich Highland GB **187** F 16
Achiemore Highland GB **186** E 13
Achill Sound Mayo IRL **218** P 3
Achiltibuie Highland GB **186** F 12
Achleck Argyll and Bute GB **174** J 10
Achmelvich Highland GB **186** F 12
Achnanellan Highland GB **160** J 12
Achnasheen Highland GB **186** G 12
Achosnich Highland GB **174** J 10
Ackergill Highland GB **187** F 16
Acklington Northumberland GB **147** M 19
Aclare Sligo IRL **206** O 5
Acle Norfolk GB **101** R 26
Acomb Northumberland GB **147** M 18
Adamstown Wexford IRL **233** S 9
Adare Limerick IRL **232** R 5
Adderley Shropshire GB **100** R 18
Addingham Bradford GB **134** P 19

Adlington Lancashire GB **119** P 17
Adrigole Cork IRL **232** T 3
Aghaboe Laois IRL **233** R 8
Aghagower Mayo IRL **218** P 4
Aghalee Antrim GB **207** N 10
Aghavannagh Wicklow IRL **233** R 10
Aghleam Mayo IRL **218** O 2
Agivey Londonderry GB **207** M 9
Aglish Waterford IRL **233** S 7
Ahascragh Galway IRL **218/219** Q 6
Ahenny Tipperary IRL **233** S 8
Ahoghill Antrim GB **207** N 10
Aikton Cumbria GB **146** N 16
Ailladie Clare IRL **218** Q 4
Ainsdale Sefton GB **119** P 16
Aird Argyll and Bute GB **174** K 11
Aird a'Mhulaidh Na h-Eileanan an Iar GB **175** G 9
Aird Mhòr Na h-Eileanan an Iar GB **175** H 8
Aird of Sleat Highland GB **175** H 11
Airdrie North Lanarkshire GB **160/161** L 15
Airidh a'Bhruaich Na h-Eileanan an Iar GB **175** F 9
Airntully Perth and Kinross GB **161** K 16
Airor Highland GB **175** H 11
Airth Falkirk GB **160/161** K 15
Airton North Yorkshire GB **147** O 18
Aisholt Somerset GB **53** U 16
Aith Orkney Islands GB **198** D 16
Aith Orkney Islands GB **198** D 17
Aith Shetland Islands GB **199** B 20
Akeld Northumberland GB **161** L 18
Akeley Buckinghamshire GB **100** S 21
Albrighton Shropshire GB **100** R 18
Albrighton Shropshire GB **87** R 17
Alcester Warwickshire GB **100** S 19
Aldbourne Wiltshire GB **70** U 19
Aldbrough East Riding of Yorkshire GB **135** P 22
Aldbrough St John North Yorkshire GB **147** O 19
Aldeburgh Suffolk GB **101** S 26
Alderley Edge Cheshire GB **134** Q 18
Aldermaston West Berkshire GB **70** U 20
Alderminster Warwickshire GB **100** S 19
Aldershot Hampshire GB **70/71** U 21

Aldford Cheshire GB **119** Q 17
Aldingham Cumbria GB **146** O 16
Aldridge Walsall GB **100** R 19
Aldsworth Gloucestershire GB **70** T 19
Alexandria West Dunbartonshire GB **160** L 13
Alford Lincolnshire GB **135** Q 23
Alford Aberdeenshire GB **187** H 17
Alfreton Derbyshire GB **134** Q 20
Alkham Kent GB **71** U 25
Allendale Town Northumberland GB **147** N 18
Allenheads Northumberland GB **147** N 18
Allenwood Kildare IRL **219** Q 9
Allerston North Yorkshire GB **134** O 21
Allhallows Medway GB **71** U 24
Allihies Cork IRL **70** T 2
Alloa Clackmannanshire GB **160/161** K 15
Allonby Cumbria GB **146** N 16
Alltnacaillich Highland GB **186** F 13
Almeley Herefordshire GB **87** S 17
Almondsbury South Gloucestershire GB **87** T 17
Alness Highland GB **186/187** G 14
Alnmouth Northumberland GB **147** M 19
Alnwick Northumberland GB **147** M 19
Alrewas Staffordshire GB **100** R 19
Alsager Cheshire GB **134** Q 18
Alston Cumbria GB **147** N 18
Altarnun Cornwall GB **52** V 13
Althorne Essex GB **71** T 24
Altnabreac Station Highland GB **187** F 15
Altnaharra Highland GB **186/187** F 14
Altnapaste Donegal IRL **206** N 7
Alton Staffordshire GB **100** R 19
Alton Hampshire GB **70** U 20
Altrincham Trafford GB **134** Q 18
Alva Clackmannanshire GB **160/161** K 15
Alvechurch Worcestershire GB **100** S 19
Alves Moray GB **187** G 16
Alveston Warwickshire GB **100** S 19
Alveston South Gloucestershire GB **87** T 17
Alvingham Lincolnshire GB **135** Q 23
Alwinton Northumberland GB **147** M 18

Alyth Perth and Kinross GB **161** J 16
Amberley West Sussex GB **70/71** V 21
Amble Northumberland GB **147** M 19
Amblecote Staffordshire GB **87** S 18
Ambleside Cumbria GB **146/147** O 17
Amcotts North Lincolnshire GB **134/135** P 21
Amersham Buckinghamshire GB **70/71** T 21
Amesbury Wiltshire GB **70** U 19
Amlwch Anglesey GB **118/119** Q 14
Ammanford Carmarthenshire GB **86/87** T 15
Ampthill Bedfordshire GB **100/101** S 22
An Baile Na h-Eileanan an Iar GB **175** H 8
An Charraig Donegal IRL **206** N 5
An Cnoc Na h-Eileanan an Iar GB **186** F 10
An Dubhcharaid Donegal IRL **206** N 6
An t-Ob Leverburgh Na h-Eileanan an Iar GB **175** G 8
Anascaul Kerry IRL **232** S 2
Ancaster Lincolnshire GB **100** R 21
Ancroft Northumberland GB **161** L 19
Ancrum Scottish Borders GB **161** L 17
Andover Hampshire GB **70** U 20
Andreas Isle of Man GB **146** O 14
Angle Pembrokeshire GB **86** T 12
Angmering West Sussex GB **71** V 22
Annagassan Louth IRL **219** P 10
Annalong Down GB **207** O 11
Annan Dumfries und Galloway GB **146** N 16
Annbank South Ayrshire GB **146** M 13
Annestown Limerick IRL **232** R 5
Annestown Waterford IRL **233** S 8
Annfield Plain Durham GB **147** N 19
Anstey Leicestershire GB **100** R 20
Anston Rotherham GB **134** Q 20
Anstruther Fife GB **161** K 17
Ansty Warwickshire GB **100** S 20
Antrim Antrim GB **207** N 10
Anwoth Dumfries und Galloway GB **146** N 14
Apley Lincolnshire GB **135** Q 22
Appleby North Lincolnshire GB **134/135** P 21

Appleby-in-Westmorland Cumbria GB **147** N 18

Applecross Highland GB **175** H 11

Appledore Devon GB **52/53** U 14

Appledore Kent GB **71** U 24

Araglin Cork IRL **232/233** S 6

Arbirlot Angus GB **161** J 18

Arbroath Angus GB **161** J 18

Arbuthnott Aberdeenshire GB **161** J 18

Archiestown Moray GB **187** H 16

Ardagh Limerick IRL **232** S 4

Ardara Donegal IRL **206** N 6

Ardarroch Highland GB **175** H 11

Ardbeg Argyll and Bute GB **174** L 10

Ardcath Meath IRL **219** P 10

Ardcharnich Highland GB **186** G 12

Ardee Louth IRL **219** P 9

Ardentinny Argyll and Bute GB **160** K 13

Ardeonaig Stirling GB **160** K 14

Ardersier Highland GB **186/187** G 14

Ardfern Argyll and Bute GB **174** K 11

Ardfert Kerry IRL **232** S 3

Ardfinnan Tipperary IRL **233** S 7

Ardgay Highland GB **186/187** G 14

Ardglass Down GB **207** O 11

Ardgroom Cork IRL **232** T 3

Ardleigh Essex GB **71** T 24

Ardley Oxfordshire GB **70** T 20

Ardlui Argyll and Bute GB **160** K 13

Ardlussa Argyll and Bute GB **174** K 11

Ardminish Argyll and Bute GB **174** L 11

Ardmolich Highland GB **174** J 11

Ardmore Waterford IRL **233** T 7

Ardnacrusha Limerick IRL **232** R 5

Ardpatrick Limerick IRL **232** S 5

Ardrahan Galway IRL **218** Q 5

Ardress Armagh GB **207** O 9

Ardrishaig Argyll and Bute GB **160** K 12

Ardrossan North Ayrshire GB **160** L 13

Ardstraw Tyrone GB **207** N 8

Ardtainaig Perth and Kinross GB **160** J 14

Ardtalla Argyll and Bute GB **174** L 10

Ardtoe Highland GB **174** J 11

Ardvasar Highland GB **175** H 11

Ardwell Dumfries und Galloway GB **146** N 13

Arinagour Argyll and Bute GB **174** J 9

Arisaig Highland GB **175** J 11

Arklow An tInbhear Mór Wicklow IRL **233** R 10

Arlecdon Cumbria GB **146** N 16

Arlosh Cumbria GB **146** N 16

Armadale West Lothian GB **160/161** L 15

Armadale Highland GB **175** H 11

Armadale Highland GB **186/187** E 14

Armagh Armagh GB **207** O 9

Armitage Staffordshire GB **100** R 19

Armoy Antrim GB **207** M 10

Armthorpe Doncaster GB **134** P 20

Arncliffe North Yorkshire GB **147** O 18

Arnisdale Highland GB **175** H 11

Arnish Highland GB **175** H 10

Arnol Na h-Eileanan an Iar GB **175** F 9

Arnold Nottinghamshire GB **134** Q 20

Arnside Cumbria GB **146/147** O 17

Arrington Cambridgeshire GB **100/101** S 22

Arrochar Argyll and Bute GB **160** K 13

Arthurstown Wexford IRL **233** S 9

Artigarvan Tyrone GB **207** N 8

Arundel West Sussex GB **70/71** V 21

Arvagh Cavan IRL **219** P 7

Ascot Windsor & Maidenhead GB **70/71** U 21

Ash Kent GB **71** U 23

Ash Mill Devon GB **53** V 15

Ashbourne Derbyshire GB **134** Q 19

Ashbourne Meath IRL **219** Q 10

Ashburton Devon GB **53** V 15

Ashbury Oxfordshire GB **70** T 19

Ashby-de-la-Zouch Leicestershire GB **100** R 20

Ashford Wicklow IRL **219** Q 10

Ashford Devon GB **52/53** U 14

Ashford Kent GB **71** U 24

Ashill Norfolk GB **101** R 24

Ashington Northumberland GB **147** M 19

Ashkirk Scottish Borders GB **146/147** M 17

Ashley Staffordshire GB **100** R 18

Ashley Devon GB **53** V 15

Ashton Devon GB **53** V 15

Ashton Keynes Wiltshire GB **70** T 19

Ashton under Hill Worcestershire GB **100** S 19

Ashton-under-Lyne Tameside GB **134** Q 18

Ashwell Rutland GB **100** R 21

Ashwell Hertfordshire GB **100/101** S 22

Ashwellthorpe Norfolk GB **101** R 25

Askam in Furness Cumbria GB **146** O 16

Askeaton Limerick IRL **232** R 5

Askern Doncaster GB **134** P 20

Askham Cumbria GB **146/147** N 17

Askrigg North Yorkshire GB **147** O 18

Askwith North Yorkshire GB **134** P 19

Aspatria Cumbria GB **146** N 16

Assington Suffolk GB **101** S 24

Aston Cheshire GB **119** Q 17

Aston Abbots Buckinghamshire GB **70/71** T 21

Aston Clinton Buckinghamshire GB **70/71** T 21

Astwood Bank Worcestershire GB **100** S 19

Athavallie Mayo IRL **218** P 4

Athboy Meath IRL **219** P 9

Athea Limerick IRL **232** S 4

Athelstaneford East Lothian GB **161** L 17

Athenry Galway IRL **218** Q 5

Atherstone Warwickshire GB **100** R 19

Atherton Wigan GB **134** P 18

Athleague Roscommon IRL **218/219** P 6

Athlone Baile Átha Luain Westmeath IRL **219** Q 7

Athy Kildare IRL **219** Q 8

Attadale Highland GB **186** H 12

Attleborough Norfolk GB **101** R 25

Attlebridge Norfolk GB **101** R 25

Atwick East Riding of Yorkshire GB **135** P 22

Atworth Wiltshire GB **70** U 18

Auchavan Angus GB **161** J 16

Auchenblae Aberdeenshire GB **161** J 18

Auchenbreck Argyll and Bute GB **160** L 12

Auchencairn Dumfries and Galloway GB **146** N 15

Auchengray South Lanarkshire GB **160/161** L 15

Auchinleck East Ayrshire GB **146** M 14

Auchleven Aberdeenshire GB **187** H 17

Auchnagatt Aberdeenshire GB **187** H 18

Aucholzie Aberdeenshire GB **161** J 16

Auchterarder Perth and Kinross GB **160/161** K 15

Auchtermuchty Fife GB **161** K 16

Auchtertool Fife GB **161** K 16

Aucloggeen Galway IRL **218** Q 5

Audlem Cheshire GB **119** R 17

Audley Staffordshire GB **134** Q 18

Augher Tyrone GB **207** O 8

Aughils Kerry IRL **232** S 3

Aughnacloy Tyrone GB **207** O 9

Aughrim Galway IRL **218/219** Q 6

Aughrim Wicklow IRL **233** R 10

Aughton Rotherham GB **134** Q 20

Auldearn Highland GB **187** G 15

Auldhouse South Lanarkshire GB **160** L 14

Aultbea Highland GB **186** G 11

Aust South Gloucestershire GB **87** T 17

Austwick North Yorkshire GB **147** O 18

Avebury Wiltshire GB **70** U 19

Avening Gloucestershire GB **70** T 18

Aviemore Highland GB **187** H 15

Avoca Wicklow IRL **233** R 10

Avoch Highland GB **186/187** G 14

Avonmouth Bristol GB **87** T 17

Avonwick Devon GB **53** W 15

Axbridge Somerset GB **53** U 17

Axminster Devon GB **53** V 17

Aylesbury Buckinghamshire GB **70/71** T 21

Aylesham Kent GB **71** U 25

Aylsham Norfolk GB **101** R 25

Ayr South Ayrshire GB **146** M 13

Aysgarth North Yorkshire GB **147** O 19

Ayton North Yorkshire GB **135** O 22

B

Bac Na h-Eileanan an Iar GB **186** F 10

Backaland Orkney Islands GB **198** D 17

Backwell North Somerset GB **53** U 17

Bacton Norfolk GB **101** R 25

Bacup Lancashire GB **134** P 18

Badachro Highland GB **186** G 11

Badby Northhamptonshire GB **100** S 20

Badcall Highland GB **186** F 12

Badcaul Highland GB **186** G 12

Badluarach Highland GB **186** G 12

Badminton South Gloucestershire GB **70** T 18

Badnabay Highland GB **186** F 12

Badrallach Highland GB **186** G 12

Bagenalstown Carlow IRL **233** R 9

Bagh a´Chaisteil Castlebay Na h-Eileanan an Iar GB **175** J 8

Bagshot Surrey GB **70/71** U 21

Baile Ailein Na h-Eileanan an Iar GB **175** F 9

Baile Mòr Argyll and Bute GB **174** K 10

Baile na Finne Donegal IRL **206** N 6

Baile nan Cailleach Na h-Eileanan an Iar GB **175** H 8

Bailieborough Cavan IRL **219** P 9

Bainbridge North Yorkshire GB **147** O 18

Bainton East Riding of Yorkshire GB **134/135** P 21

Bakewell Derbyshire GB **134** Q 19

Balbeggie Perth and Kinross GB **161** K 16

Balblair Highland GB **186/187** G 14

Balbriggan Dublin IRL **219** P 10

Balchrick Highland GB **186** E 12

Balcombe West Sussex GB **71** U 22

Balderton Nottinghamshire GB **134/135** Q 21

Balemartine Argyll and Bute GB **174** K 9

Balerno Edinburgh GB **161** L 16

Balfour Orkney Islands GB **198** D 17

Balfron Stirling GB **160** K 14

Balintore Highland GB **187** G 15

Balla Mayo IRL **218** P 4

Ballachulish Highland GB **160** J 12

Ballagh Tipperary IRL **233** R 7

Ballaghaderreen Roscommon IRL **218** P 5

Ballaghkeen Wexford IRL **233** S 10

Ballantrae South Ayrshire GB **146** M 12

Ballasalla Isle of Man GB **146** O 13

Ballater Aberdeenshire GB **187** H 16

Ballina Béal an Átha Mayo IRL **206** O 4

Ballinafad Sligo IRL **206** O 6

Ballinagar Offaly IRL **219** Q 8

Ballinagleragh Leitrim IRL **206** O 6

Ballinakill Laois IRL **233** R 8

Ballinalee Longford IRL **219** P 7

Ballinamallard Fermanagh GB **206** O 7

Ballinamore Leitrim IRL **206** O 7

Ballinasloe Béal Átha na Sluaighe Galway IRL **218/219** Q 6

Ballinclash Wicklow IRL **233** R 10

Ballincollig Cork IRL **232** T 5

Ballincurrig Cork IRL **232/233** T 6

Ballindaggan Wexford IRL **233** R 9

Ballinderry Antrim GB **207** N 10

Ballinderry Tipperary IRL **218/219** Q 6

Ballindine Mayo IRL **218** P 5

Ballineen Cork IRL **232** T 5

Ballingarry Tipperary IRL **218/219** Q 6

Ballingarry Limerick IRL **232** S 5

Ballingarry Tipperary IRL **233** R 7

Ballingeary Cork IRL **232** T 4

Ballingry Fife GB **161** K 16

Ballingurteen Cork IRL **232** T 4

Ballinhassig Cork IRL **232** T 5

Ballinlough Roscommon IRL **218** P 5

Ballinluig Perth and Kinross GB **160/161** J 15

Ballinrobe Mayo IRL **218** P 4

Ballinskelligs Kerry IRL **70** T 2

Ballinspittle Cork IRL **232** T 5

Ballintober Roscommon IRL **218/219** P 6

Ballintogher Sligo IRL **206** O 6

Ballintoy Antrim GB **207** M 10

Ballintra Donegal IRL **206** N 6

Ballinure Tipperary IRL **233** R 7

Balliokmoyler Laois IRL **233** R 9

Ballivor Meath IRL **219** P 9

Balloch West Dunbartonshire GB **160** K 13

Ballon Carlow IRL **233** R 9

Ballyagran Limerick IRL **232** S 5

Ballybay Monaghan IRL **207** O 9

Ballybofey Donegal IRL **206** N 7

Ballyboghil Dublin IRL **219** P 10

Ballybrittas Laois IRL **219** Q 8

Ballybrophy Laois IRL **233** R 7

Ballybunnion Kerry IRL **232** R 3

Ballycahill Tipperary IRL **233** R 7

Ballycarry Antrim GB **207** N 11

Ballycastle Mayo IRL **206** O 4

Ballycastle Antrim GB **207** M 10

Ballyclare Antrim GB **207** N 10

Ballyclerahan Tipperary IRL **233** S 7

Ballyclogh Cork IRL **232** S 5

Ballycolla Laois IRL **233** R 8

Ballyconneely Galway IRL **218** Q 2

Ballyconnell Cavan IRL **206** O 7

Ballycotton Cork IRL **232/233** T 6

Ballycroy Mayo IRL **218** O 3

Ballycumber Offaly IRL **219** Q 7

Ballydangan Offaly IRL **218/219** Q 6

Ballydavid Galway IRL **218/219** Q 6

Ballydehob Cork IRL **232** T 4

Ballydesmond Cork IRL **232** S 4

Ballyduff Kerry IRL **232** S 3

Ballyduff Waterford IRL **232/233** S 6

Ballyfarnan Roscommon IRL 206 O 6

Ballyfeard Cork IRL 232/233 T 6

Ballyferriter Kerry IRL 232 S 2

Ballyfin Laois IRL 219 Q 8

Ballyforan Offaly IRL 218/219 Q 6

Ballygalley Antrim GB 207 N 11

Ballygar Galway IRL 218/219 P 6

Ballygarrett Wexford IRL 233 R 10

Ballygawley Sligo IRL 206 O 6

Ballygawley Tyrone GB 207 O 8

Ballyglass Mayo IRL 218 P 4

Ballygorman Donegal IRL 207 M 8

Ballygowan Down GB 207 O 11

Ballygrant Argyll and Bute GB 174 L 10

Ballyhaise Cavan IRL 207 O 8

Ballyhalbert Down GB 207 O 12

Ballyhale Kilkenny IRL 233 S 8

Ballyhaugh Argyll and Bute GB 174 J 9

Ballyhaunis Mayo IRL 218 P 5

Ballyheige Kerry IRL 232 S 3

Ballyhooly Cork IRL 232/233 S 6

Ballyjamesduff Cavan IRL 219 P 8

Ballykelly Londonderry GB 207 M 8

Ballylanders Limerick IRL 232/233 S 6

Ballyliffin Donegal IRL 207 M 8

Ballylongford Kerry IRL 232 R 3

Ballylooby Tipperary IRL 233 S 7

Ballylynan Laois IRL 233 R 8

Ballymacarbry Waterford IRL 233 S 7

Ballymachugh Cavan IRL 219 P 8

Ballymacoda Cork IRL 233 T 7

Ballymacward Galway IRL 218/219 Q 6

Ballymahon Longford IRL 219 P 7

Ballymakeery Cork IRL 232 T 4

Ballymakenny Louth IRL 219 P 10

Ballymena Antrim GB 207 N 10

Ballymoe Galway IRL 218/219 P 6

Ballymoney Antrim GB 207 M 9

Ballymore Westmeath IRL 219 Q 7

Ballymore Eustace Kildare IRL 219 Q 9

Ballymote Sligo IRL 206 O 5

Ballymurray Roscommon IRL 218/219 P 6

Ballynabragget Down GB 207 O 10

Ballynacally Clare IRL 232 R 4

Ballynacarrigy Westmeath IRL 219 P 7

Ballynacourty Waterford IRL 233 S 7

Ballynagore Westmeath IRL 219 Q 8

Ballynahinch Down GB 207 O 11

Ballynahown Westmeath IRL 219 Q 7

Ballynamallaght Tyrone GB 207 N 8

Ballynamult Waterford IRL 233 S 7

Ballynana Kerry IRL 232 S 2

Ballyneety Limerick IRL 232 R 5

Ballynoe Cork IRL 232/233 S 6

Ballynure Antrim GB 207 N 11

Ballyporeen Tipperary IRL 232/233 S 6

Ballyragget Kilkenny IRL 233 R 8

Ballyroan Laois IRL 233 R 8

Ballyronan Londonderry GB 207 N 9

Ballyroney Down GB 207 O 10

Ballysadare Sligo IRL 206 O 5

Ballyshannon Donegal IRL 206 N 6

Ballyshrule Galway IRL 218/219 Q 6

Ballytoohy Mayo IRL 218 P 3

Ballyvaghan Clare IRL 218 Q 4

Ballyvoy Antrim GB 207 M 10

Ballywalter Down GB 146 N 12

Ballyward Down GB 207 O 10

Ballywilliam Wexford IRL 233 S 9

Balmaclellan Dumfries and Galloway GB 146 M 14

Balmaha Stirling GB 160 K 13

Balmedie Aberdeenshire GB 187 H 18

Balmerino Fife GB 161 K 16

Balnacoil Highland GB 186/187 F 14

Balnacra Highland GB 186 H 12

Balnaguard Perth and Kinross GB 160/161 J 15

Balquhidder Stirling GB 160 K 14

Balrath Meath IRL 219 P 10

Balsham Cambridgeshire GB 101 S 23

Baltasound Shetland Islands GB 199 A 21

Baltimore Cork IRL 232 U 4

Baltinglass Wicklow IRL 233 R 9

Baltonsborough Somerset GB 53 U 17

Balvicar Argyll and Bute GB 174 K 11

Bamburgh Northumberland GB 161 L 19

Bamford Derbyshire GB 134 Q 19

Bampton Cumbria GB 146/147 N 17

Bampton Devon GB 53 V 16

Bampton Oxfordshire GB 70 T 19

Banada Sligo IRL 206 O 5

Banagher Offaly IRL 219 Q 7

Banbridge Down GB 207 O 10

Banbury Oxfordshire GB 100 S 20

Banchory Aberdeenshire GB 187 H 17

Bandon Cork IRL 232 T 5

Banff Aberdeenshire GB 187 G 17

Bangor Gwynedd GB 118/119 Q 14

Bangor Down GB 207 N 11

Bangor Mayo IRL 218 O 3

Bangor-is-y-coed Wrexham GB 119 Q 17

Bankend Dumfries and Galloway GB 146 M 15

Bankfoot Perth and Kinross GB 160/161 K 15

Banks Lancashire GB 119 P 17

Banks Cumbria GB 146/147 N 17

Bankshill Dumfries and Galloway GB 146 M 16

Bannockburn Stirling GB 160/161 K 15

Bansha Tipperary IRL 232/233 S 6

Banstead Surrey GB 71 U 22

Banteer Cork IRL 232 S 5

Bantry Cork IRL 232 T 4

Barabhas Na h-Eileanan an Iar GB 186 F 10

Barbon Cumbria GB 146/147 O 17

Bardney Lincolnshire GB 135 Q 22

Bardsea Cumbria GB 146 O 16

Barefield Clare IRL 232 R 5

Barford Warwickshire GB 100 S 19

Bargoed Caerphilly GB 87 T 16

Bargrennan Dumfries and Galloway GB 146 M 13

Barham Kent GB 71 U 25

Barking Greater London GB 71 T 23

Barkston Lincolnshire GB 100 R 21

Barkway Hertfordshire GB 71 T 23

Barlaston Staffordshire GB 100 R 18

Barlborough Derbyshire GB 134 Q 20

Barlby North Yorkshire GB 134 P 20

Barlestone Leicestershire GB 100 R 20

Barley Hertfordshire GB 101 S 23

Barley Lancashire GB 134 P 18

Barmby Moor East Riding of Yorkshire GB 134/135 P 21

Barmouth Gwynedd GB 86 R 14

Barmston East Riding of Yorkshire GB 135 O 22

Barna Galway IRL 218 Q 4

Barnaderg Galway IRL 218 Q 5

Barnard Castle Durham GB 147 N 19

Barnatra Mayo IRL 218 O 3

Barnet Greater London GB 71 T 22

Barnham Suffolk GB 101 S 24

Barnham Broom Norfolk GB 101 R 25

Barnhill Moray GB 187 G 16

Barningham Suffolk GB 101 S 24

Barningham Durham GB 147 O 19

Barnoldswick Lancashire GB 134 P 18

Barnsley Barnsley GB 134 P 20

Barnsley Gloucestershire GB 70 T 19

Barnstaple Devon GB 52/53 U 14

Barr South Ayrshire GB 146 M 13

Barrhead East Renfrewshire GB 160 L 14

Barrhill South Ayrshire GB 146 M 13

Barrow Suffolk GB 101 S 24

Barrowford Lancashire GB 134 P 18

Barrow-in-Furness Cumbria GB 146 O 16

Barry Vale of Glamorgan GB 53 U 16

Bartlow Cambridgeshire GB 101 S 23

Barton-le-Clay Bedfordshire GB 71 T 22

Barton-upon-Humber North Lincolnshire GB 135 P 22

Baschurch Shropshire GB 119 R 17

Basildon Essex GB 71 T 23

Basingstoke Hampshire GB 70 U 20

Bassenthwaite Cumbria GB 146 N 16

Bassingham Lincolnshire GB 134/135 Q 21

Bastardstown Wexford IRL 233 S 9

Baston Lincolnshire GB 100/101 R 22

Bastwick Norfolk GB 101 R 26

Bath Derbyshire GB 134 Q 19

Bath Bath & NE Somerset GB 70 U 18

Bathgate West Lothian GB 160/161 L 15

Batley Kirklees GB 134 P 19

Battle East Sussex GB 71 V 23

Battlesbridge Essex GB 71 T 24

Baumber Lincolnshire GB 135 Q 22

Bawburgh Norfolk GB 101 R 25

Bawdeswell Norfolk GB 101 R 25

Bawdsey Suffolk GB 101 S 25

Bawtry Doncaster GB 134 Q 20

Baydon Wiltshire GB 70 U 19

Bayston Hill Shropshire GB 87 R 17

Beachampton Buckinghamshire GB 100 S 21

Beaconsfield Buckinghamshire GB 70/71 T 21

Beadnell Northumberland GB 161 L 19

Beal Northumberland GB 161 L 19

Bealaclugga Clare IRL 218 Q 4

Bealaha Clare IRL 232 R 3

Beaminster Dorset GB 53 V 17

Beanley Northumberland GB 147 M 19

Beare Green Surrey GB 71 U 22

Bearley Warwickshire GB 100 S 19

Bearsden East Dunbartonshire GB 160 L 14

Beattock Dumfries and Galloway GB 146 M 16

Beaulieu Hampshire GB 70 V 20

Beauly Highland GB 186 H 14

Beaumaris Anglesey GB 118/119 Q 14

Beauworth Hampshire GB 70 U 20

Bebington Wirral GB 119 Q 16

Beccles Suffolk GB 101 S 26

Beck Row Suffolk GB 101 S 23

Beckermet Cumbria GB 146 O 15

Beckfoot Cumbria GB 146 N 16

Beckingham Lincolnshire GB 134/135 Q 21

Beckingham Nottinghamshire GB 134/135 Q 21

Beckington Somerset GB 70 U 18

Bective Meath IRL 219 P 9

Bedale North Yorkshire GB 147 O 19

Beddgelert Gwynedd GB 118/119 Q 14

Beddingham East Sussex GB 71 V 23

Bedford Bedfordshire GB 100/101 S 22

Bedlington Northumberland GB 147 M 19

Bedrule Scottish Borders GB 146/147 M 17

Bedwas Caerphilly GB 87 T 16

Bedworth Warwickshire GB 100 S 20

Bedwyn Wiltshire GB 70 U 19

Beeford East Riding of Yorkshire GB 135 P 22

Beeston Nottinghamshire GB 100 R 20

Beeswing Dumfries and Galloway GB 146 M 15

Beguildy Powys GB 87 S 16

Beith North Ayrshire GB 160 L 13

Belbroughton Worcestershire GB 87 S 18

Belchford Lincolnshire GB 135 Q 22

Belcoo Fermanagh GB 206 O 7

Belderg Mayo IRL 218 O 3

Beleek Fermanagh GB 206 O 6

Belfast Antrim GB 207 N 11

Belford Northumberland GB 161 L 19

Belgooly Cork IRL 232/233 T 6

Bellacorrick Mayo IRL 218 O 3

Bellaghy Londonderry GB 207 N 9

Bellanagare Roscommon IRL 218/219 P 6

Bellanagh Cavan IRL 219 P 8

Bellanaleck Fermanagh GB 206 O 7

Bellavary Mayo IRL 218 P 4

Belleaneeny Offaly IRL 218/219 Q 6

Bellingham Northumberland GB 147 M 18

Bellshill North Lanarkshire GB 160 L 14

Belmont Blackburn with Darwen GB 119 P 17

Belmont Shetland Islands GB 199 A 21

Belmullet Mayo IRL 218 O 3

Belnacraig Aberdeenshire GB 187 H 16

Belnapaling Highland GB 186/187 G 14

Belper Derbyshire GB 134 Q 19

Belsay Northumberland GB 147 M 19

Belton Norfolk GB 101 R 26

Belton North Lincolnshire GB 134/135 P 21

Beltra Sligo IRL 206 O 5

Beltra Mayo IRL 218 P 4

Belturbet Cavan IRL 207 O 8

Belville Mayo IRL 206 O 4

Belvoir Leicestershire GB 100 R 21

Bembridge Isle of Wight GB 70 V 20

Ben Alder Lodge Highland GB 160 J 14

Benburb Tyrone GB 207 O 9

Benderloch Argyll and Bute GB 160 K 12

Benllech Anglesey GB 118/119 Q 14

Bennettsbridge Kilkenny IRL **233** R 8

Benson Oxfordshire GB **70** T 20

Bentley Doncaster GB **134** P 20

Bentley Hampshire GB **70/71** U 21

Bentpath Dumfries and Galloway GB **146** M 16

Benville Dorset GB **53** V 17

Benwick Cambridgeshire GB **100/101** S 22

Beragh Tyrone GB **207** N 8

Bere Alston Devon GB **52/53** W 14

Bere Ferrers Devon GB **52/53** W 14

Bere Regis Dorset GB **70** V 18

Berkeley Gloucestershire GB **70** T 18

Berkhamsted Hertfordshire GB **70/71** T 21

Bernisdale Highland GB **175** H 10

Berriedale Highland GB **187** F 15

Berrynarbor Devon GB **52/53** U 14

Berwick-upon-Tweed Northumberl. GB **161** L 18

Bessbrook Armagh GB **207** O 10

Bethersden Kent GB **71** U 24

Bethesda Gwynedd GB **118/119** Q 14

Bettyhill Highland GB **186/187** E 14

Bettystown Meath IRL **219** P 10

Betws-y-Coed Conwy GB **119** Q 15

Beulah Ceredigion GB **86** S 14

Beulah Powys GB **86/87** S 15

Beverley East Riding of Yorkshire GB **135** P 22

Bewcastle Cumbria GB **146/147** M 17

Bewdley Worcestershire GB **87** S 18

Bexhill East Sussex GB **71** V 23

Beyton Suffolk GB **101** S 24

Bhaltos Na h-Eileanan an Iar GB **175** F 9

Bibury Gloucestershire GB **70** T 19

Bicester Oxfordshire GB **70** T 20

Bicker Lincolnshire GB **100/101** R 22

Bickington Devon GB **53** V 15

Bickley Moss Cheshire GB **119** Q 17

Biddenden Kent GB **71** U 24

Biddulph Staffordshire GB **134** Q 18

Bideford Devon GB **52/53** U 14

Bidford-on-Avon Warwickshire GB **100** S 19

Big Sand Highland GB **186** G 11

Bigbury-on-Sea Devon GB **53** W 15

Bigby Lincolnshire GB **135** P 22

Biggar South Lanarkshire GB **160/161** L 15

Biggin Hill Greater London GB **71** U 23

Biggleswade Bedfordshire GB **100/101** S 22

Bildeston Suffolk GB **101** S 24

Billericay Essex GB **71** T 23

Billesdon Leicestershire GB **100** R 21

Billingborough Lincolnshire GB **100/101** R 22

Billinge St Helens GB **119** Q 17

Billingham Stockton-on-Tees GB **147** N 20

Billinghay Lincolnshire GB **135** Q 22

Billingshurst West Sussex GB **71** U 22

Billingsley Shropshire GB **87** S 18

Binbrook Lincolnshire GB **135** Q 22

Bingham Nottinghamshire GB **100** R 21

Bingley Bradford GB **134** P 19

Binham Norfolk GB **101** R 24

Birdhill Tipperary IRL **232/233** R 6

Birdlip Gloucestershire GB **70** T 18

Birdsall North Yorkshire GB **134** O 21

Birkenhead Wirral GB **119** Q 16

Birmingham Birmingham GB **100** S 19

Birr Offaly IRL **219** Q 7

Birtley Northumberland GB **147** M 18

Birtley Gateshead GB **147** N 19

Bishampton Worcestershire GB **87** S 18

Bishop Auckland Durham GB **147** N 19

Bishop Burton East Riding of Yorkshire GB **134/135** P 21

Bishop´s Castle Shropshire GB **87** R 16

Bishop´s Waltham Hampshire GB **70** V 20

Bishops Cannings Wiltshire GB **70** U 19

Bishop's Cleeve Gloucestershire GB **70** T 18

Bishops Lydeard Somerset GB **53** U 16

Bishop's Stortford Hertfordshire GB **71** T 23

Bishop's Tawton Devon GB **52/53** U 14

Bishopston Swansea GB **86** T 14

Bishopton Renfrewshire GB **160** L 13

Bisley Gloucestershire GB **70** T 18

Bisley Surrey GB **70/71** U 21

Bittadon Devon GB **52/53** U 14

Bitterley Shropshire GB **87** S 17

Blackburn Blackburn with Darwen GB **134** P 18

Blackburn West Lothian GB **160/161** L 15

Blackburn Aberdeen City GB **187** H 18

Blackford Cumbria GB **146/147** N 17

Blackford Perth and Kinross GB **160/161** K 15

Blackhall Durham GB **147** N 20

Blacklunans Perth and Kinross GB **161** J 16

Blacklion Cavan IRL **206** O 7

Blackmill Bridgend GB **86/87** T 15

Blackpool Blackpool GB **119** P 16

Blackpool Limerick IRL **232** S 5

Blackrock Louth IRL **219** P 10

Blackthorn Oxfordshire GB **70** T 20

Blackwater Wexford IRL **233** S 10

Blackwater Bridge Kerry IRL **232** T 3

Blackwaterfoot North Ayrshire GB **160** L 12

Blackwatertown Armagh GB **207** O 9

Bladon Oxfordshire GB **70** T 20

Blaenau Ffestiniog Gwynedd GB **119** Q 15

Blaenavon Torfaen GB **87** T 16

Blagdon North Somerset GB **53** U 17

Blaich Highland GB **160** J 12

Blaina Blaenau Gwent GB **87** T 16

Blair Atholl Perth and Kinross GB **160/161** J 15

Blairgowrie Perth and Kinross GB **161** J 16

Blakemere Herefordshire GB **87** S 17

Blakeney Norfolk GB **101** R 25

Blakeney Gloucestershire GB **70** T 18

Blakesley Northhamptonshire GB **100** S 20

Blanchland Northumberland GB **147** N 18

Blandford Forum Dorset GB **70** V 18

Blanefield Stirling GB **160** L 14

Blarnalearoch Highland GB **186** G 12

Blarney Cork IRL **232** T 5

Blaydon Gateshead GB **147** N 19

Bleadon North Somerset GB **53** U 17

Bleasby Nottinghamshire GB **134/135** Q 21

Bledington Oxfordshire GB **70** T 19

Blencarn Cumbria GB **146/147** N 17

Blessington Wicklow IRL **219** Q 9

Blewbury Oxfordshire GB **70** T 20

Blidworth Nottinghamshire GB **134** Q 20

Blisworth Northhamptonshire GB **100** S 21

Blockley Gloucestershire GB **70** T 19

Blofield Norfolk GB **101** R 25

Bloxham Oxfordshire GB **100** S 20

Blubberhouses North Yorkshire GB **134** P 19

Blue Ball Offaly IRL **219** Q 7

Bluntisham Cambridgeshire GB **101** S 23

Blyth Nottinghamshire GB **134** Q 20

Blyth Northumberland GB **147** M 20

Blythburgh Suffolk GB **101** S 26

Blythe Bridge Staffordshire GB **100** R 18

Blyton Lincolnshire GB **134/135** Q 21

Bo´ness Falkirk GB **160/161** K 15

Boarhills Fife GB **161** K 17

Boat of Garten Highland GB **187** H 15

Boath Highland GB **186/187** G 14

Bocking Churchstreet Essex GB **71** T 24

Boddam Aberdeenshire GB **187** H 19

Boddam Shetland Islands GB **199** C 20

Bodedern Anglesey GB **118** Q 13

Bodiam East Sussex GB **71** U 24

Bodmin Cornwall GB **52** W 13

Boduan Gwynedd GB **118** R 13

Bodyke Clare IRL **232** R 5

Bofin Mayo IRL **218** P 2

Bognor Regis West Sussex GB **70/71** V 21

Boharboy Louth IRL **207** O 10

Boheeshil Kerry IRL **232** T 3

Boheraphuca Offaly IRL **219** Q 7

Boherboy Cork IRL **232** S 4

Bohola Mayo IRL **218** P 4

Boldon South Tyneside GB **147** N 20

Boldre Hampshire GB **70** V 19

Bollington Cheshire GB **134** Q 18

Bolsover Derbyshire GB **134** Q 20

Boltby North Yorkshire GB **147** O 20

Bolton Bolton GB **134** P 18

Bolton Northumberland GB **147** M 19

Bolton Abbey North Yorkshire GB **134** P 19

Bolton Percy North Yorkshire GB **134** P 20

Bolton-by-Bowland Lancashire GB **134** P 18

Bolton-le-Sands Lancashire GB **146/147** O 17

Bolventor Cornwall GB **52** V 13

Bonar Bridge Highland GB **186/187** G 14

Boncath Pembrokeshire GB **86** S 13

Bonchester Bridge Scottish Borders GB **146/147** M 17

Bonhill West Dunbartonshire GB **160** L 13

Bonnington Kent GB **71** U 24

Bonnybridge Falkirk GB **160/161** L 15

Bonnyrigg Midlothian GB **161** L 16

Bont-goch or Elerch Ceredigion GB **86/87** S 15

Bonvilston Vale of Glamorgan GB **53** U 15

Boosbeck Redcar & Cleveland GB **147** N 21

Boot Cumbria GB **146** O 16

Booth of Toft Shetland Islands GB **199** B 20

Bootle Salford GB **119** Q 17

Bootle Cumbria GB **146** O 16

Borehamwood Hertfordshire GB **71** T 22

Boreland Dumfries and Galloway GB **146** M 16

Borgh Na h-Eileanan an Iar GB **175** G 8

Borgh Na h-Eileanan an Iar GB **175** J 7

Borgue Dumfries and Galloway GB **146** N 14

Boroughbridge North Yorkshire GB **147** O 20

Borreraig Highland GB **175** H 9

Borris Carlow IRL **233** R 9

Borris in Ossory Laois IRL **233** R 7

Borrisokane Tipperary IRL **232/233** R 6

Borrisoleigh Tipperary IRL **233** R 7

Borrowdale Cumbria GB **146** N 16

Borth Ceredigion GB **86** S 14

Borve Na h-Eileanan an Iar GB **175** G 8

Borve Highland GB **175** H 10

Borwick Lancashire GB **146/147** O 17

Bosbury Herefordshire GB **87** S 18

Boscastle Cornwall GB **52** V 13

Bosherston Pembrokeshire GB **86** T 13

Boston Lincolnshire GB **100/101** R 22

Boston Spa Leeds GB **134** P 20

Botesdale Suffolk GB **101** S 25

Bothel Cumbria GB **146** N 16

Botley Hampshire GB **70** V 20

Bottesford Leicestershire GB **100** R 21

Bottisham Cambridgeshire GB **101** S 23

Boulmer Northumberland GB **147** M 19

Bourne Lincolnshire GB **100/101** R 22

Bournemouth Bournemouth GB **70** V 19

Bourton Dorset GB **70** U 18

Bourton-on-the-Water Gloucestershire GB **70** T 19

Bovey Tracey Devon GB **53** V 15

Bovingdon Hertfordshire GB **70/71** T 21

Bow Orkney Islands GB **198** E 16

Bow Devon GB **53** V 15

Bowburn Durham GB **147** N 19

Bowden Scottish Borders GB **161** L 17

Bowes Durham GB **147** N 19

Bowmore Argyll and Bute GB **174** L 10

Bowness-on-Solway Cumbria GB **146** N 16

Bowness-on-Windermere Cumbria GB **146/147** O 17

Bowsden Northumberland GB **161** L 19

Box Wiltshire GB **70** U 18

Boxford Suffolk GB **101** S 24

Boyle Roscommon IRL **218/219** P 6

Boynton East Riding of Yorkshire GB **135** O 22

Boyton Cornwall GB **52/53** V 14

Bozeat Northhamptonshire GB **100** S 21

Braaid Isle of Man GB **146** O 13

Brabourne Lees Kent GB **71** U 25

Bracadale Highland GB **175** H 10

Brackley Buckinghamshire GB **100** S 20

Brackley Northhamptonshire GB **100** S 20

Bracknell Bracknell Forest GB **70/71** U 21

Braco Perth and Kinross GB **160/161** K 15

Bracora Highland GB **175** J 11

Bradford Bradford GB **134** P 19

Bradford Abbas Dorset GB **53** V 17

Bradford-on-Avon Wiltshire GB **70** U 18

Bradninch Devon GB **53** V 16

Bradwell Derbyshire GB **134** Q 19

Bradwell Waterside Essex GB **71** T 24

Bradworthy Devon GB **52/53** V 14

Brae Shetland Islands GB **199** B 20

Brae Roy Lodge Highland GB **160** J 13

Braehead South Lanarkshire GB **160/161** L 15

Braemar Aberdeenshire GB **161** H 16

Braemore Highland GB **186** G 12

Braemore Highland GB **187** F 15

Braeswick Orkney Islands GB **198** D 17

Brafferton North Yorkshire GB **147** O 20

Bragar Na h-Eileanan an Iar GB **175** F 9

Brailsford Derbyshire GB **100** R 19

Braintree Essex GB **71** T 24

Braishfield Hampshire GB **70** U 20

Braithwaite Cumbria GB **146** N 16

Braithwell Doncaster GB **134** Q 20

Bramdean Hampshire GB **70** U 20

Bramfield Suffolk GB **101** S 26

Bramford Suffolk GB **101** S 25

Bramham Leeds GB **134** P 20

Bramhope Leeds GB **134** P 19

Bramley Hampshire GB **70** U 20

Brampton Cambridgeshire GB **100/101** S 22

Brampton Suffolk GB **101** S 26

Brampton Cumbria GB **146/147** N 17

Bramshaw Hampshire GB **70** V 19

Brancaster Norfolk GB **101** R 24

Branderburgh Moray GB **187** G 16

Brandesburton East Riding of Yorkshire GB **135** P 22

Brandon Suffolk GB **101** S 24

Brandon Durham GB **147** N 19

Brandsby North Yorkshire GB **147** O 20

Branscombe Devon GB **53** V 16

Bransgore Hampshire GB **70** V 19

Branston Leicestershire GB **100** R 21

Branston Lincolnshire GB **135** Q 22

Branxton Northumberland GB **161** L 18

Brassington Derbyshire GB **134** Q 19

Bratton Clovelly Devon GB **52/53** V 14

Bratton Fleming Devon GB **53** U 15

Braughing Hertfordshire GB **71** T 23

Braunston Northhamptonshire GB **100** S 20

Braunton Devon GB **52/53** U 14

Bray Bré Wicklow IRL **219** Q 10

Brayford Devon GB **53** U 15

Breage Cornwall GB **52** W 12

Breamore Hampshire GB **70** V 19

Brean Somerset GB **53** U 16

Breanais Na h-Eileanan an Iar GB **176** F 8

Breascleit Na h-Eileanan an Iar GB **175** F 9

Brechfa Carmarthenshire GB **86** T 14

Brechin Angus GB **161** J 18

Brecon Aberhonddu Powys GB **87** T 16

Brede East Sussex GB **71** V 24

Bredgar Kent GB **71** U 24

Bredon Worcestershire GB **87** S 18

Breedon on the Hill Leicestershire GB **100** R 20

Brendon Devon GB **53** U 15

Brent Pelham Hertfordshire GB **71** T 23

Brentwood Essex GB **71** T 23

Brewood Staffordshire GB **100** R 18

Brickeens Mayo IRL **218** P 5

Bride Isle of Man GB **146** O 14

Bridestowe Devon GB **52/53** V 14

Bridge Kent GB **71** U 25

Bridge End Donegal IRL **207** M 8

Bridge of Allan Stirling GB **160/161** K 15

Bridge of Balgie Perth and Kinross GB **160** J 14

Bridge of Cally Perth and Kinross GB **161** J 16

Bridge of Dee Dumfries and Galloway GB **146** N 15

Bridge of Don Aberdeen City GB **187** H 18

Bridge of Dun Angus GB **161** J 18

Bridge of Earn Perth and Kinross GB **161** K 16

Bridge of Gaur Perth and Kinross GB **160** J 14

Bridge of Weir Renfrewshire GB **160** L 13

Bridgend Angus GB **161** J 18

Bridgend Argyll and Bute GB **174** L 10

Bridgend Moray GB **187** H 16

Bridgend Peny-y-Bont Ar Ogwr Bridgend GB **53** U 15

Bridgerule Devon GB **52/53** V 14

Bridgetown Wexford IRL **233** S 9

Bridgnorth Shropshire GB **100** R 18

Bridgwater Somerset GB **53** U 16

Bridlington East Riding of Yorkshire GB **135** O 22

Bridport Dorset GB **53** V 17

Brierfield Lancashire GB **134** P 18

Brig o'Turk Stirling GB **160** K 14

Brigg North Lincolnshire GB **135** P 22

Brigham Cumbria GB **146** N 16

Brighouse Calderdale GB **134** P 19

Brighstone Isle of Wight GB **70** V 20

Brightlingsea Essex GB **71** T 25

Brighton Cornwall GB **52** W 13

Brighton Brighton & Hove GB **71** V 22

Brigstock Northhamptonshire GB **100** S 21

Brill Buckinghamshire GB **70** T 20

Brinian Orkney Islands GB **198** D 17

Brinkhill Lincolnshire GB **135** Q 23

Brinkley Cambridgeshire GB **101** S 23

Brinklow Warwickshire GB **100** S 20

Brinkworth Wiltshire GB **70** T 19

Bristol Bristol GB **53** U 17

Brithdir Gwynedd GB **119** R 15

Briton Ferry Neath Port Talbot GB **86/87** T 15

Brittas Dublin IRL **219** Q 10

Brixham Torbay GB **53** W 15

Brixworth Northhamptonshire GB **100** S 21

Brize Norton Oxfordshire GB **70** T 19

Broad Chalke Wiltshire GB **70** U 19

Broad Haven Pembrokeshire GB **86** T 12

Broad Hinton Wiltshire GB **70** U 19

Broadclyst Devon GB **53** V 16

Broadford Highland GB **175** H 11

Broadford Clare IRL **232** R 5

Broadford Limerick IRL **232** S 5

Broadhembury Devon GB **53** V 16

Broadley Moray GB **187** G 16

Broadmayne Dorset GB **70** V 18

Broadstairs Kent GB **71** U 25

Broadway Worcestershire GB **100** S 19

Broadway Somerset GB **53** V 17

Broadwindsor Dorset GB **53** V 17

Brochel Highland GB **175** H 10

Brockenhurst Hampshire GB **70** V 19

Brodick North Ayrshire GB **160** L 12

Brodie Moray GB **187** G 15

Bromborough Wirral GB **119** Q 16

Bromfield Shropshire GB **87** S 17

Bromham Bedfordshire GB **100** S 21

Bromham Wiltshire GB **70** U 18

Bromley Greater London GB **71** U 22

Brompton North Yorkshire GB **134** O 21

Brompton North Yorkshire GB **147** O 19

Brompton North Yorkshire GB **147** O 20

Brompton Ralph Somerset GB **53** U 16

Brompton Regis Somerset GB **53** U 15

Bromsgrove Worcestershire GB **87** S 18

Bromyard Herefordshire GB **87** S 17

Brook Isle of Wight GB **70** V 20

Brooke Norfolk GB **101** R 25

Brookeborough Fermanagh GB **207** O 8

Brookhouse Lancashire GB **146/147** O 17

Brookland Kent GB **71** V 24

Broom Warwickshire GB **100** S 19

Broomfield Monaghan IRL **207** O 9

Broomfleet East Riding of Yorkshire GB **134/135** P 21

Broomhill Northumberland GB **147** M 19

Brora Highland GB **187** F 15

Broseley Shropshire GB **100** R 18

Brotton Redcar & Cleveland GB **147** N 21

Brough Cumbria GB **147** N 18

Brough Highland GB **198** E 16

Brough Shetland Islands GB **199** B 21

Broughshane Antrim GB **207** N 10

Broughton Northhamptonshire GB **100** S 21

Broughton Lancashire GB **119** P 17

Broughton Flintshire GB **119** Q 17

Broughton Scottish Borders GB **161** L 16

Broughton Hampshire GB **70** U 19

Broughton Astley Leicestershire GB **100** R 20

Broughton Poggs Oxfordshire GB **70** T 19

Broughton-in-Furness Cumbria GB **146** O 16

Broughtown Orkney Islands GB **198** D 17

Brownhills Walsall GB **100** R 19

Brownston Devon GB **53** W 15

Brownstown Meath IRL **219** P 9

Broxburn West Lothian GB **161** L 16

Bruff Limerick IRL **232** S 5

Brundall Norfolk GB **101** R 25

Brundish Suffolk GB **101** S 25

Bruree Limerick IRL **232** S 5

Bruton Somerset GB **70** U 18

Bryansford Down GB **207** O 11

Brydekirk Dumfries and Galloway GB **146** M 16

Brynamman Carmarthenshire GB **86/87** T 15

Brynmawr Blaenau Gwent GB **87** T 16

Brynsiencyn Anglesey GB **118/119** Q 14

Bubwith East Riding of Yorkshire GB **134/135** P 21

Buchlyvie Stirling GB **160** K 14

Buckden North Yorkshire GB **147** O 18

Buckfastleigh Devon GB **53** W 15

Buckhaven Fife GB **161** K 16

Buckie Moray GB **187** G 17

Buckingham Buckinghamshire GB **100** S 21

Buckland Oxfordshire GB **70** T 19

Buckland Hertfordshire GB **71** T 22

Bromyard Herefordshire GB **87** S 17

Buckland Brewer Devon GB **52/53** V 14

Bucklers Hard Hampshire GB **70** V 20

Buckley Flintshire GB **119** Q 16

Bucknall Lincolnshire GB **135** Q 22

Bucknell Shropshire GB **87** S 17

Bucksburn Aberdeen City GB **187** H 18

Bude Cornwall GB **52** V 13

Budleigh Salterton Devon GB **53** V 16

Bugbrooke Northhamptonshire GB **100** S 20

Bugle Cornwall GB **52** W 13

Builth Wells Llanfair-ym-Muallt Powys GB **87** S 16

Bulford Wiltshire GB **70** U 19

Bulkeley Cheshire GB **119** Q 17

Bulmer North Yorkshire GB **134** O 21

Bunacaimb Highland GB **175** J 11

Bunacurry Mayo IRL **218** P 3

Bunane Kerry IRL **232** T 3

Bunbeg Donegal IRL **206** M 6

Bunbrosna Westmeath IRL **219** P 8

Bunbury Cheshire GB **119** Q 17

Bunclody Wexford IRL **233** R 9

Buncrana Donegal IRL **207** M 8

Bundoran Donegal IRL **206** O 6

Bunessan Argyll and Bute GB **174** K 10

Bunmahon Waterford IRL **233** S 8

Bunnahabhain Argyll and Bute GB **174** L 10

Bunnahowen Mayo IRL **218** O 3

Bunnanaddan Sligo IRL **206** O 5

Bunratty Clare IRL **232** R 5

Buntingford Hertfordshire GB **71** T 22

Burbage Wiltshire GB **70** U 19

Bures Essex GB **71** T 24

Burford Oxfordshire GB **70** T 19

Burgess Hill West Sussex GB **71** V 22

Burgh Castle Norfolk GB **101** R 26

Burgh le Marsh Lincolnshire GB **135** Q 23

Burghead Moray GB **187** G 15

Burley Hampshire GB **70** V 19

Burley Gate Herefordshire GB **87** S 17

Burlton Shropshire GB **119** R 17

Burmington Warwickshire GB **100** S 19

Burneside Cumbria GB **146/147** O 17

Burneston North Yorkshire GB **147** O 19

Burnfoot Scottish Borders GB **146/147** M 17

Burnfoot Donegal IRL **207** M 8

Burnham Market Norfolk GB **101** R 24

Burnham-on-Crouch Essex GB **71** T 24

Burnham-on-Sea Somerset GB **53** U 16

Burnley Lancashire GB **134** P 18

Burnmouth Scottish Borders GB **161** L 18

Burnopfield Durham GB **147** N 19

Burnsall North Yorkshire GB **147** O 19

Burntisland Fife GB **161** K 16

Burrafirth Shetland Islands GB **199** A 21
Burravoe Shetland Islands GB **199** A 20
Burrelton Perth and Kinross GB **161** J 16
Burren Clare IRL **218** Q 4
Burry Port Carmarthenshire GB **86** T 14
Burton Cheshire GB **119** Q 16
Burton Agnes East Riding of Yorkshire GB **135** O 22
Burton Bradstock Dorset GB **53** V 17
Burton Constable East Riding of Yorkshire GB **135** P 22
Burton Fleming East Riding of Yorkshire GB **135** O 22
Burton in Lonsdale North Yorkshire GB **146/147** O 17
Burton Joyce Nottinghamshire GB **100** R 20
Burton Latimer Northhamptonshire GB **100** S 21
Burton Pidsea East Riding of Yorkshire GB **135** P 22
Burton upon Stather North Lincolns. GB **134/135** P 21
Burton-in-Kendal Cumbria GB **146/147** O 17
Burtonport Donegal IRL **206** N 6
Burton-upon-Trent Staffordshire GB **100** R 19
Burwardsley Cheshire GB **119** Q 17
Burwash East Sussex GB **71** U 23
Burwell Cambridgeshire GB **101** S 23
Burwick Orkney Islands GB **198** E 17
Bury Bury GB **134** P 18
Bury St. Edmunds Suffolk GB **101** S 24
Busby East Renfrewshire GB **160** L 14
Buscough Bridge Lancashire GB **119** P 17
Bushey Hertfordshire GB **71** T 22
Bushmills Antrim GB **207** M 9
Butleigh Somerset GB **53** U 17
Butlers Bridge Cavan IRL **207** O 8
Butlerstown Cork IRL **232** T 5
Butley Suffolk GB **101** S 25
Buttermere Cumbria GB **146** N 16
Butterwick Lincolnshire GB **101** R 23
Buttevant Cork IRL **232** S 5
Buxton Norfolk GB **101** R 25
Buxton Derbyshire GB **134** Q 19
Byfield Northhamptonshire GB **100** S 20
Byfleet Surrey GB **71** U 22
Bylchau Conwy GB **119** Q 15
Byrness Northumberland GB **147** M 18

C

Cabrach Moray GB **187** H 16
Cadbury Devon GB **53** V 15
Cadnam Hampshire GB **70** V 19
Caerdydd Cardiff Cardiff GB **53** U 16
Caerfyrddin Carmarthenshire GB **86** T 14

Caergwrle Flintshire GB **119** Q 16
Caergybi Holyhead Anglesey GB **118** Q 13
Caerleon Newport GB **87** T 17
Caernarfon Gwynedd GB **118/119** Q 14
Caerphilly Caerphilly GB **87** T 16
Caersws Powys GB **87** S 16
Caerwent Monmouthshire GB **87** T 17
Caerwys Flintshire GB **119** Q 16
Caherconell Clare IRL **218** Q 4
Caherconlish Limerick IRL **232/233** R 6
Cahersiveen Cathair Saidhbhín Kerry IRL **70** T 2
Cahir Tipperary IRL **233** S 7
Cairinis Na h-Eileanan an Iar GB **175** H 8
Cairnbaan Argyll and Bute GB **160** K 12
Cairncross Angus GB **161** J 18
Cairndow Argyll and Bute GB **160** K 13
Cairnryan Dumfries and Galloway GB **146** N 12
Caister-on-Sea Norfolk GB **101** R 26
Caistor Lincolnshire GB **135** Q 22
Calanais Na h-Eileanan an Iar GB **175** F 9
Calbourne Isle of Wight GB **70** V 20
Caldbeck Cumbria GB **146** N 16
Calder Bridge Cumbria GB **146** O 16
Calder Mains Highland GB **198** E 15
Caldicot Monmouthshire GB **87** T 17
Caldwell North Yorkshire GB **147** N 19
Caledon Tyrone GB **207** O 9
Calgary Argyll and Bute GB **174** J 10
Callan Kilkenny IRL **233** R 8
Callander Stirling GB **160** K 14
Callington Cornwall GB **52/53** V 14
Callow Mayo IRL **218** P 4
Calne Wiltshire GB **70** U 18
Calshot Hampshire GB **70** V 20
Calthwaite Cumbria GB **146/147** N 17
Caltra Galway IRL **218/219** Q 6
Calvine Perth and Kinross GB **160/161** J 15
Camaross Wexford IRL **233** S 9
Camastianavaig Highland GB **175** H 10
Camb Shetland Islands GB **199** A 20
Camber East Sussex GB **71** V 24
Camberley Surrey GB **70/71** U 21
Cambo Northumberland GB **147** M 19
Cambois Northumberland GB **147** M 19
Camborne Cornwall GB **52** W 12
Cambridge Cambridgeshire GB **101** S 23
Cambustbarron Stirling GB **160/161** K 15
Camelford Cornwall GB **52** V 13
Camlough Armagh GB **207** O 10

Camolin Wexford IRL **233** R 10
Camp Kerry IRL **232** S 3
Campbeltown Argyll and Bute GB **174** M 11
Camus Galway IRL **218** Q 3
Camusnagaul Highland GB **160** J 12
Camusnagaul Highland GB **186** G 12
Candlesby Lincolnshire GB **135** Q 23
Canewdon Essex GB **71** T 24
Cannich Highland GB **186** H 13
Canningstown Cavan IRL **219** P 8
Cannington Somerset GB **53** U 16
Cannock Staffordshire GB **100** R 18
Canonbie Dumfries and Galloway GB **146/147** M 17
Canterbury Kent GB **71** U 25
Cantley Norfolk GB **101** R 26
Canvey Thurrock GB **71** T 24
Caol Highland GB **160** J 12
Caolas Argyll and Bute GB **174** J 9
Capel Surrey GB **71** U 22
Capel Curig Conwy GB **119** Q 15
Capel St Mary Suffolk GB **101** S 25
Capheaton Northumberland GB **147** M 19
Cappagh White Tipperary IRL **232/233** R 6
Cappamore Limerick IRL **232/233** R 6
Cappeen Cork IRL **232** T 4
Cappercleuch Scottish Borders GB **146** M 16
Cappoquin Waterford IRL **233** S 7
Capthorne Surrey GB **71** U 22
Caputh Perth and Kinross GB **161** J 16
Caragh Lake Kerry IRL **232** S 3
Carbost Highland GB **175** H 10
Carbury Kildare IRL **219** Q 9
Cardiff Caerdydd Cardiff GB **53** U 16
Cardigan Aberteifi Ceredigion GB **86** S 13
Cardington Bedfordshire GB **100/101** S 22
Cardington Shropshire GB **87** R 17
Cardross Argyll and Bute GB **160** L 13
Carew Pembrokeshire GB **86** T 13
Carham Scottish Borders GB **161** L 18
Cark Cumbria GB **146/147** O 17
Carlabhagh Na h-Eileanan an Iar GB **175** F 9
Carlanstown Meath IRL **219** P 9
Carlingcott Bath & NE Somerset GB **70** U 18
Carlingford Louth IRL **207** O 10
Carlisle Cumbria GB **146/147** N 17
Carlops Scottish Borders GB **161** L 16
Carlow Ceatharlach Carlow IRL **233** R 9
Carlton North Yorkshire GB **134** P 20

Carlton North Yorkshire GB **147** O 19
Carlton in Cleveland North Yorkshire GB **147** O 20
Carlton in Lindrick Nottinghamshire GB **134** Q 20
Carlton-on-Trent Nottinghamshire GB **134/135** Q 21
Carluke South Lanarkshire GB **160/161** L 15
Carmarthen/ Carmarthenshire GB **86** T 14
Cárna Galway IRL **218** Q 3
Carnach Na h-Eileanan an Iar GB **175** G 9
Carnach Highland GB **186** H 12
Carnagh Armagh GB **207** O 9
Carnaross Meath IRL **219** P 9
Carnbee Fife GB **161** K 17
Carncastle Antrim GB **207** N 11
Carndonagh Donegal IRL **207** M 8
Carnew Wicklow IRL **233** R 9
Carnforth Lancashire GB **146/147** O 17
Carnlough Antrim GB **207** N 10
Carno Powys GB **86/87** R 15
Carnock Fife GB **160/161** K 15
Carnoustie Angus GB **161** K 17
Carnteel Tyrone GB **207** O 9
Carnwath South Lanarkshire GB **160/161** L 15
Carr Shield Northumberland GB **147** N 18
Carracastle Mayo IRL **218** P 5
Carradale Argyll and Bute GB **160** L 12
Carraroe Galway IRL **218** Q 3
Carrbridge Highland GB **187** H 15
Carrick Wexford IRL **233** S 9
Carrick Castle Argyll and Bute GB **160** K 13
Carrick Ho Orkney Islands GB **198** D 17
Carrickart Donegal IRL **206** M 7
Carrickfergus Antrim GB **207** N 11
Carrickmacross Monaghan IRL **219** P 9
Carrickmore Tyrone GB **207** N 8
Carrick-on-Shannon Leitrim IRL **218/219** P 6
Carrick-on-Suir Carraig na Siúre Tipperary IRL **233** S 8
Carrigaholt Clare IRL **232** R 3
Carrigahorig Tipperary IRL **218/219** Q 6
Carrigaline Cork IRL **232/233** T 6
Carrigallen Leitrim IRL **219** P 7
Carriganimmy Cork IRL **232** T 4
Carronbridge Dumfries and Galloway GB **146** M 15
Carrowbehy Roscommon IRL **218** P 5
Carrowdore Down GB **207** N 11
Carrowkeel Donegal IRL **206** M 7
Carrowmoreknock Galway IRL **218** Q 4
Carrowrory Longford IRL **219** P 7
Carryduff Down GB **207** N 11
Carsaig Argyll and Bute GB **174** K 11
Carskiey Argyll and Bute GB **174** M 11
Carsluith Dumfries and Galloway GB **146** N 14

Carspshairn Dumfries and Galloway GB **146** M 14
Carstairs South Lanarkshire GB **160/161** L 15
Carterton Oxfordshire GB **70** T 19
Cartmel Cumbria GB **146/147** O 17
Cartmel Fell Cumbria GB **146/147** O 17
Cas-Gwent Chepstow Monmouthshire GB **87** T 17
Cashel Galway IRL **218** Q 3
Cashel Tipperary IRL **233** R 7
Cashleen Galway IRL **218** P 2
Cashlie Perth and Kinross GB **160** J 14
Casla Galway IRL **218** Q 3
Casnewydd Newport Newport GB **87** T 17
Castle Acre Norfolk GB **101** R 24
Castle Bolton North Yorkshire GB **147** O 19
Castle Bytham Lincolnshire GB **100** R 21
Castle Carrock Cumbria GB **146/147** N 17
Castle Cary Somerset GB **53** U 17
Castle Donington Leicestershire GB **100** R 20
Castle Douglas Dumfries and Galloway GB **146** N 15
Castle Frome Herefordshire GB **87** S 18
Castlebaldwin Sligo IRL **206** O 6
Castlebar Caisleán an Bharráigh Mayo IRL **218** P 4
Castlebay Bagh a'Chaisteil Na h-Eileanan an Iar GB **175** J 8
Castlebellingham Louth IRL **219** P 10
Castleblayney Monaghan IRL **207** O 9
Castlebridge Wexford IRL **233** S 10
Castlecaulfield Tyrone GB **207** N 9
Castlecomer Kilkenny IRL **233** R 8
Castleconnell Limerick IRL **232/233** R 6
Castlecor Cork IRL **232** S 5
Castlederg Tyrone GB **206** N 7
Castledermot Kildare IRL **233** R 9
Castlefinn Donegal IRL **206** N 7
Castleford Wakefield GB **134** P 20
Castlefreke Cork IRL **232** T 5
Castlegregory Kerry IRL **232** S 2
Castlehill Mayo IRL **206** O 4
Castleisland Kerry IRL **232** S 4
Castlemaine Kerry IRL **232** S 3
Castlemartin Pembrokeshire GB **86** T 12
Castlemartyr Cork IRL **232/233** T 6
Castleplunket Roscommon IRL **218/219** P 6
Castlepollard Westmeath IRL **219** P 8
Castlequarter Galway IRL **218** Q 4
Castlerea Roscommon IRL **218** P 5
Castleside Durham GB **147** N 19

Castleton North Yorkshire GB **147** O 21

Castletown Isle of Man GB **146** O 13

Castletown Highland GB **198** E 16

Castletown Westmeath IRL **219** Q 8

Castletown Laois IRL **233** R 8

Castletown Bearhaven Cork IRL **232** T 3

Castletownroche Cork IRL **232** S 5

Castletownshend Cork IRL **232** T 4

Castlewellan Down GB **207** O 11

Caston Norfolk GB **101** R 24

Caterham Surrey GB **71** U 22

Catfield Norfolk GB **101** R 26

Catlowdy Cumbria GB **146/147** M 17

Catrine East Ayrshire GB **146** M 14

Catterall Lancashire GB **119** P 17

Catterick North Yorkshire GB **147** O 19

Catterick Garrison North Yorkshire GB **147** O 19

Catterline Aberdeenshire GB **161** J 18

Catton Northumberland GB **147** N 18

Caulkerbush Dumfries and Galloway GB **146** N 15

Caunton Nottinghamshire GB **134/135** Q 21

Causeway Kerry IRL **232** S 3

Cavan Cavan IRL **219** P 8

Cavendish Suffolk GB **101** S 24

Cavenham Suffolk GB **101** S 24

Cawdor Highland GB **187** G 15

Cawood North Yorkshire GB **134** P 20

Cawston Norfolk GB **101** R 25

Caypole Lincolnshire GB **134/135** Q 21

Ceann a Bhàigh Na h-Eileanan an Iar GB **175** G 8

Cearsiadair Na h-Eileanan an Iar GB **175** F 9

Celbridge Kildare IRL **219** Q 9

Cemaes Anglesey GB **118/119** Q 14

Cemmaes Powys GB **86/87** R 15

Ceòs Na h-Eileanan an Iar GB **186** F 10

Ceres Fife GB **161** K 17

Cerne Abbas Dorset GB **70** V 18

Cerrigydrudion Conwy GB **119** Q 15

Chacewater Cornwall GB **52** W 12

Chaddesley Corbett Worcestershire GB **87** S 18

Chagford Devon GB **53** V 15

Chale Isle of Wight GB **70** V 20

Chalfont St. Giles Buckinghamshire GB **70/71** T 21

Challacombe Devon GB **53** U 15

Challerton Northumberland GB **147** M 18

Chanonrock Louth IRL **219** P 9

Chapel St Leonards Lincolnshire GB **135** Q 23

Chapel-en-le-Frith Derbyshire GB **134** Q 19

Chapelton South Lanarkshire GB **160** L 14

Chapeltown Sheffield GB **134** Q 20

Chapeltown Moray GB **187** H 16

Chapmans Well Devon GB **52/53** V 14

Chard Somerset GB **53** V 17

Chardstock Devon GB **53** V 17

Charing Kent GB **71** U 24

Charlbury Oxfordshire GB **70** T 20

Charlestown Mayo IRL **218** P 5

Charlestown of Aberlour Moray GB **187** H 16

Charleville Cork IRL **232** S 5

Charlton Wiltshire GB **70** T 18

Charlton Horethorne Somerset GB **70** U 18

Charlton-on-Otmoor Oxfordshire GB **70** T 20

Charlwood Surrey GB **71** U 22

Charmouth Dorset GB **53** V 17

Charwelton Northhamptonshire GB **100** S 20

Chatburn Lancashire GB **134** P 18

Chatham Medway GB **71** U 24

Chathill Northumberland GB **161** L 19

Chatteris Cambridgeshire GB **101** S 23

Chatton Northumberland GB **161** L 19

Chawleigh Devon GB **53** V 15

Cheadle Staffordshire GB **100** R 19

Cheadle Stockport GB **134** Q 18

Chedburgh Suffolk GB **101** S 24

Cheddar Somerset GB **53** U 17

Cheddleton Staffordshire GB **134** Q 18

Chelford Cheshire GB **134** Q 18

Chellaston Derby GB **100** R 20

Chelmsford Essex GB **71** T 23

Cheltenham Gloucestershire GB **70** T 18

Chepstow Cas-Gwent Monmouthshire GB **87** T 17

Cherhill Wiltshire GB **70** U 19

Cheriton Hampshire GB **70** U 20

Cheriton Bishop Devon GB **53** V 15

Cheriton Fitzpaine Devon GB **53** V 15

Chertsey Surrey GB **70/71** U 21

Chesham Buckinghamshire GB **70/71** T 21

Cheshunt Hertfordshire GB **71** T 22

Chester Cheshire GB **119** Q 17

Chesterfield Derbyshire GB **134** Q 20

Chester-le-Street Durham GB **147** N 19

Chesters Scottish Borders GB **146/147** M 17

Cheswardine Shropshire GB **100** R 18

Cheswick Northumberland GB **161** L 19

Chevington Northumberland GB **147** M 19

Chew Magna Bath & NE Somerset GB **53** U 17

Chewton Mendip Somerset GB **53** U 17

Chichester West Sussex GB **70/71** V 21

Chickerell Dorset GB **53** V 17

Chiddingfold Surrey GB **70/71** U 21

Chigwell Essex GB **71** T 23

Chilbolton Hampshire GB **70** U 20

Child's Ercall Shropshire GB **119** R 17

Chilham Kent GB **71** U 24

Chillaton Devon GB **52/53** V 14

Chillingham Northumberland GB **161** L 19

Chinnor Oxfordshire GB **70/71** T 21

Chippenham Cambridgeshire GB **101** S 23

Chippenham Wiltshire GB **70** U 18

Chipping Lancashire GB **119** P 17

Chipping Campden Gloucestershire GB **100** S 19

Chipping Ongar Essex GB **71** T 23

Chipping Sodbury South Gloucestershire GB **70** T 18

Chipping-Norton Oxfordshire GB **70** T 19

Chirbury Shropshire GB **87** R 16

Chirk Wrexham GB **119** R 16

Chirnside Scottish Borders GB **161** L 18

Chiseldon Swindon GB **70** T 19

Chitterne Wiltshire GB **70** U 18

Chittlehampton Devon GB **53** U 15

Chobham Surrey GB **70/71** U 21

Cholderton Wiltshire GB **70** U 19

Cholsey Oxfordshire GB **70** T 20

Chopwell Gateshead GB **147** N 19

Chorley Lancashire GB **119** P 17

Chorleywood Hertfordshire GB **70/71** T 21

Chrickhowell Powys GB **87** T 16

Christchurch Cambridgeshire GB **101** R 23

Christchurch Bournemouth GB **70** V 19

Chudleigh Devon GB **53** V 15

Chulmleigh Devon GB **53** V 15

Church Eaton Staffordshire GB **100** R 18

Church Fenton North Yorkshire GB **134** P 20

Church Hill Donegal IRL **206** N 7

Church Minshull Cheshire GB **119** Q 17

Church Quarker Antrim GB **207** M 10

Church Stoke Powys GB **87** R 16

Church Stretton Shropshire GB **87** R 17

Churchdown Gloucestershire GB **70** T 18

Churchingford Somerset GB **53** V 16

Churchtown Wexford IRL **233** S 10

Churchtown Wexford IRL **233** S 9

Churston Ferrers Devon GB **53** W 15

Chwilog Gwynedd GB **118/119** R 14

Cilcain Flintshire GB **119** Q 16

Cilcennin Ceredigion GB **86** S 14

Cilfynydd Rhondda Cynon Taff GB **87** T 16

Cilgerran Pembrokeshire GB **86** S 13

Cill Charthaigh Donegal IRL **206** N 5

Cilycwm Carmarthenshire GB **86/87** S 15

Cinderford Gloucestershire GB **70** T 18

Cirencester Gloucestershire GB **70** T 19

City of London Greater London GB **71** U 22

Clabby Fermanagh GB **207** O 8

Clachaig Argyll and Bute GB **160** L 12

Clachan Argyll and Bute GB **174** L 11

Clachan Highland GB **175** H 10

Clachan of Campsie East Dunbartonshire GB **160** L 14

Clachan of Glendaruel Argyll and Bute GB **160** K 12

Cladich Argyll and Bute GB **160** K 12

Clady Donegal IRL **206** N 7

Cladymilltown Armagh GB **207** O 9

Claggan Highland GB **174** J 11

Claigan Highland GB **175** H 9

Clanabogan Tyrone GB **207** N 8

Clane Kildare IRL **219** Q 9

Clanfield Oxfordshire GB **70** T 19

Clanfield Hampshire GB **70** V 20

Claonaig Argyll and Bute GB **160** L 12

Clapham North Yorkshire GB **147** O 18

Clara Offaly IRL **219** Q 7

Clarbeston Pembrokeshire GB **86** T 13

Clare Suffolk GB **101** S 24

Clare Armagh GB **207** O 10

Clarecastle Clare IRL **232** R 5

Clareen Offaly IRL **219** Q 7

Claregalway Galway IRL **218** Q 5

Claremorris Mayo IRL **218** P 4

Clarina Limerick IRL **232** R 5

Clarinbridge Galway IRL **218** Q 5

Clashmore Waterford IRL **233** S 7

Clatt Aberdeenshire GB **187** H 17

Claudy Londonderry GB **207** N 8

Claughton Lancashire GB **146/147** O 17

Claverdon Warwickshire GB **100** S 19

Claverley Shropshire GB **100** R 18

Clawton Devon GB **52/53** V 14

Claxby Lincolnshire GB **135** Q 22

Clay Cross Derbyshire GB **134** Q 20

Claydon Suffolk GB **101** S 25

Claythorpe Lincolnshire GB **134/135** Q 21

Clayton-le-Moors Lancashire GB **134** P 18

Cleadale Highland GB **175** J 10

Cleator Cumbria GB **146** O 15

Cleator Moor Cumbria GB **146** N 15

Clee St Margaret Shropshire GB **87** S 17

Cleethorpes North East Lincolnshire GB **135** P 22

Cleggan Galway IRL **218** P 2

Cleobury Mortimer Shropshire GB **87** S 18

Clevedon North Somerset GB **53** U 17

Cleveleys Blackpool GB **119** P 16

Cliddesden Hampshire GB **70** U 20

Cliffe Medway GB **71** U 24

Cliffony Sligo IRL **206** O 6

Clifford Herefordshire GB **87** S 16

Clifton Cumbria GB **146/147** N 17

Clifton upon Teme Worcestershire GB **87** S 18

Clipston Northhamptonshire GB **100** S 21

Clitheroe Lancashire GB **134** P 18

Clive Shropshire GB **119** R 17

Clogh Antrim GB **207** N 10

Cloghan Donegal IRL **206** N 7

Cloghan Westmeath IRL **219** P 8

Cloghan Offaly IRL **219** Q 7

Cloghane Kerry IRL **232** S 2

Clogheen Tipperary IRL **233** S 7

Clogher Tyrone GB **207** O 8

Clogher Mayo IRL **218** P 4

Clogher Roscommon IRL **218/219** P 6

Clogherhead Louth IRL **219** P 10

Cloghjordan Tipperary IRL **232/233** R 6

Cloghmore Mayo IRL **218** P 3

Cloghy Down GB **207** O 12

Clonakilty Cloich na Coillte Cork IRL **232** T 5

Clonaslee Laois IRL **219** Q 7

Clonbern Galway IRL **218** P 5

Clonbulloge Offaly IRL **219** Q 8

Clonbur Galway IRL **218** P 4

Clondalkin Dublin IRL **219** Q 10

Clonea Waterford IRL **233** S 8

Clonee Meath IRL **219** Q 10

Cloneen Tipperary IRL **233** S 7

Clonegall Carlow IRL **233** R 9

Clonelly Fermanagh GB **206** N 7

Clones Monaghan IRL **207** O 8

Clonfert Galway IRL **218/219** Q 6

Clonkeevy Sligo IRL **206** O 5

Clonmacnoise Offaly IRL **219** Q 7

Clonmany Donegal IRL **207** M 8

Clonmel Cluain Meala Tipperary IRL **233** S 7

Clonmellon Westmeath IRL **219** P 8

Clonmore Carlow IRL **233** R 9

Clonroche Wexford IRL **233** S 9

Clontibret Monaghan IRL **207** O 9

Clonygowan Offaly IRL **219** Q 8

Cloonacool Sligo IRL **206** O 5

Cloone Leitrim IRL **219** P 7

Cloonfad Roscommon IRL **218** P 5

Clophill Bedfordshire GB **100/101** S 22

Close Clark Isle of Man GB **146** O 13

Closeburn Dumfries and Galloway GB **146** M 15

Clough Down GB **207** O 11

Cloughton North Yorkshire GB **135** O 22

Clousta Shetland Islands GB **199** B 20

Clova Angus GB **161** J 16

Clovelly Devon GB **52/53** V 14

Clovenfords Scottish Borders GB **161** L 17

Clowne Derbyshire GB **134** Q 20

Clows Top Worcestershire GB **87** S 18

Cloyne Cork IRL **232/233** T 6

Clun Shropshire GB **87** S 16

Clunes Highland GB **160** J 13

Clungunford Shropshire GB **87** S 17

Clutton Bath & NE Somerset GB **53** U 17

Clydach Swansea GB **86/87** T 15

Clydebank Renfrewshire GB **160** L 14

Clynnogfawr Gwynedd GB **118/119** Q 14

Clyro Powys GB **87** S 16

Coachford Cork IRL **232** T 5

Coad's Cornwall GB **52/53** V 14

Coagh Tyrone GB **207** N 9

Coalburn South Lanarkshire GB **160/161** L 15

Coalisland Tyrone GB **207** N 9

Coalville Leicestershire GB **100** R 20

Coatbridge North Lanarkshire GB **160** L 14

Coatham Redcar & Cleveland GB **147** N 20

Cobh An Cóbh Cork IRL **232/233** T 6

Cobham Surrey GB **71** U 22

Cock Bridge Aberdeenshire GB **187** H 16

Cockburnspath East Lothian GB **161** L 18

Cockenzie and Port Seton East Lothian GB **161** L 17

Cockerham Lancashire GB **119** P 17

Cockermouth Cumbria GB **146** N 16

Cockfield Suffolk GB **101** S 24

Cockfield Durham GB **147** N 19

Cocking West Sussex GB **70/71** V 21

Cockley Cley Norfolk GB **101** R 24

Cockshutt Shropshire GB **119** R 17

Coddenham Suffolk GB **101** S 25

Codsall Staffordshire GB **100** R 18

Coedpoeth Wrexham GB **119** Q 16

Coggeshall Essex GB **71** T 24

Coignafearn Lodge Highland GB **186** H 14

Col Na h-Eileanan an Iar GB **186** F 10

Colbost Highland GB **175** H 9

Colchester Essex GB **71** T 24

Cold Ashton South Gloucestershire GB **70** U 18

Cold Norton Essex GB **71** T 24

Coldbackie Highland GB **186/187** E 14

Coldingham Scottish Borders GB **161** L 18

Coldstream Scottish Borders GB **161** L 18

Coleford Gloucestershire GB **87** T 17

Coleraine Londonderry GB **207** M 9

Coleshill Warwickshire GB **100** R 19

Colintraive Argyll and Bute GB **160** L 12

Collace Perth and Kinross GB **161** K 16

Collieston Aberdeenshire GB **187** H 19

Collin Dumfries and Galloway GB **146** M 15

Collingbourne Kingston Wiltshire GB **70** U 19

Collingham Leeds GB **134** P 20

Collingham Nottinghamshire GB **134/135** Q 21

Collinstown Westmeath IRL **219** P 8

Collon Louth IRL **219** P 9

Collooney Sligo IRL **206** O 5

Colmonell South Ayrshire GB **146** M 13

Colne Lancashire GB **134** P 18

Colsterworth Lincolnshire GB **100** R 21

Colston Bassett Nottinghamshire GB **100** R 21

Coltishall Norfolk GB **101** R 25

Colwyn Bay Conwy GB **119** Q 15

Colyford Devon GB **53** V 16

Combe Martin Devon GB **52/53** U 14

Combe St. Nicholas Somerset GB **53** V 17

Comber Down GB **207** N 11

Comberton Cambridgeshire GB **101** S 23

Commondale North Yorkshire GB **147** O 21

Compton West Sussex GB **70/71** V 21

Comrie Perth and Kinross GB **160/161** K 15

Cong Galway IRL **218** P 4

Congleton Cheshire GB **134** Q 18

Congresbury North Somerset GB **53** U 17

Coningsby Lincolnshire GB **135** Q 22

Conisbrough Doncaster GB **134** Q 20

Coniston Cumbria GB **146** O 16

Conistone North Yorkshire GB **147** O 18

Conna Cork IRL **232/233** S 6

Connah's Flintshire GB **119** Q 16

Connel Argyll and Bute GB **160** K 12

Connel Park East Ayrshire GB **146** M 14

Conon Bridge Highland GB **186/187** G 14

Consett Durham GB **147** N 19

Contin Highland GB **186** G 13

Convoy Donegal IRL **206** N 7

Conwy Conwy GB **119** Q 15

Cookham Windsor & Maidenhead GB **70/71** T 21

Cookstown Tyrone GB **207** N 9

Coola Sligo IRL **206** O 6

Coolaney Sligo IRL **206** O 5

Coole Westmeath IRL **219** P 8

Coombe Cornwall GB **52** V 13

Coombe Bradley Wiltshire GB **70** U 19

Cooraclare Clare IRL **232** R 4

Cootehill Cavan IRL **207** O 8

Copdock Suffolk GB **101** S 25

Copplestone Devon GB **53** V 15

Coppull Lancashire GB **119** P 17

Copthorne West Sussex GB **71** U 22

Corbally Sligo IRL **206** O 4

Corbridge Northumberland GB **147** N 18

Corby Northhamptonshire GB **100** S 21

Corby Glen Lincolnshire GB **100** R 21

Corclogh Mayo IRL **218** O 2

Corfe Somerset GB **53** V 16

Corfe Castle Dorset GB **70** V 18

Cork Corcaigh Cork IRL **232/233** T 6

Corlea Longford IRL **219** P 7

Cornaigmore Argyll and Bute GB **174** J 9

Cornaigmore Argyll and Bute GB **174** J 9

Corner North Yorkshire GB **147** O 19

Cornhill Aberdeenshire GB **187** G 17

Cornhill-on-Tweed Northumberland GB **161** L 18

Corpach Highland GB **160** J 12

Corran Highland GB **160** J 12

Corraun Mayo IRL **218** P 3

Corrie North Ayrshire GB **160** L 12

Corrie Common Dumfries and Galloway GB **146** M 16

Corringham Lincolnshire GB **134/135** Q 21

Corris Gwynedd GB **86/87** R 15

Corrofin Clare IRL **232** R 4

Corsham Wiltshire GB **70** U 18

Corsock Dumfries and Galloway GB **146** M 15

Cortachy Angus GB **161** J 18

Corton Suffolk GB **101** R 26

Corwen Denbighshire GB **119** R 16

Coryton Thurrock GB **71** T 24

Cossington Somerset GB **53** U 17

Costessey Norfolk GB **101** R 25

Cotehill Cumbria GB **146/147** N 17

Cotgrave Nottinghamshire GB **100** R 20

Cotherstone Durham GB **147** N 19

Cotleigh Devon GB **53** V 16

Cottenham Cambridgeshire GB **101** S 23

Cottered Hertfordshire GB **71** T 22

Cottingham Northhamptonshire GB **100** R 21

Cottingham Kingston upon Hull GB **135** P 22

Coulport Argyll and Bute GB **160** K 13

Coulter South Lanarkshire GB **160/161** L 15

Countesthorpe Leicestershire GB **100** R 20

Countisbury Devon GB **53** U 15

Coupar Angus Perth and Kinross GB **161** J 16

Courtmacsherry Cork IRL **232** T 5

Courtown Wexford IRL **233** R 10

Cove Highland GB **186** G 11

Cove Bay Aberdeen City GB **187** H 18

Coventry Coventry GB **100** S 19

Coverack Cornwall GB **52** W 12

Cowbit Lincolnshire GB **100/101** R 22

Cowbridge Vale of Glamorgan GB **53** U 16

Cowdenbeath Fife GB **161** K 16

Cowesby North Yorkshire GB **147** O 20

Cowfold West Sussex GB **71** V 22

Coxwold North Yorkshire GB **147** O 20

Coylton South Ayrshire GB **146** M 14

Cradley Herefordshire GB **87** S 18

Crai Powys GB **86/87** T 15

Craigavon Down GB **207** O 10

Craigellachie Moray GB **187** H 16

Craigendoran Argyll and Bute GB **160** L 13

Craighouse Argyll and Bute GB **174** L 11

Craigie South Ayrshire GB **160** L 13

Craignure Argyll and Bute GB **174** K 11

Craik Scottish Borders GB **146** M 16

Crail Fife GB **161** K 17

Crailing Scottish Borders GB **161** L 18

Cramlington Northumberland GB **147** M 19

Cranagh Tyrone GB **207** N 8

Cranborne Dorset GB **70** V 19

Cranbrook Kent GB **71** U 24

Cranfield Bedfordshire GB **100** S 21

Cranford Donegal IRL **206** M 7

Cranford St Andrew Northhamptonshire GB **100** S 21

Cranleigh Surrey GB **70/71** U 21

Crannogeboy Donegal IRL **206** N 5

Cranshaws Scottish Borders GB **161** L 17

Crask Inn Highland GB **186** F 13

Craster Northumberland GB **147** M 19

Crathes Aberdeenshire GB **187** H 18

Crathie Aberdeenshire GB **187** H 16

Crathorne North Yorkshire GB **147** O 20

Craven Arms Shropshire GB **87** S 17

Crawford South Lanarkshire GB **146** M 15

Crawfordjohn South Lanarkshire GB **160/161** L 15

Crawley Hampshire GB **70** U 20

Crawley West Sussex GB **71** U 22

Creag Ghoraidh Na h-Eileanan an Iar GB **175** H 8

Crean's Cross Roads Cork IRL **232** T 5

Crediton Devon GB **53** V 15

Creegh Clare IRL **232** R 4

Creegs Passage Galway IRL **218/219** P 6

Creeslough Donegal IRL **206** M 7

Creetown Dumfries and Galloway GB **146** N 14

Creggan Tyrone GB **207** N 8

Cregganbaun Mayo IRL **218** P 3

Creggans Argyll and Bute GB **160** K 12

Cressage Shropshire GB **87** R 17

Cresswell Northumberland GB **147** M 19

Crewe Cheshire GB **134** Q 18

Crewkerne Somerset GB **53** V 17

Crianlarich Stirling GB **160** K 13

Cribyn Ceredigion GB **86** S 14

Criccieth Gwynedd GB **118/119** R 14

Crich Derbyshire GB **134** Q 20

Crick Northhamptonshire GB **100** S 20

Cricklade Wiltshire GB **70** T 19

Crieff Perth and Kinross GB **160/161** K 15

Crimond Aberdeenshire GB **187** G 19

Crinan Argyll and Bute GB **174** K 11

Crocketford Dumfries and Galloway GB **146** M 15

Crockham Hill Kent GB **71** U 23

Croft-on-Tees North Yorkshire GB **147** O 19

Croggan Argyll and Bute GB **174** K 11

Croglin Cumbria GB **146/147** N 17

Croick Highland GB **186** G 13

Cromarty Highland GB **186/187** G 14

Cromer Norfolk GB **101** R 25

Cromor Na h-Eileanan an Iar GB **186** F 10

Crook Durham GB **147** N 19

Crookedwood Westmeath IRL **219** P 8

Crookham Northumberland GB **161** L 18

Crookhaven Cork IRL **232** U 3

Crookstown Kildare IRL **219** Q 9

Crookstown Cork IRL **232** T 5

Croom Limerick IRL **232** R 5

Cropredy Oxfordshire GB **100** S 20

Crosbost Na h-Eileanan an Iar GB **186** F 10

Crosby Salford GB **119** Q 16

Crosby Isle of Man GB **146** O 13

Crosby Cumbria GB **147** O 18

Crosby Ravensworth Cumbria GB **146/147** N 17

Crosby-on-Eden Cumbria GB **146/147** N 17

Cross Barry Cork IRL **232** T 5

Cross Hands Carmarthenshire GB **86** T 14

Cross Keys Cavan IRL **219** P 8

Cross Keys Meath IRL **219** P 8

Crossaig Argyll and Bute GB **160** L 12

Crossakeel Meath IRL **219** P 8

Crossdoney Cavan IRL **219** P 8

Crossens Sefton GB **119** P 17

Crossford South Lanarkshire GB **160/161** L 15

Crossgar Down GB **207** O 11

Crossgates Fife GB **161** K 16

Crossgates Powys GB **87** S 16

Crosshaven Cork IRL **232/233** T 6

Crosshill South Ayrshire GB **146** M 13

Crossmaglen Armagh GB **207** O 9

Crossmichael Dumfries and Galloway GB **146** N 15
Crossmolina Mayo IRL **206** O 4
Crosthwaite Cumbria GB **146/147** O 17
Croston Lancashire GB **119** P 17
Croughton Oxfordshire GB **70** T 20
Crowan Cornwall GB **52** W 12
Crowborough East Sussex GB **71** U 23
Crowland Lincolnshire GB **100/101** R 22
Crowlas Cornwall GB **52** W 12
Crowle North Lincolnshire GB **134/135** P 21
Crowle Worcestershire GB **87** S 18
Croxton North Lincolnshire GB **135** P 22
Croxton Kerrial Leicestershire GB **100** R 21
Croy Highland GB **186** H 14
Croyde Devon GB **52/53** U 14
Croydon Greater London GB **71** U 22
Cruden Bay Aberdeenshire GB **187** H 19
Crudgington Shropshire GB **119** R 17
Crudgington Telford and Wrekin GB **87** R 17
Crudwell Wiltshire GB **70** T 18
Crulabhig Na h-Eileanan an Iar GB **175** F 9
Crumlin Antrim GB **207** N 10
Crusheen Clare IRL **232** R 5
Crymych Pembrokeshire GB **86** T 13
Crynant Neath Port Talbot GB **86/87** T 15
Cubert Cornwall GB **52** W 12
Cuckfield West Sussex GB **71** U 22
Cuckney Nottinghamshire GB **134** Q 20
Cudworth Barnsley GB **134** P 20
Culbokie Highland GB **186/187** G 14
Culdaff Donegal IRL **207** M 8
Culford Suffolk GB **101** S 24
Culkein Highland GB **186** F 12
Cullaville Armagh GB **207** O 9
Culleens Sligo IRL **206** O 5
Cullen Moray GB **187** G 17
Cullicudden Highland GB **186/187** G 14
Cullipool Argyll and Bute GB **174** K 11
Cullivoe Shetland Islands GB **199** A 20
Cullomane Cross Roads Cork IRL **232** T 4
Cullompton Devon GB **53** V 16
Cullybackey Antrim GB **207** N 10
Culmington Shropshire GB **87** S 17
Culmstock Devon GB **53** V 16
Culnacraig Highland GB **186** G 12
Culrain Highland GB **186/187** G 14
Culross Fife GB **160/161** K 15
Culswick Shetland Islands GB **199** B 19
Cults Aberdeen City GB **187** H 18
Culworth Northhamptonshire GB **100** S 20

Cumbernauld North Lanarkshire GB **160/161** L 15
Cuminestown Aberdeenshire GB **187** G 18
Cumnock East Ayrshire GB **146** M 14
Cumnor Oxfordshire GB **70** T 20
Cumrew Cumbria GB **146/147** N 17
Cumwhitton Cumbria GB **146/147** N 17
Cupar Fife GB **161** K 16
Curracloe Wexford IRL **233** S 10
Curraghalicky Cork IRL **232** T 4
Curraghroe Roscommon IRL **218/219** P 6
Curry Sligo IRL **218** P 5
Cushendall Antrim GB **207** M 10
Cushendun Antrim GB **207** M 10
Cushina Offaly IRL **219** Q 8
Cwmbran Torfaen GB **87** T 16
Cwmffrwd Carmarthenshire GB **86** T 14
Cyffylliog Denbighshire GB **119** Q 16
Cymmer Neath Port Talbot GB **86/87** T 15
Cynghordy Carmarthenshire GB **86/87** S 15
Cynwyd Denbighshire GB **119** R 16
Cynwyl Elfed Carmarthenshire GB **86** T 14

D

Dacre Cumbria GB **146/147** N 17
Dagenham Greater London GB **71** T 23
Daglingworth Gloucestershire GB **70** T 18
Dagnall Buckinghamshire GB **70/71** T 21
Dail bho Dheas Na h-Eileanan an Iar GB **186** F 10
Dailly South Ayrshire GB **146** M 13
Daingean Offaly IRL **219** Q 8
Dairsie or Osnaburgh Fife GB **161** K 17
Dalabrog Na h-Eileanan an Iar GB **175** H 8
Dalbeattie Dumfries and Galloway GB **146** N 15
Dalchork Highland GB **186/187** F 14
Dalchreichart Highland GB **186** H 13
Dalchruin Perth and Kinross GB **160** K 14
Dale Pembrokeshire GB **86** T 12
Dale of Walls Shetland Islands GB **199** B 19
Dalhavaig Highland GB **187** F 15
Dalkeith Midlothian GB **161** L 16
Dalkey Dublin IRL **219** Q 10
Dallas Moray GB **187** G 16
Dalleagles East Ayrshire GB **146** M 14
Dalmally Argyll and Bute GB **160** K 13
Dalmellington East Ayrshire GB **146** M 14
Dalnavie Highland GB **186/187** G 14
Dalnawillan Lodge Highland GB **187** F 15
Dalreavoch Highland GB **186/187** F 14

Dalry North Ayrshire GB **160** L 13
Dalrymple East Ayrshire GB **146** M 13
Dalston Cumbria GB **146/147** N 17
Dalswinton Dumfries and Galloway GB **146** M 15
Dalton Dumfries and Galloway GB **146** M 16
Dalton-in-Furness Cumbria GB **146** O 16
Dalwhinnie Highland GB **160** J 14
Dalwood Devon GB **53** V 16
Dalystown Westmeath IRL **219** Q 8
Damerham Hampshire GB **70** V 19
Danbury Essex GB **71** T 24
Darenth Kent GB **71** U 23
Darfield Barnsley GB **134** P 20
Darlington Darlington GB **147** N 19
Dartford Kent GB **71** U 23
Dartington Devon GB **53** W 15
Dartmeet Devon GB **53** V 15
Dartmouth Devon GB **53** W 15
Darvel East Ayrshire GB **160** L 14
Darwen Blackburn with Darwen GB **134** P 18
Davenham Cheshire GB **119** Q 17
Daventry Northhamptonshire GB **100** S 20
Davidstow Cornwall GB **52** V 13
Davington Dumfries and Galloway GB **146** M 16
Daviot Highland GB **187** H 14
Dawley Shropshire GB **100** R 18
Dawley Telford and Wrekin GB **100** R 18
Dawlish Devon GB **53** V 16
Deal Kent GB **71** U 25
Deanich Lodge Highland GB **186** G 13
Dearham Cumbria GB **146** N 16
Debenham Suffolk GB **101** S 25
Deddington Oxfordshire GB **70** T 20
Deeping St Nicholas Lincolnshire GB **100/101** R 22
Defford Worcestershire GB **87** S 18
Deiniolen Gwynedd GB **118/119** Q 14
Delabole Cornwall GB **52** V 13
Delgany Wicklow IRL **219** Q 10
Delphi Mayo IRL **218** P 3
Delvin Westmeath IRL **219** P 8
Denbigh Denbighshire GB **119** Q 16
Denby Dale Kirklees GB **134** P 19
Denholm Scottish Borders GB **146/147** M 17
Denny Falkirk GB **160/161** K 15
Denshaw Oldham GB **134** P 18
Dent Cumbria GB **147** O 18
Denton Lincolnshire GB **100** R 21
Denton Norfolk GB **101** S 25
Derby Derby GB **100** R 20
Dereham Norfolk GB **101** R 24
Derrybeg Donegal IRL **206** M 6
Derrybrien Galway IRL **218** Q 5
Derrygolan Westmeath IRL **219** Q 8

Derrygonnelly Fermanagh GB **206** O 7
Derrykeighan Antrim GB **207** M 10
Derrylin Fermanagh GB **206** O 7
Derryrush Galway IRL **218** Q 3
Dersingham Norfolk GB **101** R 24
Dervaig Argyll and Bute GB **174** J 10
Dervock Antrim GB **207** M 10
Desborough Northhamptonshire GB **100** S 21
Desertmartin Londonderry GB **207** N 9
Desford Leicestershire GB **100** R 20
Devil's Bridge Ceredigion GB **86/87** S 15
Devizes Wiltshire GB **70** U 19
Dewsbury Kirklees GB **134** P 19
Dickleburgh Norfolk GB **101** S 25
Didcot Oxfordshire GB **70** T 20
Digby Lincolnshire GB **135** Q 22
Dinas Gwynedd GB **118** R 13
Dinas Cross Pembrokeshire GB **86** S 13
Dinas Mawddwy Gwynedd GB **86/87** R 15
Dinas Powys Vale of Glamorgan GB **53** U 16
Dingle Kerry IRL **232** S 2
Dingwall Highland GB **186/187** G 14
Dinnet Aberdeenshire GB **187** H 17
Dinnington Rotherham GB **134** Q 20
Dinnington Newcastle upon Tyne GB **147** M 19
Dinton Wiltshire GB **70** U 19
Dippen Argyll and Bute GB **174** L 11
Dirleton East Lothian GB **161** K 17
Dishforth North Yorkshire GB **147** O 20
Diss Norfolk GB **101** S 25
Distington Cumbria GB **146** N 15
Ditchling East Sussex GB **71** V 22
Ditton Priors Shropshire GB **87** R 17
Doagh Antrim GB **207** N 10
Doagh Beg Donegal IRL **206** M 7
Dobwalls Cornwall GB **52** W 13
Doc Penfro Pembroke Dock Pembrokeshire GB **86** T 13
Docking Norfolk GB **101** R 24
Dockray Cumbria GB **146/147** N 17
Doddington Cambridgeshire GB **101** S 23
Doddington Northumberland GB **161** L 19
Doddington Kent GB **71** U 24
Dodleston Cheshire GB **119** Q 17
Dodworth Barnsley GB **134** P 19
Dogdyke Lincolnshire GB **135** Q 22
Dolanog Powys GB **87** R 16
Dolfor Powys GB **87** S 16
Dolgarrog Conwy GB **119** Q 15
Dolgellau Gwynedd GB **119** R 15
Dolla Tipperary IRL **232/233** R 6
Dollar Clackmannanshire GB **160/161** K 15

Dolphinholme Lancashire GB **119** P 17
Dolphinton South Lanarkshire GB **161** L 16
Dolton Devon GB **52/53** V 14
Dolwyddelan Conwy GB **119** Q 15
Donabate Dublin IRL **219** Q 10
Donadea Kildare IRL **219** Q 9
Donaghadee Down GB **207** N 11
Doncaster Doncaster GB **134** P 20
Donegal Dún na nGall Donegal IRL **206** N 6
Doneraile Cork IRL **232** S 5
Donington Lincolnshire GB **100/101** R 22
Donnington Shropshire GB **100** R 18
Donnington Telford and Wrekin GB **100** R 18
Donohill Tipperary IRL **232/233** R 6
Donoughmore Cork IRL **232** T 5
Doogort Mayo IRL **218** O 2
Doolin Clare IRL **218** Q 4
Doon Limerick IRL **232/233** R 6
Doona Mayo IRL **218** O 3
Doonaha Clare IRL **232** R 3
Doonbeg Clare IRL **232** R 3
Dorchester Oxfordshire GB **70** T 20
Dorchester Dorset GB **70** V 18
Dores Highland GB **186** H 14
Dorking Surrey GB **71** U 22
Dornie Highland GB **186** H 12
Dornoch Highland GB **186/187** G 14
Dorstone Herefordshire GB **87** S 16
Douglas Isle of Man GB **146** O 14
Douglas South Lanarkshire GB **160/161** L 15
Dounby Orkney Islands GB **198** D 16
Doune Stirling GB **160** K 14
Dounreay Highland GB **198** E 15
Dove Holes Derbyshire GB **134** Q 19
Dover Kent GB **71** U 25
Doveridge Derbyshire GB **100** R 19
Downderry Cornwall GB **52/53** W 14
Downham Market Norfolk GB **101** R 23
Downhill Londonderry GB **207** M 9
Downies Donegal IRL **206** M 7
Downpatrick Down GB **207** O 11
Downton Wiltshire GB **70** V 19
Dowra Leitrim IRL **206** O 6
Draperstown Londonderry GB **207** N 9
Drax North Yorkshire GB **134/135** P 21
Draycott Somerset GB **53** U 17
Draycott in the Clay Staffordshire GB **100** R 19
Drem East Lothian GB **161** K 17
Driffield East Riding of Yorkshire GB **135** P 22
Drigg Cumbria GB **146** O 16
Drimnin Highland GB **174** J 11
Drimoleague Cork IRL **232** T 4
Dring Longford IRL **219** P 7
Dripsey Cork IRL **232** T 5

Drogheda Droichead Átha Louth IRL **219** P 10
Droitwich Spa Worcestershire GB **87** S 18
Dromahair Leitrim IRL **206** O 6
Dromara Down GB **207** O 11
Dromcolliher Limerick IRL **232** S 5
Dromina Cork IRL **232** S 5
Dromod Leitrim IRL **219** P 7
Dromore Down GB **207** O 10
Dromore Tyrone GB **207** O 8
Dromore West Sligo IRL **206** O 5
Dronfield Derbyshire GB **134** Q 20
Drum Monaghan IRL **207** O 8
Drumandoora Clare IRL **218** Q 5
Drumaroad Down GB **207** O 11
Drumbeg Highland GB **186** F 12
Drumburgh Cumbria GB **146** N 16
Drumcliffe Sligo IRL **206** O 5
Drumclog South Lanarkshire GB **160** L 14
Drumcondra Meath IRL **219** P 9
Drumelzier Scottish Borders GB **161** L 16
Drumfearn Highland GB **175** H 11
Drumfin Sligo IRL **206** O 6
Drumfree Donegal IRL **207** M 8
Drumkeeran Leitrim IRL **206** O 6
Drumlamford House South Ayrshire GB **146** M 13
Drumlish Longford IRL **219** P 7
Drumlithie Aberdeenshire GB **161** J 18
Drummore Dumfries and Galloway GB **146** N 13
Drumnadrochit Highland GB **186** H 14
Drumquin Tyrone GB **207** N 8
Drumrunie Highland GB **186** G 12
Drumshanbo Leitrim IRL **206** O 6
Drumsna Leitrim IRL **219** P 6
Drymen Stirling GB **160** K 14
Drynoch Highland GB **175** H 10
Duagh Kerry IRL **232** S 4
Dublin Baile Átha Cliath Dublin IRL **219** Q 10
Duchally Highland GB **186** F 13
Ducklington Oxfordshire GB **70** T 20
Duddington Northhamptonshire GB **100** R 21
Duddo Northumberland GB **161** L 18
Dudley Dudley GB **100** R 18
Duffield Derbyshire GB **100** R 20
Dufftown Moray GB **187** H 16
Duffus Moray GB **187** G 16
Dufton Cumbria GB **147** N 18
Duirinish Highland GB **175** H 11
Dukinfield Tameside GB **134** Q 18
Duleek Meath IRL **219** P 10
Dulford Devon GB **53** V 16
Dullingham Cambridgeshire GB **101** S 23
Dulnain Bridge Highland GB **187** H 15
Dulverton Somerset GB **53** U 15
Dumbarton West Dunbartonshire GB **160** L 13
Dumfries Dumfries and Galloway GB **146** M 15

Dún Laoghaire Dublin IRL **219** Q 10
Dunan Highland GB **175** H 10
Dunbar East Lothian GB **161** K 17
Dunbeath Highland GB **187** F 16
Dunblane Stirling GB **160/161** K 15
Dunboyne Meath IRL **219** Q 10
Duncannon Wexford IRL **233** S 9
Dunchurch Warwickshire GB **100** S 20
Duncormick Wexford IRL **233** S 9
Duncow Dumfries and Galloway GB **146** M 15
Duncton West Sussex GB **70/71** V 21
Dundalk Dun Dealgan Louth IRL **207** O 10
Dundee Dundee City GB **161** K 17
Dundonald South Ayrshire GB **160** L 13
Dundonald Down GB **207** N 11
Dundonnell Highland GB **186** G 12
Dundrennan Dumfries and Galloway GB **146** N 15
Dundrod Antrim GB **207** N 10
Dundrum Down GB **207** O 11
Dundrum Tipperary IRL **232/233** R 6
Dunecht Aberdeenshire GB **187** H 18
Dunfanaghy Donegal IRL **206** M 7
Dunfermline Fife GB **161** K 16
Dungannon Tyrone GB **207** O 9
Dungarvan Kilkenny IRL **233** R 8
Dungarvan Dún Garbhán Waterford IRL **233** S 7
Dungiven Londonderry GB **207** N 9
Dunglow Donegal IRL **206** N 6
Dungourney Cork IRL **232/233** T 6
Dunguin Kerry IRL **232** S 2
Dunholme Lincolnshire GB **135** Q 22
Dunino Fife GB **161** K 17
Dunkeld Perth and Kinross GB **160/161** J 15
Dunkerrin Offaly IRL **233** R 7
Dunkeswell Devon GB **53** V 16
Dunkineely Donegal IRL **206** N 6
Dunlavin Wicklow IRL **219** Q 9
Dunleer Louth IRL **219** P 10
Dunlop East Ayrshire GB **160** L 13
Dunloy Antrim GB **207** N 10
Dunmanway Cork IRL **232** T 4
Dunmore Galway IRL **218** P 5
Dunmore East Waterford IRL **233** S 9
Dunmurry Antrim GB **207** N 10
Dunnamanagh Tyrone GB **207** N 8
Dunnet Highland GB **198** E 16
Dunning Perth and Kinross GB **160/161** K 15
Dunoon Argyll and Bute GB **160** L 13
Dunragit Dumfries and Galloway GB **146** N 13
Duns Scottish Borders GB **161** L 18
Dunsby Lincolnshire GB **100/101** R 22

Dunscore Dumfries and Galloway GB **146** M 15
Dunsford Devon GB **53** V 15
Dunshaughlin Meath IRL **219** P 9
Dunstable Bedfordshire GB **70/71** T 21
Dunster Somerset GB **53** U 16
Dunston Lincolnshire GB **135** Q 22
Dunsyre South Lanarkshire GB **161** L 16
Duntish Dorset GB **70** V 18
Dunure South Ayrshire GB **146** M 13
Dunvegan Highland GB **175** H 9
Dunwich Suffolk GB **101** S 26
Durham Durham GB **147** N 19
Durisdeer Dumfries and Galloway GB **146** M 15
Durness Highland GB **186** E 13
Durrington Wiltshire GB **70** U 19
Durrow Laois IRL **233** R 8
Durrus Cork IRL **232** T 3
Dursley Gloucestershire GB **70** T 18
Durweston Dorset GB **70** V 18
Duthil Highland GB **187** H 15
Duxford Cambridgeshire GB **101** S 23
Dyce Aberdeen City GB **187** H 18
Dyffryn Ardudwy Gwynedd GB **86** R 14
Dyke Moray GB **187** G 15
Dykehead Angus GB **161** J 16
Dykends Angus GB **161** J 16
Dylife Powys GB **86/87** R 15
Dymchurch Kent GB **71** U 24
Dymock Gloucestershire GB **70** T 18
Dysart Fife GB **161** K 16
Dyserth Denbighshire GB **119** Q 16

E

Eaglesfield Dumfries and Galloway GB **146** M 16
Eaglesfield Dean Cumbria GB **146** N 16
Eaglesham East Renfrewshire GB **160** L 14
Eakring Nottinghamshire GB **134** Q 20
Earby Lancashire GB **134** P 18
Eardisley Herefordshire GB **87** S 17
Earith Cambridgeshire GB **101** S 23
Earl Shilton Leicestershire GB **100** R 20
Earl Soham Suffolk GB **101** S 25
Earl Stonham Suffolk GB **101** S 25
Earlish Highland GB **186** G 10
Earls Barton Northhamptonshire GB **100** S 21
Earls Colne Essex GB **71** T 24
Earlsferry Fife GB **161** K 17
Earlston Scottish Borders GB **161** L 17
Easington East Riding of Yorkshire GB **135** P 23
Easington Durham GB **147** N 20
Easingwold North Yorkshire GB **147** O 20
Easky Sligo IRL **206** O 5
Eassie Angus GB **161** J 16
East Barkwith Lincolnshire GB **135** Q 22

East Bergholt Suffolk GB **71** T 24
East Brent Somerset GB **53** U 17
East Bridgford Nottinghamshire GB **100** R 21
East Challow Oxfordshire GB **70** T 20
East Chinnock Somerset GB **53** V 17
East Cowes Isle of Wight GB **70** V 20
East Cowton North Yorkshire GB **147** O 19
East Croachy Highland GB **186** H 14
East Dean East Sussex GB **71** V 23
East Grinstead West Sussex GB **71** U 23
East Haddon Northhamptonshire GB **100** S 20
East Halton North Lincolnshire GB **135** P 22
East Hanney Oxfordshire GB **70** T 20
East Harling Norfolk GB **101** S 24
East Harlsey North Yorkshire GB **147** O 20
East Hauxwell North Yorkshire GB **147** O 19
East Hoathly East Sussex GB **71** V 23
East Ilsey West Berkshire GB **70** T 20
East Kilbride South Lanarkshire GB **160** L 14
East Knoyle Wiltshire GB **70** U 18
East Leake Nottinghamshire GB **100** R 20
East Linton East Lothian GB **161** L 17
East Markham Nottinghamshire GB **134/135** Q 21
East Meon Hampshire GB **70** V 20
East Morton Bradford GB **134** P 19
East Norton Leicestershire GB **100** R 21
East Portlemouth Devon GB **53** W 15
East Raynham Norfolk GB **101** R 24
East Rhidorroch Lodge Highland GB **186** G 13
East Rudham Norfolk GB **101** R 24
East Saltoun East Lothian GB **161** L 17
East Wemyss Fife GB **161** K 16
East Wittering West Sussex GB **70/71** V 21
East Witton North Yorkshire GB **147** O 19
East Wretham Norfolk GB **101** S 24
Eastbourne East Sussex GB **71** V 23
Eastchurch Kent GB **71** U 24
Easter Compton South Gloucestershire GB **87** T 17
Eastgate Durham GB **147** N 18
Eastleigh Hampshire GB **70** V 20
Eastnor Herefordshire GB **87** S 18
Eastoft North Lincolnshire GB **134/135** P 21

Easton Dorset GB **70** V 18
Easton on the Hill Northhamptonshire GB **100/101** R 22
Eastry Kent GB **71** U 25
Eastville Lincolnshire GB **135** Q 23
Eastwood Nottinghamshire GB **100** R 20
Ebbw Vale Blaenau Gwent GB **87** T 16
Ebchester Durham GB **147** N 19
Ecclefechan Dumfries and Galloway GB **146** M 16
Eccles Scottish Borders GB **161** L 18
Eccleshall Staffordshire GB **100** R 18
Eccleston Lancashire GB **119** P 17
Eccleston Cheshire GB **119** Q 17
Echt Aberdeenshire GB **187** H 18
Eckford Scottish Borders GB **161** L 18
Eckington Derbyshire GB **134** Q 20
Edale Derbyshire GB **134** Q 19
Edderton Highland GB **186/187** G 14
Eddleston Scottish Borders GB **161** L 16
Edenbridge Kent GB **71** U 23
Edenderry Offaly IRL **219** Q 8
Edenham Lincolnshire GB **100/101** R 22
Edensor Derbyshire GB **134** Q 19
Edern Gwynedd GB **118** R 13
Ederny Fermanagh GB **206** N 7
Edgeworthstown Longford IRL **219** P 7
Edgmond Shropshire GB **100** R 18
Edgmond Telford and Wrekin GB **100** R 18
Edgworth Blackburn with Darwen GB **134** P 18
Edinbane Highland GB **175** H 10
Edinburgh Edinburgh GB **161** L 16
Edington Wiltshire GB **70** U 18
Edington Burtle Somerset GB **53** U 17
Edlingham Northumberland GB **147** M 19
Edmonstone Orkney Islands GB **198** D 17
Edmundbyers Durham GB **147** N 19
Ednam Scottish Borders GB **161** L 18
Edrom Scottish Borders GB **161** L 18
Edwinstowe Nottinghamshire GB **134** Q 20
Edzell Angus GB **161** J 18
Egglescliffe Stockton-on-Tees GB **147** N 20
Eggleston Durham GB **147** N 19
Egham Surrey GB **70/71** U 21
Eglingham Northumberland GB **147** M 19
Eglinton Londonderry GB **207** M 8
Egloskerry Cornwall GB **52/53** V 14
Eglwys Fach Ceredigion GB **86/87** R 15
Eglwysbach Conwy GB **119** Q 15

Eglwyswrw Pembrokeshire GB **86** S 13

Egremont Cumbria GB **146** O 15

Egton North Yorkshire GB **134** O 21

Eileanach Highland GB **186/187** G 14

Eisgein Na h-Eileanan an Iar GB **175** F 9

Elan Village Powys GB **86/87** S 15

Elgin Moray GB **187** G 16

Elgol Highland GB **175** H 10

Elham Kent GB **71** U 25

Elie Fife GB **161** K 17

Elishadder Highland GB **186** G 10

Elland Calderdale GB **134** P 19

Ellastone Staffordshire GB **100** R 19

Ellesmere Shropshire GB **119** R 17

Ellesmere Port Cheshire GB **119** Q 17

Ellingham Northumberland GB **161** L 19

Ellington Northumberland GB **147** M 19

Ellon Aberdeenshire GB **187** H 18

Elmdon Essex GB **101** S 23

Elmswell Suffolk GB **101** S 24

Elphin Highland GB **186** F 12

Elphin Roscommon IRL **218/219** P 6

Elrig Dumfries and Galloway GB **146** N 13

Elsdon Northumberland GB **147** M 18

Elsenham Essex GB **71** T 23

Elsham North Lincolnshire GB **135** P 22

Elsrickle South Lanarkshire GB **160/161** L 15

Elstead Surrey GB **70/71** U 21

Elston Nottinghamshire GB **134/135** Q 21

Elstree Hertfordshire GB **71** T 22

Elswick Lancashire GB **119** P 17

Elsworth Cambridgeshire GB **100/101** S 22

Eltisley Cambridgeshire GB **100/101** S 22

Elton Northhamptonshire GB **100/101** R 22

Elvanfoot South Lanarkshire GB **146** M 15

Elveden Suffolk GB **101** S 24

Elvington York GB **134/135** P 21

Elwick Hartlepool GB **147** N 20

Ely Cambridgeshire GB **101** S 23

Embleton Northumberland GB **161** L 19

Embo Highland GB **187** G 15

Embsay North Yorkshire GB **134** P 19

Emly Tipperary IRL **232/233** S 6

Emmoo Roscommon IRL **218/219** P 6

Emneth Norfolk GB **101** R 23

Empingham Rutland GB **100** R 21

Emsworth Hampshire GB **70/71** V 21

Emyvale Monaghan IRL **207** O 9

Endon Staffordshire GB **134** Q 18

Enfield Greater London GB **71** T 22

Ennis Inis Clare IRL **232** R 5

Enniscorthy Inis Córthaidh Wexford IRL **233** R 9

Enniskean Cork IRL **232** T 5

Enniskerry Wicklow IRL **219** Q 10

Enniskillen Fermanagh GB **206** O 7

Ennistimon Clare IRL **232** R 4

Enochdhu Perth and Kinross GB **160/161** J 15

Enstone Oxfordshire GB **70** T 20

Enterkinfoot Dumfries and Galloway GB **146** M 15

Eòropaidh Na h-Eileanan an Iar GB **186** E 10

Epping Essex GB **71** T 23

Epsom Greater London GB **71** U 22

Epworth North Lincolnshire GB **134/135** P 21

Erbusaig Highland GB **175** H 11

Eriboll Highland GB **186** F 13

Ermington Devon GB **53** W 15

Erpingham Norfolk GB **101** R 25

Errogie Highland GB **186** H 14

Errol Perth and Kinross GB **161** K 16

Escrick North Yorkshire GB **134** P 20

Esh Winning Durham GB **147** N 19

Esher Surrey GB **71** U 22

Eshnadarragh Fermanagh GB **207** O 8

Eskdalemuir Dumfries and Galloway GB **146** M 16

Essendine Rutland GB **100/101** R 22

Essich Highland GB **186** H 14

Etal Northumberland GB **161** L 18

Eton Windsor & Maidenhead GB **70/71** U 21

Ettington Warwickshire GB **100** S 19

Ettrickbridge Scottish Borders GB **161** L 17

Etwall Derbyshire GB **100** R 19

Euxton Lancashire GB **119** P 17

Evanton Highland GB **186/187** G 14

Evercreech Somerset GB **53** U 17

Everdon Northhamptonshire GB **100** S 20

Everingham East Riding of Yorkshire GB **134/135** P 21

Everleigh Wiltshire GB **70** U 19

Eversden Cambridgeshire GB **100/101** S 22

Evershot Dorset GB **53** V 17

Evesham Worcestershire GB **100** S 19

Ewes Dumfries and Galloway GB **146** M 16

Ewhurst Surrey GB **71** U 22

Exbourne Devon GB **53** V 15

Exbury Hampshire GB **70** V 20

Exeter Devon GB **53** V 15

Exford Somerset GB **53** U 15

Exminster Devon GB **53** V 15

Exmouth Devon GB **53** V 16

Exton Somerset GB **53** U 15

Eyam Derbyshire GB **134** Q 19

Eye Peterborough GB **100/101** R 22

Eye Suffolk GB **101** S 25

Eyemouth Scottish Borders GB **161** L 18

Eyeries Cork IRL **232** T 3

Eynort Highland GB **175** H 10

Eynsford Kent GB **71** U 23

Eynsham Oxfordshire GB **70** T 20

Eyrecourt Galway IRL **218/219** Q 6

F

Fahamore Kerry IRL **232** S 2

Fahan Donegal IRL **207** M 8

Fairbourne Gwynedd GB **86** R 14

Fairford Gloucestershire GB **70** T 19

Fairlie North Ayrshire GB **160** L 13

Fairlight East Sussex GB **71** V 24

Fakenham Norfolk GB **101** R 24

Fala Midlothian GB **161** L 17

Falcarragh Donegal IRL **206** M 6

Faldingworth Lincolnshire GB **135** Q 22

Falfield South Gloucestershire GB **70** T 18

Falkirk Falkirk GB **160/161** L 15

Falkland Fife GB **161** K 16

Falmer East Sussex GB **71** V 22

Falmouth Cornwall GB **52** W 12

Falstone Northumberland GB **147** M 18

Fangfoss East Riding of Yorkshire GB **134/135** P 21

Farcet Cambridgeshire GB **100/101** R 22

Fareham Hampshire GB **70** V 20

Faringdon Oxfordshire GB **70** T 19

Farlam Cumbria GB **146/147** N 17

Farnaght Leitrim IRL **219** P 7

Farnborough Hampshire GB **70/71** U 21

Farnell Angus GB **161** J 18

Farnham Surrey GB **70/71** U 21

Farningham Kent GB **71** U 23

Farnworth Bolton GB **134** P 18

Farr Highland GB **186** H 14

Farranfore Kerry IRL **232** S 3

Farringdon Hampshire GB **70/71** U 21

Farthinghoe Northhamptonshire GB **100** S 20

Fascadale Highland GB **174** J 10

Fauldhouse West Lothian GB **160/161** L 15

Faversham Kent GB **71** U 24

Fawley Hampshire GB **70** V 20

Faxfleet East Riding of Yorkshire GB **134/135** P 21

Fazeley Staffordshire GB **100** R 19

Feakle Clare IRL **232** R 5

Fearnmore Highland GB **186** G 11

Featherstone Wakefield GB **134** P 20

Feckenham Worcestershire GB **100** S 19

Fedamore Limerick IRL **232** R 5

Feeard Clare IRL **232** R 3

Feeny Londonderry GB **207** N 8

Feetham North Yorkshire GB **147** O 18

Felixstowe Suffolk GB **71** T 25

Felton Northumberland GB **147** M 19

Feltwell Norfolk GB **101** S 24

Fenagh Leitrim IRL **206** O 7

Fenit Kerry IRL **232** S 3

Fennagh Carlow IRL **233** R 9

Fennor Waterford IRL **233** S 8

Fenwick East Ayrshire GB **160** L 14

Feochaig Argyll and Bute GB **174** M 11

Feolin Ferry Argyll and Bute GB **174** L 10

Ferbane Offaly IRL **219** Q 7

Fermoy Cork IRL **232/233** S 6

Fern Angus GB **161** J 18

Ferndown Dorset GB **70** V 19

Ferness Highland GB **187** H 15

Fernhurst West Sussex GB **70/71** U 21

Ferns Wexford IRL **233** R 9

Ferryhill Durham GB **147** N 19

Fethard Tipperary IRL **233** S 7

Fethard Wexford IRL **233** S 9

Fetterangus Aberdeenshire GB **187** G 18

Fettercairn Aberdeenshire GB **161** J 18

Fewston North Yorkshire GB **134** P 19

Ffarmers Carmarthenshire GB **86/87** S 15

Ffostrasol Ceredigion GB **86** S 14

Fiddown Kilkenny IRL **233** S 8

Filby Norfolk GB **101** R 26

Filey North Yorkshire GB **135** O 22

Fillongley Warwickshire GB **100** S 19

Fincham Norfolk GB **101** R 23

Finchingfield Essex GB **71** T 23

Findhom Moray GB **187** G 15

Findochty Moray GB **187** G 17

Findon West Sussex GB **71** V 22

Finedon Northhamptonshire GB **100** S 21

Finnea Westmeath IRL **219** P 8

Finningham Suffolk GB **101** S 25

Finningley Doncaster GB **134/135** Q 21

Finstown Orkney Islands GB **198** D 16

Fintona Tyrone GB **207** O 8

Fintry Stirling GB **160** K 14

Finuge Kerry IRL **232** S 3

Finvoy Antrim GB **207** M 10

Fionnphort Argyll and Bute GB **174** K 10

Fionnsabhagh Na h-Eileanan an Iar GB **175** G 9

Fishbourne Isle of Wight GB **70** V 20

Fishguard Abergwaun Pembrokeshire GB **86** T 13

Fishlake Doncaster GB **134** P 20

Fiskavaig Highland GB **175** H 10

Fittleworth West Sussex GB **70/71** V 21

Fiunary Highland GB **174** J 11

Fivemiletown Fermanagh GB **207** O 8

Fladdabister Shetland Islands GB **199** B 20

Flagmount Clare IRL **232** R 5

Flamborough East Riding of Yorkshire GB **135** O 22

Flash Staffordshire GB **134** Q 19

Flawith North Yorkshire GB **147** O 20

Flaxton North Yorkshire GB **134** O 21

Fleet Hampshire GB **70/71** U 21

Fleetwood Lancashire GB **119** P 16

Flimby Cumbria GB **146** N 15

Flimwell East Sussex GB **71** U 23

Flint Flintshire GB **119** Q 16

Flintham Nottinghamshire GB **100** R 21

Flitwick Bedfordshire GB **71** T 22

Flixborough North Lincolnshire GB **134/135** P 21

Flodden Northumberland GB **161** L 18

Flookburgh Cumbria GB **146** O 16

Florence Court Fermanagh GB **206** O 7

Fobbing Thurrock GB **71** T 23

Fochabers Moray GB **187** G 16

Folda Angus GB **161** J 16

Folkestone Kent GB **71** U 25

Folkingham Lincolnshire GB **100/101** R 22

Fontstown Kildare IRL **219** Q 9

Ford Argyll and Bute GB **160** K 12

Ford Northumberland GB **161** L 18

Ford End Essex GB **71** T 23

Fordham Cambridgeshire GB **101** S 23

Fordingbridge Hampshire GB **70** V 19

Fordoun Aberdeenshire GB **161** J 18

Fordstown Meath IRL **219** P 9

Fordyce Aberdeenshire GB **187** G 17

Fore Westmeath IRL **219** P 8

Forest Row East Sussex GB **71** U 23

Forfar Angus GB **161** J 18

Forgandenny Perth and Kinross GB **160/161** K 15

Forkill Armagh GB **207** O 10

Formby Sefton GB **119** P 16

Forres Moray GB **187** G 15

Forsinard Highland GB **187** F 15

Forss Highland GB **198** E 15

Fort Augustus Highland GB **186** H 13

Fort George Highland GB **186/187** G 14

Fort William Highland GB **160** J 12

Forter Angus GB **161** J 16

Forteviot Perth and Kinross GB **160/161** K 15

Forth South Lanarkshire GB **160/161** L 15

Fortingall Perth and Kinross GB **160** J 14

Fortrose Highland GB **186/187** G 14

Fortuneswell Dorset GB **70** V 18

Fosdyke Lincolnshire GB **100/101** R 22

Foss Perth and Kinross GB **160/161** J 15

Fotherby Lincolnshire GB **135** Q 22

Foulden Scottish Borders GB **161** L 18

Foulsham   Norfolk   GB   **101**   R 25

Fountainhall   Scottish Borders GB   **161**   L 17

Four Mile House   Roscommon IRL   **218/219**   P 6

Foveran   Aberdeenshire   GB   **187** H 18

Fowey   Cornwall   GB   **52**   W 13

Fownhope   Herefordshire   GB   **87** S 17

Foxdale   Isle of Man   GB   **146**   O 13

Foxford   Mayo   IRL   **218**   P 4

Foxholes   North Yorkshire   GB   **135** O 22

Foyers   Highland   GB   **186**   H 14

Foynes   Limerick   IRL   **232**   R 4

Framlingham   Suffolk   GB   **101** S 25

Frampton   Dorset   GB   **53**   V 17

Frampton on Severn Gloucestershire   GB   **70**   T 18

Fraserburgh   Aberdeenshire GB   **187**   G 19

Freckleton   Lancashire   GB   **119** P 17

Freemount   Cork   IRL   **232**   S 5

Frenchpark   Roscommon IRL   **218/219**   P 6

Frensham   Surrey   GB   **70/71**   U 21

Freshford   Kilkenny   IRL   **233**   R 8

Freshwater   Isle of Wight   GB   **70** V 19

Fressingfield   Suffolk   GB   **101** S 25

Freswick   Highland   GB   **198**   E 16

Friday Bridge   Cambridgeshire GB   **101**   R 23

Fridaythorpe   East Riding of Yorkshire   GB   **134**   O 21

Frinton-on-Sea   Essex   GB   **71**   T 25

Friockheim   Angus   GB   **161**   J 18

Frisby on the Wreake   Leicestershire GB   **100**   R 21

Friskney   Lincolnshire   GB   **135** Q 23

Frizington   Cumbria   GB   **146**   N 16

Frodsham   Cheshire   GB   **119**   Q 17

Frome   Somerset   GB   **70**   U 18

Frongoch   Gwynedd   GB   **119**   R 15

Frosterley   Durham   GB   **147**   N 19

Froxfield   Wiltshire   GB   **70**   U 19

Fulbourn   Cambridgeshire   GB   **101** S 23

Fulstow   Lincolnshire   GB   **135** Q 23

Fulwood   Lancashire   GB   **119**   P 17

Funzie   Shetland Islands   GB   **199** A 21

Furnace   Argyll and Bute   GB   **160** K 12

Fyfield   Essex   GB   **71**   T 23

Fyvie   Aberdeenshire   GB   **187** H 18

G

Gabwell   Devon   GB   **53**   V 15

Gaick Lodge   Highland   GB   **160** J 14

Gainsborough   Lincolnshire GB   **134/135**   Q 21

Gairloch   Highland   GB   **186**   G 11

Gairlochy   Highland   GB   **160**   J 12

Gairnshiel Lodge   Aberdeenshire GB   **187**   H 16

Gaitsgill   Cumbria   GB   **146/147** N 17

Galashiels   Scottish Borders GB   **161**   L 17

Galbally   Limerick   IRL   **232/233** S 6

Galgate   Lancashire   GB   **119**   P 17

Galmisdale   Highland   GB   **175** J 10

Galston   East Ayrshire   GB   **160** L 14

Galway Gaillimh   Galway   IRL   **218** Q 4

Gamblesby   Cumbria   GB   **146/147** N 17

Gamlingay   Cambridgeshire GB   **100/101**   S 22

Gamston   Nottinghamshire GB   **134/135**   Q 21

Gaoth Dobhair   Donegal   IRL   **206** M 6

Garagie Lodge   Highland   GB   **186** H 14

Garbhallt   Argyll and Bute   GB   **160** K 12

Garboldisham   Norfolk   GB   **101** S 24

Gardenstown   Aberdeenshire GB   **187**   G 18

Garelochhead   Argyll and Bute GB   **160**   K 13

Garforth   Leeds   GB   **134**   P 20

Gargrave   North Yorkshire   GB   **134** P 18

Gargunnock   Stirling   GB   **160** K 14

Garlieston   Dumfries and Galloway GB   **146**   N 14

Garmouth   Moray   GB   **187**   G 16

Garrabost   Na h-Eileanan an Iar GB   **186**   F 10

Garrafrauns   Galway   IRL   **218**   P 5

Garras   Cornwall   GB   **52**   W 12

Garreg   Gwynedd   GB   **118/119** R 14

Garrett   Cumbria   GB   **147**   O 18

Garrigill   Cumbria   GB   **147**   N 18

Garrison   Fermanagh   GB   **206**   O 6

Garristown   Dublin   IRL   **219**   P 10

Garros   Highland   GB   **186**   G 10

Garryvoe   Cork   IRL   **232/233**   T 6

Garsdale Head   Cumbria   GB   **147** O 18

Garstang   Lancashire   GB   **119** P 17

Garth   Powys   GB   **86/87**   S 15

Garthmyl   Powys   GB   **87**   R 16

Garthorpe   North Lincolnshire GB   **134/135**   P 21

Gartmore   Stirling   GB   **160**   K 14

Gartocharn   West Dunbartonshire GB   **160**   K 13

Garton   East Riding of Yorkshire GB   **135**   P 22

Garton-on-the-Wolds   East Riding of Yorkshire   GB   **135**   O 22

Garvagh   Londonderry   GB   **207** N 9

Garvagh   Leitrim   IRL   **219**   P 7

Garvaghy   Tyrone   GB   **207** O 8

Garvald   East Lothian   GB   **161** L 17

Garvard   Argyll and Bute   GB   **174** K 10

Garve   Highland   GB   **186**   G 13

Gatehouse   Northumberland GB   **147**   M 18

Gatehouse of Fleet   Dumfries and Galloway   GB   **146**   N 14

Gateshead   Gateshead   GB   **147** N 19

Gawsworth   Cheshire   GB   **134** Q 18

Gaybrook   Westmeath   IRL   **219** Q 8

Gaydon   Warwickshire   GB   **100** S 20

Gayton   Norfolk   GB   **101**   R 24

Gearraidh na h-Aibhne   Na h-Eileanan an Iar   GB   **175**   F 9

Geddington   Northhamptonshire GB   **100**   S 21

Gedney Drove End   Lincolnshire GB   **101**   R 23

Gedney Hill   Lincolnshire GB   **100/101**   R 22

Geirinis   Na h-Eileanan an Iar GB   **175**   H 8

Gelston   Dumfries and Galloway GB   **146**   N 15

Georgeham   Devon   GB   **52/53** U 14

Gerrards Cross   Buckinghamshire GB   **70/71**   T 21

Gibstown   Meath   IRL   **219**   P 9

Gifford   East Lothian   GB   **161**   L 17

Gilcrux   Cumbria   GB   **146**   N 16

Gilford   Down   GB   **207**   O 10

Gill   Durham   GB   **147**   N 19

Gilling East   North Yorkshire GB   **147**   O 20

Gilling West   North Yorkshire GB   **147**   O 19

Gillingham   Norfolk   GB   **101**   S 26

Gillingham   Dorset   GB   **70**   U 18

Gillingham   Medway   GB   **71**   U 24

Gills   Highland   GB   **198**   E 16

Gilmerton   Perth and Kinross GB   **160/161**   K 15

Gilmorton   Leicestershire   GB   **100** S 20

Gilsland   Cumbria   GB   **146/147** N 17

Gilwern   Monmouthshire   GB   **87** T 16

Girvan   South Ayrshire   GB   **146** M 13

Gisburn   Lancashire   GB   **134**   P 18

Gladestry   Powys   GB   **87**   S 16

Glaisdale   North Yorkshire   GB   **134** O 21

Glamis   Angus   GB   **161**   J 16

Glanaman   Carmarthenshire GB   **86/87**   T 15

Glandore   Cork   IRL   **232**   T 4

Glangevlin   Cavan   IRL   **206**   O 7

Glanton   Northumberland   GB   **147** M 19

Glanworth   Cork   IRL   **232/233**   S 6

Glasgow   Glasgow City   GB   **160** L 14

Glaslough   Monaghan   IRL   **207** O 9

Glassan   Westmeath   IRL   **219**   Q 7

Glassford   South Lanarkshire GB   **160**   L 14

Glasson   Lancashire   GB   **119**   P 17

Glassonby   Cumbria   GB   **146/147** N 17

Glastonbury   Somerset   GB   **53** U 17

Gleann an Muaidhe   Mayo   IRL   **218** O 3

Glebe   Londonderry   GB   **207**   M 9

Glemsford   Suffolk   GB   **101**   S 24

Glen   Donegal   IRL   **206**   M 7

Glenancross   Highland   GB   **175** J 11

Glenariff   Antrim   GB   **207**   M 10

Glenarm   Antrim   GB   **207**   N 11

Glenavy   Antrim   GB   **207**   N 10

Glenbarr   Argyll and Bute   GB   **174** L 11

Glenbeigh   Kerry   IRL   **232**   S 3

Glenborrodale   Highland   GB   **174** J 11

Glenbrittle   Highland   GB   **175** H 10

Glenbuck   East Ayrshire GB   **160/161**   L 15

Glencaple   Dumfries and Galloway GB   **146**   M 15

Glencarse   Perth and Kinross GB   **161**   K 16

Glencoe   Highland   GB   **160**   J 12

Glencolumbkille   Donegal   IRL   **206** N 5

Glenderry   Kerry   IRL   **232**   S 3

Glendevon   Perth and Kinross GB   **160/161**   K 15

Glenealy   Wicklow   IRL   **233**   R 10

Gleneely   Donegal   IRL   **207**   M 8

Glenegedale   Argyll and Bute GB   **174**   L 10

Glenelg   Highland   GB   **175**   H 11

Glenfarg   Perth and Kinross GB   **161**   K 16

Glenfeshie Lodge   Highland GB   **160**   H 15

Glenfinnan   Highland   GB   **160** J 12

Glengarriff   Cork   IRL   **232**   T 3

Glenkindie   Aberdeenshire   GB   **187** H 17

Glenlivet   Moray   GB   **187**   H 16

Glenluce   Dumfries and Galloway GB   **146**   N 13

Glenmaye   Isle of Man   GB   **146** O 13

Glenmore   Highland   GB   **187**   H 15

Glenmore   Kilkenny   IRL   **233**   S 8

Glennamaddy   Galway   IRL   **218** P 5

Glenntrool Lodge   Dumfries and Galloway   GB   **146**   M 14

Glenprosen Village   Angus   GB   **161** J 16

Glenrothes   Fife   GB   **161**   K 16

Glentane   Galway   IRL   **218/219** Q 6

Glentham   Lincolnshire GB   **134/135**   Q 21

Glenties   Donegal   IRL   **206**   N 6

Glenville   Cork   IRL   **232/233**   S 6

Gletness   Shetland Islands   GB   **199** B 20

Glin   Limerick   IRL   **232**   R 4

Glinsk   Galway   IRL   **218**   Q 3

Glossop   Derbyshire   GB   **134**   Q 19

Gloucester   Gloucestershire   GB   **70** T 18

Gloup   Shetland Islands   GB   **199** A 20

Glusburn   Bradford   GB   **134**   P 19

Glutt Lodge   Highland   GB   **187** F 15

Glyn Ceiriog   Wrexham   GB   **119** R 16

Glynde   East Sussex   GB   **71**   V 23

Glyndyfrdwy   Denbighshire GB   **119**   R 16

Glynn   Antrim   GB   **207**   N 11

Glynn   Wexford   IRL   **233**   S 9

Glynneath   Neath Port Talbot GB   **86/87**   T 15

Gnosall   Staffordshire   GB   **100** R 18

Goathland   North Yorkshire GB   **134**   O 21

Gobhig   Na h-Eileanan an Iar GB   **175**   G 8

Godalming   Surrey   GB   **70/71** U 21

Godmanchester   Cambridgeshire GB   **100/101**   S 22

Godshill   Isle of Wight   GB   **70** V 20

Godstone   Surrey   GB   **71**   U 22

Goginan   Ceredigion   GB   **86/87** S 15

Golborne   Wigan   GB   **119**   Q 17

Goldcliff   Newport   GB   **87**   T 17

Golden   Tipperary   IRL   **233**   R 7

Goldhanger   Essex   GB   **71**   T 24

Goleen   Cork   IRL   **232**   U 3

Golspie   Highland   GB   **187**   G 15

Gonfirth   Shetland Islands   GB   **199** B 20

Goodrich   Herefordshire   GB   **87** T 17

Goodwick   Pembrokeshire   GB   **86** S 13

Goole   East Riding of Yorkshire GB   **134/135**   P 21

Goonhavern   Cornwall   GB   **52** W 12

Goosnargh   Lancashire   GB   **119** P 17

Gordon   Scottish Borders   GB   **161** L 17

Gorebridge   Midlothian   GB   **161** L 16

Gorey   Wexford   IRL   **233**   R 10

Gorey   Channel Islands   GB   **66** Y 18

Goring   Oxfordshire   GB   **70**   T 20

Gormanston   Meath   IRL   **219**   P 10

Gorran Haven   Cornwall   GB   **52** W 13

Gorseinon   Swansea   GB   **86**   T 14

Gorseness   Orkney Islands   GB   **198** D 17

Gorstan   Highland   GB   **186**   G 13

Gort   Galway   IRL   **218**   Q 5

Gortahork   Donegal   IRL   **206**   M 6

Gortantaoid   Argyll and Bute GB   **174**   L 10

Gorteen   Sligo   IRL   **218**   P 5

Gorteen   Galway   IRL   **218**   Q 5

Gortin   Tyrone   GB   **207**   N 8

Gortmore   Mayo   IRL   **206**   O 4

Gortnahoo   Tipperary   IRL   **233**   R 7

Gosberton   Lincolnshire GB   **100/101**   R 22

Gosforth   Cumbria   GB   **146**   O 16

Gosport   Hampshire   GB   **70**   V 20

Goswick   Northumberland   GB   **161** L 19

Goudhurst   Kent   GB   **71**   U 23

Gourdon   Aberdeenshire   GB   **161** J 18

Gourock   Inverclyde   GB   **160**   L 13

Gowran   Kilkenny   IRL   **233**   R 8

Goxhill   North Lincolnshire GB   **135**   P 22

Grabhair   Na h-Eileanan an Iar GB   **186**   F 10

Graiguenamanagh   Kilkenny IRL   **233**   R 9

Grain   Medway   GB   **71**   U 24

Grainthorpe   Lincolnshire   GB   **135** Q 23

Grampound   Cornwall   GB   **52** W 13

Granard   Longford   IRL   **219**   P 7

Grandtully   Perth and Kinross GB **160/161** J 15

Grange   Cumbria GB **146** N 16

Grange   Sligo IRL **206** O 5

Grangebellew   Louth IRL **219** P 10

Grangemouth   Falkirk GB **160/161** K 15

Grange-over-Sands   Cumbria GB **146/147** O 17

Grantham   Lincolnshire GB **100** R 21

Grantown-on-Spey   Highland GB **187** H 15

Grantshouse   Scottish Borders GB **161** L 18

Grasby   Lincolnshire GB **135** P 22

Grasmere   Cumbria GB **146** O 16

Grassington   North Yorkshire GB **147** O 19

Gravesend   Kent GB **71** U 23

Grayrigg   Cumbria GB **146/147** O 17

Grays   Thurrock GB **71** U 23

Great Altcar   Lancashire GB **119** P 16

Great Asby   Cumbria GB **146/147** N 17

Great Ayton   North Yorkshire GB **147** O 20

Great Baddow   Essex GB **71** T 23

Great Bardfield   Essex GB **71** T 23

Great Barford   Bedfordshire GB **100/101** S 22

Great Bircham   Norfolk GB **101** R 24

Great Brickhill   Buckinghamshire GB **70/71** T 21

Great Broughton   Cumbria GB **146** N 16

Great Broughton   North Yorkshire GB **147** O 20

Great Budworth   Cheshire GB **134** Q 18

Great Carlton   Lincolnshire GB **135** Q 23

Great Chesterford   Essex GB **101** S 23

Great Clifton   Cumbria GB **146** N 16

Great Coates   North East Lincolnshire GB **135** P 22

Great Dalby   Leicestershire GB **100** R 21

Great Dunmow   Essex GB **71** T 23

Great Eccleston   Lancashire GB **119** P 17

Great Gidding   Cambridgeshire GB **100/101** S 22

Great Glen   Leicestershire GB **100** R 20

Great Grandsen   Cambridgeshire GB **100/101** S 22

Great Hampden   Buckinghamshire GB **70/71** T 21

Great Harrowden   Northhamptons. GB **100** S 21

Great Harwood   Lancashire GB **134** P 18

Great Langton   North Yorkshire GB **147** O 19

Great Leighs   Essex GB **71** T 23

Great Limber   Lincolnshire GB **135** P 22

Great Malvern   Worcestershire GB **87** S 18

Great Massingham   Norfolk GB **101** R 24

Great Missenden   Buckinghamshire GB **70/71** T 21

Great Mitton   Lancashire GB **134** P 18

Great Oakley   Essex GB **71** T 25

Great Offley   Hertfordshire GB **71** T 22

Great Ormside   Cumbria GB **147** N 18

Great Orton   Cumbria GB **146** N 16

Great Ponton   Lincolnshire GB **100** R 21

Great Rissington   Gloucestershire GB **70** T 19

Great Ryburgh   Norfolk GB **101** R 24

Great Salkeld   Cumbria GB **146/147** N 17

Great Sampford   Essex GB **71** T 23

Great Shefford   West Berkshire GB **70** U 20

Great Shelford   Cambridgeshire GB **101** S 23

Great Smeaton   North Yorkshire GB **147** O 20

Great Staughton   Cambridgeshire GB **100/101** S 22

Great Strickland   Cumbria GB **146/147** N 17

Great Tew   Oxfordshire GB **70** T 20

Great Torrington   Devon GB **52/53** V 14

Great Wakering   Essex GB **71** T 24

Great Waltham   Essex GB **71** T 23

Great Whittington   Northumberland GB **147** M 19

Great Witley   Worcestershire GB **87** S 18

Great Wolford   Gloucestershire GB **70** T 19

Great Yarmouth   Norfolk GB **101** R 26

Great Yeldham   Essex GB **101** S 24

Greatham   Hartlepool GB **147** N 20

Green   Cornwall GB **52/53** V 14

Green Hammerton   North Yorkshire GB **147** O 20

Greencastle   Donegal IRL **207** M 9

Greencastle   Tyrone GB **207** N 8

Greencastle   Down GB **207** O 10

Greenhaugh   Northumberland GB **147** M 18

Greenhead   Northumberland GB **146/147** N 17

Greenholm   East Ayrshire GB **160** L 14

Greenisland   Antrim GB **207** N 11

Greenlaw   Scottish Borders GB **161** L 18

Greenloaning   Perth and Kinross GB **160/161** K 15

Greenock   Inverclyde GB **160** L 13

Greenodd   Cumbria GB **146** O 16

Greetham   Rutland GB **100** R 21

Grenagh   Cork IRL **232** S 5

Greosabhagh   Na h-Eileanan an Iar GB **175** G 9

Gresford   Wrexham GB **119** Q 17

Greshornish   Highland GB **175** H 10

Gretna   Dumfries and Galloway GB **146** N 16

Gretton   Northhamptonshire GB **100** R 21

Greyabbey   Down GB **207** N 11

Greystoke   Cumbria GB **146/147** N 17

Greystone   Angus GB **161** J 18

Greystone   Tyrone GB **207** O 9

Greystones   Wicklow IRL **219** Q 10

Grimister   Shetland Islands GB **199** A 20

Grimoldby   Lincolnshire GB **135** Q 23

Grimsby   North East Lincolnshire GB **135** P 22

Grimston   Norfolk GB **101** R 24

Grindleton   Lancashire GB **134** P 18

Grindon   Northumberland GB **161** L 18

Gringley on the Hill   Nottinghams. GB **134/135** Q 21

Grinton   North Yorkshire GB **147** O 19

Gritley   Orkney Islands GB **198** E 17

Grizebeck   Cumbria GB **146** O 16

Groby   Leicestershire GB **100** R 20

Grogport   Argyll and Bute GB **160** L 12

Grosmont   North Yorkshire GB **134** O 21

Grove   Cheshire GB **134** Q 18

Grove   Kent GB **71** U 25

Grundisburgh   Suffolk GB **101** S 25

Gruting   Shetland Islands GB **199** B 20

Grutness   Shetland Islands GB **199** C 20

Gualachulain   Highland GB **160** J 12

Guildford   Surrey GB **70/71** U 21

Guildtown   Perth and Kinross GB **161** K 16

Guilsfield   Powys GB **87** R 16

Guisborough   Redcar & Cleveland GB **147** N 20

Guiseley   Leeds GB **134** P 19

Guist   Norfolk GB **101** R 24

Guiting Power   Gloucestershire GB **70** T 19

Gulladuff   Londonderry GB **207** N 9

Gullane   East Lothian GB **161** K 17

Gunnislake   Cornwall GB **52/53** V 14

Gunnista   Shetland Islands GB **199** B 20

Gusserane   Wexford IRL **233** S 9

Gutcher   Shetland Islands GB **199** A 20

Guthrie   Angus GB **161** J 18

Guyhirn   Cambridgeshire GB **101** R 23

Gwalchmai   Anglesey GB **118/119** Q 14

Gweek   Cornwall GB **52** W 12

Gweesalia   Mayo IRL **218** O 3

Gwernymynydd   Flintshire GB **119** Q 16

Gwyddelwern   Denbighshire GB **119** Q 16

Gwytherin   Conwy GB **119** Q 15

Gyleen   Cork IRL **232/233** T 6

H

Habrough   North East Lincolnshire GB **135** P 22

Hacketstown   Carlow IRL **233** R 9

Hackness   North Yorkshire GB **135** O 21

Haddenham   Cambridgeshire GB **101** S 23

Haddenham   Buckinghamshire GB **70/71** T 21

Haddington   East Lothian GB **161** L 17

Haddiscoe   Norfolk GB **101** R 26

Hadleigh   Suffolk GB **101** S 24

Hadleigh   Southend-on-Sea GB **71** T 24

Hadnall   Shropshire GB **119** R 17

Hagley   Herefordshire GB **87** S 17

Hagley   Worcestershire GB **87** S 18

Haile   Cumbria GB **146** O 16

Hailsham   East Sussex GB **71** V 23

Hale   Trafford GB **134** Q 18

Hales   Norfolk GB **101** R 26

Halesowen   Dudley GB **87** S 18

Halesworth   Suffolk GB **101** S 26

Halford   Warwickshire GB **100** S 19

Halifax   Calderdale GB **134** P 19

Halkirk   Highland GB **198** E 16

Halland   East Sussex GB **71** V 23

Hallaton   Leicestershire GB **100** R 21

Hallbankgate   Cumbria GB **146/147** N 17

Hallington   Northumberland GB **147** M 18

Hallsands   Devon GB **53** W 15

Halsham   East Riding of Yorkshire GB **135** P 22

Halstead   Essex GB **71** T 24

Haltham   Lincolnshire GB **135** Q 22

Halton Gill   North Yorkshire GB **147** O 18

Halton Lea Gate   Northumberland GB **146/147** N 17

Haltwhistle   Northumberland GB **147** N 18

Halvergate   Norfolk GB **101** R 26

Halwell   Devon GB **53** W 15

Halwill   Devon GB **52/53** V 14

Ham   Shetland Islands GB **199** B 18

Hamble le Rice   Hampshire GB **70** V 20

Hambledon   Hampshire GB **70** V 20

Hambleton   Lancashire GB **119** P 17

Hambleton   North Yorkshire GB **134** P 20

Hamilton   South Lanarkshire GB **160** L 14

Hamnavoe   Shetland Islands GB **199** B 20

Hamnavoe   Shetland Islands GB **199** B 20

Hamsterley   Durham GB **147** N 19

Hamstreet   Kent GB **71** U 24

Handforth   Cheshire GB **134** Q 18

Hanslope   Milton Keynes GB **100** S 21

Happisburgh   Norfolk GB **101** R 26

Harbottle   Northumberland GB **147** M 18

Harbury   Warwickshire GB **100** S 20

Harby   Leicestershire GB **100** R 21

Harby   Nottinghamshire GB **100** R 21

Hardraw   North Yorkshire GB **147** O 18

Harewood   Leeds GB **134** P 19

Harlech   Gwynedd GB **86** R 14

Harleston   Norfolk GB **101** S 25

Harlosh   Highland GB **175** H 9

Harlow   Essex GB **71** T 23

Harmston   Lincolnshire GB **134/135** Q 21

Haroldswick   Shetland Islands GB **199** A 21

Harpenden   Hertfordshire GB **71** T 22

Harpley   Norfolk GB **101** R 24

Harrietfield   Perth and Kinross GB **160/161** K 15

Harrietsham   Kent GB **71** U 24

Harrington   Cumbria GB **146** N 15

Harringworth   Northhamptonshire GB **100** R 21

Harrogate   North Yorkshire GB **134** P 19

Harrold   Bedfordshire GB **100** S 21

Harrow   Greater London GB **71** T 22

Hart   Hartlepool GB **147** N 20

Hartburn   Northumberland GB **147** M 19

Hartest   Suffolk GB **101** S 24

Hartfield   East Sussex GB **71** U 23

Hartford   Cambridgeshire GB **100/101** S 22

Harthill   West Lothian GB **160/161** L 15

Hartington   Derbyshire GB **134** Q 19

Hartland   Devon GB **52/53** V 14

Hartlepool   Hartlepool GB **147** N 20

Hartley Whitney   Hampshire GB **70/71** U 21

Hartpury   Gloucestershire GB **70** T 18

Harvington   Worcestershire GB **100** S 19

Harwel   Oxfordshire GB **70** T 20

Harwich   Essex GB **71** T 25

Harwood Dale   North Yorkshire GB **134** O 21

Harworth   Nottinghamshire GB **134** Q 20

Haslemere   Surrey GB **70/71** U 21

Haslingden   Lancashire GB **134** P 18

Hastings   East Sussex GB **71** V 24

Haswell   Durham GB **147** N 20

Hatch Beauchamp   Somerset GB **53** V 17

Hatfield   Doncaster GB **134** P 20

Hatfield   Hertfordshire   GB   **71**   T 22

Hatfield   Herefordshire   GB   **87**   S 17

Hatfield Broad Oak   Essex   GB   **71**   T 23

Hatfield Peverel   Essex   GB   **71**   T 24

Hatherleigh   Devon   GB   **52/53**   V 14

Hathern   Leicestershire   GB   **100**   R 20

Hatherop   Gloucestershire   GB   **70**   T 19

Hathersage   Derbyshire   GB   **134**   Q 19

Hatton   Warwickshire   GB   **100**   S 19

Hatton   Aberdeenshire   GB   **187**   H 19

Hatton of Fintray   Aberdeenshire   GB   **187**   H 18

Haugh of Urr   Dumfries and Galloway   GB   **146**   N 15

Haughton   Staffordshire   GB   **100**   R 18

Havant   Hampshire   GB   **70**   V 20

Haverfordwet Hwlffordd   Pembrokeshire   GB   **86**   T 13

Haverhill   Essex   GB   **101**   S 23

Haverhill   Suffolk   GB   **101**   S 23

Hawarden   Flintshire   GB   **119**   Q 16

Hawes   North Yorkshire   GB   **147**   O 18

Hawick   Scottish Borders   GB   **146/147**   M 17

Hawkhurst   Kent   GB   **71**   U 24

Hawkinge   Kent   GB   **71**   U 25

Hawkshead   Cumbria   GB   **146/147**   O 17

Hawnby   North Yorkshire   GB   **147**   O 20

Haworth   Bradford   GB   **134**   P 19

Hawsker   North Yorkshire   GB   **134**   O 21

Haxby   York   GB   **147**   O 20

Haxey   North Lincolnshire   GB   **134/135**   Q 21

Haydon Bridge   Northumberland   GB   **147**   N 18

Hayfield   Derbyshire   GB   **134**   Q 19

Hayle   Cornwall   GB   **52**   W 12

Hay-on-Wye   Powys   GB   **87**   S 16

Hayton   East Riding of Yorkshire   GB   **134/135**   P 21

Hayton   Nottinghamshire   GB   **134/135**   Q 21

Hayton   Cumbria   GB   **146/147**   N 17

Haywards Heath   West Sussex   GB   **71**   U 22

Hazel Grove   Stockport   GB   **134**   Q 18

Hazelbury Bryan   Dorset   GB   **70**   V 18

Hazlemere   Buckinghamshire   GB   **70/71**   T 21

Heacham   Norfolk   GB   **101**   R 23

Headcorn   Kent   GB   **71**   U 24

Headford   Galway   IRL   **218**   Q 4

Headford   Kerry   IRL   **232**   S 4

Healey   North Yorkshire   GB   **147**   O 19

Heanor   Derbyshire   GB   **134**   Q 20

Heast   Highland   GB   **175**   H 11

Heath End   West Berkshire   GB   **70**   U 20

Heathfield   East Sussex   GB   **71**   V 23

Hebden Bridge   Calderdale   GB   **134**   P 18

Heckington   Lincolnshire   GB   **100/101**   R 22

Hedge End   Hampshire   GB   **70**   V 20

Hedon   East Riding of Yorkshire   GB   **135**   P 22

Heighington   Lincolnshire   GB   **135**   Q 22

Heighington   Durham   GB   **147**   N 19

Helensburgh   Argyll and Bute   GB   **160**   K 13

Hellingly   East Sussex   GB   **71**   V 23

Helmdon   Northhamptonshire   GB   **100**   S 20

Helmsdale   Highland   GB   **187**   F 15

Helmsley   North Yorkshire   GB   **147**   O 20

Helpringham   Lincolnshire   GB   **100/101**   R 22

Helpston   Peterborough   GB   **100/101**   R 22

Helsby   Cheshire   GB   **119**   Q 17

Helston   Cornwall   GB   **52**   W 12

Hemel Hempstead   Hertfordshire   GB   **71**   T 22

Hemingbrough   North Yorkshire   GB   **134/135**   P 21

Hempnall   Norfolk   GB   **101**   S 25

Hemsby   Norfolk   GB   **101**   R 26

Hemsworth   Wakefield   GB   **134**   P 20

Hemyock   Devon   GB   **53**   V 16

Henfield   West Sussex   GB   **71**   V 22

Hengoed   Shropshire   GB   **119**   R 16

Henley-in-Arden   Warwickshire   GB   **100**   S 19

Henley-on-Thames   Oxfordshire   GB   **70/71**   T 21

Henllan   Conwy   GB   **119**   Q 16

Henshaw   Northumberland   GB   **147**   N 18

Henstridge   Somerset   GB   **70**   V 18

Hepple   Northumberland   GB   **147**   M 18

Herbertstown   Limerick   IRL   **232/233**   R 6

Hereford   Herefordshire   GB   **87**   S 17

Heriot   Scottish Borders   GB   **161**   L 17

Hermitage   West Berkshire   GB   **70**   U 20

Herne Bay   Kent   GB   **71**   U 25

Herriard   Hampshire   GB   **70**   U 20

Herstmonceux   East Sussex   GB   **71**   V 23

Herston   Orkney Islands   GB   **198**   E 16

Hertford   Hertfordshire   GB   **71**   T 22

Hesketh Bank   Lancashire   GB   **119**   P 17

Hessle   Kingston upon Hull   GB   **135**   P 22

Heswall   Wirral   GB   **119**   Q 16

Hethersett   Norfolk   GB   **101**   R 25

Hethersgill   Cumbria   GB   **146/147**   M 17

Hetton-le-Hole   Sunderland   GB   **147**   N 20

Heveningham   Suffolk   GB   **101**   S 25

Hexham   Northumberland   GB   **147**   N 18

Heylor   Shetland Islands   GB   **199**   A 20

Heytesbury   Wiltshire   GB   **70**   U 18

Heywood   Rochdale   GB   **134**   P 18

Hibaldstow   North Lincolnshire   GB   **134/135**   P 21

Hickling   Norfolk   GB   **101**   R 26

High Ackworth   Wakefield   GB   **134**   P 20

High Bentham   North Yorkshire   GB   **146/147**   O 17

High Bradfield   Sheffield   GB   **134**   Q 19

High Dougarie   North Ayrshire   GB   **160**   L 12

High Ercall   Shropshire   GB   **119**   R 17

High Ercall   Telford and Wrekin   GB   **119**   R 17

High Ham   Somerset   GB   **53**   U 17

High Hesket   Cumbria   GB   **146/147**   N 17

High Newton-by-the-Sea   Northumberl.   GB   **161**   L 19

High Roding   Essex   GB   **71**   T 23

High Wycombe   Buckinghamshire   GB   **70/71**   T 21

Higham   Derbyshire   GB   **134**   Q 20

Higham Ferrers   Northhamptonshire   GB   **100**   S 21

Highampton   Devon   GB   **52/53**   V 14

Highbridge   Somerset   GB   **53**   U 17

Highclere   Hampshire   GB   **70**   U 20

Higher Town   Isles of Scilly   GB   **52**   X 10

Highley   Shropshire   GB   **87**   S 18

Hightae   Dumfries and Galloway   GB   **146**   M 16

Highworth   Swindon   GB   **70**   T 19

Hilborough   Norfolk   GB   **101**   R 24

Hildenborough   Kent   GB   **71**   U 23

Hilderstone   Staffordshire   GB   **100**   R 18

Hilgay   Norfolk   GB   **101**   R 23

Hill   South Gloucestershire   GB   **87**   T 17

Hill of Fearn   Highland   GB   **187**   G 15

Hillington   Norfolk   GB   **101**   R 24

Hillsborough   Down   GB   **207**   O 10

Hillside   Angus   GB   **161**   J 17

Hillswick   Shetland Islands   GB   **199**   B 19

Hilltown   Down   GB   **207**   O 10

Hilmarton   Wiltshire   GB   **70**   U 19

Hilton   Cumbria   GB   **147**   N 18

Hilton of Cadboll   Highland   GB   **187**   G 15

Hinckley   Leicestershire   GB   **100**   R 20

Hinderwell   North Yorkshire   GB   **147**   N 21

Hindhead   Hampshire   GB   **70/71**   U 21

Hindley   Wigan   GB   **119**   P 17

Hindolveston   Norfolk   GB   **101**   R 25

Hindon   Wiltshire   GB   **70**   U 18

Hingham   Norfolk   GB   **101**   R 24

Hinstock   Shropshire   GB   **100**   R 18

Hintlesham   Suffolk   GB   **101**   S 25

Hirnant   Powys   GB   **119**   R 16

Hirwaun   Rhondda Cynon Taff   GB   **86/87**   T 15

Histon   Cambridgeshire   GB   **101**   S 23

Hitcham   Suffolk   GB   **101**   S 24

Hitchin   Hertfordshire   GB   **71**   T 22

Hockley   Essex   GB   **71**   T 24

Hockley Heath   Warwickshire   GB   **100**   S 19

Hockliffe   Bedfordshire   GB   **70/71**   T 21

Hockwold cum Wilton   Norfolk   GB   **101**   S 24

Hoddesdon   Hertfordshire   GB   **71**   T 22

Hodnet   Shropshire   GB   **119**   R 17

Holbeach   Lincolnshire   GB   **101**   R 23

Holbeach St Johns   Lincolnshire   GB   **100/101**   R 22

Holbeach St Matthew   Lincolnshire   GB   **101**   R 23

Holbrook   Suffolk   GB   **71**   T 25

Holcombe Rogus   Devon   GB   **53**   V 16

Holford   Somerset   GB   **53**   U 16

Hollandstoun   Orkney Islands   GB   **198**   D 18

Hollesley   Suffolk   GB   **101**   S 25

Hollingbourne   Kent   GB   **71**   U 24

Hollingworth   Derbyshire   GB   **134**   Q 19

Hollym   East Riding of Yorkshire   GB   **135**   P 23

Hollymount   Mayo   IRL   **218**   P 4

Hollywood   Wicklow   IRL   **219**   Q 9

Holme   Cambridgeshire   GB   **100/101**   S 22

Holme next the Sea   Norfolk   GB   **101**   R 24

Holme-on-Spalding-Moor   East Riding of Yorkshire   GB   **134/135**   P 21

Holmes Chapel   Cheshire   GB   **134**   Q 18

Holmfirth   Kirklees   GB   **134**   P 19

Holmsfield   Derbyshire   GB   **134**   Q 19

Holsworthy   Devon   GB   **52/53**   V 14

Holsworthy Beacon   Devon   GB   **52/53**   V 14

Holt   Norfolk   GB   **101**   R 25

Holt   Wrexham   GB   **119**   Q 17

Holt Heath   Worcestershire   GB   **87**   S 18

Holy Island   Northumberland   GB   **161**   L 19

Holycross   Tipperary   IRL   **233**   R 7

Holyhead Caergybi   Anglesey   GB   **118**   Q 13

Holystone   Northumberland   GB   **147**   M 18

Holywell   Flintshire   GB   **119**   Q 16

Holywell   Dorset   GB   **53**   V 17

Holywood   Dumfries and Galloway   GB   **146**   M 15

Holywood   Down   GB   **207**   N 11

Honing   Norfolk   GB   **101**   R 25

Honingham   Norfolk   GB   **101**   R 25

Honington   Lincolnshire   GB   **100**   R 21

Honiton   Devon   GB   **53**   V 16

Hoo St Werburgh   Medway   GB   **71**   U 24

Hook   East Riding of Yorkshire   GB   **134/135**   P 21

Hook   Hampshire   GB   **70/71**   U 21

Hook Norton   Oxfordshire   GB   **70**   T 20

Hope   Flintshire   GB   **119**   Q 16

Hope   Derbyshire   GB   **134**   Q 19

Hope Bowdler   Shropshire   GB   **87**   R 17

Hope under Dinmore   Herefordshire   GB   **87**   S 17

Hopeman   Moray   GB   **187**   G 16

Hopton-on-Sea   Norfolk   GB   **101**   R 26

Hordley   Shropshire   GB   **119**   R 17

Horley   Surrey   GB   **71**   U 22

Hornby   Lancashire   GB   **146/147**   O 17

Horncastle   Lincolnshire   GB   **135**   Q 22

Horncliffe   Northumberland   GB   **161**   L 18

Horndean   Hampshire   GB   **70**   V 20

Horningsham   Wiltshire   GB   **70**   U 18

Hornsea   East Riding of Yorkshire   GB   **135**   P 22

Horrabridge   Devon   GB   **52/53**   V 14

Horse   Tipperary   IRL   **233**   R 7

Horsehouse   North Yorkshire   GB   **147**   O 19

Horseleap   Offaly   IRL   **219**   Q 7

Horsey   Norfolk   GB   **101**   R 26

Horsforth   Leeds   GB   **134**   P 19

Horsham   West Sussex   GB   **71**   U 22

Horsham St Faith   Norfolk   GB   **101**   R 25

Horsley   Northumberland   GB   **147**   N 19

Horsley   Gloucestershire   GB   **70**   T 18

Horsted Keynes   West Sussex   GB   **71**   U 22

Horton   Dorset   GB   **70**   V 19

Horton in Ribblesdale   North Yorkshire   GB   **147**   O 18

Horwich   Bolton   GB   **119**   P 17

Hospital   Limerick   IRL   **232/233**   S 6

Hoswick   Shetland Islands   GB   **199**   B 20

Hotham   East Riding of Yorkshire   GB   **134/135**   P 21

Houghton-le-Spring   Sunderland   GB   **147**   N 20

Hourn   Highland   GB   **186**   H 12

Housay   Shetland Islands   GB   **199**   B 21

Houston   Renfrewshire   GB   **160**   L 13

Houstry   Highland   GB   **187**   F 16

Houton   Orkney Islands   GB   **198**   E 16

Hove   Brighton & Hove   GB   **71**   V 22

Hovingham   North Yorkshire   GB   **134**   O 21

Hovnam   Scottish Borders   GB   **147**   M 18

Howden   East Riding of Yorkshire   GB   **134/135**   P 21

Howgate   Midlothian   GB   **161**   L 16

Howick Northumberland GB **147** M 19

Howth Dublin IRL **219** Q 10

Howwood Renfrewshire GB **160** L 13

Hoxa Orkney Islands GB **198** E 17

Hoxne Suffolk GB **101** S 25

Hoylake Wirral GB **119** Q 16

Hoyland Barnsley GB **134** Q 20

Hoyland Barnsley GB **134** Q 20

Hubbert's Bridge Lincolnshire GB **100/101** R 22

Hucknall Nottinghamshire GB **134** Q 20

Huddersfield Kirklees GB **134** P 19

Huggate East Riding of Yorkshire GB **134/135** P 21

Hugh Town Isles of Scilly GB **52** X 10

Huish Champflower Somerset GB **53** U 16

Huisinis Na h-Eileanan an Iar GB **175** G 8

Hullavington Wiltshire GB **70** T 18

Hulwer Street Suffolk GB **101** S 26

Humberston North East Lincolnshire GB **135** P 22

Humbie East Lothian GB **161** L 17

Humshaugh Northumberland GB **147** M 18

Huna Highland GB **198** E 16

Hundon Suffolk GB **101** S 24

Hungerford West Berkshire GB **70** U 19

Hunmanby North Yorkshire GB **135** O 22

Hunstanton Norfolk GB **101** R 23

Hunter's Quay Argyll and Bute GB **160** L 13

Huntingdon Cambridgeshire GB **100/101** S 22

Huntley Gloucestershire GB **70** T 18

Huntly Aberdeenshire GB **187** H 17

Hurlers Cross Clare IRL **232** R 5

Hurliness Orkney Islands GB **198** E 16

Hurn Dorset GB **70** V 19

Hursley Hampshire GB **70** U 20

Hurst Green East Sussex GB **71** U 23

Hurstbourne Priors Hampshire GB **70** U 20

Hurstbourne Tarrant Hampshire GB **70** U 20

Hurstpierpoint West Sussex GB **71** V 22

Hurworth-on-Tees Durham GB **147** O 20

Husbands Bosworth Leicestershire GB **100** S 20

Husthwaite North Yorkshire GB **147** O 20

Huttoft Lincolnshire GB **135** Q 23

Hutton Scottish Borders GB **161** L 18

Hutton Cranswick East Riding of Yorkshire GB **135** P 22

Hutton-le-Hole North Yorkshire GB **134** O 21

Hwlfforddd Haverfordwet Pembrokeshire GB **86** T 13

Hyde Derbyshire GB **134** Q 18

Hynish Argyll and Bute GB **174** K 9

Hythe Hampshire GB **70** V 20

Hythe Kent GB **71** U 25

I

Ibsley Hampshire GB **70** V 19

Ibstock Leicestershire GB **100** R 20

Icklingham Suffolk GB **101** S 24

Ide Devon GB **53** V 15

Ideford Devon GB **53** V 15

Idminston Wiltshire GB **70** U 19

Ightfield Shropshire GB **119** R 17

Ightham Kent GB **71** U 23

Ilchester Somerset GB **53** V 17

Ilderton Northumberland GB **147** M 19

Ilfracombe Devon GB **52/53** U 14

Ilkeston Derbyshire GB **100** R 20

Ilkley Bradford GB **134** P 19

Ilmington Warwackshire GB **100** S 19

Ilminster Somerset GB **53** V 17

Immingham North East Lincolnshire GB **135** P 22

Inagh Clare IRL **232** R 4

Inch Kerry IRL **232** S 3

Inch Wexford IRL **233** R 10

Inchbare Angus GB **161** J 18

Inchigeelagh Cork IRL **232** T 4

Inchnadamph Highland GB **186** F 13

Inchture Perth and Kinross GB **161** K 16

Ingatestone Essex GB **71** T 23

Ingham Suffolk GB **101** S 24

Ingleton North Yorkshire GB **147** O 18

Inglewhite Lancashire GB **119** P 17

Ingoldmells Lincolnshire GB **135** Q 23

Ingoldsby Lincolnshire GB **100** R 21

Ingram Northumberland GB **147** M 19

Inishannon Cork IRL **232** T 5

Inishcrone Sligo IRL **206** O 4

Iniskeen Monaghan IRL **219** P 9

Inistioge Kilkenny IRL **233** S 8

Inkberrow Worcestershire GB **100** S 19

Innellan Argyll and Bute GB **160** L 13

Innerleithen Scottish Borders GB **161** L 16

Innermessan Dumfries and Galloway GB **146** N 13

Innerwick East Lothian GB **161** L 18

Innfield Meath IRL **219** Q 9

Insch Aberdeenshire GB **187** H 17

Insh Highland GB **187** H 15

Inskip Lancashire GB **119** P 17

Instow Devon GB **52/53** U 14

Inver Perth and Kinross GB **160/161** J 15

Inver Highland GB **187** G 15

Inveralligin Highland GB **186** G 11

Inverallochy Aberdeenshire GB **187** G 19

Inveran Highland GB **186/187** G 14

Inveran Galway IRL **218** Q 4

Inverarity Angus GB **161** J 18

Inverbervie Aberdeenshire GB **161** J 18

Invercassley Highland GB **186** G 13

Inverdruie Highland GB **187** H 15

Invereray Argyll and Bute GB **160** K 12

Inverey Aberdeenshire GB **160/161** J 15

Invergarry Highland GB **186** H 13

Invergordon Highland GB **186/187** G 14

Inverie Highland GB **175** H 11

Inverkeilor Angus GB **161** J 18

Inverkeithing Fife GB **161** K 16

Inverkeithny Aberdeenshire GB **187** G 17

Inverkip Inverclyde GB **160** L 13

Inverkirkaig Highland GB **186** F 12

Invermoriston Highland GB **186** H 13

Inverness Highland GB **186** H 14

Inversnaid Stirling GB **160** K 13

Inveruglas Argyll and Bute GB **160** K 13

Inverurie Aberdeenshire GB **187** H 18

Invervar Perth and Kinross GB **160** J 14

Ipplepen Devon GB **53** W 15

Ipstones Staffordshire GB **134** Q 19

Ipswich Suffolk GB **101** S 25

Ireby Cumbria GB **146** N 16

Ireleth Cumbria GB **146** O 16

Iron Acton South Gloucestershire GB **70** T 18

Ironbridge Shropshire GB **100** R 18

Ironbridge Telford and Wrekin GB **100** R 18

Irthington Cumbria GB **146/147** N 17

Irthlingborough Northhamptonshire GB **100** S 21

Irvine North Ayrshire GB **160** L 13

Irvinestown Tyrone GB **206** O 7

Isbister Shetland Islands GB **199** B 21

Island Medway GB **71** U 24

Isle of Whithorn Dumfries and Galloway GB **146** N 14

Isleham Cambridgeshire GB **101** S 23

Isleornsay Highland GB **175** H 11

Islibhig Na h-Eileanan an Iar GB **175** F 8

Iver Buckinghamshire GB **70/71** T 21

Ivinghoe Buckinghamshire GB **70/71** T 21

Ivybridge Devon GB **53** W 15

Iwerne Minster Dorset GB **70** V 18

Ixworth Suffolk GB **101** S 24

J

Jamestown West Dunbartonshire GB **160** L 13

Jedburgh Scottish Borders GB **146/147** M 17

Jemimaville Highland GB **186/187** G 14

Jerrettspass Armagh GB **207** O 10

John O'Groats Highland GB **198** E 16

Johnshaven Aberdeenshire GB **161** J 18

Johnston Pembrokeshire GB **86** T 13

Johnstone Renfrewshire GB **160** L 14

Johnstonebridge Dumfries and Galloway GB **146** M 16

Johnstown Kilkenny IRL **233** R 7

Julianstown Meath IRL **219** P 10

K

Kanturk Cork IRL **232** S 5

Katesbridge Down GB **207** O 10

Keadew Roscommon IRL **206** O 6

Keady Armagh GB **207** O 9

Keal Lincolnshire GB **135** Q 23

Kealkill Cork IRL **232** T 4

Keel Mayo IRL **218** P 2

Keelby Lincolnshire GB **135** P 22

Keenagh Longford IRL **219** P 7

Kegworth Leicestershire GB **100** R 20

Keig Aberdeenshire GB **187** H 17

Keighley Bradford GB **134** P 19

Keillmore Argyll and Bute GB **174** L 11

Keiss Highland GB **198** E 16

Keith Moray GB **187** G 17

Keld North Yorkshire GB **147** O 18

Kelham Nottinghamshire GB **134/135** Q 21

Kells Antrim GB **207** N 10

Kells Meath IRL **219** P 9

Kells Kilkenny IRL **233** R 8

Kellys Grove Galway IRL **218/219** Q 6

Kelmscott Oxfordshire GB **70** T 19

Kelsall Cheshire GB **119** Q 17

Kelso Scottish Borders GB **161** L 18

Keltneyburn Perth and Kinross GB **160** J 14

Kelty Fife GB **161** K 16

Kelvedon Essex GB **71** T 24

Kemble Gloucestershire GB **70** T 19

Kemnay Aberdeenshire GB **187** H 18

Kempsey Worcestershire GB **87** S 18

Kempston Bedfordshire GB **100** S 21

Kemsing Kent GB **71** U 23

Kendal Cumbria GB **146/147** O 17

Kenfig Bridgend GB **86/87** T 15

Kenilworth Warwickshire GB **100** S 19

Kenmare Kerry IRL **232** T 3

Kenmore Perth and Kinross GB **160/161** J 15

Kennacraig Argyll and Bute GB **160** L 12

Kennethmont Aberdeenshire GB **187** H 17

Kenninghall Norfolk GB **101** S 25

Kennoway Fife GB **161** K 16

Kensaleyre Highland GB **175** H 10

Kentford Suffolk GB **101** S 24

Kentisbury Devon GB **53** U 15

Kentmere Cumbria GB **146/147** O 17

Kenton Devon GB **53** V 16

Kentra Highland GB **174** J 11

Kerry Powys GB **87** S 16

Kershopefoot Cumbria GB **146/147** M 17

Kesh Fermanagh GB **206** N 7

Keshcarrigan Leitrim IRL **206** O 7

Kessingland Suffolk GB **101** S 26

Keswick Cumbria GB **146** N 16

Kettering Northhamptonshire GB **100** S 21

Kettletoft Orkney Islands GB **198** D 17

Kettlewell North Yorkshire GB **147** O 18

Ketton Rutland GB **100** R 21

Keynsham Bath & NE Somerset GB **53** U 17

Keyworth Nottinghamshire GB **100** R 20

Kibworth Harcourt Leicestershire GB **100** R 21

Kidderminster Worcestershire GB **87** S 18

Kidlington Oxfordshire GB **70** T 20

Kidsgrove Staffordshire GB **134** Q 18

Kidwelly Carmarthenshire GB **86** T 14

Kielder Northumberland GB **146/147** M 17

Kilbaha Clare IRL **232** R 3

Kilbarchan Renfrewshire GB **160** L 13

Kilbeggan Westmeath IRL **219** Q 8

Kilberry Argyll and Bute GB **174** L 11

Kilberry Meath IRL **219** P 9

Kilbirnie North Ayrshire GB **160** L 13

Kilbride Argyll and Bute GB **160** K 12

Kilbride Wicklow IRL **219** Q 10

Kilbride Wicklow IRL **233** R 10

Kilbrittain Cork IRL **232** T 5

Kilchattan Bay Argyll and Bute GB **160** L 12

Kilchenzie Argyll and Bute GB **174** M 11

Kilchiaran Argyll and Bute GB **174** L 10

Kilchoan Highland GB **174** J 10

Kilchoman Argyll and Bute GB **174** L 10

Kilchreest Galway IRL **218** Q 5

Kilchrenan Argyll and Bute GB **160** K 12

Kilclief Down GB **207** O 11

Kilcock Meath IRL **219** Q 9

Kilcolgan Galway IRL **218** Q 5

Kilconnell Galway IRL **218/219** Q 6

Kilconquhar Fife GB **161** K 17

Kilcormac Offaly IRL **219** Q 7

Kilcreggan Argyll and Bute GB **160** L 13

Kilcrohane Cork IRL **232** T 3

Kilcullen Kildare IRL **219** Q 9

Kildale North Yorkshire GB 147 O 20

Kildare Kildare IRL 219 Q 9

Kildary Highland GB 186/187 G 14

Kildavanan Argyll and Bute GB 160 L 12

Kildermorie Lodge Highland GB 186/187 G 14

Kildonan North Ayrshire GB 174 M 12

Kildonan Lodge Highland GB 187 F 15

Kildorrery Cork IRL 232/233 S 6

Kildrummy Aberdeenshire GB 187 H 17

Kilfenora Clare IRL 232 R 4

Kilfiernan Dublin IRL 219 Q 10

Kilfinan Argyll and Bute GB 160 L 12

Kilfinnane Limerick IRL 232/233 S 6

Kilgarvan Kerry IRL 232 T 4

Kilgetty Pembrokeshire GB 86 T 13

Kilglass Sligo IRL 206 O 4

Kilham East Riding of Yorkshire GB 135 O 22

Kilham Northumberland GB 161 L 18

Kilkee Clare IRL 232 R 3

Kilkeel Down GB 207 O 11

Kilkelly Mayo IRL 218 P 5

Kilkenny Cill Chainnigh Kilkenny IRL 233 R 8

Kilkerrin Galway IRL 218 P 5

Kilkhampton Cornwall GB 52/53 V 14

Kilkieran Galway IRL 218 Q 3

Kilkinlea Limerick IRL 232 S 4

Kilkishen Clare IRL 232 R 5

Kill Waterford IRL 233 S 8

Killadeas Fermanagh GB 206 O 7

Killadoon Mayo IRL 218 P 3

Killadysert Clare IRL 232 R 4

Killala Mayo IRL 206 O 4

Killaloe Clare IRL 232/233 R 6

Killamarsh Derbyshire GB 134 Q 20

Killarga Leitrim IRL 206 O 6

Killarney Cill Áirne Kerry IRL 232 S 3

Killashandra Cavan IRL 206 O 7

Killashee Longford IRL 219 P 7

Killavally Mayo IRL 218 P 4

Killavullen Cork IRL 232 S 5

Killead Antrim GB 207 N 10

Killeagh Cork IRL 232/233 T 6

Killean Argyll and Bute GB 174 L 11

Killearn Stirling GB 160 K 14

Killeigh Offaly IRL 219 Q 8

Killen Tyrone GB 206 N 7

Killenaule Tipperary IRL 233 R 7

Killeter Tyrone GB 206 N 7

Killichonan Perth and Kinross GB 160 J 14

Killiecrankie Perth and Kinross GB 160/161 J 15

Killilan Highland GB 186 H 12

Killimer Clare IRL 232 R 4

Killimor Galway IRL 218/219 Q 6

Killin Stirling GB 160 K 14

Killinaboy Clare IRL 232 R 4

Killiney Dublin IRL 219 Q 10

Killorglin Cill Orglan Kerry IRL 232 S 3

Killough Down GB 207 O 11

Killsallaghan Dublin IRL 219 Q 10

Killucan Westmeath IRL 219 P 8

Killybegs Donegal IRL 206 N 6

Killyleagh Down GB 207 O 11

Killyon Offaly IRL 219 Q 7

Kilmacolm Inverclyde GB 160 L 13

Kilmacrenan Donegal IRL 206 M 7

Kilmacthomas Waterford IRL 233 S 8

Kilmaganny Kilkenny IRL 233 S 8

Kilmaine Mayo IRL 218 P 4

Kilmallock Limerick IRL 232 S 5

Kilmaluag Highland GB 186 G 10

Kilmanagh Kilkenny IRL 233 R 8

Kilmarnock East Ayrshire GB 160 L 14

Kilmartin Argyll and Bute GB 160 K 12

Kilmaurs East Ayrshire GB 160 L 13

Kilmeedy Limerick IRL 232 S 5

Kilmelford Argyll and Bute GB 160 K 12

Kilmichael Cork IRL 232 T 4

Kilmichael Glassary Argyll and Bute GB 160 K 12

Kilmichael of Inverlussa Argyll and Bute GB 174 L 11

Kilmihil Clare IRL 232 R 4

Kilmorack Highland GB 186 H 13

Kilmore Quay Wexford IRL 233 S 9

Kilmory Argyll and Bute GB 174 L 11

Kilmory North Ayrshire GB 174 M 12

Kilmory Highland GB 175 H 10

Kilmuckridge Wexford IRL 233 R 10

Kilmun Argyll and Bute GB 160 L 13

Kilmurvy Galway IRL 218 Q 3

Kilnave Argyll and Bute GB 174 L 10

Kilncadzow South Lanarkshire GB 160/161 L 15

Kilninian Argyll and Bute GB 174 J 10

Kilninver Argyll and Bute GB 174 K 11

Kilnsea East Riding of Yorkshire GB 135 P 23

Kiloran Argyll and Bute GB 174 K 10

Kilrea Londonderry GB 207 N 9

Kilreekill Galway IRL 218/219 Q 6

Kilronan Galway IRL 218 Q 3

Kilross Donegal IRL 206 N 7

Kilrush Clare IRL 232 R 4

Kilsby Northhamptonshire GB 100 S 20

Kilsheelan Tipperary IRL 233 S 7

Kilskeery Fermanagh GB 206 O 7

Kilsyth North Lanarkshire GB 160 L 14

Kiltamagh Mayo IRL 218 P 4

Kiltarlity Highland GB 186 H 14

Kiltealy Wexford IRL 233 R 9

Kilteel Kildare IRL 219 Q 9

Kiltegan Wicklow IRL 233 R 9

Kiltoom Offaly IRL 218/219 Q 6

Kiltormer Galway IRL 218/219 Q 6

Kiltullagh Galway IRL 218 Q 5

Kiltyclogher Leitrim IRL 206 O 6

Kilvaxter Highland GB 186 G 10

Kilwaughter Antrim GB 207 N 11

Kilwinning North Ayrshire GB 160 L 13

Kilworth Cork IRL 232/233 S 6

Kimbolton Cambridgeshire GB 100/101 S 22

Kimmendge Dorset GB 70 V 18

Kimpton Hertfordshire GB 71 T 22

Kinauchdrachd Argyll and Bute GB 174 K 11

Kinawley Fermanagh GB 206 O 7

Kinbrace Highland GB 187 F 15

Kinbuck Stirling GB 160/161 K 15

Kincardine Fife GB 186/187 G 14

Kincardine Highland GB 186/187 G 14

Kincraig Highland GB 187 H 15

Kineton Warwickshire GB 100 S 19

Kinfauns Perth and Kinross GB 161 K 16

King´s Bromley Staffordshire GB 100 R 19

King´s Cliffe Northhamptonshire GB 100 R 21

King´s Lynn Norfolk GB 101 R 23

Kingarth Argyll and Bute GB 160 L 12

Kinghorn Fife GB 161 K 16

Kings Caple Herefordshire GB 87 T 17

Kings Langley Hertfordshire GB 71 T 22

King´s Somborne Hampshire GB 70 U 20

Kings Sutton Northhamptonshire GB 100 S 20

Kingsbarns Fife GB 161 K 17

Kingsbridge Devon GB 53 W 15

Kingsbury Warwickshire GB 100 R 19

Kingsbury Episcopi Somerset GB 53 V 17

Kingsclere Hampshire GB 70 U 20

Kingscourt Cavan IRL 219 P 9

Kingshouse Stirling GB 160 K 14

Kingskerswell Devon GB 53 V 15

Kingsland Roscommon IRL 218/219 P 6

Kingsland Herefordshire GB 87 S 17

Kingsley Staffordshire GB 134 Q 19

Kingsteignton Devon GB 53 V 15

Kingston Moray GB 187 G 16

Kingston Devon GB 53 W 15

Kingston Bagpuize Oxfordshire GB 70 T 20

Kingston upon Thames Greater London GB 71 U 22

Kingstone Herefordshire GB 87 S 17

Kingston-upon-Hull Kingston upon Hull GB 135 P 22

Kingswear Devon GB 53 W 15

Kingswood Bristol GB 53 U 17

Kington Herefordshire GB 87 S 16

Kingussie Highland GB 187 H 14

Kinkell Bridge Perth and Kinross GB 160/161 K 15

Kinloch Highland GB 175 H 10

Kinloch Highland GB 186 F 13

Kinloch Highland GB 186 H 12

Kinloch Rannoch Perth and Kinross GB 160 J 14

Kinlochard Stirling GB 160 K 14

Kinlochbervie Highland GB 186 F 12

Kinlocheil Highland GB 160 J 12

Kinlochewe Highland GB 186 G 12

Kinlochleven Highland GB 160 J 13

Kinloss Moray GB 187 G 15

Kinlough Leitrim IRL 206 O 6

Kinnaird Perth and Kinross GB 161 K 16

Kinneff Aberdeenshire GB 161 J 18

Kinnegad Westmeath IRL 219 Q 8

Kinnerley Shropshire GB 119 R 17

Kinnitty Offaly IRL 219 Q 7

Kinross Perth and Kinross GB 161 K 16

Kinsale Cork IRL 232 T 5

Kinsalebeg Waterford IRL 233 T 7

Kintbury West Berkshire GB 70 U 20

Kintore Aberdeenshire GB 187 H 18

Kinvarra Galway IRL 218 Q 3

Kinvarra Galway IRL 218 Q 5

Kinver Staffordshire GB 87 S 18

Kippen Stirling GB 160 K 14

Kirby Grindalythe North Yorkshire GB 134 O 21

Kirby Malham North Yorkshire GB 147 O 18

Kirby Misperton North Yorkshire GB 134 O 21

Kircubbin Down GB 207 O 11

Kirk Derbyshire GB 100 R 19

Kirk North Yorkshire GB 134 P 20

Kirk Highland GB 198 E 16

Kirk Ireton Derbyshire GB 134 Q 19

Kirk Michael Isle of Man GB 146 O 13

Kirk of Shotts North Lanarkshire GB 160/161 L 15

Kirkabister Shetland Islands GB 199 B 20

Kirkbampton Cumbria GB 146 N 16

Kirkbean Dumfries and Galloway GB 146 N 15

Kirkbride Cumbria GB 146 N 16

Kirkburn East Riding of Yorkshire GB 135 P 22

Kirkburton Kirklees GB 134 P 19

Kirkby Knowsley GB 119 Q 17

Kirkby Cumbria GB 147 O 18

Kirkby in Ashfield Nottinghamshire GB 134 Q 20

Kirkby Lonsdale Cumbria GB 146/147 O 17

Kirkby Malzeard North Yorkshire GB 147 O 19

Kirkby Thore Cumbria GB 146/147 N 17

Kirkbymoorside North Yorkshire GB 134 O 21

Kirkcaldy Fife GB 161 K 16

Kirkcambeck Cumbria GB 146/147 M 17

Kirkcolm Dumfries and Galloway GB 146 N 12

Kirkconnel Dumfries and Galloway GB 146 M 15

Kirkcowan Dumfries and Galloway GB 146 N 13

Kirkcudbright Dumfries and Galloway GB 146 N 14

Kirkgunzeon Dumfries and Galloway GB 146 N 15

Kirkham Lancashire GB 119 P 17

Kirkheaton Northumberland GB 147 M 19

Kirkhill Highland GB 186 H 14

Kirkinner Dumfries and Galloway GB 146 N 14

Kirkintilloch East Dunbartonshire GB 160 L 14

Kirkland Dumfries and Galloway GB 146 M 15

Kirklington Nottinghamshire GB 134/135 Q 21

Kirkmaiden Dumfries and Galloway GB 146 N 13

Kirkmichael South Ayrshire GB 146 M 13

Kirkmichael Perth and Kinross GB 161 J 16

Kirknewton West Lothian GB 161 L 16

Kirknewton Northumberland GB 161 L 18

Kirkoswald South Ayrshire GB 146 M 13

Kirkoswald Cumbria GB 146/147 N 17

Kirkpatrick Durham Dumfries and Galloway GB 146 M 15

Kirkpatrick-Fleming Dumfries and Galloway GB 146 M 16

Kirksanton Cumbria GB 146 O 16

Kirkton Scottish Borders GB 146/147 M 17

Kirkton Angus GB 161 J 18

Kirkton Highland GB 175 H 11

Kirkton Aberdeenshire GB 187 H 18

Kirkton Manor Scottish Borders GB 161 L 16

Kirkton of Airlie Angus GB 161 J 16

Kirkton of Alvah Aberdeenshire GB 187 G 17

Kirkton of Auchterless Aberdeenshire GB 187 H 17

Kirkton of Culsalmond Aberdeenshire GB 187 H 17

Kirkton of Durris Aberdeenshire GB 187 G 17

Kirkton of Kingoldrum Angus GB 161 J 16

Kirktown of Deskford Moray GB 187 G 17

Kirkwall Orkney Islands GB 198 E 17

Kirkwhelpington Northumberland GB 147 M 19

Kirriemuir Angus GB 161 J 16

Kirtlebridge Dumfries and Galloway GB 146 M 16

Kirtlington Oxfordshire GB 70 T 20

Kirtomy Highland GB 186/187 E 14

Kirton Lincolnshire GB **100/101**
R 22

Kirton Nottinghamshire
GB **134/135** Q 21

Kirton in Lindsey North Lincolns.
GB **134/135** Q 21

Knaresborough North Yorkshire
GB **147** O 20

Knarsdale Northumberland
GB **146/147** N 17

Knebworth Hertfordshire GB **71**
T 22

Kneesall Nottinghamshire
GB **134/135** Q 21

Knighton Powys GB **87** S 16

Knight's Town Kerry IRL **232** T 2

Kniveton Derbyshire GB **134**
Q 19

Knock Argyll and Bute GB **174**
K 11

Knock Moray GB **187** G 17

Knock Mayo IRL **218** P 5

Knock Clare IRL **232** R 4

Knockaderry Limerick IRL **232**
S 5

Knockandhu Moray GB **187** H 16

Knockanevin Cork IRL **232/233**
S 6

Knocklong Limerick IRL **232/233**
S 6

Knocknagree Cork IRL **232** S 4

Knocktopher Kilkenny IRL **233**
S 8

Knockvicar Roscommon
IRL **218/219** P 6

Knossington Rutland GB **100**
R 21

Knott End-on-Sea Lancashire
GB **119** P 17

Knottingley Wakefield GB **134**
P 20

Knowehead Dumfries and Galloway
GB **146** M 14

Knowle Solihull GB **100** S 19

Knucklas Powys GB **87** S 16

Knutsford Cheshire GB **134** Q 18

Kyle of Lochalsh Highland GB **175**
H 11

Kyleakin Highland GB **175** H 11

Kylebrack Galway IRL **218/219**
Q 6

Kylerhea Highland GB **175** H 11

Kylestrome Highland GB **186**
F 12

L

Labasheeda Clare IRL **232** R 4

Lacasaidh Na h-Eileanan an Iar
GB **175** F 9

Laceby North East Lincolnshire
GB **135** P 22

Lack Fermanagh GB **206** N 7

Lacock Wiltshire GB **70** U 18

Ladybank Fife GB **161** K 16

Ladysbridge Cork IRL **232/233**
T 6

Lagavulin Argyll and Bute GB **174**
L 10

Lagg Argyll and Bute GB **174**
L 11

Laggan Highland GB **160** H 13

Laggan Highland GB **160** H 14

Laghy Donegal IRL **206** N 6

Lagney Corner Tyrone GB **207**
O 9

Lahinch Clare IRL **232** R 4

Laide Highland GB **186** G 11

Lair Highland GB **186** H 12

Lairg Highland GB **186/187** F 14

Lakenheath Suffolk GB **101** S 24

Lamberhurst Kent GB **71** U 23

Lambert Falkirk GB **160/161** K 15

Lambourn West Berkshire GB **70**
T 19

Lamington South Lanarkshire
GB **160/161** L 15

Lamlash North Ayrshire GB **160**
L 12

Lamonby Cumbria GB **146/147**
N 17

Lampeter Ceredigion GB **86** S 14

Lamplugh Cumbria GB **146** N 16

Lamport Northhamptonshire
GB **100** S 21

Lanark South Lanarkshire
GB **160/161** L 15

Lancaster Lancashire GB **146/147**
O 17

Lanchester Durham GB **147** N 19

Lane End Buckinghamshire
GB **70/71** T 21

Lanesborough Longford
IRL **218/219** P 6

Langdale End North Yorkshire
GB **134** O 21

Langdon Beck Durham GB **147**
N 18

Langford Devon GB **53** V 16

Langford Budville Somerset
GB **53** U 16

Langholm Dumfries and Galloway
GB **146/147** M 17

Langley Derbyshire GB **100** R 19

Langley Essex GB **71** T 23

Langport Somerset GB **53** U 17

Langrick Lincolnshire GB **135**
Q 22

Langsett Barnsley GB **134** P 19

Langshaw Scottish Borders
GB **161** L 17

Langthwaite North Yorkshire
GB **147** O 19

Langtoft East Riding of Yorkshire
GB **135** O 22

Langton North Yorkshire GB **134**
O 21

Langwathby Cumbria GB **146/147**
N 17

Lanivet Cornwall GB **52** W 13

Lanreath Cornwall GB **52** W 13

Lanton Scottish Borders
GB **146/147** M 17

Lapford Devon GB **53** V 15

Laracor Meath IRL **219** P 9

Laragh Wicklow IRL **219** Q 10

Largowald Fife GB **161** K 17

Largs North Ayrshire GB **160**
L 13

Larkhall South Lanarkshire
GB **160/161** L 15

Larne Antrim GB **207** N 11

Lasham Hampshire GB **70** U 20

Lasswade Midlothian GB **161**
L 16

Latheron Highland GB **187** F 16

Lauder Scottish Borders GB **161**
L 17

Laugharne Carmarthenshire
GB **86** T 14

Launceston Cornwall GB **52/53**
V 14

Lauragh Kerry IRL **232** T 3

Laurencekirk Aberdeenshire
GB **161** J 18

Laurencetown Galway
IRL **218/219** Q 6

Laurieston Dumfries and Galloway
GB **146** N 14

Lavendon Milton Keynes GB **100**
S 21

Lavenham Suffolk GB **101** S 24

Lawers Perth and Kinross GB **160**
J 14

Laxey Isle of Man GB **146** O 14

Laxfield Suffolk GB **101** S 25

Laxo Shetland Islands GB **199**
B 20

Laxton East Riding of Yorkshire
GB **134/135** P 21

Laxton Nottinghamshire
GB **134/135** Q 21

Layer de la Haye Essex GB **71**
T 24

Lazonby Cumbria GB **146/147**
N 17

Lea Herefordshire GB **70** T 18

Leabgarrow Donegal IRL **206**
N 5

Leadburn Scottish Borders
GB **161** L 16

Leaden Roding Essex GB **71** T 23

Leadenham Lincolnshire
GB **134/135** Q 21

Leadgate Cumbria GB **147** N 18

Leadhills South Lanarkshire
GB **146** M 15

Leafield Oxfordshire GB **70** T 19

Lealholm North Yorkshire GB **147**
O 21

Leap Cork IRL **232** T 4

Leasingham Lincolnshire GB **135**
Q 22

Leatherhead Surrey GB **71** U 22

Leavening North Yorkshire GB **134**
O 21

Lecarrow Roscommon
IRL **218/219** P 6

Lechlade Gloucestershire GB **70**
T 19

Leckmelm Highland GB **186**
G 12

Leconfield East Riding of Yorkshire
GB **135** P 22

Ledbury Herefordshire GB **87**
S 18

Ledmore Highland GB **186** F 13

Lee Lancashire GB **119** P 17

Leebotwood Shropshire GB **87**
R 17

Leeds Leeds GB **134** P 19

Leeds Kent GB **71** U 24

Leedstown Cornwall GB **52** W 12

Leek Staffordshire GB **134** Q 18

Leenane Galway IRL **218** P 3

Lee-on-the-Solent Hampshire
GB **70** V 20

Legbourne Lincolnshire GB **135**
Q 23

Legerwood Scottish Borders
GB **161** L 17

Leicester Leicester GB **100**
R 20

Leigh Wigan GB **119** Q 17

Leigh Surrey GB **71** U 22

Leigh Kent GB **71** U 23

Leighlinbridge Carlow IRL **233**
R 9

Leighterton Gloucestershire
GB **70** T 18

Leighton Buzzard Bedfordshire
GB **70/71** T 21

Leintwardine Herefordshire GB **87**
S 17

Leiston Suffolk GB **101** S 26

Leitholm Scottish Borders GB **161**
L 18

Leitrim Leitrim IRL **218/219** P 6

Lemybrien Waterford IRL **233**
S 7

Lendalfoot South Ayrshire GB **146**
M 13

Lenham Kent GB **71** U 24

Lennoxtown East Dunbartonshire
GB **160** L 14

Leominster Herefordshire GB **87**
S 17

Leperstown Waterford IRL **233**
S 8

Lerryn Cornwall GB **52** W 13

Lerwick Shetland Islands GB **199**
B 20

Lesbury Northumberland GB **147**
M 19

Leslie Fife GB **161** K 16

Leslie Aberdeenshire GB **187**
H 17

Lesmahagow South Lanarkshire
GB **160/161** L 15

Leswalt Dumfries and Galloway
GB **146** N 12

Letchworth Garden City
Hertfordshire GB **71** T 22

Letham Angus GB **161** J 18

Letterfearn Highland GB **175**
H 11

Letterfrack Galway IRL **218** P 3

Letterkenny Leitir Ceanainn Donegal
IRL **206** N 7

Lettermulan Galway IRL **218** Q 3

Letterston Pembrokeshire GB **86**
T 13

Leuchars Fife GB **161** K 17

Leumrabhagh Na h-Eileanan an Iar
GB **186** F 10

Leven East Riding of Yorkshire
GB **135** P 22

Leven Fife GB **161** K 17

Levens Cumbria GB **146/147**
O 17

Leverburgh An t-Ob Na h-Eileanan
an Iar GB **175** G 8

Lewannick Cornwall GB **52/53**
V 14

Lewes East Sussex GB **71** V 23

Lewtrenchard Devon GB **52/53**
V 14

Leyburn North Yorkshire GB **147**
O 19

Leyland Lancashire GB **119** P 17

Leysdown on Sea Kent GB **71**
U 24

Lhanbryde Moray GB **187** G 16

Libberton South Lanarkshire
GB **160/161** L 15

Lichfield Staffordshire GB **100**
R 19

Lidgate Suffolk GB **101** S 24

Liff Angus GB **161** K 16

Lifford Donegal IRL **207** N 8

Lifton Devon GB **52/53** V 14

Lilliesleaf Scottish Borders
GB **161** L 17

Limavady Londonderry GB **207**
M 9

Limerick Luimneach Limerick
IRL **232** R 5

Lincoln Lincolnshire GB **134/135**
Q 21

Lindale Cumbria GB **146/147**
O 17

Lingen Herefordshire GB **87**
S 17

Lingfield Surrey GB **71** U 23

Linlithgow West Lothian
GB **160/161** L 15

Linton Cambridgeshire GB **101**
S 23

Linton North Yorkshire GB **147**
O 18

Linton Scottish Borders GB **161**
L 18

Linton Kent GB **71** U 24

Lional Na h-Eileanan an Iar
GB **186** F 10

Liphook West Sussex GB **70/71**
U 21

Lisbellaw Fermanagh GB **206**
O 7

Lisburn Antrim GB **207** N 10

Liscannor Clare IRL **232** R 4

Liscarney Mayo IRL **218** P 3

Liscarroll Cork IRL **232** S 5

Lisdoonvarna Clare IRL **218** Q 4

Lisduff Cavan IRL **219** P 8

Liskeard Cornwall GB **52/53**
W 14

Lismore Waterford IRL **233** S 7

Lisnacree Down GB **207** O 10

Lisnarick Fermanagh GB **206** O 7

Lisnaskea Fermanagh GB **207**
O 8

Lispatrick Cork IRL **232** T 5

Liss Hampshire GB **70/71** U 21

Lissatinnig Br. Kerry IRL **232** T 3

Lissycasey Clare IRL **232** R 4

Listowel Kerry IRL **232** S 4

Lisvarrinane Tipperary
IRL **232/233** S 6

Litcham Norfolk GB **101** R 24

Little Ayre Orkney Islands GB **198**
E 16

Little Berkhamsted Hertfordshire
GB **71** T 22

Little Bytham Lincolnshire
GB **100/101** R 22

Little Compton Warwickshire
GB **70** T 19

Little Downham Cambridgeshire
GB **101** S 23

Little Missenden Buckinghamshire
GB **70/71** T 21

Little Strickland Cumbria
GB **146/147** N 17

Little Walsingham Norfolk GB **101**
R 24

Little Waltham Essex GB **71** T 23

Littleborough Rochdale GB **134**
P 18

Littleferry Highland GB **186/187**
G 14

Littlehampton West Sussex
GB **70/71** V 21

Littlemill Highland GB **187** G 15

Littleport Cambridgeshire GB **101**
S 23

Littleton Tipperary IRL **233** R 7

Litton North Yorkshire GB **147**
O 18

Litton Cheney Dorset GB **53** V 17

Liurbost Na h-Eileanan an Iar
GB **186** F 10

Liverpool Liverpool GB **119** Q 17

Livingston West Lothian GB **161**
L 16

Lixnaw Kerry IRL **232** S 3

Lizard Cornwall GB **52** X 12

Llan Ffestiniog Gwynedd GB **119**
R 15

Llanaber Gwynedd GB **118/119**
R 14

Llanaelhaearn Gwynedd
GB **118/119** R 14
Llanarmon Dyffryn Ceiriog
Wrexham GB **119** R 16
Llanarmon-yn-Ial Denbighshire
GB **119** Q 16
Llanarth Ceredigion GB **86** S 14
Llanasa Flintshire GB **119** Q 16
Llanbadarn Fynydd Powys GB **87**
S 16
Llanbedr Gwynedd GB **86** R 14
Llanbedrog Gwynedd GB **118/119**
R 14
Llanberis Gwynedd GB **118/119**
Q 14
Llanbister Powys GB **87** S 16
Llanboidy Carmarthenshire GB **86**
T 13
Llanbrynmair Powys GB **86/87**
R 15
Llanddarog Carmarthenshire
GB **86** T 14
Llandderfel Gwynedd GB **119**
R 15
Llanddewi Brefi Ceredigion
GB **86/87** S 15
Llanddewi Ystradenni Powys
GB **87** S 16
Llandefaelog Powys GB **87** T 16
Llandeilo Carmarthenshire
GB **86/87** T 15
Llandinam Powys GB **87** S 16
Llandovery Llanymddyfi
Carmarthenshire GB **86/87** T 15
Llandrillo Denbighshire GB **119**
R 16
Llandrindod Powys GB **87** S 16
Llandudno Conwy GB **119** Q 15
Llandwrog Gwynedd GB **118/119**
Q 14
Llandybie Carmarthenshire
GB **86/87** T 15
Llandyfaelog Carmarthenshire
GB **86** T 14
Llandyrnog Denbighshire GB **119**
Q 16
Llandyssil Powys GB **119** R 16
Llandysul Ceredigion GB **86**
S 14
Llanegryn Gwynedd GB **86** R 14
Llanelidan Denbighshire GB **119**
Q 16
Llanelltyd Gwynedd GB **119** R 15
Llanerchymedd Anglesey
GB **118/119** Q 14
Llanfachraeth Anglesey GB **118**
Q 13
Llanfaelog Anglesey GB **118/119**
Q 14
Llanfaethlu Anglesey GB **118**
Q 13
Llanfair Clydogau Ceredigion
GB **86** S 14
Llanfair Talhaiarn Conwy GB **119**
Q 15
Llanfair-Caereinion Powys GB **87**
R 16
Llanfairfechan Conwy GB **119**
Q 15
Llanfair-ym-Muallt Builth Wells
Powys GB **87** S 16
Llanfechain Powys GB **119** R 16
Llanfihangel Nant Bran Powys
GB **86/87** T 15
Llanfihangel-nant-Melan Powys
GB **87** S 16
Llanfihangel-yng-Ngwynfa Powys
GB **87** R 16

Llanfihangel-y-pennant Gwynedd
GB **86/87** R 15
Llanfrynach Powys GB **87** T 16
Llanfyllin Powys GB **119** R 16
Llanfynydd Carmarthenshire
GB **86** T 14
Llanfyrnach Pembrokeshire GB **86**
T 13
Llangadfan Powys GB **87** R 16
Llangadog Carmarthenshire
GB **86/87** T 15
Llangain Carmarthenshire GB **86**
T 14
Llangefni Anglesey GB **118/119**
Q 14
Llangeler Carmarthenshire GB **86**
S 14
Llangennech Carmarthenshire
GB **86** T 14
Llangernyw Conwy GB **119** Q 15
Llanglydwen Carmarthenshire
GB **86** T 13
Llangoed Anglesey GB **118/119**
Q 14
Llangollen Denbighshire GB **119**
R 16
Llangors Powys GB **87** T 16
Llangower Gwynedd GB **119**
R 15
Llangranog Ceredigion GB **86**
S 14
Llangunllo Powys GB **87** S 16
Llangunnor Carmarthenshire
GB **86** T 14
Llangurig Powys GB **86/87** S 15
Llangwm Conwy GB **119** R 15
Llangybi Ceredigion GB **86** S 14
Llangynidr Powys GB **87** T 16
Llangynin Carmarthenshire GB **86**
T 13
Llangynog Powys GB **119** R 16
Llanharry Rhondda Cynon Taff
GB **87** T 16
Llanidloes Powys GB **86/87** S 15
Llanilar Ceredigion GB **86** S 14
Llanllugan Powys GB **87** R 16
Llanmadoc Swansea GB **86** T 14
Llannon Carmarthenshire GB **86**
T 14
Llanon Ceredigion GB **86** S 14
Llanpumsaint Carmarthenshire
GB **86** T 14
Llanrhaeadr Denbighshire GB **119**
Q 16
Llanrhaeadr-ym-Mochnant Powys
GB **119** R 16
Llanrhain Pembrokeshire GB **86**
T 12
Llanrhidian Swansea GB **86** T 14
Llanrhystud Ceredigion GB **86**
S 14
Llanrug Gwynedd GB **118/119**
Q 14
Llanrwst Conwy GB **119** Q 15
Llansanffraid Glan Conwy Conwy
GB **119** Q 15
Llansannan Conwy GB **119** Q 15
Llansilin Powys GB **119** R 16
Llansteffan Carmarthenshire
GB **86** T 14
Llanthony Monmouthshire GB **87**
T 16
Llantrisant Rhondda Cynon Taff
GB **87** T 16
Llantrisant Monmouthshire GB **87**
T 17
Llantwit Major Vale of Glamorgan
GB **53** U 16

Llanuwchllyn Gwynedd GB **119**
R 15
Llanvihangel Gobion
Monmouthshire GB **87** T 17
Llanwddyn Powys GB **119** R 16
Llanwenog Ceredigion GB **86**
S 14
Llanwnog Powys GB **87** R 16
Llanwrda Carmarthenshire
GB **86/87** T 15
Llanwrin Powys GB **86/87** R 15
Llanwrthwl Powys GB **87** S 16
Llanwrtyd Wells Powys GB **86/87**
S 15
Llanybydder Carmarthenshire
GB **86** S 14
Llanycefn Pembrokeshire GB **86**
T 13
Llanychaer Pembrokeshire GB **86**
T 13
Llanymawddwy Gwynedd
GB **86/87** R 15
Llanymddyfi Llandovery
Carmarthens. GB **86/87** T 15
Llawhaden Pembrokeshire GB **86**
T 13
Lledrod Ceredigion GB **86** S 14
Llithfaen Gwynedd GB **118/119**
R 14
Lloonfower Roscommon IRL **218**
P 5
Llwyndafydd Ceredigion GB **86**
S 14
Llwyngwril Gwynedd GB **86**
R 14
Llysfaen Conwy GB **119** Q 15
Llyswen Powys GB **87** S 16
Loanhead Midlothian GB **161**
L 16
Loch Baghasdail Lochboisdale Na h-
Eileanan an Iar GB **175** H 8
Loch Choire Lodge Highland
GB **186/187** F 14
Loch Euphort Na h-Eileanan an Iar
GB **175** G 8
Loch Gowna Cavan IRL **219** P 7
Loch nam Madadh Lochmaddy
Na h-Eileanan an Iar
GB **175** G 8
Loch Sgioport Na h-Eileanan an Iar
GB **175** H 8
Lochailort Highland GB **175** J 11
Lochaline Highland GB **174** J 11
Lochboisdale Loch Baghasdail Na h-
Eileanan an Iar GB **175** H 8
Lochbuie Argyll and Bute GB **174**
K 11
Lochcarron Highland GB **186**
H 12
Lochdon Argyll and Bute GB **174**
K 11
Lochearnhead Stirling GB **160**
K 14
Locherben Dumfries and Galloway
GB **146** M 15
Lochgair Argyll and Bute GB **160**
K 12
Lochgelly Fife GB **161** K 16
Lochgilphead Argyll and Bute
GB **160** K 12
Lochgoilhead Argyll and Bute
GB **160** K 13
Lochinver Highland GB **186** F 12
Lochmaben Dumfries and Galloway
GB **146** M 16
Lochmaddy Loch nam Madadh
Na h-Eileanan an Iar
GB **175** G 8

Lochportain Na h-Eileanan an Iar
GB **175** G 8
Lochranza North Ayrshire GB **160**
L 12
Lochwinnoch Renfrewshire
GB **160** L 13
Lockerbie Dumfries and Galloway
GB **146** M 16
Lockton North Yorkshire GB **134**
O 21
Loddiswell Devon GB **53** W 15
Loddon Norfolk GB **101** R 25
Loftus Redcar & Cleveland
GB **147** N 21
Logie of Coldstone Aberdeenshire
GB **187** H 17
Login Carmarthenshire GB **86**
T 13
Lombardstown Cork IRL **232** S 5
Lon. Colney Hertfordshire GB **71**
T 22
London Greater London GB **71**
T 22
Londonderry Londonderry
GB **207** N 8
Long Buckby Northhamptonshire
GB **100** S 20
Long Compton Warwickshire
GB **70** T 19
Long Crendon Buckinghamshire
GB **70** T 20
Long Eaton Derbyshire GB **100**
R 20
Long Marston Warwickshire
GB **100** S 19
Long Marston North Yorkshire
GB **134** P 20
Long Marton Cumbria
GB **146/147** N 17
Long Melford Suffolk GB **101**
S 24
Long Preston North Yorkshire
GB **147** O 18
Long Riston East Riding of
Yorkshire GB **135** P 22
Long Stratton Norfolk GB **101**
S 25
Long Sutton Lincolnshire GB **101**
R 23
Long Sutton Somerset GB **53**
U 17
Longbridge Deverill Wiltshire
GB **70** U 18
Longdon Worcestershire GB **87**
S 18
Longdon Derbyshire GB **100**
R 19
Longford Longford IRL **219**
P 7
Longformacus Scottish Borders
GB **161** L 18
Longframlington Northumberland
GB **147** M 19
Longhirst Northumberland
GB **147** M 19
Longhope Orkney Islands GB **198**
E 16
Longhorsley Northumberland
GB **147** M 19
Longhoughton Northumberland
GB **147** M 19
Longmanhill Aberdeenshire
GB **187** G 18
Longmorn Moray GB **187** G 16
Longney Gloucestershire GB **70**
T 18
Longniddry East Lothian GB **161**
L 17

Longnor Staffordshire GB **134**
Q 19
Longridge Lancashire GB **119**
P 17
Longridge West Lothian
GB **160/161** L 15
Longside Aberdeenshire GB **187**
G 19
Longton Lancashire GB **119** P 17
Longtown Cumbria GB **146/147**
M 17
Longtown Herefordshire GB **87**
T 17
Longwood Meath IRL **219** Q 9
Looe Cornwall GB **52/53** W 14
Loose Kent GB **71** U 24
Lorton Cumbria GB **146** N 16
Lossiemouth Moray GB **187**
G 16
Lostwithiel Cornwall GB **52** W 13
Lothmore Highland GB **187** F 15
Loughanavally Offaly IRL **219**
Q 7
Loughborough Leicestershire
GB **100** R 20
Loughbrickland Down GB **207**
O 10
Loughglinn Roscommon IRL **218**
P 5
Loughrea Galway IRL **218** Q 5
Loughshinny Dublin IRL **219**
P 10
Louisburgh Mayo IRL **218** P 3
Louth Lincolnshire GB **135** Q 23
Louth Louth IRL **219** P 9
Low Row Cumbria GB **146/147**
N 17
Lowdham Nottinghamshire
GB **134** Q 20
Lower Antrim GB **207** N 10
Lower Diabaig Highland GB **186**
G 11
Lower Heyford Oxfordshire GB **70**
T 20
Lower Higham Kent GB **71** U 23
Lower Killeyan Argyll and Bute
GB **174** L 10
Lower Largo Fife GB **161** K 17
Lowestoft Suffolk GB **101** S 26
Loweswater Cumbria GB **146**
N 16
Lowgill Cumbria GB **146/147**
O 17
Lowick Northumberland GB **161**
L 19
Lucan Dublin IRL **219** Q 10
Luccombe Somerset GB **53** U 15
Lucker Northumberland GB **161**
L 19
Ludag Na h-Eileanan an Iar
GB **175** H 8
Ludborough Lincolnshire GB **135**
Q 22
Ludford Lincolnshire GB **135**
Q 22
Ludgershall Wiltshire GB **70**
U 19
Ludham Norfolk GB **101** R 26
Ludlow Shropshire GB **87** S 17
Lugar East Ayrshire GB **146**
M 14
Lugton East Ayrshire GB **160**
L 13
Luib Highland GB **175** H 10
Lumphanan Aberdeenshire
GB **187** H 17
Lumsden Aberdeenshire GB **187**
H 17

Lunan Angus GB **161** J 18
Lund East Riding of Yorkshire
GB **134/135** P 21
Lundie Angus GB **161** J 16
Lunna Shetland Islands GB **199**
B 20
Lunning Shetland Islands GB **199**
B 20
Lurgan Down GB **207** O 10
Lusk Dublin IRL **219** P 10
Luss Argyll and Bute GB **160**
K 13
Lusta Highland GB **175** G 9
Lustleigh Devon GB **53** V 15
Luthrie Fife GB **161** K 16
Luton Luton GB **71** T 22
Lutterworth Leicestershire GB **100**
S 20
Lutton Northhamptonshire
GB **100/101** S 22
Lutton Lincolnshire GB **101** R 23
Lutton Devon GB **53** W 15
Luxborough Somerset GB **53**
U 16
Lybster Highland GB **187** F 16
Lydbury North Shropshire GB **87**
S 17
Lydd Kent GB **71** V 24
Lydford Devon GB **52/53** V 14
Lydford Somerset GB **53** U 17
Lydham Shropshire GB **87** R 17
Lydlinch Dorset GB **70** V 18
Lydney Gloucestershire GB **87**
T 17
Lyminge Kent GB **71** U 25
Lymington Hampshire GB **70**
V 19
Lymm Warrington GB **134** Q 18
Lympne Kent GB **71** U 25
Lympstone Devon GB **53** V 16
Lyndhurst Hampshire GB **70**
V 19
Lyneham Wiltshire GB **70** T 19
Lynemouth Northumberland
GB **147** M 19
Lyness Orkney Islands GB **198**
E 16
Lyng Norfolk GB **101** R 25
Lyng Somerset GB **53** U 17
Lynmouth Devon GB **53** U 15
Lynton Devon GB **53** U 15
Lytchett Matravers Dorset GB **70**
V 18
Lytchett Minster Dorset GB **70**
V 18
Lytham Lancashire GB **119** P 17
Lytham St. Anne's Lancashire
GB **119** P 16
Lythe North Yorkshire GB **147**
N 21

M

Maam Cross Galway IRL **218** Q 3
Maas Donegal IRL **206** N 6
Mablethorpe Lincolnshire GB **135**
Q 23
Macclesfield Cheshire GB **134**
Q 18
Macduff Aberdeenshire GB **187**
G 17
Macharioch Argyll and Bute
GB **174** M 11
Machrihanish Argyll and Bute
GB **174** M 11
Machynlleth Powys GB **86/87**
R 15
Macosquin Londonderry GB **207**
M 9

Macroom Cork IRL **232** T 5
Madderty Perth and Kinross
GB **160/161** K 15
Madeley Heath Staffordshire
GB **134** Q 18
Madley Herefordshire GB **87**
S 17
Maenclochog Pembrokeshire
GB **86** T 13
Maentwrog Gwynedd GB **119**
R 15
Maesteg Bridgend GB **86/87**
T 15
Maganey Kildare IRL **233** R 9
Maghera Londonderry GB **207**
N 9
Magherafelt Londonderry GB **207**
N 9
Magheraveely Fermanagh GB **207**
O 8
Maghull Sefton GB **119** P 17
Magor Monmouthshire GB **87**
T 17
Maguiresbridge Fermanagh
GB **207** O 8
Mahoonagh Limerick IRL **232**
S 5
Maiden Bradley Wiltshire GB **70**
U 18
Maiden Newton Dorset GB **53**
V 17
Maidenhead Windsor &
Maidenhead GB **70/71** T 21
Maidens South Ayrshire GB **146**
M 13
Maidstone Kent GB **71** U 24
Malahide Dublin IRL **219** Q 10
Maldon Essex GB **71** T 24
Malham North Yorkshire GB **147**
O 18
Malin Donegal IRL **207** M 8
Malin Beg Donegal IRL **206** N 5
Mallaig Highland GB **175** H 11
Mallaranny Mayo IRL **218** P 3
Mallow Mala Cork IRL **232** S 5
Mallwyd Gwynedd GB **119** R 15
Malmesbury Wiltshire GB **70**
T 18
Malpas Cheshire GB **119** Q 17
Maltby Rotherham GB **134** Q 20
Maltby le Marsh Lincolnshire
GB **135** Q 23
Malton North Yorkshire GB **134**
O 21
Malzie Dumfries and Galloway
GB **146** N 13
Manaccan Cornwall GB **52** W 12
Manafon Powys GB **87** R 16
Manais Na h-Eileanan an Iar
GB **175** G 9
Manchester Manchester GB **134**
Q 18
Manea Cambridgeshire GB **101**
S 23
Mangotsfield Bristol GB **53** U 17
Manningtree Essex GB **71** T 25
Manorbier Pembrokeshire GB **86**
T 13
Manorhamilton Leitrim IRL **206**
O 6
Mansfield Nottinghamshire
GB **134** Q 20
Mansfield Woodhouse Nottingham-
shire GB **134** Q 20
Mantor Rutland GB **100** R 21
Marazion Cornwall GB **52** W 12
March Cambridgeshire GB **101**
R 23

Marden Kent GB **71** U 24
Maresfield East Sussex GB **71**
V 23
Margam Neath Port Talbot
GB **86/87** T 15
Margate Kent GB **71** U 25
Marham Norfolk GB **101** R 24
Marhamchurch Cornwall GB **52**
V 13
Marholm Peterborough
GB **100/101** R 22
Mark Somerset GB **53** U 17
Market Bosworth Leicestershire
GB **100** R 20
Market Deeping Lincolnshire
GB **100/101** R 22
Market Drayton Shropshire
GB **100** R 18
Market Harborough Leicestershire
GB **100** R 21
Market Lavington Wiltshire GB **70**
U 19
Market Rasen Lincolnshire
GB **135** Q 22
Market Warsop Nottinghamshire
GB **134** Q 20
Market Weighton East Riding of
Yorkshire GB **134/135** P 21
Markethill Armagh GB **207** O 9
Markinch Fife GB **161** K 16
Marks Tey Essex GB **71** T 24
Marksbury Bath & NE Somerset
GB **53** U 17
Marlborough Wiltshire GB **70**
U 19
Marloes Pembrokeshire GB **86**
T 12
Marlow Buckinghamshire
GB **70/71** T 21
Marple Stockport GB **134** Q 18
Marsden Kirklees GB **134** P 19
Marsh Gibbon Buckinghamshire
GB **70** T 20
Marshalstown Wexford IRL **233**
R 9
Marshaw Lancashire GB **119**
P 17
Marshchapel Lincolnshire GB **135**
Q 23
Marshfield South Gloucestershire
GB **70** U 18
Marshwood Dorset GB **53** V 17
Marske North Yorkshire GB **147**
O 19
Marske-by-the-Sea Redcar &
Cleveland GB **147** N 20
Marston Magna Somerset GB **53**
U 17
Martham Norfolk GB **101** R 26
Martin Hampshire GB **70** V 19
Martinhoe Devon GB **53** U 15
Martlesham Suffolk GB **101** S 25
Martley Worcestershire GB **87**
S 18
Martock Somerset GB **53** V 17
Marton Lincolnshire GB **134/135**
Q 21
Marton North Yorkshire GB **147**
O 20
Marwood Devon GB **52/53** U 14
Mary Tavy Devon GB **52/53** V 14
Marybank Highland GB **186** G 13
Marykirk Aberdeenshire GB **161**
J 18
Marypark Moray GB **187** H 16
Maryport Cumbria GB **146** N 15
Marywell Aberdeenshire GB **187**
H 17

Masham North Yorkshire GB **147**
O 19
Matfen Northumberland GB **147**
M 19
Mathry Pembrokeshire GB **86**
T 12
Matlaske Norfolk GB **101** R 25
Matlock Derbyshire GB **134** Q 19
Mauchline East Ayrshire GB **160**
L 14
Maud Aberdeenshire GB **187**
G 18
Maughold Isle of Man GB **146**
O 14
Maum Galway IRL **218** P 3
Maumtrasna Mayo IRL **218** P 3
Mawbray Cumbria GB **146** N 16
Mawnan Cornwall GB **52** W 12
Maxton Scottish Borders GB **161**
L 17
Maybole South Ayrshire GB **146**
M 13
Mayfield Staffordshire GB **134**
Q 19
Mayfield East Sussex GB **71**
U 23
Maynooth Kildare IRL **219** Q 9
Mayobridge Down GB **207** O 10
Mealsgate Cumbria GB **146** N 16
Meanus Limerick IRL **232** R 5
Meare Somerset GB **53** U 17
Mearns East Renfrewshire
GB **160** L 14
Mears Ashby Northhamptonshire
GB **100** S 21
Measham Leicestershire GB **100**
R 19
Medbourne Leicestershire GB **100**
R 21
Medstead Hampshire GB **70**
U 20
Meenlaragh Donegal IRL **206**
M 6
Meidrim Carmarthenshire GB **86**
T 13
Meifod Powys GB **87** R 16
Meigle Perth and Kinross GB **161**
J 16
Meikle Aberdeenshire GB **187**
H 18
Meikleour Perth and Kinross
GB **161** J 16
Melbourn Cambridgeshire GB **101**
S 23
Melbourne Derbyshire GB **100**
R 20
Meldon Northumberland GB **147**
M 19
Meldreth Cambridgeshire GB **101**
S 23
Melgarve Highland GB **160** H 13
Melin-y-ddol Powys GB **87** R 16
Melksham Wiltshire GB **70** U 18
Melling Lancashire GB **146/147**
O 17
Mellis Suffolk GB **101** S 25
Mellon Charles Highland GB **186**
G 11
Mellon Udrigle Highland GB **186**
G 11
Mells Somerset GB **70** U 18
Melmerby Cumbria GB **146/147**
N 17
Melrose Scottish Borders GB **161**
L 17
Meltham Kirklees GB **134** P 19
Melton Constable Norfolk GB **101**
R 25

Melton Mowbray Leicestershire
GB **100** R 21
Melvaig Highland GB **186** G 11
Melvich Highland GB **198** E 15
Memsie Aberdeenshire GB **187**
G 18
Menai Bridge Anglesey
GB **118/119** Q 14
Mendlesham Suffolk GB **101**
S 25
Menlough Galway IRL **218** Q 5
Mennock Dumfries and Galloway
GB **146** M 15
Menston Bradford GB **134** P 19
Mentmore Buckinghamshire
GB **70/71** T 21
Meonstoke Hampshire GB **70**
V 20
Meopham Kent GB **71** U 23
Mepal Cambridgeshire GB **101**
S 23
Mere Wiltshire GB **70** U 18
Mereworth Kent GB **71** U 23
Meriden Solihull GB **100** S 19
Merriott Somerset GB **53** V 17
Merthyr Cynog Powys GB **87**
S 16
Merthyr Tydfil Merthyr Tydfil
GB **87** T 16
Merton Devon GB **52/53** V 14
Merton Greater London GB **71**
U 22
Meshaw Devon GB **53** V 15
Messingham North Lincolnshire
GB **134/135** P 21
Metfield Suffolk GB **101** S 25
Metheringham Lincolnshire
GB **135** Q 22
Methil Fife GB **161** K 16
Methlick Aberdeenshire GB **187**
H 18
Methven Perth and Kinross
GB **160/161** K 15
Methwold Norfolk GB **101** R 24
Mevagissey Cornwall GB **52**
W 13
Mey Highland GB **198** E 16
Miabhaig Na h-Eileanan an Iar
GB **175** F 9
Miabhaig Na h-Eileanan an Iar
GB **175** G 9
Michaelchurch Escley Herefordshire
GB **87** T 16
Mickleton Gloucestershire GB **100**
S 19
Mickley North Yorkshire GB **147**
O 19
Mid Calder West Lothian GB **161**
L 16
Mid Yell Shetland Islands GB **199**
A 20
Midbea Orkney Islands GB **198**
D 17
Middle Barton Oxfordshire GB **70**
T 20
Middle Tysoe Warwickshire
GB **100** S 19
Middle Wallop Hampshire GB **70**
U 19
Middlebie Dumfries and Galloway
GB **146** M 16
Middleham North Yorkshire
GB **147** O 19
Middlesbrough Middlesbrough
GB **147** N 20
Middlesmoor North Yorkshire
GB **147** O 19
Middleton Norfolk GB **101** R 23

Middleton Oldham GB **134** P 18

Middleton Cumbria GB **146/147** O 17

Middleton Northumberland GB **161** L 18

Middleton Argyll and Bute GB **174** K 9

Middleton Cheney Northhamptonshire GB **100** S 20

Middleton-in-Teesdale Durham GB **147** N 18

Middleton-on-the-Wolds East Riding of Yorkshire GB **134/135** P 21

Middletown Armagh GB **207** O 9

Middletown Powys GB **87** R 16

Middlewich Cheshire GB **134** Q 18

Midhurst West Sussex GB **70/71** V 21

Midlem Scottish Borders GB **161** L 17

Midleton Cork IRL **232/233** T 6

Midsomer Norton Bath & NE Somerset GB **70** U 18

Midtown Highland GB **186** G 11

Migvie Aberdeenshire GB **187** H 17

Milborne Port Somerset GB **70** V 18

Milbourne Northumberland GB **147** M 19

Milburn Cumbria GB **146/147** N 17

Mildenhall Suffolk GB **101** S 24

Milestone Tipperary IRL **232/233** R 6

Milfield Northumberland GB **161** L 18

Milford Cork IRL **232** S 5

Milford Haven Aberdaugleddau Pembrokeshire GB **86** T 12

Milford on Sea Hampshire GB **70** V 19

Millbrook Cornwall GB **52/53** W 14

Millford Donegal IRL **206** M 7

Millhouse Argyll and Bute GB **160** L 12

Millington East Riding of Yorkshire GB **134/135** P 21

Millisle Down GB **207** N 11

Millom Cumbria GB **146** O 16

Millport North Ayrshire GB **160** L 13

Mills Antrim GB **207** N 10

Millstreet Cork IRL **232** S 4

Milltown Dumfries and Galloway GB **146** M 16

Milltown Galway IRL **218** P 5

Milltown Kerry IRL **232** S 3

Milltown Malbay Clare IRL **232** R 4

Milltown of Rothiemay Aberdeenshire GB **187** G 17

Milnathort Perth and Kinross GB **161** K 16

Milngavie East Dunbartonshire GB **160** L 14

Milnthorpe Cumbria GB **146/147** O 17

Milovaig Highland GB **175** H 9

Milton Highland GB **186** G 13

Milton Highland GB **186** H 13

Milton Highland GB **186/187** G 14

Milton Abbas Dorset GB **70** V 18

Milton Abbot Devon GB **52/53** V 14

Milton Bryan Bedfordshire GB **70/71** T 21

Milton Ernest Bedfordshire GB **100** S 21

Milton Keynes Milton Keynes GB **100** S 21

Minard Argyll and Bute GB **160** K 12

Minchinhampton Gloucestershire GB **70** T 18

Minehead Somerset GB **53** U 16

Minety Wiltshire GB **70** T 19

Minnigaff Dumfries and Galloway GB **146** N 14

Minskip North Yorkshire GB **147** O 20

Minstead Hampshire GB **70** V 19

Minster Kent GB **71** U 24

Minster Kent GB **71** U 25

Minsterley Shropshire GB **87** R 17

Mintlaw Aberdeenshire GB **187** G 18

Minto Scottish Borders GB **146/147** M 17

Mirfield Kirklees GB **134** P 19

Misson Nottinghamshire GB **134/135** Q 21

Misterton Nottinghamshire GB **134/135** Q 21

Mistley Essex GB **71** T 25

Mitcheldean Gloucestershire GB **70** T 18

Mitchelstown Cork IRL **232/233** S 6

Mitford Northumberland GB **147** M 19

Moate Westmeath IRL **219** Q 7

Mochrum Dumfries and Galloway GB **146** N 13

Modbury Devon GB **53** W 15

Moelfre Anglesey GB **118/119** Q 14

Moffat Dumfries and Galloway GB **146** M 16

Mohill Leitrim IRL **219** P 7

Moira Down GB **207** O 10

Mold Yr Wyddgrug Flintshire GB **119** Q 16

Monaghan Muineachán Monaghan IRL **207** O 9

Monamolin Wexford IRL **233** R 10

Monasteraden Sligo IRL **218** P 5

Monasterevin Kildare IRL **219** Q 8

Moneygall Offaly IRL **233** R 7

Moneymore Londonderry GB **207** N 9

Moneyslane Down GB **207** O 10

Moniaive Dumfries and Galloway GB **146** M 15

Monimail Fife GB **161** K 16

Monivea Galway IRL **218** Q 5

Monkland Herefordshire GB **87** S 17

Monksilver Somerset GB **53** U 16

Monmouth Trefynwy Monmouthshire GB **87** T 17

Monreith Dumfries and Galloway GB **146** N 13

Montacute Somerset GB **53** V 17

Montain Ash Rhondda Cynon Taff GB **87** T 16

Montgomery Powys GB **119** R 16

Montpelier Limerick IRL **232** R 5

Montrose Angus GB **161** J 18

Monzie Perth and Kinross GB **160/161** K 15

Moorfields Antrim GB **207** N 10

Moorlinch Somerset GB **53** U 17

Morchard Bishop Devon GB **53** V 15

Mordiford Herefordshire GB **87** S 17

Morebath Devon GB **53** U 16

Morebattle Scottish Borders GB **161** L 18

Morecambe Lancashire GB **146/147** O 17

Moreton Dorset GB **70** V 18

Moreton Essex GB **71** T 23

Moretonhampstead Devon GB **53** V 15

Morland Cumbria GB **146/147** N 17

Morley Leeds GB **134** P 19

Mornymusk Aberdeenshire GB **187** H 17

Moroe Limerick IRL **232/233** R 6

Morpeth Northumberland GB **147** M 19

Mortehoe Devon GB **52/53** U 14

Mortimer's Cross Herefordshire GB **87** S 17

Morton Lincolnshire GB **100/101** R 22

Morvich Highland GB **186** H 12

Morville Shropshire GB **100** R 18

Morwenstow Cornwall GB **52** V 13

Mosedale Cumbria GB **146** N 16

Mosstodloch Moray GB **187** G 16

Mostyn Flintshire GB **119** Q 16

Motherwell North Lanarkshire GB **160/161** L 15

Moulton Northhamptonshire GB **100** S 21

Moulton Lincolnshire GB **100/101** R 22

Moulton Suffolk GB **101** S 24

Moulton North Yorkshire GB **147** O 19

Mount Bellew Bridge Galway IRL **218** Q 5

Mountcharles Donegal IRL **206** N 6

Mountfield Tyrone GB **207** N 8

Mountmellick Laois IRL **219** Q 8

Mountnorris Armagh GB **207** O 10

Mountrath Laois IRL **219** Q 8

Mountshannon Clare IRL **232/233** R 6

Mountsorrel Leicestershire GB **100** R 20

Mousehole Cornwall GB **52** W 11

Mouswald Dumfries and Galloway GB **146** M 16

Moville Donegal IRL **207** M 8

Mow Cop Cheshire GB **134** Q 18

Moy Armagh GB **207** O 9

Moy Lodge Highland GB **160** J 13

Moyard Galway IRL **218** P 2

Moyasta Clare IRL **232** R 3

Moycullen Galway IRL **218** Q 4

Moylgrove Pembrokeshire GB **86** S 13

Moylough Galway IRL **218** Q 5

Moynalty Meath IRL **219** P 9

Moyne Longford IRL **219** P 7

Moyvore Westmeath IRL **219** P 7

Muasdale Argyll and Bute GB **174** L 11

Much Hadham Hertfordshire GB **71** T 23

Much Marcle Herefordshire GB **70** T 18

Much Wenlock Shropshire GB **87** R 17

Muchalls Aberdeenshire GB **161** H 18

Muff Donegal IRL **207** M 8

Muie Highland GB **186/187** F 14

Muir of Ord Highland GB **186/187** G 14

Muirdrum Angus GB **161** J 18

Muirhead Angus GB **161** K 16

Muirkirk East Ayrshire GB **160** L 14

Muirton Perth and Kinross GB **160/161** K 15

Muker North Yorkshire GB **147** O 18

Mullagh Cavan IRL **219** P 9

Mullagh Meath IRL **219** Q 9

Mullaghboy Antrim GB **207** N 11

Mullaghmore Sligo IRL **206** O 6

Mullany's Cross Sligo IRL **206** O 5

Mullinahone Tipperary IRL **233** R 8

Mullinavat Kilkenny IRL **233** S 8

Mullingar An Muileann gCearr Westmeath IRL **219** P 8

Mullion Cornwall GB **52** W 12

Multyfarnham Westmeath IRL **219** P 8

Mundesley Norfolk GB **101** R 25

Mundford Norfolk GB **101** R 24

Munlochy Highland GB **186/187** G 14

Murrisk Mayo IRL **218** P 3

Murrow Cambridgeshire GB **101** R 23

Murton Cumbria GB **147** N 18

Murton Durham GB **147** N 20

Musbury Devon GB **53** V 16

Musselburgh East Lothian GB **161** L 16

Muthill Perth and Kinross GB **160/161** K 15

Mybster Highland GB **187** F 16

Myddfai Carmarthenshire GB **86/87** T 15

Myddle Shropshire GB **119** R 17

Mydroilyn Ceredigion GB **86** S 14

Myshall Carlow IRL **233** R 9

N

Na Gearrannan Na h-Eileanan an Iar GB **175** F 9

Naas An Nás Kildare IRL **219** Q 9

Naburn York GB **134** P 20

Nacton Suffolk GB **101** S 25

Nafferton East Riding of Yorkshire GB **135** O 22

Nailsea North Somerset GB **53** U 17

Nailsworth Gloucestershire GB **70** T 18

Nairn Highland GB **187** G 15

Nant y-moel Bridgend GB **86/87** T 15

Nantmel Powys GB **87** S 16

Nantwich Cheshire GB **119** Q 17

Nantyffyllon Bridgend GB **86/87** T 15

Naran Donegal IRL **206** N 6

Narberth Pembrokeshire GB **86** T 13

Narborough Leicestershire GB **100** R 20

Narborough Norfolk GB **101** R 24

Naseby Northhamptonshire GB **100** S 21

Nateby Cumbria GB **147** O 18

Naul Dublin IRL **219** P 10

Navan An Uaimh Meath IRL **219** P 9

Navenby Lincolnshire GB **134/135** Q 21

Nazeing Essex GB **71** T 23

Neale Mayo IRL **218** P 4

Neap Shetland Islands GB **199** B 20

Neath Neath Port Talbot GB **86/87** T 15

Necton Norfolk GB **101** R 24

Needham Market Suffolk GB **101** S 25

Nefyn Gwynedd GB **118** R 13

Neilston East Renfrewshire GB **160** L 14

Nelson Lancashire GB **134** P 18

Nenagh Tipperary IRL **232/233** R 6

Nenthead Cumbria GB **147** N 18

Nesscliffe Shropshire GB **119** R 17

Neston Cheshire GB **119** Q 16

Nether Stowey Somerset GB **53** U 16

Nether Wasdale Cumbria GB **146** O 16

Netheravon Wiltshire GB **70** U 19

Netherton Northumberland GB **147** M 19

Netherwitton Northumberland GB **147** M 19

Nethy Bridge Highland GB **187** H 15

Nettlebed Oxfordshire GB **70/71** T 21

Nettleham Lincolnshire GB **135** Q 22

New Abbey Dumfries and Galloway GB **146** N 15

New Aberdour Aberdeenshire GB **187** G 18

New Addington Greater London GB **71** U 22

New Alresford Hampshire GB **70** U 20

New Buckenham Norfolk GB **101** S 25

New Buildings Londonderry GB **207** N 8

New Byth Aberdeenshire GB **187** G 18

New Cumnock East Ayrshire GB **146** M 14

New Deer Aberdeenshire GB **187** G 18

New Galloway Dumfries and Galloway GB **146** M 14

New Holland North Lincolnshire GB **135** P 22

New Inn Galway IRL **218/219** Q 6

New Inn Cavan IRL **219** P 8

New Kildimo Limerick IRL **232** R 5

New Leeds   Aberdeenshire   GB   **187**
G 18
New Luce   Dumfries and Galloway
GB   **146**   N 13
New Mills   Derbyshire   GB   **134**
Q 19
New Milton   Hampshire   GB   **70**
V 19
New Pallas Green   Limerick
IRL   **232/233**   R 6
New Pitsligo   Aberdeenshire
GB   **187**   G 18
New Quay   Ceredigion   GB   **86**
S 14
New Radnor   Powys   GB   **87**   S 16
New Romney   Kent   GB   **71**   V 24
New Ross Ross Mhic Thriúin
Wexford   IRL   **233**   S 9
New Scone   Perth and Kinross
GB   **161**   K 16
New Twopothouse Village   Cork
IRL   **232**   S 5
Newark-on-Trent   Nottinghamshire
GB   **134/135**   Q 21
Newbiggin   Durham   GB   **147**   N 18
Newbiggin-by-the-Sea
Northumberland   GB   **147**   M 20
Newbigging   South Lanarkshire
GB   **160/161**   L 15
Newbliss   Monaghan   IRL   **207**   O 8
Newbridge   Galway   IRL   **218/219**
P 6
Newbridge Droichead Nua   Kildare
IRL   **219**   Q 9
Newbridge   Caerphilly   GB   **87**
T 16
Newbridge on-Wye   Powys   GB   **87**
S 16
Newburgh   Fife   GB   **161**   K 16
Newburgh   Aberdeenshire   GB   **187**
H 19
Newbury   West Berkshire   GB   **70**
U 20
Newby   Cumbria   GB   **146/147**
N 17
Newby Bridge   Cumbria
GB   **146/147**   O 17
Newcastle   Down   GB   **207**   O 11
Newcastle   Wicklow   IRL   **219**   Q 10
Newcastle   Tipperary   IRL   **233**   S 7
Newcastle   Shropshire   GB   **87**
S 16
Newcastle Emlyn   Carmarthenshire
GB   **86**   S 14
Newcastle upon Tyne   Newcastle
upon Tyne   GB   **147**   N 19
Newcastle West   Limerick   IRL   **232**
S 4
Newcastleton or Copshaw Holm
Scottish Borders
GB   **146/147**   M 17
Newcastle-under-Lyme
Staffordshire   GB   **134**   Q 18
Newchurch   Powys   GB   **87**   S 16
Newent   Gloucestershire   GB   **70**
T 18
Newham   Northumberland
GB   **161**   L 19
Newhaven   East Sussex   GB   **71**
V 23
Newick   East Sussex   GB   **71**   V 22
Newington   Kent   GB   **71**   U 24
Newinn   Tipperary   IRL   **233**   S 7
Newlot   Orkney Islands   GB   **198**
D 17
Newlyn   Cornwall   GB   **52**   W 11
Newmachar   Aberdeenshire
GB   **187**   H 18

Newmains   North Lanarkshire
GB   **160/161**   L 15
Newmarket   Suffolk   GB   **101**   S 23
Newmarket   Na h-Eileanan an Iar
GB   **186**   F 10
Newmarket   Cork   IRL   **232**   S 4
Newmarket on Fergus   Clare
IRL   **232**   R 5
Newmill   Scottish Borders
GB   **146/147**   M 17
Newmilns   East Ayrshire   GB   **160**
L 14
Newport   Shropshire   GB   **100**
R 18
Newport   Telford and Wrekin
GB   **100**   R 18
Newport   Mayo   IRL   **218**   P 3
Newport   Tipperary   IRL   **232/233**
R 6
Newport   Isle of Wight   GB   **70**
V 20
Newport   Essex   GB   **71**   T 23
Newport   Pembrokeshire   GB   **86**
S 13
Newport Casnewydd   Newport
GB   **87**   T 17
Newport Pagnell   Milton Keynes
GB   **100**   S 21
Newport Trench   Tyrone   GB   **207**
N 9
Newport-on-Tay   Fife   GB   **161**
K 17
Newquay   Cornwall   GB   **52**   W 12
Newry   Down   GB   **207**   O 10
Newton   Lancashire   GB   **134**   P 18
Newton   Dumfries and Galloway
GB   **146**   M 16
Newton   Cumbria   GB   **146**   N 16
Newton   Argyll and Bute   GB   **160**
K 12
Newton   East Renfrewshire
GB   **160**   L 14
Newton   Pembrokeshire   GB   **86**
T 12
Newton Abbot   Devon   GB   **53**
V 15
Newton Aycliffe   Durham   GB   **147**
N 19
Newton Ferrers   Devon   GB   **52/53**
W 14
Newton Flotman   Norfolk   GB   **101**
R 25
Newton on Trent   Lincolnshire
GB   **134/135**   Q 21
Newton on-the-Moor   Northumberl.
GB   **147**   M 19
Newton Poppleford   Devon   GB   **53**
V 16
Newton Reigny   Cumbria
GB   **146/147**   N 17
Newton Stewart   Dumfries and
Galloway   GB   **146**   N 13
Newton Tracey   Devon   GB   **52/53**
U 14
Newtongrange   Midlothian
GB   **161**   L 16
Newtonhill   Aberdeenshire   GB   **161**
H 18
Newton-le-Willows   St Helens
GB   **119**   Q 17
Newtonmore   Highland   GB   **187**
H 14
Newton-on-Ouse   North Yorkshire
GB   **147**   O 20
Newton-on-Rawcliffe   North
Yorkshire   GB   **134**   O 21
Newtown   Wicklow   IRL   **219**   Q 10
Newtown   Laois   IRL   **233**   R 8

Newtown Y Drenewydd   Powys
GB   **87**   R 16
Newtown Cunningham   Donegal
IRL   **206**   N 7
Newtown Forbes   Longford
IRL   **219**   P 7
Newtown Gore   Leitrim   IRL   **206**
O 7
Newtownabbey   Antrim   GB   **207**
N 11
Newtownards   Down   GB   **207**
N 11
Newtownbutler   Fermanagh
GB   **207**   O 8
Newtown-Crommelin   Antrim
GB   **207**   M 10
Newtownhamilton   Armagh
GB   **207**   O 9
Newtownsands   Kerry   IRL   **232**
R 4
Newtownstewart   Tyrone   GB   **207**
N 8
Newtyle   Angus   GB   **161**   J 16
Neyland   Pembrokeshire   GB   **86**
T 13
Nigg   Highland   GB   **186/187**   G 14
Ninemilehouse   Tipperary   IRL   **233**
S 8
Ninfield   East Sussex   GB   **71**   V 23
Nisbet   Scottish Borders   GB   **161**
L 17
Niwbwrch   Anglesey   GB   **118/119**
Q 14
Nobber   Meath   IRL   **219**   P 9
Nohaval   Cork   IRL   **232/233**
T 6
Nolton   Pembrokeshire   GB   **86**
T 12
Norham   Northumberland   GB   **161**
L 18
Normanby   North Yorkshire
GB   **134**   O 21
Normanton   Wakefield   GB   **134**
P 20
North Ballachulish   Highland
GB   **160**   J 12
North Berwick   East Lothian
GB   **161**   K 17
North Brentor   Devon   GB   **52/53**
V 14
North Cave   East Riding of Yorkshire
GB   **134/135**   P 21
North Cerney   Gloucestershire
GB   **70**   T 19
North Charlton   Northumberland
GB   **161**   L 19
North Collafirth   Shetland Islands
GB   **199**   A 20
North Crawley   Milton Keynes
GB   **100**   S 21
North Creake   Norfolk   GB   **101**
R 24
North Curry   Somerset   GB   **53**
U 17
North Dalton   East Riding of
Yorkshire   GB   **134/135**   P 21
North Elmham   Norfolk   GB   **101**
R 24
North Frodingham   East Riding of
Yorkshire   GB   **135**   P 22
North Grimston   North Yorkshire
GB   **134**   O 21
North Hill   Cornwall   GB   **52/53**
V 14
North Hykeham   Lincolnshire
GB   **134/135**   Q 21
North Kessock   Highland
GB   **186/187**   G 14

North Kilworth   Leicestershire
GB   **100**   S 20
North Kyme   Lincolnshire   GB   **135**
Q 22
North Leverton   Nottinghamshire
GB   **134/135**   Q 21
North Luffenham   Rutland   GB   **100**
R 21
North Marston   Buckinghamshire
GB   **70/71**   T 21
North Molton   Devon   GB   **53**   U 15
North Newbald   East Riding of
Yorkshire   GB   **134/135**   P 21
North Nibley   Gloucestershire
GB   **70**   T 18
North Petherton   Somerset   GB   **53**
U 16
North Queensferry   Fife   GB   **161**
K 16
North Roe   Shetland Islands
GB   **199**   A 20
North Scarle   Lincolnshire
GB   **134/135**   Q 21
North Sunderland   Northumberland
GB   **161**   L 19
North Tamerton   Cornwall
GB   **52/53**   V 14
North Tawton   Devon   GB   **53**   V 15
North Thoresby   Lincolnshire
GB   **135**   Q 22
North Walsham   Norfolk   GB   **101**
R 25
North Wheatley   Nottinghamshire
GB   **134/135**   Q 21
North Wootton   Somerset   GB   **53**
U 17
Northallerton   North Yorkshire
GB   **147**   O 20
Northam   Devon   GB   **52/53**   U 14
Northampton   Northhamptonshire
GB   **100**   S 21
Northchapel   West Sussex
GB   **70/71**   U 21
Northiam   East Sussex   GB   **71**
V 24
Northleach   Gloucestershire   GB   **70**
T 19
Northleigh   Devon   GB   **53**   V 16
Northlew   Devon   GB   **52/53**   V 14
Northmuir   Angus   GB   **161**   J 16
Northpunds   Shetland Islands
GB   **199**   C 20
Northwall   Orkney Islands   GB   **198**
D 18
Northwich   Cheshire   GB   **119**   Q 17
Northwold   Norfolk   GB   **101**   R 24
Northwood   Shropshire   GB   **119**
R 17
Norton   Gloucestershire   GB   **70**
T 18
Norton   Oxfordshire   GB   **70**   T 20
Norton   Powys   GB   **87**   S 16
Norton Fitzwarren   Somerset
GB   **53**   U 16
Norton St. Philip   Somerset   GB   **70**
U 18
Norton-on-Dervent   North Yorkshire
GB   **134**   O 21
Norwich   Norfolk   GB   **101**   R 25
Norwick   Shetland Islands   GB   **199**
A 21
Nottingham   Nottingham   GB   **100**
R 20
Nuneaton   Warwickshire   GB   **100**
R 20
Nunney   Somerset   GB   **70**   U 18
Nunnington   North Yorkshire
GB   **147**   O 20

Nybster   Highland   GB   **198**   E 16

O

Oadby   Leicestershire   GB   **100**
R 20
Oakford   Devon   GB   **53**   V 15
Oakham   Rutland   GB   **100**   R 21
Oakington   Cambridgeshire
GB   **101**   S 23
Oakley   Buckinghamshire   GB   **70**
T 20
Oakworth   Bradford   GB   **134**   P 19
Oban   Argyll and Bute   GB   **160**
K 12
O'Briensbridge   Clare   IRL   **232**   R 5
O'Callaghansmills   Clare   IRL   **232**
R 5
Ochiltree   East Ayrshire   GB   **146**
M 14
Ockle   Highland   GB   **174**   J 11
Ockley   Surrey   GB   **71**   U 22
Odiham   Hampshire   GB   **70/71**
U 21
of Rayne   Aberdeenshire   GB   **187**
H 18
Offord D'Arcy   Cambridgeshire
GB   **100/101**   S 22
Offton   Suffolk   GB   **101**   S 25
Ogle   Northumberland   GB   **147**
M 19
Ogonnelloe   Clare   IRL   **232/233**
R 6
Oilgate   Wexford   IRL   **233**   S 9
Okehampton   Devon   GB   **52/53**
V 14
Old Bolingbroke   Lincolnshire
GB   **135**   Q 23
Old Deer   Aberdeenshire   GB   **187**
G 18
Old Fletton   Peterborough
GB   **100/101**   R 22
Old Town   Cumbria   GB   **146/147**
O 17
Old Town   Isles of Scilly   GB   **52**
X 10
Oldcastle   Meath   IRL   **219**   P 8
Oldham   Oldham   GB   **134**   P 18
Oldhamstocks   East Lothian
GB   **161**   L 18
Oldland   South Gloucestershire
GB   **70**   U 18
Oldmeldrum   Aberdeenshire
GB   **187**   H 18
Oldshoremore   Highland   GB   **186**
F 12
Olgrinmore   Highland   GB   **187**
F 15
Ollaberry   Shetland Islands
GB   **199**   A 20
Ollach   Highland   GB   **175**   H 10
Ollerton   Nottinghamshire   GB   **134**
Q 20
Olney   Milton Keynes   GB   **100**
S 21
Omagh   Tyrone   GB   **207**   N 8
Ombersley   Worcestershire   GB   **87**
S 18
Omeath   Louth   IRL   **207**   O 10
Onchan   Isle of Man   GB   **146**   O 14
Onich   Highland   GB   **160**   J 12
Oranmore   Galway   IRL   **218**   Q 5
Orford   Suffolk   GB   **101**   S 26
Orleton   Herefordshire   GB   **87**
S 17
Ormesby St Margaret   Norfolk
GB   **101**   R 26
Ormskirk   Lancashire   GB   **119**
P 17

Orpington   Greater London   GB   **71**   U 23

Orsett   Thurrock   GB   **71**   T 23

Orston   Nottinghamshire   GB   **100**   R 21

Orton   Cumbria   GB   **146/147**   O 17

Orwell   Cambridgeshire   GB   **101**   S 23

Osbournby   Lincolnshire   GB   **100/101**   R 22

Oskamull   Argyll and Bute   GB   **174**   K 10

Osmington   Dorset   GB   **70**   V 18

Osmotherley   North Yorkshire   GB   **147**   O 20

Ossett   Wakefield   GB   **134**   P 19

Oswaldtwistle   Lancashire   GB   **134**   P 18

Oswestry   Shropshire   GB   **119**   R 16

Othery   Somerset   GB   **53**   U 17

Otley   Suffolk   GB   **101**   S 25

Otley   Leeds   GB   **134**   P 19

Otter Ferry   Argyll and Bute   GB   **160**   K 12

Otterburn   Northumberland   GB   **147**   M 18

Otterswick   Shetland Islands   GB   **199**   A 20

Otterton   Devon   GB   **53**   V 16

Ottery St Mary   Devon   GB   **53**   V 16

Ottringham   East Riding of Yorkshire   GB   **135**   P 22

Oughterard   Galway   IRL   **218**   Q 4

Oulart   Wexford   IRL   **233**   R 10

Oulton   Cumbria   GB   **146**   N 16

Oundle   Northhamptonshire   GB   **100/101**   S 22

Outwell   Norfolk   GB   **101**   R 23

Outwood   Surrey   GB   **71**   U 22

Ovens   Cork   IRL   **232**   T 5

Over Kellet   Lancashire   GB   **146/147**   O 17

Overbister   Orkney Islands   GB   **198**   D 17

Overseal   Derbyshire   GB   **100**   R 19

Overstrand   Norfolk   GB   **101**   R 25

Overton   Wrexham   GB   **119**   R 17

Overton   Lancashire   GB   **146/147**   O 17

Overton   Hampshire   GB   **70**   U 20

Owston Ferry   North Lincolnshire   GB   **134/135**   Q 21

Oxborough   Norfolk   GB   **101**   R 24

Oxenhope   Bradford   GB   **134**   P 19

Oxford   Oxfordshire   GB   **70**   T 20

Oxnam   Scottish Borders   GB   **147**   M 18

Oxted   Surrey   GB   **71**   U 23

Oxton   Nottinghamshire   GB   **134**   Q 20

Oxton   Scottish Borders   GB   **161**   L 17

Oykel Bridge   Highland   GB   **186**   G 13

Oyne   Aberdeenshire   GB   **187**   H 17

P

Pabail larach   Na h-Eileanan an Iar   GB   **186**   F 10

Padbury   Buckinghamshire   GB   **70/71**   T 21

Paddock Wood   Kent   GB   **71**   U 23

Padiham   Lancashire   GB   **134**   P 18

Padstow   Cornwall   GB   **52**   V 13

Pagham   West Sussex   GB   **70/71**   V 21

Paignton   Torbay   GB   **53**   W 15

Pailton   Warwickshire   GB   **100**   S 20

Painscastle   Powys   GB   **87**   S 16

Painswick   Gloucestershire   GB   **70**   T 18

Paisley   Renfrewshire   GB   **160**   L 14

Pallas Green   Limerick   IRL   **232/233**   R 6

Pallaskenry   Limerick   IRL   **232**   R 5

Palnackie   Dumfries and Galloway   GB   **146**   N 15

Palnure   Dumfries and Galloway   GB   **146**   N 14

Pandy   Monmouthshire   GB   **87**   T 17

Pangbourne   West Berkshire   GB   **70**   U 20

Pant   Shropshire   GB   **87**   R 16

Pant Glas   Gwynedd   GB   **118/119**   Q 14

Papworth Everard   Cambridgeshire   GB   **100/101**   S 22

Parbold   Lancashire   GB   **119**   P 17

Park   Londonderry   GB   **207**   N 8

Parkend   Gloucestershire   GB   **87**   T 17

Parkgate   Dumfries and Galloway   GB   **146**   M 15

Parknasilla   Kerry   IRL   **232**   T 3

Parracombe   Devon   GB   **53**   U 15

Partney   Lincolnshire   GB   **135**   Q 23

Parton   Dumfries and Galloway   GB   **146**   M 14

Parton   Cumbria   GB   **146**   N 15

Partry   Mayo   IRL   **218**   P 4

Parwich   Derbyshire   GB   **134**   Q 19

Passage East   Waterford   IRL   **233**   S 9

Passage West   Cork   IRL   **232/233**   T 6

Pateley Bridge   North Yorkshire   GB   **147**   O 19

Path of Condie   Perth and Kinross   GB   **160/161**   K 15

Pathead   Midlothian   GB   **161**   L 17

Patna   East Ayrshire   GB   **146**   M 14

Patrick   North Yorkshire   GB   **147**   O 19

Patrikswell   Limerick   IRL   **232**   R 5

Patrington   East Riding of Yorkshire   GB   **135**   P 23

Patterdale   Cumbria   GB   **146/147**   N 17

Paxton   Scottish Borders   GB   **161**   L 18

Peacehaven   East Sussex   GB   **71**   V 23

Peak Forest   Derbyshire   GB   **134**   Q 19

Peakirk   Peterborough   GB   **100/101**   R 22

Peasenhall   Suffolk   GB   **101**   S 25

Peasmarsh   East Sussex   GB   **71**   V 24

Peat Inn   Fife   GB   **161**   K 17

Peebles   Scottish Borders   GB   **161**   L 16

Peel   Isle of Man   GB   **146**   O 13

Peinchorran   Highland   GB   **175**   H 10

Pelton   Durham   GB   **147**   N 19

Pembrey   Carmarthenshire   GB   **86**   T 14

Pembridge   Herefordshire   GB   **87**   S 17

Pembroke   Pembrokeshire   GB   **86**   T 13

Pembroke Dock   Doc Penfro   Pembrokeshire   GB   **86**   T 13

Penarth   Vale of Glamorgan   GB   **53**   U 16

Pencaitland   East Lothian   GB   **161**   L 17

Pencoed   Bridgend   GB   **86/87**   T 15

Pendeen   Cornwall   GB   **52**   W 11

Penderyn   Rhondda Cynon Taff   GB   **86/87**   T 15

Pendine   Carmarthenshire   GB   **86**   T 13

Penicuik   Midlothian   GB   **161**   L 16

Peniston   Barnsley   GB   **134**   P 19

Penkridge   Staffordshire   GB   **100**   R 18

Penley   Wrexham   GB   **119**   R 17

Penmachno   Conwy   GB   **119**   Q 15

Penmaenmawr   Conwy   GB   **119**   Q 15

Pennal   Gwynedd   GB   **86/87**   R 15

Pennan   Aberdeenshire   GB   **187**   G 18

Penpont   Dumfries and Galloway   GB   **146**   M 15

Penrhyn-deudraeth   Gwynedd   GB   **118/119**   R 14

Penrith   Cumbria   GB   **146/147**   N 17

Penruddock   Cumbria   GB   **146/147**   N 17

Penryn   Cornwall   GB   **52**   W 12

Pensford   Bath & NE Somerset   GB   **53**   U 17

Penshurst   Kent   GB   **71**   U 23

Pensilva   Cornwall   GB   **52/53**   W 14

Pentraeth   Anglesey   GB   **118/119**   Q 14

Pentrefoelas   Conwy   GB   **119**   Q 15

Penybont   Powys   GB   **87**   S 16

Penygroes   Gwynedd   GB   **118/119**   Q 14

Peny-y-Bont Ar Ogwr Bridgend   Bridgend   GB   **53**   U 15

Penzance   Cornwall   GB   **52**   W 11

Perranporth   Cornwall   GB   **52**   W 12

Pershore   Worcestershire   GB   **87**   S 18

Perth   Perth and Kinross   GB   **161**   K 16

Peterborough   Peterborough   GB   **100/101**   R 22

Peterculter   Aberdeenshire   GB   **187**   H 18

Peterhead   Aberdeenshire   GB   **187**   G 19

Peterlee   Durham   GB   **147**   N 20

Petersfield   Hampshire   GB   **70/71**   V 21

Peterstow   Herefordshire   GB   **87**   T 17

Petham   Kent   GB   **71**   U 25

Pettigo   Donegal   IRL   **206**   N 7

Petworth   West Sussex   GB   **70/71**   V 21

Pevensey   East Sussex   GB   **71**   V 23

Pewsey   Wiltshire   GB   **70**   U 19

Pickering   North Yorkshire   GB   **134**   O 21

Piddletrenthide   Dorset   GB   **70**   V 18

Piercetown   Wexford   IRL   **233**   S 10

Pierowall   Orkney Islands   GB   **198**   D 17

Pilling   Lancashire   GB   **119**   P 17

Pilton   Somerset   GB   **53**   U 17

Pinchbeck   Lincolnshire   GB   **100/101**   R 22

Pinchbeck West   Lincolnshire   GB   **100/101**   R 22

Pinwherry   South Ayrshire   GB   **146**   M 13

Pirbright   Surrey   GB   **70/71**   U 21

Pirnmill   North Ayrshire   GB   **160**   L 12

Pitcox   East Lothian   GB   **161**   L 17

Pittenweem   Fife   GB   **161**   K 17

Pitlochry   Perth and Kinross   GB   **160/161**   J 15

Pitmedden   Aberdeenshire   GB   **187**   H 18

Pitscottie   Fife   GB   **161**   K 17

Pittentrail   Highland   GB   **186/187**   G 14

Pittington   Durham   GB   **147**   N 19

Plean   Stirling   GB   **160/161**   K 15

Pleasley   Nottinghamshire   GB   **134**   Q 20

Plenmeller   Northumberland   GB   **147**   N 18

Plockton   Highland   GB   **175**   H 11

Pluckley   Kent   GB   **71**   U 24

Plumbland   Cumbria   GB   **146**   N 16

Plumbridge   Tyrone   GB   **207**   N 8

Plumpton   Cumbria   GB   **146/147**   N 17

Plymouth   Plymouth   GB   **52/53**   W 14

Plympton   Plymouth   GB   **52/53**   W 14

Pocklington   East Riding of Yorkshire   GB   **134/135**   P 21

Point   Donegal   IRL   **207**   M 8

Polbain   Highland   GB   **186**   F 12

Polbathic   Cornwall   GB   **52/53**   W 14

Polegate   East Sussex   GB   **71**   V 23

Polesworth   Warwickshire   GB   **100**   R 19

Pollatomish   Mayo   IRL   **218**   O 3

Polmont   Falkirk   GB   **160/161**   L 15

Polperro   Cornwall   GB   **52**   W 13

Polruan   Cornwall   GB   **52**   W 13

Polwarth   Scottish Borders   GB   **161**   L 18

Polzeath   Cornwall   GB   **52**   V 13

Pomeroy   Tyrone   GB   **207**   N 9

Pontardawe   Neath Port Talbot   GB   **86/87**   T 15

Pontardulais   Swansea   GB   **86**   T 14

Pontefract   Wakefield   GB   **134**   P 20

Ponteland   Northumberland   GB   **147**   M 19

Ponterwyd   Ceredigion   GB   **86/87**   S 15

Pontesbury   Shropshire   GB   **87**   R 17

Pontllanfraith   Caerphilly   GB   **87**   T 16

Pontoon   Mayo   IRL   **218**   P 4

Pontrhydfendigaid   Ceredigion   GB   **86/87**   S 15

Pontrilas   Herefordshire   GB   **87**   T 17

Pontsticill   Powys   GB   **87**   T 16

Pontyates   Carmarthenshire   GB   **86**   T 14

Pontycymer   Bridgend   GB   **86/87**   T 15

Pontypool   Torfaen   GB   **87**   T 16

Pontypridd   Rhondda Cynon Taff   GB   **87**   T 16

Pool   North Yorkshire   GB   **134**   P 19

Poole   Poole   GB   **70**   V 19

Poolewe   Highland   GB   **186**   G 11

Pooley Bridge   Cumbria   GB   **146/147**   N 17

Poppleton   York   GB   **134**   P 20

Porlock   Somerset   GB   **53**   U 15

Port Bannatyne   Argyll and Bute   GB   **160**   L 12

Port Carlisle   Cumbria   GB   **146**   N 16

Port Charlotte   Argyll and Bute   GB   **174**   L 10

Port Ellen   Argyll and Bute   GB   **174**   L 10

Port Erin   Isle of Man   GB   **146**   O 13

Port Glasgow   Inverclyde   GB   **160**   L 13

Port Henderson   Highland   GB   **186**   G 11

Port Isaac   Cornwall   GB   **52**   V 13

Port Lamont   Argyll and Bute   GB   **160**   L 12

Port Laoise   Laois   IRL   **219**   Q 8

Port Logan   Dumfries and Galloway   GB   **146**   N 13

Port nan Giuran Portnaguran   Na h-Eileanan an Iar   GB   **186**   F 10

Port nan Long   Na h-Eileanan an Iar   GB   **175**   G 8

Port Nis Port of Ness   Na h-Eileanan an Iar   GB   **186**   E 10

Port of Menteith   Stirling   GB   **160**   K 14

Port of Ness Port Nis   Na h-Eileanan an Iar   GB   **186**   E 10

Port Talbot   Neath Port Talbot   GB   **86/87**   T 15

Port William   Dumfries and Galloway   GB   **146**   N 13

Portacloy   Mayo   IRL   **218**   O 3

Portadown   Armagh   GB   **207**   O 10

Portaferry   Down   GB   **207**   O 11

Portaleen   Donegal   IRL   **207**   M 8

Portarlington   Offaly   IRL   **219**   Q 8

Portavadie   Argyll and Bute   GB   **160**   L 12

Portesham   Dorset   GB   **53**   V 17

Port Eynon   Swansea   GB   **86**   T 14

Portglenone   Antrim   GB   **207**   N 10

Porth   Rhondda Cynon Taff   GB   **87**   T 16

Porthcawl   Bridgend   GB   **53**   U 15

Porthleven   Cornwall   GB   **52**   W 12

Porthmadog   Gwynedd   GB   **118/119**   R 14

Porthmeor   Cornwall   GB   **52**   W 11

Portishead   North Somerset   GB   **53**   U 17

Portknockie   Moray   GB   **187**   G 17

Portlaw   Waterford   IRL   **233**   S 8

Portlethen   Aberdeenshire   GB   **187**   H 18

Portmagee   Kerry   IRL   **70**   T 2

Portmahomack   Highland   GB   **187**   G 15

Portmarnock Dublin IRL **219** Q 10

Portnaguran Port nan Giuran Na h-Eileanan an Iar GB **186** F 10

Portnahaven Argyll and Bute GB **174** L 9

Portnalong Highland GB **175** H 10

Portpatrick Dumfries and Galloway GB **146** N 12

Portreath Cornwall GB **52** W 12

Portree Highland GB **175** H 10

Portroe Tipperary IRL **232/233** R 6

Portrush Antrim GB **207** M 9

Portsalon Donegal IRL **206** M 7

Portscatho Cornwall GB **52** W 13

Portskerra Highland GB **198** E 15

Portslade-by-Sea Brighton & Hove GB **71** V 22

Portsmouth Portsmouth GB **70** V 20

Portsoy Aberdeenshire GB **187** G 17

Port St. Mary Isle of Man GB **146** O 13

Portstewart Londonderry GB **207** M 9

Portumna Galway IRL **218/219** Q 6

Porturlin Mayo IRL **218** O 3

Potterhanworth Lincolnshire GB **135** Q 22

Potters Bar Hertfordshire GB **71** T 22

Potton Bedfordshire GB **100/101** S 22

Poulgorm Br. Kerry IRL **232** T 4

Poulton Gloucestershire GB **70** T 19

Poulton-le-Fylde Lancashire GB **119** P 17

Poundstock Cornwall GB **52** V 13

Powerstock Dorset GB **53** V 17

Powick Worcestershire GB **87** S 18

Poynton Cheshire GB **134** Q 18

Poyntz Pass Armagh GB **207** O 10

Prees Shropshire GB **119** R 17

Preesall Lancashire GB **119** P 17

Prendwick Northumberland GB **147** M 19

Prenteg Gwynedd GB **118/119** R 14

Prescot Knowsley GB **119** Q 17

Prestatyn Denbighshire GB **119** Q 16

Presteigne Powys GB **87** S 17

Preston Rutland GB **100** R 21

Preston Lancashire GB **119** P 17

Preston Scottish Borders GB **161** L 18

Preston Dorset GB **70** V 18

Preston Candover Hampshire GB **70** U 20

Prestonpans East Lothian GB **161** L 17

Prestwick South Ayrshire GB **146** M 13

Prickwillow Cambridgeshire GB **101** S 23

Princes Risborough Buckinghamshire GB **70/71** T 21

Princethorpe Warwickshire GB **100** S 20

Princetown Devon GB **52/53** V 14

Priors Marston Warwickshire GB **100** S 20

Probus Cornwall GB **52** W 13

Proncy Highland GB **186/187** G 14

Prudhoe Northumberland GB **147** N 19

Puckaun Tipperary IRL **232/233** R 6

Puckerridge Hertfordshire GB **71** T 23

Puddletown Dorset GB **70** V 18

Pudsey Leeds GB **134** P 19

Pulborough West Sussex GB **70/71** V 21

Pulham Norfolk GB **101** S 25

Pumsaint Carmarthenshire GB **86/87** S 15

Puncheston Pembrokeshire GB **86** T 13

Purfleet Thurrock GB **71** U 23

Puriton Somerset GB **53** U 17

Purley Greater London GB **71** U 22

Purton Wiltshire GB **70** T 19

Puttenham Surrey GB **70/71** U 21

Pwllheli Gwynedd GB **118/119** R 14

Pyle Bridgend GB **86/87** T 15

Q

Quainton Buckinghamshire GB **70/71** T 21

Quantoxhead Somerset GB **53** U 16

Quarndon Derbyshire GB **100** R 20

Quay Flintshire GB **119** Q 16

Queenborough Kent GB **71** U 24

Queensbury Bradford GB **134** P 19

Queensferry Flintshire GB **119** Q 16

Queensferry Edinburgh GB **161** L 16

Quendale Shetland Islands GB **199** C 20

Quendon Essex GB **71** T 23

Quigley's Donegal IRL **207** M 8

Quilty Clare IRL **232** R 4

Quin Clare IRL **232** R 5

Quorn Leicestershire GB **100** R 20

Quoyness Orkney Islands GB **198** E 16

R

Rackenford Devon GB **53** V 15

Rackwick Orkney Islands GB **198** E 16

Radcliffe on Trent Nottinghamshire GB **100** R 20

Radlett Hertfordshire GB **71** T 22

Radstock Bath & NE Somerset GB **70** U 18

Rafford Moray GB **187** G 15

Raghly Sligo IRL **206** O 5

Raglan Monmouthshire GB **87** T 17

Rahaghy Meath IRL **219** P 8

Rainham Greater London GB **71** T 23

Rainworth Nottinghamshire GB **134** Q 20

Rait Perth and Kinross GB **161** K 16

Ramasaig Highland GB **175** H 9

Rame Cornwall GB **52** W 12

Rame Cornwall GB **52/53** W 14

Ramsbottom Bury GB **134** P 18

Ramsbury Wiltshire GB **70** U 19

Ramsey Cambridgeshire GB **100/101** S 22

Ramsey Isle of Man GB **146** O 14

Ramsey Essex GB **71** T 25

Ramseycleuch Scottish Borders GB **146** M 16

Ramsgate Kent GB **71** U 25

Ramsgill North Yorkshire GB **147** O 19

Ranais Na h-Eileanan an Iar GB **186** F 10

Randalstown Antrim GB **207** N 10

Rankinston East Ayrshire GB **146** M 14

Rannoch Station Perth and Kinross GB **160** J 13

Ranskill Nottinghamshire GB **134** Q 20

Rapness Orkney Islands GB **198** D 17

Rasharkin Antrim GB **207** N 10

Rashedoge Donegal IRL **206** N 7

Ratallen Cross Roads Roscommon IRL **218/219** P 6

Rathangan Kildare IRL **219** Q 9

Rathconrath Westmeath IRL **219** P 7

Rathcoole Dublin IRL **219** Q 10

Rathcormack Cork IRL **232/233** S 6

Rathdowney Laois IRL **233** R 7

Rathdrum Wicklow IRL **233** R 10

Rathen Aberdeenshire GB **187** G 18

Rathfeigh Meath IRL **219** P 10

Rathfriland Down GB **207** O 10

Rathkeale Limerick IRL **232** R 5

Rathlackan Mayo IRL **206** O 4

Rathmelton Donegal IRL **206** M 7

Rathmolyon Meath IRL **219** Q 9

Rathmore Meath IRL **219** P 9

Rathmore Kerry IRL **232** S 4

Rathmullan Donegal IRL **206** M 7

Rathnew Wicklow IRL **233** R 10

Rathnure Wexford IRL **233** S 9

Rathowen Westmeath IRL **219** P 7

Rathvilly Carlow IRL **233** R 9

Ratoath Meath IRL **219** P 10

Rattlesden Suffolk GB **101** S 24

Rattray Perth and Kinross GB **161** J 16

Raunds Northhamptonshire GB **100** S 21

Ravenglass Cumbria GB **146** O 16

Ravenscar North Yorkshire GB **135** Q 22

Ravensworth North Yorkshire GB **147** O 19

Ravyenstonedale Cumbria GB **147** O 18

Rawcliffe East Riding of Yorkshire GB **134/135** P 21

Rawmarsh Rotherham GB **134** Q 20

Rawtenstall Lancashire GB **134** P 18

Rayleigh Essex GB **71** T 24

Reading Reading GB **70/71** U 21

Rear Cross Tipperary IRL **232/233** R 6

Rearsby Leicestershire GB **100** R 20

Reawick Shetland Islands GB **199** B 20

Reay Highland GB **198** E 15

Reculver Kent GB **71** U 25

Red Roses Carmarthenshire GB **86** T 13

Red Row Northumberland GB **147** M 19

Redcar Redcar & Cleveland GB **147** N 20

Redditch Worcestershire GB **100** S 19

Redesmouth Northumberland GB **147** M 18

Redgrave Suffolk GB **101** S 25

Redhill Surrey GB **71** U 22

Redland Orkney Islands GB **198** D 16

Redlynch Wiltshire GB **70** V 19

Redmire North Yorkshire GB **147** O 19

Redpoint Highland GB **186** G 11

Redruth Cornwall GB **52** W 12

Redwick Newport GB **87** T 17

Reedham Norfolk GB **101** R 26

Reepham Norfolk GB **101** R 25

Reepham Lincolnshire GB **135** Q 22

Reeth North Yorkshire GB **147** O 19

Regaba Isle of Man GB **146** O 14

Reiff Highland GB **186** F 12

Reigate Surrey GB **71** U 22

Reighton North Yorkshire GB **135** O 22

Reiss Highland GB **187** F 16

Rendlesham Suffolk GB **101** S 25

Renfrew Renfrewshire GB **160** L 14

Renhold Bedfordshire GB **100/101** S 22

Rennington Northumberland GB **147** M 19

Renton West Dunbartonshire GB **160** L 13

Renwick Cumbria GB **146/147** N 17

Rescobie Angus GB **161** J 18

Resolven Neath Port Talbot GB **86/87** T 15

Reston Scottish Borders GB **161** L 18

Retford Nottinghamshire GB **134/135** Q 21

Rettendon Essex GB **71** T 24

Revesby Lincolnshire GB **135** Q 22

Reynoldston Swansea GB **86** T 14

Rhaeadr Gwy Rhayader Powys GB **86/87** S 15

Rhandirmwyn Carmarthenshire GB **86/87** S 15

Rhayader Rhaeadr Gwy Powys GB **86/87** S 15

Rhewl Denbighshire GB **119** Q 16

Rhiconich Highland GB **186** F 13

Rhiw Gwynedd GB **118** R 13

Rhode Offaly IRL **219** Q 8

Rhondda Rhondda Cynon Taff GB **87** T 16

Rhoose Vale of Glamorgan GB **53** U 16

Rhos Carmarthenshire GB **86** T 14

Rhoscolyn Anglesey GB **118** Q 13

Rhosllanerchrugog Wrexham GB **119** Q 16

Rhosneigr Anglesey GB **118** Q 13

Rhossili Swansea GB **86** T 14

Rhostryfan Gwynedd GB **118/119** Q 14

Rhu Argyll and Bute GB **160** K 13

Rhubodach Argyll and Bute GB **160** L 12

Rhuddlan Denbighshire GB **119** Q 16

Rhuthun Ruthin Denbighshire GB **119** Q 16

Rhydcymerau Carmarthenshire GB **86** S 14

Rhydymwyn Flintshire GB **119** Q 16

Rhymney Caerphilly GB **87** T 16

Rhynie Aberdeenshire GB **187** H 17

Ribblehead North Yorkshire GB **147** O 18

Ribchester Lancashire GB **119** P 17

Riccall North Yorkshire GB **134** P 20

Richhill Armagh GB **207** O 9

Richmond North Yorkshire GB **147** O 19

Richmond Greater London GB **71** U 22

Rickmansworth Hertfordshire GB **70/71** T 21

Ridgewell Essex GB **101** S 24

Ridgmont Bedfordshire GB **100** S 21

Riding Mill Northumberland GB **147** N 19

Ridsdale Northumberland GB **147** M 18

Rigg Dumfries and Galloway GB **146** N 16

Rigside South Lanarkshire GB **160/161** L 15

Rillington North Yorkshire GB **134** O 21

Rimington Lancashire GB **134** P 18

Ringaskiddy Cork IRL **232/233** T 6

Ringford Dumfries and Galloway GB **146** N 14

Ringmer East Sussex GB **71** V 23

Ringsend Londonderry GB **207** M 9

Ringstead Norfolk GB **101** R 24

Ringville Waterford IRL **233** S 7

Ringwood Hampshire GB **70** V 19

Ripley Derbyshire GB **134** Q 20

Ripley North Yorkshire GB **147** O 19

Ripley Surrey GB **70/71** U 21

Ripon North Yorkshire GB **147** O 19

Ripponden Calderdale GB **134** P 19

Risca Caerphilly GB **87** T 16

Rishton Lancashire GB **134** P 18

Riverchapel Wexford IRL **233** R 10

Roade Northhamptonshire GB **100** S 21
Roadside Highland GB **198** E 16
Roadside of Kinneff Aberdeenshire GB **161** J 18
Roberton Scottish Borders GB **146/147** M 17
Roberton South Lanarkshire GB **160/161** L 15
Robertsbridge East Sussex GB **71** V 23
Robertstown Kildare IRL **219** Q 9
Robin Hood's Bay North Yorkshire GB **135** O 21
Roborough Devon GB **52/53** V 14
Rocester Staffordshire GB **100** R 19
Roch Pembrokeshire GB **86** T 12
Rochdale Rochdale GB **134** P 18
Rochester Northumberland GB **147** M 18
Rochester Medway GB **71** U 23
Rochford Essex GB **71** T 24
Rochfortbridge Westmeath IRL **219** Q 8
Rock Cornwall GB **52** V 13
Rockbeare Devon GB **53** V 16
Rockchapel Cork IRL **232** S 4
Rockcliffe Dumfries and Galloway GB **146** N 15
Rockcliffe Cumbria GB **146** N 16
Rockcorry Monaghan IRL **207** O 8
Rockhill Limerick IRL **232** S 5
Rockingham Northhamptonshire GB **100** R 21
Rodington Shropshire GB **119** R 17
Rodington Telford and Wrekin GB **87** R 17
Roesound Shetland Islands GB **199** B 20
Rogart Highland GB **186/187** F 14
Roghadal Na h-Eileanan an Iar GB **175** G 9
Rolvenden Kent GB **71** U 24
Romaldkirk Durham GB **147** N 18
Romsey Hampshire GB **70** V 19
Rookhope Durham GB **147** N 18
Rooks Bridge Somerset GB **53** U 17
Roonah Quay Mayo IRL **218** P 3
Roos East Riding of Yorkshire GB **135** P 22
Rootpark South Lanarkshire GB **160/161** L 15
Ropley Hampshire GB **70** U 20
Ropsley Lincolnshire GB **100** R 21
Rora Aberdeenshire GB **187** G 19
Roscommon Ros Comáin Roscommon IRL **218/219** P 6
Roscrea Tipperary IRL **233** R 7
Rosedale Abbey North Yorkshire GB **134** O 21
Rosegreen Tipperary IRL **233** S 7
Rosehearty Aberdeenshire GB **187** G 18
Rosemarkie Highland GB **186/187** G 14
Rosenallis Laois IRL **219** Q 8
Roskhill Highland GB **175** H 9
Rosley Cumbria GB **146** N 16

Roslin Midlothian GB **161** L 16
Rosneath Argyll and Bute GB **160** K 13
Ross Northumberland GB **161** L 19
Ross Meath IRL **219** P 8
Ross Carbery Cork IRL **232** T 4
Rossaveel Galway IRL **218** Q 3
Rosses Point Sligo IRL **206** O 5
Rossington Doncaster GB **134** Q 20
Rossinver Leitrim IRL **206** O 6
Rosslare Wexford IRL **233** S 10
Rosslare Harbour Calafort Ros Láir Wexford IRL **233** S 10
Rosslea Fermanagh GB **207** O 8
Rossnowlagh Donegal IRL **206** N 6
Ross-on-Wye Herefordshire GB **87** T 17
Rostrevor Down GB **207** O 10
Rosyth Fife GB **161** K 16
Rothbury Northumberland GB **147** M 19
Rotherfield East Sussex GB **71** U 23
Rotherham Rotherham GB **134** Q 20
Rothes Moray GB **187** G 16
Rothesay Argyll and Bute GB **160** L 12
Rothienorman Aberdeenshire GB **187** H 18
Rothiesholm Orkney Islands GB **198** D 17
Rothwell Northhamptonshire GB **100** S 21
Rothwell Leeds GB **134** P 20
Rottal Angus GB **161** J 16
Rottingdean Brighton & Hove GB **71** V 22
Roughsike Cumbria GB **146/147** M 17
Roughton Norfolk GB **101** R 25
Roundstone Galway IRL **218** Q 3
Roundwood Wicklow IRL **219** Q 10
Rounton North Yorkshire GB **147** O 20
Rousdon Devon GB **53** V 16
Rousky Tyrone GB **207** N 8
Rowanburn Dumfries and Galloway GB **146/147** M 17
Rowardennan Stirling GB **160** K 13
Rowlands Gateshead GB **147** N 19
Rowsley Derbyshire GB **134** Q 19
Roxburgh Scottish Borders GB **161** L 18
Roxton Bedfordshire GB **100/101** S 22
Roxwell Essex GB **71** T 23
Royal Leamington Spa Warwickshire GB **100** S 19
Royal Tunbridge Wells Kent GB **71** U 23
Roybridge Highland GB **160** J 13
Royston Hertfordshire GB **100/101** S 22
Royston Barnsley GB **134** P 20
Royton Oldham GB **134** P 18
Ruabon Wrexham GB **119** R 16
Ruan Minor Cornwall GB **52** X 12
Ruddington Nottinghamshire GB **100** R 20

Rudgwick West Sussex GB **71** U 22
Rudston East Riding of Yorkshire GB **135** O 22
Rudyard Staffordshire GB **134** Q 18
Rufford Lancashire GB **119** P 17
Rugby Warwickshire GB **100** S 20
Rugeley Staffordshire GB **100** R 19
Rumbling Bridge Perth and Kinross GB **160/161** K 15
Rumburgh Suffolk GB **101** S 25
Runcorn Halton GB **119** Q 17
Rush Dublin IRL **219** P 10
Rushden Northhamptonshire GB **100** S 21
Ruskington Lincolnshire GB **135** Q 22
Ruswarp North Yorkshire GB **134** O 21
Rutherglen South Lanarkshire GB **160** L 14
Ruthin Rhuthun Denbighshire GB **119** Q 16
Ruthwell Dumfries and Galloway GB **146** N 16
Ryal Northumberland GB **147** M 18
Ryde Isle of Wight GB **70** V 20
Rye East Sussex GB **71** V 24
Ryhill Wakefield GB **134** P 20
Ryhope Sunderland GB **147** N 20
Rylane Cork IRL **232** T 5
Rylstone North Yorkshire GB **147** O 18
Ryton Gateshead GB **147** N 19

S

Sabden Lancashire GB **134** P 18
Sacriston Durham GB **147** N 19
Sadberge Durham GB **147** N 20
Saddell Argyll and Bute GB **174** L 11
Sadgill Cumbria GB **146/147** O 17
Saffron Walden Essex GB **101** S 23
Saggart Dublin IRL **219** Q 10
Saintfield Down GB **207** O 11
Salcombe Devon GB **53** W 15
Salcott Essex GB **71** T 24
Salen Argyll and Bute GB **174** J 11
Salen Highland GB **174** J 11
Salford Trafford GB **134** Q 18
Salfords Surrey GB **71** U 22
Saline Fife GB **160/161** K 15
Salisbury Wiltshire GB **70** U 19
Sallachy Highland GB **186** H 12
Sallins Kildare IRL **219** Q 9
Saltash Cornwall GB **52/53** W 14
Saltburn-by-the-Sea Redcar & Cleveland GB **147** N 21
Saltcoats North Ayrshire GB **160** L 13
Saltdean East Sussex GB **71** V 22
Saltfleet Lincolnshire GB **135** Q 23
Saltfleetby St Peter Lincolnshire GB **135** Q 23
Saltford Bath & NE Somerset GB **70** U 18
Salton North Yorkshire GB **134** O 21

Samhia Na h-Eileanan an Iar GB **175** G 8
Sampford Peverell Devon GB **53** V 16
Sanaigmore Argyll and Bute GB **174** L 10
Sand Shetland Islands GB **199** B 20
Sand Hutton North Yorkshire GB **134** O 21
Sandbach Cheshire GB **134** Q 18
Sandbank Argyll and Bute GB **160** L 13
Sandford North Somerset GB **53** U 17
Sandhaven Aberdeenshire GB **187** G 18
Sandhead Dumfries and Galloway GB **146** N 13
Sandhoe Northumberland GB **147** N 18
Sandhurst Hampshire GB **70/71** U 21
Sandness Shetland Islands GB **199** B 19
Sandon Staffordshire GB **100** R 18
Sandown Isle of Wight GB **70** V 20
Sandplace Cornwall GB **52/53** W 14
Sandringham Norfolk GB **101** R 24
Sandwell Sandwell GB **87** S 18
Sandwich Kent GB **71** U 25
Sandwick Shetland Islands GB **199** B 20
Sandy Bedfordshire GB **100/101** S 22
Sandygate Isle of Man GB **146** O 13
Sanndabhaig Na h-Eileanan an Iar GB **175** H 8
Sanquhar Dumfries and Galloway GB **146** M 15
Sarclet Highland GB **187** F 16
Sarn Meyllteyrn Gwynedd GB **118** R 13
Sarnesfield Herefordshire GB **87** S 17
Sarre Kent GB **71** U 25
Satley Durham GB **147** N 19
Satterthwaite Cumbria GB **146** O 16
Saul Down GB **207** O 11
Saundersfoot Pembrokeshire GB **86** T 13
Sawbridgeworth Hertfordshire GB **71** T 23
Sawrey Cumbria GB **146/147** O 17
Sawston Cambridgeshire GB **101** S 23
Sawtry Cambridgeshire GB **100/101** S 22
Saxby Leicestershire GB **100** R 21
Saxelbye Leicestershire GB **100** R 21
Saxilby Lincolnshire GB **134/135** Q 21
Saxmundham Suffolk GB **101** S 25
Saxthorpe Norfolk GB **101** R 25
Saxton North Yorkshire GB **134** P 20
Scalasaig Argyll and Bute GB **174** K 10

Scalby North Yorkshire GB **135** O 22
Scaleby Hill Cumbria GB **146/147** N 17
Scalford Leicestershire GB **100** R 21
Scalloway Shetland Islands GB **199** B 20
Scamblesby Lincolnshire GB **135** Q 22
Scar Orkney Islands GB **198** D 17
Scarborough North Yorkshire GB **135** O 22
Scardroy Highland GB **186** G 12
Scarfskerry Highland GB **198** E 16
Scarinish Argyll and Bute GB **174** K 9
Scarriff Clare IRL **232** R 5
Scartaglin Kerry IRL **232** S 4
Scarva Down GB **207** O 10
Scawby North Lincolnshire GB **134/135** P 21
Scole Norfolk GB **101** S 25
Scotch Corner North Yorkshire GB **147** O 19
Scotstown Highland GB **174** J 11
Scotter Lincolnshire GB **134/135** Q 21
Scourie Highland GB **186** F 12
Scousburgh Shetland Islands GB **199** C 20
Scrabster Highland GB **198** E 15
Scramoge Roscommon IRL **218/219** P 6
Scremerston Northumberland GB **161** L 19
Scruton North Yorkshire GB **147** O 19
Sculthorpe Norfolk GB **101** R 24
Scunthorpe North Lincolnshire GB **134/135** P 21
Sea Palling Norfolk GB **101** R 26
Seaford East Sussex GB **71** V 23
Seaham Durham GB **147** N 20
Seahouses Northumberland GB **161** L 19
Seamer North Yorkshire GB **135** O 22
Seamer North Yorkshire GB **147** O 20
Seascale Cumbria GB **146** O 16
Seathwaite Cumbria GB **146** O 16
Seaton Devon GB **53** V 16
Seaton Carew Hartlepool GB **147** N 20
Seaton Delaval Northumberland GB **147** M 19
Seaton Sluice Northumberland GB **147** M 20
Seatown Dorset GB **53** V 17
Seave Green North Yorkshire GB **147** O 20
Seaview Isle of Wight GB **70** V 20
Sebergham Cumbria GB **146** N 16
Sedbergh Cumbria GB **146/147** O 17
Sedgebrook Lincolnshire GB **100** R 21
Sedgefield Durham GB **147** N 20
Sedgeford Norfolk GB **101** R 24
Sedgley Dudley GB **100** R 18
Seend Wiltshire GB **70** U 18
Selattyn Shropshire GB **119** R 16

Selborne Hampshire GB 70/71 U 21

Selby North Yorkshire GB 134 P 20

Selkirk Scottish Borders GB 161 L 17

Sellafirth Shetland Islands GB 199 A 20

Selsey West Sussex GB 70/71 V 21

Senghenydd Caerphilly GB 87 T 16

Sennen Cornwall GB 52 W 11

Sennybridge Powys GB 86/87 T 15

Seskinore Tyrone GB 207 N 8

Sessay North Yorkshire GB 147 O 20

Settle North Yorkshire GB 147 O 18

Seven Sisters Neath Port Talbot GB 86/87 T 15

Sevenoaks Kent GB 71 U 23

Sgiogarstaigh Na h-Eileanan an Iar GB 186 F 10

Shaftesbury Dorset GB 70 U 18

Shalbourne Wiltshire GB 70 U 19

Shalfleet Isle of Wight GB 70 V 20

Shanagolden Limerick IRL 232 R 4

Shanavogh Clare IRL 232 R 4

Shandon Argyll and Bute GB 160 K 13

Shanklin Isle of Wight GB 70 V 20

Shanlaragh Cork IRL 232 T 4

Shannon Sionainn Clare IRL 232 R 5

Shannonbridge Offaly IRL 218/219 Q 6

Shantonagh Monaghan IRL 207 O 9

Shap Cumbria GB 146/147 N 17

Shapwick Somerset GB 53 U 17

Sharlston Wakefield GB 134 P 20

Sharnbrook Bedfordshire GB 100 S 21

Sharpness Gloucestershire GB 70 T 18

Shavington Cheshire GB 134 Q 18

Shaw Oldham GB 134 P 18

Shawbury Shropshire GB 119 R 17

Shawhead Dumfries and Galloway GB 146 M 15

Shebbear Devon GB 52/53 V 14

Shebster Highland GB 198 E 15

Shedfield Hampshire GB 70 V 20

Sheepwash Devon GB 52/53 V 14

Sheerness Kent GB 71 U 24

Sheffield Sheffield GB 134 Q 20

Shefford Bedfordshire GB 100/101 S 22

Sheldwich Kent GB 71 U 24

Shelf Calderdale GB 134 P 19

Shelve Shropshire GB 87 R 17

Shenley Hertfordshire GB 71 T 22

Sheperdswell Kent GB 71 U 25

Shepreth Cambridgeshire GB 101 S 23

Shepshed Leicestershire GB 100 R 20

Shepton Mallet Somerset GB 53 U 17

Sherborne Dorset GB 53 V 17

Sherborne St. John Hampshire GB 70 U 20

Sherburn North Yorkshire GB 135 O 21

Sherburn in Elmet North Yorkshire GB 134 P 20

Shercock Cavan IRL 219 P 9

Sherfield on Loddon Hampshire GB 70 U 20

Sheriff Hutton North Yorkshire GB 147 O 20

Sheriffhales Shropshire GB 100 R 18

Sheringham Norfolk GB 101 R 25

Sherington Milton Keynes GB 100 S 21

Sherston Wiltshire GB 70 T 18

Shiel Bridge Highland GB 186 H 12

Shieldaig Highland GB 186 G 11

Shieldhill Falkirk GB 160/161 L 15

Shifnal Shropshire GB 100 R 18

Shilbottle Northumberland GB 147 M 19

Shildon Durham GB 147 N 19

Shillelagh Wicklow IRL 233 R 9

Shillingstone Dorset GB 70 V 18

Shillington Bedfordshire GB 71 T 22

Shinness Highland GB 186/187 F 14

Shinrone Offaly IRL 233 R 7

Shipbourne Kent GB 71 U 23

Shipdham Norfolk GB 101 R 24

Shipley Bradford GB 134 P 19

Shipston-on-Stour Warwickshire GB 100 S 19

Shipton North Yorkshire GB 147 O 20

Shipton-under-Wychwood Oxfordshire GB 70 T 19

Shirebrook Derbyshire GB 134 Q 20

Shirenewton Monmouthshire GB 87 T 17

Shobdon Herefordshire GB 87 S 17

Shoreham-by-Sea West Sussex GB 71 V 22

Shorwell Isle of Wight GB 70 V 20

Shotley Bridge Durham GB 147 N 19

Shotley Gate Suffolk GB 71 T 25

Shotts North Lanarkshire GB 160/161 L 15

Shrewsbury Shropshire GB 87 R 17

Shrewton Wiltshire GB 70 U 19

Shrivenham Oxfordshire GB 70 T 19

Shrule Galway IRL 218 P 4

Siabost Na h-Eileanan an Iar GB 175 F 9

Siadar Na h-Eileanan an Iar GB 186 F 10

Sible Hedingham Essex GB 71 T 24

Sibsey Lincolnshire GB 135 Q 23

Sidbury Devon GB 53 V 16

Sidmouth Devon GB 53 V 16

Sigglesthorne East Riding of Yorkshire GB 135 P 22

Sileby Leicestershire GB 100 R 20

Silloth Cumbria GB 146 N 16

Silsden Bradford GB 134 P 19

Silverdale Lancashire GB 146/147 O 17

Silvermines Tipperary IRL 232/233 R 6

Silverstone Northhamptonshire GB 100 S 20

Silverton Devon GB 53 V 16

Simonburn Northumberland GB 147 M 18

Simonsbath Somerset GB 53 U 15

Singleton West Sussex GB 70/71 V 21

Sinnington North Yorkshire GB 134 O 21

Sion Mills Tyrone GB 207 N 8

Sittingbourne Kent GB 71 U 24

Six Crosses Kerry IRL 232 S 3

Sixmilebridge Clare IRL 232 R 5

Sixmilecross Tyrone GB 207 N 8

Sixpenny Handley Dorset GB 70 V 19

Skaill Orkney Islands GB 198 D 17

Skaill Orkney Islands GB 198 E 17

Skares East Ayrshire GB 146 M 14

Skegness Lincolnshire GB 135 Q 23

Skelmanthorpe Wakefield GB 134 P 19

Skelmersdale Lancashire GB 119 P 17

Skelpick Highland GB 186/187 F 14

Skelton Redcar & Cleveland GB 147 N 21

Skelwith Bridge Cumbria GB 146 O 16

Skerray Highland GB 186/187 E 14

Skerries Dublin IRL 219 P 10

Skewen Neath Port Talbot GB 86/87 T 15

Skibbereen Cork IRL 232 T 4

Skidby East Riding of Yorkshire GB 135 P 22

Skillington Lincolnshire GB 100 R 21

Skinburness Cumbria GB 146 N 16

Skipness Argyll and Bute GB 160 L 12

Skipsea East Riding of Yorkshire GB 135 P 22

Skipton North Yorkshire GB 134 P 18

Skipwith North Yorkshire GB 134/135 P 21

Skirling Scottish Borders GB 161 L 16

Skirwith Cumbria GB 146/147 N 17

Skripton-on-Swale North Yorkshire GB 147 O 20

Skulamish Highland GB 175 H 11

Skull Cork IRL 232 T 3

Slaggyford Northumberland GB 146/147 N 17

Slaidburn Lancashire GB 134 P 18

Slaithwaite Kirklees GB 134 P 19

Slaley Northumberland GB 147 N 18

Slamannan Falkirk GB 160/161 L 15

Slane Meath IRL 219 P 9

Slapton Devon GB 53 W 15

Sleaford Lincolnshire GB 100/101 R 22

Sledmere East Riding of Yorkshire GB 134 O 21

Sleights North Yorkshire GB 134 O 21

Sligachan Highland GB 175 H 10

Sligo Sligeach Sligo IRL 206 O 6

Slindon West Sussex GB 70/71 V 21

Slough Slough GB 70/71 T 21

Smailholm Scottish Borders GB 161 L 17

Smallburgh Norfolk GB 101 R 25

Smeaton North Yorkshire GB 134 P 20

Smeeth Kent GB 71 U 24

Smeircleit Na h-Eileanan an Iar GB 175 H 8

Smithborough Monaghan IRL 207 O 8

Smithfield Cumbria GB 146/147 N 17

Snainton North Yorkshire GB 134 O 21

Snaith East Riding of Yorkshire GB 134 P 20

Snape Suffolk GB 101 S 25

Snape North Yorkshire GB 147 O 19

Sneem Kerry IRL 232 T 3

Snelland Lincolnshire GB 135 Q 22

Snettisham Norfolk GB 101 R 24

Snitter Northumberland GB 147 M 19

Snodland Kent GB 71 U 23

Snouldham Norfolk GB 101 R 23

Soham Cambridgeshire GB 101 S 23

Solas Na h-Eileanan an Iar GB 175 G 8

Solihull Solihull GB 100 S 19

Solva Pembrokeshire GB 86 T 12

Somersham Cambridgeshire GB 101 S 23

Somerton Norfolk GB 101 R 26

Somerton Somerset GB 53 U 17

Somerton Oxfordshire GB 70 T 20

Sopley Dorset GB 70 V 19

Sorbie Dumfries and Galloway GB 146 N 14

Sorisdale Argyll and Bute GB 174 J 10

Sorn East Ayrshire GB 160 L 14

Sortat Highland GB 198 E 16

Soulby Cumbria GB 147 N 18

Sourton Devon GB 52/53 V 14

Soutergate Cumbria GB 146 O 16

South Benfleet Essex GB 71 T 24

South Brent Devon GB 53 W 15

South Cave East Riding of Yorkshire GB 134/135 P 21

South Creake Norfolk GB 101 R 24

South Ferriby North Lincolnshire GB 134/135 P 21

South Harting West Sussex GB 70/71 V 21

South Hayling Hampshire GB 70/71 V 21

South Kelsey Lincolnshire GB 135 Q 22

South Kirkby Wakefield GB 134 P 20

South Kyme Lincolnshire GB 135 Q 22

South Littleton Worcestershire GB 100 S 19

South Molton Devon GB 53 V 15

South Otterington North Yorkshire GB 147 O 20

South Oxhey Hertfordshire GB 71 T 22

South Petherton Somerset GB 53 V 17

South Shields South Tyneside GB 147 N 20

South Skirlaugh East Riding of Yorkshire GB 135 P 22

South Thoresby Lincolnshire GB 135 Q 23

South View Shetland Islands GB 199 B 20

South Wingfield Derbyshire GB 134 Q 20

South Woodham Ferrers Essex GB 71 T 24

South Wootton Norfolk GB 101 R 23

South Zeal Devon GB 53 V 15

Southam Warwickshire GB 100 S 20

Southampton Southampton GB 70 V 20

Southborough Kent GB 71 U 23

Southend Argyll and Bute GB 174 M 11

Southend-on-Sea Southend-on-Sea GB 71 T 24

Southerness Dumfries and Galloway GB 146 N 15

Southery Norfolk GB 101 R 23

Southminster Essex GB 71 T 24

Southport Sefton GB 119 P 16

Southwell Nottinghamshire GB 134/135 Q 21

Southwick West Sussex GB 71 V 22

Southwold Suffolk GB 101 S 26

Sowerby Bridge Calderdale GB 134 P 19

Spalding Lincolnshire GB 100/101 R 22

Spaldwick Cambridgeshire GB 100/101 S 22

Spanish Point Clare IRL 232 R 4

Sparkford Somerset GB 53 U 17

Spean Bridge Highland GB 160 J 13

Speke Liverpool GB 119 Q 17

Spennymoor Durham GB 147 N 19

Spetchley Worcestershire GB 87 S 18

Spetisbury Dorset GB 70 V 18

Spey Bay Moray GB 187 G 16

Spiddle Galway IRL 218 Q 4

Spilsby Lincolnshire GB 135 Q 23

Spinningdale Highland GB 186/187 G 14

Spittal Pembrokeshire GB 86 T 13

Spittal of Glenshee Perth and Kinross GB 161 J 16

Spofforth North Yorkshire GB **134** P 20

Spratton Northhamptonshire GB **100** S 21

Spreyton Devon GB **53** V 15

Spridlington Lincolnshire GB **135** Q 22

Springfield Fife GB **161** K 16

Sproatley East Riding of Yorkshire GB **135** P 22

Sprouston Scottish Borders GB **161** L 18

Sprowston Norfolk GB **101** R 25

Sproxton North Yorkshire GB **147** O 20

Sraith Salach Galway IRL **218** Q 3

St. Abbs Scottish Borders GB **161** L 18

St. Agnes Cornwall GB **52** W 12

St. Albans Hertfordshire GB **71** T 22

St. Andrews Fife GB **161** K 17

St. Ann's Dumfries and Galloway GB **146** M 16

St. Arvans Monmouthshire GB **87** T 17

St. Asaph Denbighshire GB **119** Q 16

St. Aubin Channel Islands GB **66** Y 18

St. Austell Cornwall GB **52** W 13

St. Bees Cumbria GB **146** O 15

St. Blazey Cornwall GB **52** W 13

St. Boswells Scottish Borders GB **161** L 17

St. Brelade Channel Islands GB **66** Y 18

St. Briavels Gloucestershire GB **87** T 17

St. Bride's Major Vale of Glamorgan GB **53** U 15

St. Buryan Cornwall GB **52** W 11

St. Catherines Argyll and Bute GB **160** K 12

St. Clears Carmarthenshire GB **86** T 14

St. Clément Channel Islands GB **66** Y 18

St. Clether Cornwall GB **52** V 13

St. Columb Major Cornwall GB **52** W 13

St. Combs Aberdeenshire GB **187** G 19

St. Cyrus Aberdeenshire GB **161** J 18

St. David's Pembrokeshire GB **86** T 12

St. Dennis Cornwall GB **52** W 13

St. Dogmaels Pembrokeshire GB **86** S 13

St. Donats Vale of Glamorgan GB **53** U 15

St. Fergus Aberdeenshire GB **187** G 19

St. Fillans Perth and Kinross GB **160** K 14

St. Gennys Cornwall GB **52** V 13

St. Harmon Powys GB **86/87** S 15

St. Helens St Helens GB **119** Q 17

St. Helens Isle of Wight GB **70** V 20

St. Helier Channel Islands GB **66** Y 18

St. Issey Cornwall GB **52** W 13

St. Ive Cornwall GB **52/53** W 14

St. Ives Cambridgeshire GB **100/101** S 22

St. Ives Cornwall GB **52** W 12

St. John Channel Islands GB **66** Y 18

St. John's Chapel Durham GB **147** N 18

St. John´s Town of Dalry Dumfries and Galloway GB **146** M 14

St. John's Isle of Man GB **146** O 13

St. Johnstown Donegal IRL **207** N 8

St. Just Cornwall GB **52** W 11

St. Keverne Cornwall GB **52** W 12

St. Margaret's at Cliffe Kent GB **71** U 25

St. Margaret's Hope Orkney Islands GB **198** E 17

St. Martin Channel Islands GB **66** Y 17

St. Martin Channel Islands GB **66** Y 18

St. Martin´s Shropshire GB **119** R 16

St. Mary's Orkney Islands GB **198** E 17

St. Mary's Bay Kent GB **71** U 24

St. Mawes Cornwall GB **52** W 13

St. Mellion Cornwall GB **52/53** W 14

St. Mellons Cardiff GB **87** T 16

St. Merryn Cornwall GB **52** V 12

St. Minver Cornwall GB **52** V 13

St. Monans Fife GB **161** K 17

St. Mullin's Carlow IRL **233** S 9

St. Neot Cornwall GB **52** W 13

St. Neots Cambridgeshire GB **100/101** S 22

St. Nicholas Pembrokeshire GB **86** T 12

St. Osyth Essex GB **71** T 25

St. Peter Channel Islands GB **66** Y 18

St. Peter Port Channel Islands GB **66** Y 17

St. Sampson Channel Islands GB **66** Y 17

St. Stephen Cornwall GB **52** W 13

St. Teath Cornwall GB **52** V 13

St. Vigeans Angus GB **161** J 18

St. Weonards Herefordshire GB **87** T 17

Stadhampton Oxfordshire GB **70** T 20

Stadhlaigearraidh Na h-Eileanan an Iar GB **175** H 8

Staffin Highland GB **186** G 10

Stafford Staffordshire GB **100** R 18

Stagsden Bedfordshire GB **100** S 21

Staindrop Durham GB **147** N 19

Staines Surrey GB **71** U 22

Stainforth North Yorkshire GB **147** O 18

Stainton Stockton-on-Tees GB **147** O 20

Staintondale North Yorkshire GB **135** O 22

Staithes North Yorkshire GB **147** N 21

Stalbridge Dorset GB **70** V 18

Stalham Norfolk GB **101** R 26

Stalling Busk North Yorkshire GB **147** O 18

Stamford Lincolnshire GB **100/101** R 22

Stamford Bridge East Riding of Yorkshire GB **134/135** P 21

Stamfordham Northumberland GB **147** M 19

Standish Wigan GB **119** P 17

Standlake Oxfordshire GB **70** T 20

Standon Staffordshire GB **100** R 18

Standon Hertfordshire GB **71** T 23

Stanford-le-Hope Thurrock GB **71** U 23

Stanhope Durham GB **147** N 18

Stanley Durham GB **147** N 19

Stanley Perth and Kinross GB **161** K 16

Stannington Northumberland GB **147** M 19

Stansted Mountfitchet Essex GB **71** T 23

Stanton Suffolk GB **101** S 24

Stanton Harcourt Oxfordshire GB **70** T 20

Stanton St John Oxfordshire GB **70** T 20

Stanway Gloucestershire GB **70** T 19

Staoinebrig Na h-Eileanan an Iar GB **175** H 8

Staple Fitzpaine Somerset GB **53** V 16

Stapleford Nottinghamshire GB **100** R 20

Stapleford Wiltshire GB **70** U 19

Staplehurst Kent GB **71** U 24

Starcross Devon GB **53** V 16

Stathern Leicestershire GB **100** R 21

Staunton Gloucestershire GB **70** T 18

Staunton-on-Wye Herefordshire GB **87** S 17

Staveley Derbyshire GB **134** Q 20

Staveley Cumbria GB **146/147** O 17

Staverton Gloucestershire GB **70** T 18

Staxigoe Highland GB **187** F 16

Staxton North Yorkshire GB **135** O 22

Ste. Anne Channel Islands GB **66** X 18

Stebbing Essex GB **71** T 23

Steeple Bumpstead Essex GB **101** S 23

Steeple Claydon Buckinghamshire GB **70/71** T 21

Steeple Morden Cambridgeshire GB **100/101** S 22

Stenton East Lothian GB **161** L 17

Steornabhagh Stornoway Na h-Eileanan an Iar GB **186** F 10

Stephen Cumbria GB **147** O 18

Stevenage Hertfordshire GB **71** T 22

Stevenston North Ayrshire GB **160** L 13

Steventon Oxfordshire GB **70** T 20

Stevning West Sussex GB **71** V 22

Stewarton East Ayrshire GB **160** L 14

Stewarton Argyll and Bute GB **174** M 11

Stewartstown Tyrone GB **207** N 9

Stewkley Buckinghamshire GB **70/71** T 21

Stibb Cross Devon GB **52/53** V 14

Stichill Scottish Borders GB **161** L 18

Sticker Cornwall GB **52** W 13

Stickford Lincolnshire GB **135** Q 23

Stickney Lincolnshire GB **135** Q 23

Stillington North Yorkshire GB **147** O 20

Stilton Cambridgeshire GB **100/101** S 22

Stirling Stirling GB **160/161** K 15

Stobo Scottish Borders GB **161** L 16

Stock Essex GB **71** T 23

Stockbridge Hampshire GB **70** U 20

Stockland Devon GB **53** V 16

Stockland Bristol Somerset GB **53** U 16

Stockport Stockport GB **134** Q 18

Stocksbridge Sheffield GB **134** Q 19

Stockton Wiltshire GB **70** U 18

Stockton-on-Tees Stockton-on-Tees GB **147** N 20

Stockwith Nottinghamshire GB **134/135** Q 21

Stoer Highland GB **186** F 12

Stoke Medway GB **71** U 24

Stoke Albany Northhamptonshire GB **100** S 21

Stoke Ferry Norfolk GB **101** R 24

Stoke Fleming Devon GB **53** W 15

Stoke Golding Leicestershire GB **100** R 20

Stoke Hammond Buckinghamshire GB **70/71** T 21

Stoke Prior Worcestershire GB **87** S 18

Stoke-by-Nayland Suffolk GB **71** T 24

Stokenchurch Buckinghamshire GB **70/71** T 21

Stoke-on-Trent Stoke-on-Trent GB **134** Q 18

Stokesley North Yorkshire GB **147** O 20

Stone Staffordshire GB **100** R 18

Stone Gloucestershire GB **70** T 18

Stone Buckinghamshire GB **70/71** T 21

Stonehaugh Northumberland GB **147** M 18

Stonehaven Aberdeenshire GB **161** J 18

Stonehouse South Lanarkshire GB **160/161** L 15

Stonehouse Gloucestershire GB **70** T 18

Stoneleigh Warwickshire GB **100** S 19

Stoneykirk Dumfries and Galloway GB **146** N 13

Stoneywood Aberdeen City GB **187** H 18

Stonor Oxfordshire GB **70/71** T 21

Stony Stratford Milton Keynes GB **100** S 21

Stonybreck Shetland Islands GB **199** C 19

Stornoway Steornabhagh Na h-Eileanan an Iar GB **186** F 10

Storrington West Sussex GB **71** V 22

Stotfold Bedfordshire GB **100/101** S 22

Stourbridge Dudley GB **87** S 18

Stourport-on-Severn Worcestershire GB **87** S 18

Stourton Wiltshire GB **70** U 18

Stow Scottish Borders GB **161** L 17

Stowmarket Suffolk GB **101** S 24

Stow-on-the-Wold Gloucestershire GB **70** T 19

Strabane Tyrone GB **207** N 8

Strachan Aberdeenshire GB **187** H 17

Strachur Argyll and Bute GB **160** K 12

Stradbally Kerry IRL **232** S 2

Stradbally Laois IRL **233** R 8

Stradbally Waterford IRL **233** S 8

Stradbroke Suffolk GB **101** S 25

Strade Mayo IRL **218** P 4

Stradone Cavan IRL **219** P 8

Straiton South Ayrshire GB **146** M 13

Strandhill Sligo IRL **206** O 5

Strangford Down GB **207** O 11

Stranocum Antrim GB **207** M 10

Stranorlar Donegal IRL **206** N 7

Stranraer Dumfries and Galloway GB **146** N 12

Stratfield Mortimer West Berkshire GB **70** U 20

Stratford Wicklow IRL **219** Q 9

Stratford St. Mary Essex GB **71** T 24

Stratford-upon-Avon Warwickshire GB **100** S 19

Strath Kanaird Highland GB **186** G 12

Strathan Highland GB **160** J 12

Strathaven South Lanarkshire GB **160** L 14

Strathblane Stirling GB **160** L 14

Strathcarron Highland GB **186** H 12

Strathdon Aberdeenshire GB **187** H 16

Strathkinness Fife GB **161** K 17

Strathmiglo Fife GB **161** K 16

Strathpeffer Highland GB **186** G 13

Strathy Highland GB **198** E 15

Strathyre Stirling GB **160** K 14

Stratton Cornwall GB **52** V 13

Stratton Audley Oxfordshire GB **70** T 20

Streatley Bedfordshire GB **71** T 22

Street Somerset GB **53** U 17

Strensall York GB **147** O 20

Strete Devon GB **53** W 15

Stretham Cambridgeshire GB **101** S 23

Stretton Rutland GB **100** R 21

Stretton Warrington GB **119** Q 17

Stretton Sugwas Herefordshire GB **87** S 17

Strichen Aberdeenshire GB **187** G 18

Strokestown Roscommon IRL **218/219** P 6
Stromeferry Highland GB **175** H 11
Stromemore Highland GB **175** H 11
Stromness Orkney Islands GB **198** E 16
Stronachlachar Stirling GB **160** K 13
Strontian Highland GB **174** J 11
Strood Medway GB **71** U 23
Stroud Gloucestershire GB **70** T 18
Struy Highland GB **186** H 13
Stuartfield Aberdeenshire GB **187** H 18
Studland Dorset GB **70** V 19
Studley Warwickshire GB **100** S 19
Sturminster Newton Dorset GB **70** V 18
Sturry Kent GB **71** U 25
Sturton by Stow Lincolnshire GB **134/135** Q 21
Sudbury Derbyshire GB **100** R 19
Sudbury Suffolk GB **101** S 24
Sulaisiadar Na h-Eileanan an Iar GB **186** F 10
Sulby Isle of Man GB **146** O 14
Sullom Shetland Islands GB **199** B 20
Sully Vale of Glamorgan GB **53** U 16
Summer Bridge North Yorkshire GB **147** O 19
Summerhill Meath IRL **219** Q 9
Sunbury Surrey GB **71** U 22
Sunderland Sunderland GB **147** N 20
Sunk Island East Riding of Yorkshire GB **135** P 22
Sunningdale Windsor & Maidenhead GB **70/71** U 21
Sutterton Lincolnshire GB **100/101** R 22
Sutton Cambridgeshire GB **101** S 23
Sutton Nottinghamshire GB **134/135** Q 21
Sutton West Sussex GB **70/71** V 21
Sutton Greater London GB **71** U 22
Sutton Bridge Lincolnshire GB **101** R 23
Sutton Coldfield Birmingham GB **100** R 19
Sutton in Ashfield Nottinghamshire GB **134** Q 20
Sutton on Sea Lincolnshire GB **135** Q 23
Sutton Scotney Hampshire GB **70** U 20
Sutton St James Lincolnshire GB **101** R 23
Sutton Valence Kent GB **71** U 24
Sutton Wick Bath & NE Somerset GB **53** U 17
Sutton-on—the-Forest North Yorkshire GB **147** O 20
Sutton-under-Whitestonecliffe North Yorkshire GB **147** O 20
Swadlincote Derbyshire GB **100** R 19
Swaffham Norfolk GB **101** R 24

Swainby North Yorkshire GB **147** O 20
Swainshill Herefordshire GB **87** S 17
Swalcliffe Oxfordshire GB **100** S 20
Swallow North East Lincolnshire GB **135** P 22
Swallowcliffe Wiltshire GB **70** U 18
Swan Laois IRL **233** R 8
Swanage Dorset GB **70** V 19
Swanbister Orkney Islands GB **198** E 16
Swanley Kent GB **71** U 23
Swanlinbar Cavan IRL **206** O 7
Swansea Abertawe Swansea GB **86/87** T 15
Swanton Morley Norfolk GB **101** R 24
Swardeston Norfolk GB **101** R 25
Swatragh Londonderry GB **207** N 9
Swavesey Cambridgeshire GB **101** S 23
Sway Hampshire GB **70** V 19
Swayfield Lincolnshire GB **100** R 21
Swimbridge Devon GB **53** U 15
Swindon Swindon GB **70** T 19
Swineshead Lincolnshire GB **100/101** R 22
Swineshead Bedfordshire GB **100/101** S 22
Swinford Leicestershire GB **100** S 20
Swinford Mayo IRL **218** P 5
Swinton Scottish Borders GB **161** L 18
Swords Dublin IRL **219** Q 10
Syderstone Norfolk GB **101** R 24
Sykehouse Doncaster GB **134** P 20
Symbister Shetland Islands GB **199** B 20
Symington South Ayrshire GB **160** L 13
Symington South Lanarkshire GB **160/161** L 15
Syre Highland GB **186/187** F 14
Syresham Northhamptonshire GB **100** S 20
Syston Leicestershire GB **100** R 20

T
Tadcaster North Yorkshire GB **134** P 20
Taddington Derbyshire GB **134** Q 19
Tadworth Surrey GB **71** U 22
Taghmon Wexford IRL **233** S 9
Tagoat Wexford IRL **233** S 10
Tain Highland GB **186/187** G 14
Tairbeart Tarbert Na h-Eileanan an Iar GB **175** G 9
Takeley Essex GB **71** T 23
Talaton Devon GB **53** V 16
Talgarth Powys GB **87** T 16
Talisker Highland GB **175** H 10
Talladale Highland GB **186** G 11
Tallaght Dublin IRL **219** Q 10
Talley Carmarthenshire GB **86/87** T 15
Tallow Waterford IRL **232/233** S 6
Talmine Highland GB **186/187** E 14

Talsarnau Gwynedd GB **118/119** R 14
Talwrn Anglesey GB **118/119** Q 14
Tal-y-bont Ceredigion GB **86/87** S 15
Tal-y-cafn Conwy GB **119** Q 15
Talysarn Gwynedd GB **118/119** Q 14
Tamerton Foliot Plymouth GB **52/53** W 14
Tamworth Staffordshire GB **100** R 19
Tandragee Armagh GB **207** O 10
Tang Westmeath IRL **219** P 7
Tangwick Shetland Islands GB **199** B 19
Tannadice Angus GB **161** J 18
Taobh Tuath Na h-Eileanan an Iar GB **175** G 8
Tara Meath IRL **219** P 9
Tarbert Argyll and Bute GB **160** L 12
Tarbert Tairbeart Na h-Eileanan an Iar GB **175** G 9
Tarbert Kerry IRL **232** R 4
Tarbet Argyll and Bute GB **160** K 13
Tarbet Highland GB **186** F 12
Tarbolton South Ayrshire GB **160** L 14
Tarfside Angus GB **161** J 18
Tarland Aberdeenshire GB **187** H 17
Tarleton Lancashire GB **119** P 17
Tarporley Cheshire GB **119** Q 17
Tarskavaig Highland GB **175** H 11
Tarves Aberdeenshire GB **187** H 18
Tarvin Cheshire GB **119** Q 17
Tattenhall Cheshire GB **119** Q 17
Taunton Somerset GB **53** U 16
Tavernspite Pembrokeshire GB **86** T 13
Tavistock Devon GB **52/53** V 14
Tawny Donegal IRL **206** M 7
Tawnyinah Mayo IRL **218** P 5
Tayinloan Argyll and Bute GB **174** L 11
Taynuilt Argyll and Bute GB **160** K 12
Tayport Fife GB **161** K 17
Tayvallich Argyll and Bute GB **174** K 11
Tealby Lincolnshire GB **135** Q 22
Teangue Highland GB **175** H 11
Tebay Cumbria GB **146/147** O 17
Tedavnet Monaghan IRL **207** O 8
Tedburn St. Mary Devon GB **53** V 15
Teelin Donegal IRL **206** N 5
Teignmouth Devon GB **53** V 16
Telford Shropshire GB **100** R 18
Telford Telford and Wrekin GB **100** R 18
Templand Dumfries and Galloway GB **146** M 16
Temple Midlothian GB **161** L 16
Temple Hirst North Yorkshire GB **134** P 20
Templeboy Sligo IRL **206** O 5
Templecombe Somerset GB **70** V 18
Templemartin Cork IRL **232** T 5
Templemore Tipperary IRL **233** R 7
Templenoe Kerry IRL **232** T 3

Templepatrick Antrim GB **207** N 10
Templeton Pembrokeshire GB **86** T 13
Templetouhy Tipperary IRL **233** R 7
Tempo Fermanagh GB **207** O 8
Tenbury Wells Worcestershire GB **87** S 17
Tenby Pembrokeshire GB **86** T 13
Tenterden Kent GB **71** U 24
Terling Essex GB **71** T 24
Termonfeckin Louth IRL **219** P 10
Ternhill Shropshire GB **119** R 17
Terrington North Yorkshire GB **134** O 21
Terrington St Clement Norfolk GB **101** R 23
Tetbury Gloucestershire GB **70** T 18
Tetney Lincolnshire GB **135** Q 22
Tetsworth Oxfordshire GB **70** T 20
Teviothead Scottish Borders GB **146/147** M 17
Tewkesbury Gloucestershire GB **70** T 18
Teynham Kent GB **71** U 24
Thame Oxfordshire GB **70/71** T 21
Thankerton South Lanarkshire GB **160/161** L 15
Thatcham West Berkshire GB **70** U 20
Thaxted Essex GB **71** T 23
The Barony Orkney Islands GB **198** D 16
The Cronk Isle of Man GB **146** O 13
The Downs Westmeath IRL **219** P 8
The Drones Antrim GB **207** M 10
The Hill Cumbria GB **146** O 16
The Loup Londonderry GB **207** N 9
The Mumbles Swansea GB **86** T 14
The Sheddings Antrim GB **207** N 10
The Temple Down GB **207** O 11
Theale West Berkshire GB **70** U 20
Therfield Hertfordshire GB **100/101** S 22
Thetford Norfolk GB **101** S 24
Thimbleby Lincolnshire GB **135** Q 22
Thirsk North Yorkshire GB **147** O 20
Thixendale North Yorkshire GB **134** O 21
Thomastown Kilkenny IRL **233** R 8
Thompson Norfolk GB **101** R 24
Thoresway Lincolnshire GB **135** Q 22
Thornbury South Gloucestershire GB **87** T 17
Thornby Northhamptonshire GB **100** S 20
Thorncombe Dorset GB **53** V 17
Thorndon Suffolk GB **101** S 25
Thorne Doncaster GB **134/135** P 21
Thorney Peterborough GB **100/101** R 22

Thornhill Dumfries and Galloway GB **146** M 15
Thornhill Stirling GB **160** K 14
Thornley Durham GB **147** N 20
Thornton Lancashire GB **119** P 17
Thornton Fife GB **161** K 16
Thornton Curtis North Lincolnshire GB **135** P 22
Thornton-in-Craven North Yorkshire GB **134** P 18
Thornton-le-Dale North Yorkshire GB **134** O 21
Thorpe on the Hill Lincolnshire GB **134/135** Q 21
Thorpe Thewles Stockton-on-Tees GB **147** N 20
Thorpe-le-Soken Essex GB **71** T 25
Thorpeness Suffolk GB **101** S 26
Thorrington Essex GB **71** T 25
Thorverton Devon GB **53** V 15
Thrapston Northamptonshire GB **100** S 21
Threapwood Cheshire GB **119** R 17
Threecastles Kilkenny IRL **233** R 8
Threlkeld Cumbria GB **146** N 16
Threshfield North Yorkshire GB **147** O 18
Thropton Northumberland GB **147** M 19
Thrumster Highland GB **187** F 16
Thruxton Hampshire GB **70** U 19
Thurlby Lincolnshire GB **100/101** R 22
Thurles Durlas Tipperary IRL **233** R 7
Thurlestone Devon GB **53** W 15
Thurlow Suffolk GB **101** S 23
Thursby Cumbria GB **146** N 16
Thurso Highland GB **198** E 15
Thurstaston Wirral GB **119** Q 16
Thwaite North Yorkshire GB **147** O 18
Tibbermore Perth and Kinross GB **160/161** K 15
Tibberton Gloucestershire GB **70** T 18
Tibshelf Derbyshire GB **134** Q 20
Ticehurst East Sussex GB **71** U 23
Tickhill Doncaster GB **134** Q 20
Tideswell Derbyshire GB **134** Q 19
Tidworth Wiltshire GB **70** U 19
Tigerton Angus GB **161** J 18
Tigh a Ghearraidh Tigharry Na h-Eileanan an Iar GB **175** G 7
Tigharry Tigh a Ghearraidh Na h-Eileanan an Iar GB **175** G 7
Tigley Devon GB **53** W 15
Tilbury Thurrock GB **71** U 23
Tildarg Antrim GB **207** N 10
Tillicoultry Clackmannanshire GB **160/161** K 15
Tillingham Essex GB **71** T 24
Tillyfourie Aberdeenshire GB **187** H 17
Tilshead Wiltshire GB **70** U 19
Tilstock Shropshire GB **119** R 17
Tilston Cheshire GB **119** Q 17
Timahoe Laois IRL **233** R 8
Timberscombe Somerset GB **53** U 15
Timoleague Cork IRL **232** T 5
Timolin Kildare IRL **233** R 9

Timsgearraidh Na h-Eileanan an lar GB **175** F 8

Tinahely Wicklow IRL **233** R 10

Tingewick Buckinghamshire GB **70** T 20

Tingwall Orkney Islands GB **198** D 16

Tintagel Cornwall GB **52** V 13

Tintern Monmouthshire GB **87** T 17

Tinwald Dumfries and Galloway GB **146** M 15

Tipperary Tipperary IRL **232/233** S 6

Tiptree Essex GB **71** T 24

Tirabad Powys GB **86/87** S 15

Tissington Derbyshire GB **134** Q 19

Tiverton Devon GB **53** V 15

Toab Shetland Islands GB **199** C 20

Tobercurry Sligo IRL **206** O 5

Tobermore Londonderry GB **207** N 9

Tobermory Argyll and Bute GB **174** J 10

Toberonochy Argyll and Bute GB **174** K 11

Tobha Mòr Na h-Eileanan an lar GB **175** H 8

Tockwith North Yorkshire GB **134** P 20

Todmorden Calderdale GB **134** P 18

Togher Louth IRL **219** P 10

Togher Cork IRL **232** T 4

Tollerton North Yorkshire GB **147** O 20

Tollesbury Essex GB **71** T 24

Tolleshunt D'Arcy Essex GB **71** T 24

Tolstadh bho Thuath Na h-Eileanan an lar GB **186** F 10

Tomatin Highland GB **187** H 14

Tomdoun Highland GB **186** H 12

Tomich Highland GB **186** H 13

Tomintoul Moray GB **187** H 16

Tomnavoulin Moray GB **187** H 16

Tonbridge Kent GB **71** U 23

Tondu Bridgend GB **86/87** T 15

Tongham Surrey GB **70/71** U 21

Tongland Dumfries and Galloway GB **146** N 14

Tongue Highland GB **186/187** F 14

Tonyrefail Rhondda Cynon Taff GB **87** T 16

Toombeola Galway IRL **218** Q 3

Toome Antrim GB **207** N 10

Toomyvara Tipperary IRL **232/233** R 6

Toormakeady Mayo IRL **218** P 4

Toormore Cork IRL **232** T 3

Topcliffe North Yorkshire GB **147** O 20

Topsham Devon GB **53** V 16

Torcross Devon GB **53** W 15

Tore Highland GB **186/187** G 14

Tormarton South Gloucestershire GB **70** U 18

Torphichen West Lothian GB **160/161** L 15

Torphins Aberdeenshire GB **187** H 17

Torpoint Cornwall GB **52/53** W 14

Torquay Torbay GB **53** W 16

Torridon Highland GB **186** G 12

Torrin Highland GB **175** H 11

Torthorwald Dumfries and Galloway GB **146** M 15

Torver Cumbria GB **146** O 16

Toscaig Highland GB **175** H 11

Totegan Highland GB **186/187** E 14

Totland Isle of Wight GB **70** V 19

Totnes Devon GB **53** W 15

Tottington Bury GB **134** P 18

Totton Hampshire GB **70** V 20

Tow Law Durham GB **147** N 19

Towcester Northhamptonshire GB **100** S 20

Towie Aberdeenshire GB **187** H 17

Town Yetholm Scottish Borders GB **161** L 18

Tralee Trá-Lí Kerry IRL **232** S 3

Tramore Waterford IRL **233** S 8

Tranent East Lothian GB **161** L 17

Trapp Carmarthenshire GB **86/87** T 15

Traquair Scottish Borders GB **161** L 16

Trawden Lancashire GB **134** P 18

Trawsfynydd Gwynedd GB **119** R 15

Trearddur Anglesey GB **118** Q 13

Treburley Cornwall GB **52/53** V 14

Trecastle Powys GB **86/87** T 15

Tredegar Blaenau Gwent GB **87** T 16

Treen Cornwall GB **52** W 11

Trefeglwys Powys GB **86/87** R 15

Treffgarne Pembrokeshire GB **86** T 13

Trefnant Denbighshire GB **119** Q 16

Trefonen Shropshire GB **119** R 16

Trefnwy Monmouth Monmouthshire GB **87** T 17

Tregaron Ceredigion GB **86/87** S 15

Tregonetha Cornwall GB **52** W 13

Tregony Cornwall GB **52** W 13

Tregynon Powys GB **87** R 16

Treherbert Rhondda Cynon Taff GB **86/87** T 15

Trelech Carmarthenshire GB **86** T 14

Treleddydfawr Pembrokeshire GB **86** T 12

Trelleck Monmouthshire GB **87** T 17

Trenance Cornwall GB **52** W 12

Tressait Perth and Kinross GB **160/161** J 15

Tresta Shetland Islands GB **199** A 21

Treuddyn Flintshire GB **119** Q 16

Trillick Tyrone GB **207** O 8

Trim Baile Atha Troim Meath IRL **219** P 9

Trimdon Durham GB **147** N 20

Trimingham Norfolk GB **101** R 25

Trinafour Perth and Kinross GB **160** J 14

Tring Hertfordshire GB **70/71** T 21

Trinity Channel Islands GB **66** Y 18

Trochry Perth and Kinross GB **160/161** J 15

Troon South Ayrshire GB **160** L 13

Troutbeck Bridge Cumbria GB **146/147** O 17

Trowbridge Wiltshire GB **70** U 18

Trull Somerset GB **53** V 16

Trumpan Highland GB **175** G 9

Trumpington Cambridgeshire GB **101** S 23

Trunch Norfolk GB **101** R 25

Truro Cornwall GB **52** W 12

Tuam Galway IRL **218** P 5

Tuddenham Suffolk GB **101** S 24

Tuddenham St Martin Suffolk GB **101** S 25

Tudhoe Durham GB **147** N 19

Tudweiliog Gwynedd GB **118** R 13

Tulla Clare IRL **232** R 5

Tullaghought Kilkenny IRL **233** S 8

Tullamore Tulach Mhor Offaly IRL **219** Q 8

Tullaree Kerry IRL **232** S 3

Tulloch Highland GB **160** J 13

Tullow Carlow IRL **233** R 9

Tullynessle Aberdeenshire GB **187** H 17

Tulsk Roscommon IRL **218/219** P 6

Tumble Carmarthenshire GB **86** T 14

Tummel Bridge Perth and Kinross GB **160/161** J 15

Tunga Na h-Eileanan an lar GB **186** F 10

Tunstall Suffolk GB **101** S 25

Tunstall East Riding of Yorkshire GB **135** P 23

Tuosist Kerry IRL **232** T 3

Turloughmore Galway IRL **218** Q 5

Turnberry South Ayrshire GB **146** M 13

Turnditch Derbyshire GB **134** Q 19

Turriff Aberdeenshire GB **187** G 18

Turvey Bedfordshire GB **100** S 21

Tutbury Staffordshire GB **100** R 19

Tuxford Nottinghamshire GB **134/135** Q 21

Twatt Orkney Islands GB **198** D 16

Tweedmouth Northumberland GB **161** L 19

Tweedsmuir Scottish Borders GB **161** L 16

Two Bridges Devon GB **53** V 15

Twycross Leicestershire GB **100** R 19

Twyford Leicestershire GB **100** R 21

Twyford Hampshire GB **70** U 20

Twyford Wokingham GB **70/71** U 21

Twynholm Dumfries and Galloway GB **146** N 14

Tydd St Giles Cambridgeshire GB **101** R 23

Tydd St Mary Lincolnshire GB **101** R 23

Tynagh Galway IRL **218/219** Q 6

Tyndrum Stirling GB **160** K 13

Tynemouth North Tyneside GB **147** M 20

Tynron Dumfries and Galloway GB **146** M 15

Tyrella Down GB **207** O 11

Tyrrellspass Westmeath IRL **219** Q 8

Tywyn Gwynedd GB **86** R 14

U

Uachdar Na h-Eileanan an lar GB **175** H 8

Uckfield East Sussex GB **71** V 23

Udny Aberdeenshire GB **187** H 18

Uffculme Devon GB **53** V 16

Uffington Oxfordshire GB **70** T 19

Ufford Peterborough GB **100/101** R 22

Ufford Suffolk GB **101** S 25

Ugthorpe North Yorkshire GB **147** O 21

Uig Highland GB **186** G 10

Ulbster Highland GB **187** F 16

Ulceby North Lincolnshire GB **135** P 22

Uldale Cumbria GB **146** N 16

Uley Gloucestershire GB **70** T 18

Ulgham Northumberland GB **147** M 19

Ullapool Highland GB **186** G 12

Ullesthorpe Leicestershire GB **100** S 20

Ullock Cumbria GB **146** N 16

Ulpha Cumbria GB **146** O 16

Ulsta Shetland Islands GB **199** B 20

Ulverston Cumbria GB **146** O 16

Umberleigh Devon GB **53** V 15

Unapool Highland GB **186** F 12

Up Holland Lancashire GB **119** P 17

Upavon Wiltshire GB **70** U 19

Upham Hampshire GB **70** V 20

Uplawmoor East Renfrewshire GB **160** L 14

Upottery Devon GB **53** V 16

Upper Antrim GB **207** N 10

Upper Broughton Leicestershire GB **100** R 21

Upper Chapel Powys GB **87** S 16

Upper Knockando Moray GB **187** H 16

Upper Largo Fife GB **161** K 17

Upper Tean Staffordshire GB **100** R 19

Upperchurch Tipperary IRL **232/233** R 6

Upperlands Londonderry GB **207** N 9

Uppingham Rutland GB **100** R 21

Upton Wirral GB **119** Q 16

Upton Oxfordshire GB **70** T 20

Upton under Severn Worcestershire GB **87** S 18

Upwell Norfolk GB **101** R 23

Urchfont Wiltshire GB **70** U 19

Urlingford Kilkenny IRL **233** R 7

Urquhart Moray GB **187** G 16

Usk Monmouthshire GB **87** T 17

Uttoxeter Staffordshire GB **100** R 19

Uxbridge Greater London GB **71** T 22

Uyeasound Shetland Islands GB **199** A 21

V

Vale Channel Islands GB **66** X 17

Ventnor Isle of Wight GB **70** V 20

Ventry Kerry IRL **232** S 2

Vernham Dean Hampshire GB **70** U 19

Verwood Dorset GB **70** V 19

Vickerstown Cumbria GB **146** O 16

Victoria Cornwall GB **52** W 13

Vidlin Shetland Islands GB **199** B 20

Virginia Cavan IRL **219** P 8

Voe Shetland Islands GB **199** B 20

Vowchurch Herefordshire GB **87** S 17

W

Waddesdon Buckinghamshire GB **70/71** T 21

Waddeton Devon GB **53** W 15

Waddingham Lincolnshire GB **134/135** Q 21

Waddington Lancashire GB **134** P 18

Waddington Lincolnshire GB **134/135** Q 21

Wadebridge Cornwall GB **52** V 13

Wadhurst East Sussex GB **71** U 23

Wadworth Doncaster GB **134** Q 20

Wainfleet All Saints Lincolnshire GB **135** Q 23

Wainhouse Corner Cornwall GB **52** V 13

Wakefield Wakefield GB **134** P 19

Wakes Colne Essex GB **71** T 24

Walberswick Suffolk GB **101** S 26

Walcott Lincolnshire GB **135** Q 22

Wales Rotherham GB **134** Q 20

Walford Herefordshire GB **87** S 17

Walgherton Cheshire GB **134** Q 18

Walkerburn Scottish Borders GB **161** L 16

Walkeringham Nottinghamshire GB **134/135** Q 21

Walkern Hertfordshire GB **71** T 22

Walkington East Riding of Yorkshire GB **135** P 22

Wall Northumberland GB **147** M 18

Wallasey Wirral GB **119** Q 16

Wallingford Oxfordshire GB **70** T 20

Walls Shetland Islands GB **199** B 19

Walmer Kent GB **71** U 25

Walpole Norfolk GB **101** R 23

Walsden Calderdale GB **134** P 18

Walshall Walsall GB **100** R 19

Walsham le Willows Suffolk GB **101** S 24

Waltham North East Lincolnshire GB **135** P 22

Waltham Essex GB **71** T 23

Waltham Kent GB **71** U 25

Waltham on the Wolds Leicestershire GB **100** R 21

Walton Cumbria GB **146/147** N 17

Walton Powys GB **87** S 16

Walton-on-Thames Surrey GB **71** U 22

Walton-on-the-Naze Essex GB **71** T 25

Walton-on-Trent Derbyshire GB **100** R 19

Wanborough Swindon GB **70** T 19

Wangford Suffolk GB **101** S 26

Wanlockhead South Lanarkshire GB **146** M 15

Wansford Northhamptonshire GB **100/101** R 22

Wanstrow Somerset GB **70** U 18

Wantage Oxfordshire GB **70** T 20

Warboys Cambridgeshire GB **100/101** S 22

Warbstow Cornwall GB **52** V 13

Warcop Cumbria GB **147** N 18

Ware Hertfordshire GB **71** T 22

Wareham Dorset GB **70** V 18

Wargrave Wokingham GB **70/71** T 21

Wark Northumberland GB **147** M 18

Warkworth Northumberland GB **147** M 19

Warlingham Surrey GB **71** U 22

Warmington Northhamptonshire GB **100/101** R 22

Warminster Wiltshire GB **70** U 18

Warrenpoint Down GB **207** O 10

Warrington Warrington GB **119** Q 17

Warsash Hampshire GB **70** V 20

Warslow Staffordshire GB **134** Q 19

Warter East Riding of Yorkshire GB **134/135** P 21

Wartle Aberdeenshire GB **187** H 18

Warwick Warwickshire GB **100** S 19

Warwick-on-Eden Cumbria GB **146/147** N 17

Wasbister Orkney Islands GB **198** D 16

Wasdale Head Cumbria GB **146** O 16

Washford Somerset GB **53** U 16

Washington Sunderland GB **147** N 19

Washington West Sussex GB **71** V 22

Watchet Somerset GB **53** U 16

Waterbeach Cambridgeshire GB **101** S 23

Waterbeck Dumfries and Galloway GB **146** M 16

Waterford Port Láirge Waterford IRL **233** S 8

Watergrasshill Cork IRL **232/233** S 6

Waterhouses Staffordshire GB **134** Q 19

Wateringbury Kent GB **71** U 23

Waterlooville Hampshire GB **70** V 20

Waterrow Somerset GB **53** U 16

Waterside East Ayrshire GB **146** M 14

Waterville Kerry IRL **70** T 2

Watford Hertfordshire GB **71** T 22

Watlington Oxfordshire GB **70** T 20

Watlington Norfolk GB **101** R 24

Watten Highland GB **187** F 16

Watton Norfolk GB **101** R 24

Watton at Stone Hertfordshire GB **71** T 22

Waverton Cumbria GB **146** N 16

Wawne Kingston upon Hull GB **135** P 22

Weasenham Norfolk GB **101** R 24

Weaverham Cheshire GB **119** Q 17

Weaverthorpe North Yorkshire GB **135** O 21

Wedmore Somerset GB **53** U 17

Wednesbury Wolverhampton GB **100** R 18

Weedon Bec Northhamptonshire GB **100** S 20

Weeley Essex GB **71** T 25

Weem Perth and Kinross GB **160/161** J 15

Weeton North Yorkshire GB **134** P 19

Welbury North Yorkshire GB **147** O 20

Welby Lincolnshire GB **100** R 21

Weldon Northhamptonshire GB **100** S 21

Welford Northhamptonshire GB **100** S 20

Well North Yorkshire GB **147** O 19

Welland Worcestershire GB **87** S 18

Wellesbourne Warwickshire GB **100** S 19

Wellingborough Northhamptonshire GB **100** S 21

Wellington Shropshire GB **100** R 18

Wellington Telford and Wrekin GB **100** R 18

Wellington Somerset GB **53** V 16

Wellington Herefordshire GB **87** S 17

Wellingtonbridge Wexford IRL **233** S 9

Wells Somerset GB **53** U 17

Wells Powys GB **87** S 16

Wells-next-the-Sea Norfolk GB **101** R 24

Welney Norfolk GB **101** R 23

Welshampton Shropshire GB **119** R 17

Welshpool Y Trallwng Powys GB **87** R 16

Welton East Riding of Yorkshire GB **134/135** P 21

Welwyn Hertfordshire GB **71** T 22

Welwyn Garden City Hertfordshire GB **71** T 22

Wem Shropshire GB **119** R 17

Wembley Greater London GB **71** T 22

Wendens Ambo Essex GB **71** T 23

Wendling Norfolk GB **101** R 24

Wendover Buckinghamshire GB **70/71** T 21

Wensley North Yorkshire GB **147** O 19

Wenvoe Vale of Glamorgan GB **53** U 16

Weobley Herefordshire GB **87** S 17

Wernyss Bay Inverclyde GB **160** L 13

West Auckland Durham GB **147** N 19

West Bay Dorset GB **53** V 17

West Bergholt Essex GB **71** T 24

West Bexington Dorset GB **53** V 17

West Burrafirth Shetland Islands GB **199** B 19

West Calder West Lothian GB **160/161** L 15

West Chevington Northumberland GB **147** M 19

West Dean Wiltshire GB **70** U 19

West Down Devon GB **52/53** U 14

West Felton Shropshire GB **119** R 17

West Grinstead West Sussex GB **71** V 22

West Haddon Northhamptonshire GB **100** S 20

West Harptree Bath & NE Somerset GB **53** U 17

West Heslerton North Yorkshire GB **134** O 21

West Hoathly West Sussex GB **71** U 22

West Horsley Surrey GB **71** U 22

West Kilbride North Ayrshire GB **160** L 13

West Kirby Wirral GB **119** Q 16

West Linton Scottish Borders GB **161** L 16

West Lulworth Dorset GB **70** V 18

West Lutton North Yorkshire GB **134** O 21

West Malling Kent GB **71** U 23

West Meon Hampshire GB **70** U 20

West Mersea Essex GB **71** T 24

West Moors Dorset GB **70** V 19

West Overton Wiltshire GB **70** U 19

West Rasen Lincolnshire GB **135** Q 22

West Rudham Norfolk GB **101** R 24

West Saltoun East Lothian GB **161** L 17

West Sandwick Shetland Islands GB **199** A 20

West Tanfield North Yorkshire GB **147** O 19

West Tarbert Argyll and Bute GB **160** L 12

West Thorney West Sussex GB **70/71** V 21

West Town Donegal IRL **206** M 6

West Wellow Hampshire GB **70** V 19

West Wemyss Fife GB **161** K 16

West Wittering West Sussex GB **70/71** V 21

West Witton North Yorkshire GB **147** O 19

West Woodburn Northumberland GB **147** M 18

Westbury Wiltshire GB **70** U 18

Westbury Shropshire GB **87** R 17

Westbury-sub-Mendip Somerset GB **53** U 17

Wester Quarff Shetland Islands GB **199** B 20

Westerdale North Yorkshire GB **134** O 21

Westerdale Highland GB **187** F 15

Westerfield Shetland Islands GB **199** B 20

Westerham Kent GB **71** U 23

Westerleigh South Gloucestershire GB **70** T 18

Westfield Highland GB **198** E 15

Westgate Durham GB **147** N 18

Westhill Aberdeen City GB **187** H 18

Westing Shetland Islands GB **199** A 21

Westleton Suffolk GB **101** S 26

Westminster Greater London GB **71** T 22

Westnewton Cumbria GB **146** N 16

Weston Lincolnshire GB **100/101** R 22

Weston Underwood Derbyshire GB **100** R 19

Weston-super-Mare North Somerset GB **53** U 17

Westonzoyland Somerset GB **53** U 17

Westport Cathair na Mart Mayo IRL **218** P 3

Westruther Scottish Borders GB **161** L 17

Westward Ho! Devon GB **52/53** U 14

Wetheral Cumbria GB **146/147** N 17

Wetherby Leeds GB **134** P 20

Wetwang East Riding of Yorkshire GB **134** O 21

Wexford Loch Garman Wexford IRL **233** S 10

Weyhill Hampshire GB **70** U 19

Weymouth Dorset GB **70** V 18

Whaley Bridge Derbyshire GB **134** Q 19

Whalley Lancashire GB **134** P 18

Whalton Northumberland GB **147** M 19

Whaplode Lincolnshire GB **100/101** R 22

Whauphill Dumfries and Galloway GB **146** N 14

Wheathampstead Hertfordshire GB **71** T 22

Wheatley Oxfordshire GB **70** T 20

Wheaton Aston Staffordshire GB **100** R 18

Wheldrake York GB **134/135** P 21

Whickham Gateshead GB **147** N 19

Whissendine Rutland GB **100** R 21

Whissonsett Norfolk GB **101** R 24

Whitbeck Cumbria GB **146** O 16

Whitbourne Herefordshire GB **87** S 18

Whitburn South Tyneside GB **147** N 20

Whitburn West Lothian GB **160/161** L 15

Whitby North Yorkshire GB **134** O 21

Whitchurch Shropshire GB **119** R 17

Whitchurch Hampshire GB **70** U 20

Whitchurch Buckinghamshire GB **70/71** T 21

Whitchurch Herefordshire GB **87** T 17

White Notley Essex GB **71** T 24

Whitegate Clare IRL **232/233** R 6

Whitegate Cork IRL **232/233** T 6

Whitehall Orkney Islands GB **198** D 17

Whitehall Westmeath IRL **219** P 8

Whitehall Kilkenny IRL **233** R 8

Whitehaven Cumbria GB **146** N 15

Whitehead Antrim GB **207** N 11

Whitehills Aberdeenshire GB **187** G 17

Whitehouse Argyll and Bute GB **160** L 12

Whitekirk East Lothian GB **161** K 17

Whiteparish Wiltshire GB **70** U 19

White's Cross Cork IRL **232/233** T 6

Whitesides Corner Antrim GB **207** N 10

Whitfield Northumberland GB **147** N 18

Whithersfield Suffolk GB **101** S 23

Whithorn Dumfries and Galloway GB **146** N 14

Whiting Bay North Ayrshire GB **174** M 12

Whitland Carmarthenshire GB **86** T 13

Whitley Bay North Tyneside GB **147** M 20

Whitley Chapel Northumberland GB **147** N 18

Whitmore Staffordshire GB **100** R 18

Whitney-on-Wye Herefordshire GB **87** S 16

Whitsome Scottish Borders GB **161** L 18

Whitstable Kent GB **71** U 25

Whitstone Cornwall GB **52/53** V 14

Whittingham Northumberland GB **147** M 19

Whittington Staffordshire GB **100** R 19

Whittington Shropshire GB **119** R 16

Whittington Derbyshire GB **134** Q 20

Whittlebury Northhamptonshire GB **100** S 21

Whittle-le-Woods Lancashire GB **119** P 17

Whittlesey Cambridgeshire GB **100/101** R 22

Whitton North Lincolnshire GB **134/135** P 21

Whitton Powys GB **87** S 16

Whitwell Derbyshire GB **134** Q 20

Whitwell Isle of Wight GB **70** V 20

Whitwell Hertfordshire GB **71** T 22

Whitwick Leicestershire GB **100** R 20

Whitworth Lancashire GB **134** P 18

Wick Highland GB **187** F 16

Wick Vale of Glamorgan GB **53** U 15

Wick South Gloucestershire GB **70** U 18

Wicken Cambridgeshire GB **101** S 23

Wickford Essex GB **71** T 24

Wickham Market Suffolk GB **101** S 25

Wickhambrook Suffolk GB **101** S 24

Wicklow Wicklow IRL **233** R 10

Wickwar South Gloucestershire GB **70** T 18

Widdrington Northumberland GB **147** M 19

Widecombe in the Moor Devon GB **53** V 15

Widegates Cornwall GB **52/53** W 14

Wideopen North Tyneside GB **147** M 19

Widford Hertfordshire GB **71** T 23

Widnes Halton GB **119** Q 17

Wigan Wigan GB **119** P 17

Wiggenhall St Germans Norfolk GB **101** R 23

Wigglesworth North Yorkshire GB **147** O 18

Wighill North Yorkshire GB **134** P 20

Wigmore Herefordshire GB **87** S 17

Wigston Leicestershire GB **100** R 20

Wigton Cumbria GB **146** N 16

Wigtown Dumfries and Galloway GB **146** N 14

Wilberfoss East Riding of Yorkshire GB **134/135** P 21

Wilkhaven Highland GB **187** G 15

Wilkinstown Meath IRL **219** P 9

Willaston Cheshire GB **119** Q 17

Willersey Gloucestershire GB **100** S 19

Williamstown Galway IRL **218** P 5

Willingham Cambridgeshire GB **101** S 23

Willingham by Stow Lincolnshire GB **134/135** Q 21

Willington Derbyshire GB **100** R 19

Willington Durham GB **147** N 19

Williton Somerset GB **53** U 16

Willoughby Lincolnshire GB **135** Q 23

Willoughby-on-the-Wolds Nottinghamshire GB **100** R 20

Wilmslow Cheshire GB **134** Q 18

Wilton Wiltshire GB **70** U 19

Wimblington Cambridgeshire GB **101** R 23

Wimborne Minster Dorset GB **70** V 18

Wincanton Somerset GB **70** U 18

Winchcombe Gloucestershire GB **70** T 19

Winchelsea East Sussex GB **71** V 24

Winchester Hampshire GB **70** U 20

Windermere Cumbria GB **146/147** O 17

Windlesham Surrey GB **70/71** U 21

Windsor Windsor & Maidenhead GB **70/71** U 21

Wing Buckinghamshire GB **70/71** T 21

Wingate Durham GB **147** N 20

Wingham Kent GB **71** U 25

Winkfield Bracknell Forest GB **70/71** U 21

Winkleigh Devon GB **53** V 15

Winksley North Yorkshire GB **147** O 19

Winscombe North Somerset GB **53** U 17

Winsford Cheshire GB **119** Q 17

Winsford Somerset GB **53** U 15

Winsham Somerset GB **53** V 17

Winslow Buckinghamshire GB **70/71** T 21

Winster Derbyshire GB **134** Q 19

Winster Cumbria GB **146/147** O 17

Winston Durham GB **147** N 19

Winstone Gloucestershire GB **70** T 18

Winterborne Stickland Dorset GB **70** V 18

Winterbourne South Gloucestershire GB **70** T 18

Winterbourne Abbas Dorset GB **53** V 17

Winteringham North Lincolnshire GB **134/135** P 21

Winterton-on-Sea Norfolk GB **101** R 26

Winton Cumbria GB **147** O 18

Wintringham North Yorkshire GB **134** O 21

Wirksworth Derbyshire GB **134** Q 19

Wisbech Cambridgeshire GB **101** R 23

Wisbech St Mary Cambridgeshire GB **101** R 23

Wisborough Green West Sussex GB **71** U 22

Wishaw North Lanarkshire GB **160/161** L 15

Wistanstow Shropshire GB **87** S 17

Wiston South Lanarkshire GB **160/161** L 15

Wiston Pembrokeshire GB **86** T 13

Wistow North Yorkshire GB **134** P 20

Witchampton Dorset GB **70** V 18

Witchford Cambridgeshire GB **101** S 23

Witham Essex GB **71** T 24

Witham Friary Somerset GB **70** U 18

Witheridge Devon GB **53** V 15

Withernsea East Riding of Yorkshire GB **135** P 23

Withernwick East Riding of Yorkshire GB **135** P 22

Withington Gloucestershire GB **70** T 19

Withington Herefordshire GB **87** S 17

Withleigh Devon GB **53** V 15

Withnell Lancashire GB **119** P 17

Withycombe Somerset GB **53** U 16

Withypool Somerset GB **53** U 15

Witley Surrey GB **70/71** U 21

Witney Oxfordshire GB **70** T 19

Wittersham Kent GB **71** U 24

Witton Park Durham GB **147** N 19

Witton-le-Wear Durham GB **147** N 19

Wiveliscomba Somerset GB **53** U 16

Wivenhoe Essex GB **71** T 24

Wix Essex GB **71** T 25

Woburn Bedfordshire GB **70/71** T 21

Woburn Sands Milton Keynes GB **100** S 21

Woking Surrey GB **70/71** U 21

Wokingham Wokingham GB **70/71** U 21

Wold Newton North East Lincolnshire GB **135** Q 22

Wolferton Norfolk GB **101** R 23

Wollaston Northhamptonshire GB **100** S 21

Wolsingham Durham GB **147** N 19

Wolverhampton Wolverhampton GB **100** R 18

Wolverton Milton Keynes GB **100** S 21

Wolvey Warwickshire GB **100** S 20

Wolviston Stockton-on-Tees GB **147** N 20

Wombourne Staffordshire GB **100** R 18

Wombwell Barnsley GB **134** P 20

Wonersh Surrey GB **70/71** U 21

Wooburn Buckinghamshire GB **70/71** T 21

Woodbridge Suffolk GB **101** S 25

Woodchester Gloucestershire GB **70** T 18

Woodchurch Kent GB **71** U 24

Woodcote Oxfordshire GB **70** T 20

Woodenbridge Wicklow IRL **233** R 10

Woodford Galway IRL **218/219** Q 6

Woodford Halse Northhamptonshire GB **100** S 20

Woodhall Spa Lincolnshire GB **135** Q 22

Woodland Durham GB **147** N 19

Woodseaves Staffordshire GB **100** R 18

Woodstock Oxfordshire GB **70** T 20

Woodton Norfolk GB **101** R 25

Woofferton Shropshire GB **87** S 17

Wookey Somerset GB **53** U 17

Wool Dorset GB **70** V 18

Woolacombe Devon GB **52/53** U 14

Wooler Northumberland GB **161** L 18

Woolfardisworthy Devon GB **52/53** V 14

Wooperton Northumberland GB **147** M 19

Woore Shropshire GB **100** R 18

Wootton Oxfordshire GB **70** T 20

Wootton Oxfordshire GB **70** T 20

Wootton Bassett Wiltshire GB **70** T 19

Wootton Wawen Warwickshire GB **100** S 19

Worcester Worcestershire GB **87** S 18

Workington Cumbria GB **146** N 15

Worksop Nottinghamshire GB **134** Q 20

Worlaby North Lincolnshire GB **135** P 22

Wormit Fife GB **161** K 17

Wormshill Kent GB **71** U 24

Worplesdon Surrey GB **70/71** U 21

Worthing West Sussex GB **71** V 22

Wotton-under-Edge Gloucestershire GB **70** T 18

Wouldham Kent GB **71** U 23

Wragby Lincolnshire GB **135** Q 22

Wrangle Lincolnshire GB **135** Q 23

Wray Lancashire GB **146/147** O 17

Wrea Green Lancashire GB **119** P 17

Wreay Cumbria GB **146/147** N 17

Wrecsam Wrexham Wrexham GB **119** Q 17

Wrelton North Yorkshire GB **134** O 21

Wrentham Suffolk GB **101** S 26

Wressle East Riding of Yorkshire GB **134/135** P 21

Wrexham Wrecsam Wrexham GB **119** Q 17

Writtle Essex GB **71** T 23

Wrotham Kent GB **71** U 23

Wroughton Swindon GB **70** T 19

Wroxham Norfolk GB **101** R 25

Wroxton Oxfordshire GB **100** S 20

Wye Kent GB **71** U 24

Wylye Wiltshire GB **70** U 19

Wymeswold Leicestershire GB **100** R 20

Wymondham Leicestershire GB **100** R 21

Wymondham Norfolk GB **101** R 25

Wyre Piddle Worcestershire GB **87** S 18

Wyvis Lodge Highland GB **186** G 13

Y

Y Bala Gwynedd GB **119** R 15

Y Drenewydd Newtown Powys GB **87** R 16

Y Fali Anglesey GB **118** Q 13

Y Felinheli Gwynedd GB **118/119** Q 14

Y Fenni Abergavenny Monmouthshire GB **87** T 17

Y Ferwig Ceredigion GB **86** S 13

Y Ffor Gwynedd GB **118/119** R 14

Y Trallwng Welshpool Powys GB **87** R 16

Yalding Kent GB **71** U 23

Yarcombe Devon GB **53** V 16

Yardley Hastings Northhamptonshire GB **100** S 21

Yarmouth Isle of Wight GB **70** V 20

Yarrow Scottish Borders GB **161** L 16

Yate South Gloucestershire GB **70** T 18

Yattendon West Berkshire GB **70** U 20

Yatton North Somerset GB **53** U 17

Yaxley Cambridgeshire GB **100/101** R 22

Yeadon Leeds GB **134** P 19

Yealmpton Devon GB **53** W 15

Yedingham North Yorkshire GB **134** O 21

Yelvertoft Northhamptonshire GB **100** S 20

Yelverton Devon GB **52/53** W 14

Yeoford Devon GB **53** V 15

Yeovil Somerset GB **53** V 17

Yesnaby Orkney Islands GB **198** D 16

Yetminster Dorset GB **53** V 17

Yetts o'Monans Clackmannanshire GB **160/161** K 15

Ynysybwl Rhondda Cynon Taff GB **87** T 16

York York GB **134** P 20

Yorkton Gloucestershire GB **87** T 17

Youghal Eochaill Cork IRL **233** T 7

Youlgrave Derbyshire GB **134** Q 19

Yoxall Staffordshire GB **100** R 19

Yoxford Suffolk GB **101** S 26

Yr Wyddgrug Mold Flintshire GB **119** Q 16

Ysbyty Ifan Conwy GB **119** Q 15

Ysbyty Ystwyth Ceredigion GB **86/87** S 15

Ystalyfera Neath Port Talbot GB **86/87** T 15

Ystrad Aeron Ceredigion GB **86** S 14

Ystradfellte Powys GB **86/87** T 15

Ystradgynlais Powys GB **86/87** T 15

Ythanbank Aberdeenshire GB **187** H 18

Ythanwells Aberdeenshire GB **187** H 17

Z

Zennor Cornwall GB **52** W 11

Acknowledgements

The Aerial Atlas of Great Britain & Ireland

© 2005 Wissen Media Verlag GmbH, Gütersloh/Munich

© Cartography: 2005 Wissen Media Verlag GmbH Gütersloh/Munich

All rights reserved

The Aerial Atlas of Great Britain & Ireland was commissioned, edited, designed and typeset by Book Creation Illustrated Ltd, Mitre House, 44–46 Fleet Street, London EC4Y 1BN

www.bookcreation.com

BOOK CREATION ILLUSTRATED LTD

Managing Editor
David Popey

Assistant Editors
Rosemary Browne and David Halford

Copy Editor
Elizabeth Loving

Art Editor
Keith Miller

Picture Research
David Halford and David Popey; special thanks to Kevin Davidson at The GeoInformation Group

Publishing Director
Hal Robinson

Contributors
Chris Cooper, Jonathan Dore, David Halford, Elizabeth Loving, Keith Miller, Charles Phillips, David Popey

WISSEN MEDIA VERLAG

Chief Cartographer
Glenn Riedel

Editor
Irmgard Sigg

Digital Cartography
Liana Steinborn

Data Management/DTP
Klaus Jost

Picture Credits
(l=left, r=right, t=top, c=centre, b=bottom)

© Kevin Allen www.kevinallenphotography.co.uk 115(t); Imagery supplied by BKS Surveys Ltd. www.bks.co.uk 128, 130, 210, 212, 214, 226, 234, 238; Copyright Hans Bracker 194; Cities Revealed Aerial Photography © Copyright The GeoInformation Group 50–51(c), 56, 76, 80, 82–83(b), 90–91, 92, 102, 104, 106, 108, 114, 124–125, 138, 140, 142, 154, 156, 164, 166, 168, 188, 208, 220, Cover (main); Photography © CUCAP and with permission of Scottish Natural Heritage 178, 200, 202, 204; © Digimap Ltd 67–69; © Copyright DigitalGlobe 182; © Copyright Kevin Dwyer 19(t), 50(tr), 221(t & b), 223, 229, 230–231, 237, 239, 240–241; Kenneth Ferguson Photography; 164 (inset) and 165; Forewick Stud 205(b); FreeFoto.com 155(b), 169(t & b); Glasgow School of Art Collection 167(t); Glastonbury Festivals Ltd 63(b) © Copyright David Halford 105(c & b); www.jasonhawkes.com 18(bl), 19(r), 51(cr & b), 77, 79, 89, 93, 98–99, 103, 123, 137, 143, 163, 172–173, 189(b), 193, 196–197, 216–217, 225, 227; Courtesy of David Houlston Photography and the Ironbridge Gorge Museum Trust 96(b); © Infoterra Ltd 88, 94, 113, 122, 126, 136, 148, 150, 170; © Infoterra Ltd (supplied by Skyscan Ltd) 192, 194; © Copyright Isle of Man Tourist Board 129(r), 131(r & b); courtesy of www.kilkennytourism.ie 235; © Last Refuge – Dae Sasitorn and Adrian Warren 8–17, 18(tl & bl), 19(c & bl), 50(cl & cr) 54, 55, 59(t), 61(t), 62, 64–65, 72, 75, 78, 81(b), 83(r), 84–85, 91(b), 95, 97(t), 111, 113, 116–117, 121(t), 127(t), 132–133, 139, 144–145, 151, 152, 157(t), 158–159, 171, back cover (r); Image courtesy of Mapflow 2005 224; The Mersey Partnership (TMP) 125(b); Courtesy of the Northern Ireland Tourist Board www.discovernorthernireland.com 209(b), 211, 213, 215; © Ordnance Survey Ireland 222, 228, 236; © Mike Page 107(t & b); Parks Trust, Milton Keynes 109(t) image by Nick Bland, 109(b) image by Anne Robinson; www.graeme–peacock.com 153; Pictures of Britain 18(c), 57(t & b), 59(b), 61(b), 73, 81(t), 115(b), 121(c & b), 127(b), 141 (t & c), 149, 155(t), 157(b), 163, 177, 191 Redferns Music Picture Library Ltd 63(t); Science Photo Library 50(tl & br), 51(tl & c), 162, 176, 180, 190, 209(t) Scotpix/Colin J. Smith 189(t); © Simmons Aerofilms 51(tr), 184–185; © www.charles–tait.co.uk 179(t, c & b), 181, 183, 193(t), 201(t & b), 203(t, c & b), 205(t); Imagery provided by UKPerspectives.com 58, 60, 74, 96, 110, 120

Satellite images (pages 20–49)
© WorldSat International, Inc., 2005
www.worldsat.ca
All rights reserved